# BEN
# JONSON

*Ben Jonson
from a portrait by Gerard Honthorst
in the collection of Lord Sackville at Knole*

# BEN JONSON

*Edited by* C. H. HERFORD
*and* PERCY SIMPSON

VOLUMES I & II
The Man and his Work

*The first Volume*

OXFORD
At the Clarendon Press

Oxford University Press, Amen House, London E.C.4
*Glasgow   New York   Toronto   Melbourne   Wellington*
*Bombay   Calcutta   Madras   Karachi   Cape Town   Ibadan*
Geoffrey Cumberlege Publisher to the UNIVERSITY

FIRST EDITION 1925
REPRINTED LITHOGRAPHICALLY IN GREAT BRITAIN AT THE
UNIVERSITY PRESS, OXFORD, FROM CORRECTED SHEETS OF
THE FIRST EDITION
1954

# PREFACE

THE present two volumes are the first instalment of an edition of Jonson's entire Works, which will eventually extend to ten. They are occupied in the main with editorial matter. This comprises: the Life; Introductions to the several Plays, to the Masques, the Poems, and the Prose works; and a series of Appendices, in which the whole of the extant and accessible documents bearing upon Jonson are reproduced *in extenso*. These comprise the Drummond *Conversations*, now reprinted in a critical text with full commentary; the authentic Letters of Jonson, including several hitherto unknown or unpublished; a catalogue of the books which can be shown to have been in Jonson's library; and a number of extracts from public records, furnishing evidence for conclusions advanced, or new facts embodied, in the text. The illustrations include, besides the well-known portrait at Knole, reproduced by the kind permission of Lord Sackville, five of Inigo Jones's designs, hitherto unpublished, for the Masques of *Oberon* and *Chloridia*. The originals are in the collection of the Duke of Devonshire at Chatsworth, and we are deeply indebted to His Grace for the privilege of reproducing them.

The remaining volumes will contain, together with the text of the works, a complete critical apparatus and a full commentary.

It appears desirable to give some indication of the nature of the collaboration between the two editors.

In a work carried on, as the present has been, for a number of years, with constant consultation and exchange of views, it is impracticable, even if it were desirable, to assign exact shares. But, with this proviso, it may be stated that the commentary and critical apparatus (for the most part still to appear), all that concerns the textual and bibliographical data (including the quotations throughout), and the first four Appendices are due to the one editor; the Introductions, except those to the *Discoveries* and the *Grammar*, with the five Appendices on the Plays, to the other. In the *Life* both have co-operated. It has been planned and written by a single hand. But the material incorporated in it has been enlarged at very many points by investigations and discoveries due solely to the editor of the commentary.

A word may be added in regard to the arrangement of the present volumes. The whole of the biographical and quasi-biographical matter is given first. The Introductions to the Plays, which follow, are not designed to form a continuous critical account of Jonson's drama, but, strictly, to 'introduce' the several pieces. Matter is therefore often repeated from a previous Introduction where it is equally relevant. The other Introductions are single, continuous essays.

It remains to acknowledge the help we have received. One collector in America, who owns an unprinted letter of Jonson, has refused to answer an inquiry about it; one collector in England has withheld a manuscript note of a contemporary of Jonson giving a new fact about his life. With these two exceptions we have experienced the utmost generosity at the hands of collectors and scholars. For access to the Drummond Manuscript of the *Conversations* in the Advocates' Library at Edinburgh, and permission to take a rotograph of it, we have to thank the keeper, Dr. W. K. Dickson. This Library, which is destined to become the National Library of Scotland, has been prematurely so described on page 129. The Council of the Society of Antiquaries of Scotland kindly allowed access to the Drummond Manuscripts in their collection. For leave to examine the manuscripts at Dulwich College, including Henslowe's *Diary*, we have to thank Mr. Gilbert Stretton and Mr. E. M. Everett, past and present librarians. Archdeacon Plume's *Notes* are reprinted from his notebooks in the Plume Library at Maldon by permission of the librarian, the Rev. I. L. Seymour, vicar of Maldon. The *Memorandums of the Immortal Ben* are printed, by Professor Bang-Kaup's permission, from a photograph of the manuscript which he supplied.

For the characteristic group of letters relating to the *Eastward Ho* imprisonment we are indebted to Mr. William Augustus White of New York, who further helped us by checking a typed copy of the text with the originals. Six of these letters are printed from Mr. White's manuscript, three of them for the first time. The text of the second letter is taken from the autograph at Hatfield House. The late Marquess of Salisbury kindly allowed access to the Cecil Papers, and when the transcript was lost in a fire—for one of the editors suffered equally with Jonson a visitation of Vulcan—the present Marquess of Salisbury allowed a new copy to be taken. To the former secretary and librarian at Hatfield, Mr. R. T. Gunton, we are indebted for this transcript; and to the present librarian, the Rev. W. Stanhope-Lovell, for checking the text. Dr. W. W. Greg kindly gave a photograph of the tenth letter. Mr. D. T. B. Wood, assistant keeper of the manuscripts in the British Museum, checked the text of the Museum manuscripts.

Of the legal documents printed in Appendix III, a number are preserved in the Public Record Office. We are greatly indebted to Mr. Hilary Jenkinson, officer in charge of the literary search-room, for help in working at these, and especially for obtaining the Chancery deposition

## Preface

(iv) and the deed of assignment (x) printed for the first time. The latter was unearthed from a bundle of miscellaneous papers which Mr. Jenkinson thought might contain something about Jonson; the former was found after a prolonged search, begun by Mr. Simpson and carried to a successful close by Miss E. Salisbury, who also checked the text of all the state papers printed in this appendix. The indictment for manslaughter of Gabriel Spencer (ii) is printed by the permission of Mr. G. S. W. Hart, clerk of the peace to the City of Westminster. The citations of Jonson and his wife for recusancy (iii) are printed by permission of the Right Honourable Sir Henry Duke, President of the Probate Court. The discoverer of this document, Mr. F. W. X. Fincham, superintendent of the department of literary inquiry in the Principal Probate Registry, Somerset House, and his successor, Mr. G. Hudson, also claim our thanks. For access to the notices of Jonson in the city archives of Edinburgh (vii) we are indebted to the late Sir Thomas Hunter, writer to the signet, town clerk of the city of Edinburgh. For permission to print the official record of Jonson's honorary degree at Oxford (viii) we are indebted to Dr. R. L. Poole, keeper of the archives of the University. The documents relating to Jonson's appointment as city chronologer (xii) are printed by permission of the Corporation of the City of London; we acknowledge the courteous help of the records clerk, Mr. A. H. Thomas. The grant to Jonson in 1629 recorded in the muniments of Westminster Abbey (xiv) is printed by permission of the Venerable R. H. Charles, archdeacon of Westminster and keeper of the muniments; for access to the document we are indebted to the assistant keeper, Canon W. F. Westlake.

Much general help in tracing books formerly in Jonson's library was given by the late Charles Sayle, of the Cambridge University Library, and by Mr. Sidney Grose, librarian of Christ's College, Cambridge, both of whom took the keenest interest in this inquiry. At Oxford our thanks are due to two former librarians of St. John's College, the late C. F. Burney, and the late W. H. Stevenson, vice-president of the College, and to their successor in the librarianship, Mr. H. Last; to Mr. A. W. Pickard-Cambridge, librarian of Balliol College; and to Mr. J. R. H. Weaver, librarian of Trinity College. At Cambridge to Mr. A. F. Scholfield in a twofold capacity, first as librarian of Trinity College, and since as the University librarian; to Mr. O. F. Morshead, librarian of the Pepys Library at Magdalene College; to Mr. P. W. Wood, librarian of Emmanuel College; to Mr. W. L. Mollison, the Master of Clare; and to the late J. Bass Mullinger, librarian of St. John's College. We are indebted to several owners of these old books, to Mr. Sydney Cockerell, Mr. T. Loveday, and Mr. William Augustus White; to the librarian of Eton College, Mr. H. Broadbent; to Messrs. Sotheby, Mr. F. Sabin, and Mr. F. Edwards, the booksellers; to Mr. H. H. Champion, Mr. J. Isaacs, and Mr. T. Kingdom. For help of a miscellaneous character, extending over a number of years, we are indebted to the late Bertram Dobell and his son, Mr. Percy J. Dobell, Dr. W. W. Greg, and Mr. G. Thorn-Drury, K.C.

Our debt to our predecessors is acknowledged wherever we have made use of them, but it is right to add here an express acknowledgement of the labours of William Gifford, the doughty champion of Jonson, whose edition of 1816 still holds the field.

The Introduction to Jonson's *English Grammar* was read in proof by Sir Mark Hunter, who made some suggestive criticisms.

Finally, a work involving such varied and prolonged labour could not have been carried through without access to those great collections which lie open to every student. The 'spadework', not only for these two volumes, but also for the remaining eight, has been done year after year in the British Museum and the Bodleian Libraries, and to a less extent in the Cambridge University Library and in the Dyce Library at South Kensington. It would be a grave oversight, in acknowledging specific debts, to pass by the wider and continuous obligation to these unfailing literary stores.

To the readers of the Clarendon Press we are indebted for a close scrutiny of our difficult proofs, and we wish specially to acknowledge the help rendered from time to time by Mr. Frederick Page, of the London branch of the Press, in investigating special points and ensuring the accuracy of texts.

C. H. H.<br>P. S.

# CONTENTS

## VOLUME I

## LIFE OF BEN JONSON

|     |     |
| --- | --- |
|     | PAGE |
| I. EARLY LIFE |  |
|    I. Origins. School | 1 |
|    II. Bricklaying. Flanders | 4 |
|    III. London in the 90's | 9 |
|    IV. The Actor | 12 |
| II. THE HUMOUR PLAYS |  |
|    I. *Every Man in his Humour*. *The Case is Altered* | 18 |
|    II. *Every Man out of his Humour* | 22 |
|    III. Stage Quarrel. *Cynthia's Revels*. *Poetaster* | 24 |
|    IV. With D'Aubigny | 31 |
| III. THE NEW REIGN. FROM 'SEJANUS' TO 'CATILINE' |  |
|    I. *Sejanus*; and sequel | 35 |
|    II. *Eastward Ho*; and sequel | 38 |
|    III. Gunpowder plot commission | 40 |
|    IV. *Volpone*. *Epicoene*. *The Alchemist*. Masques. *Catiline* | 43 |
| IV. JONSON'S SOCIETY: 1603–12 |  |
|    I. Friends: The Mermaid. Donne, Roe | 48 |
|    II. Court circles. Lady Bedford, Rutland, &c. The Universities | 52 |
|    III. Fellow-artists; Inigo Jones, Ferrabosco | 59 |

## V. LATER MATURITY: 1612–25

  I. Journey to France . . . . . 64
  II. *Bartholomew Fair.* *The Devil is an Ass.*
    Masques. Literary occupations 1616–25   69
  III. Scottish Journey . . . . . 75
  IV. Oxford. The Apollo . . . . 84

## VI. RETURN TO THE STAGE

  I. *The Staple of News.* The new reign . 89
  II. *The New Inn.* Quarrels. Later Masques 93
  III. *The Magnetic Lady.* *A Tale of a Tub* . 99

## VII. THE LAST PHASE: JONSON AND HIS FRIENDS

  I. Outward history. *Discoveries. Grammar* 103
  II. Friends . . . . . . . 105
  III. His Sons . . . . . . . 108
  IV. The end . . . . . . . 114

## VIII. FINAL APPRECIATION

  I. Ben Jonson's 'rarity' . . . . 119
  II. Yet of his age . . . . . . 121
  III. Drama, scholarship, satire . . . 123
  IV. Limitations . . . . . . 125
  V. Position in after-criticism . . . . 126

## APPENDICES

### I. CONTEMPORARY NOTES AND RECORDS

  I. Ben Jonson's Conversations with William
    Drummond of Hawthornden . . 128
  II. John Aubrey's Notes on Ben Jonson . 178
  III. Archdeacon Plume's Notes on Ben Jonson 184
  IV. Memorandums of the Immortal Ben . 188

## Contents

|  | PAGE |
|---|---|
| II. LETTERS OF JONSON, including the Drummond Correspondence | 190 |
|    I. To an Unnamed Lord (probably the Earl of Suffolk), 1605 | 193 |
|    II. To the Earl of Salisbury, 1605 | 194 |
|    III. To an Unnamed Lord, 1605 | 196 |
|    IV. To an Unnamed Lady (probably the Countess of Bedford), 1605 | 197 |
|    V. To Esme, Lord D'Aubigny? 1605 | 198 |
|    VI. To the Earl of Montgomery, 1605 | 199 |
|    VII. To the Earl of Pembroke, 1605 | 199 |
|    VIII. To Mr. Leech | 200 |
|    IX. To Mr. Thomas Bond | 201 |
|    X. To the Earl of Salisbury, 1605 | 202 |
|    XI. To Doctor Donne | 203 |
|    XII. William Drummond to Jonson, 1619 | 204 |
|    XIII. William Drummond to Jonson, 1619 | 205 |
|    XIV. To William Drummond, 1619 | 207 |
|    XV. William Drummond to Jonson, 1619 | 208 |
|    XVI. To the Earl of Newcastle, 1631 | 210 |
|    XVII. To the Earl of Newcastle, 1631 | 211 |
|    XVIII. To the Earl of Newcastle, 1631 | 211 |
|    XIX. To the Earl of Newcastle | 212 |
|    XX. To the Earl of Newcastle, 1631 | 213 |
|    XXI. To Sir Robert Cotton | 215 |
|    XXII. Letter written in a corner of Thomas Farnaby's edition of Martial, 1615 | 215 |
| III. LEGAL AND OFFICIAL DOCUMENTS | |
|    I. Official Papers relating to Jonson's imprisonment for his share in *The Isle of Dogs*, 1597 | 217 |
|    II. Indictment against Ben Jonson for the manslaughter of Gabriel Spencer on September 22, 1598, at Shordiche | 219 |

|     |                                                                                  | PAGE |
| --- | -------------------------------------------------------------------------------- | ---- |
| III. | Citations of Jonson and his Wife for Recusancy, 1606 . . . . . | 220 |
| IV. | Jonson's Deposition in the Chancery suit William Roe *versus* Walter Garland, 1610 . . . . . . . | 223 |
| V. | The Patent for Jonson's Pension of 1616 . | 231 |
| VI. | Notices from the Exchequer of Receipt Miscellanea, 1617 . . . . . | 232 |
| VII. | Notices of Ben Jonson in the City Archives of Edinburgh, 1618 . . . . | 233 |
| VIII. | Jonson's Honorary Degree at Oxford, 1619 | 234 |
| IX. | Thomas Cooke's Bill, 1620 . . . | 235 |
| X. | Deed of Assignment to John Hull, 1621 . | 236 |
| XI. | Warrant for the Reversion of the Office of the Master of the Revels, October 5, 1621 | 237 |
| XII. | Documents relating to Jonson's appointment as Chronologer to the City of London, 1628, 1631, and 1634 . . | 240 |
| XIII. | Examination of Jonson by the Attorney-General on October 26, 1629 . . | 242 |
| XIV. | Grant from the Dean and Chapter of Westminster to Jonson in his Sickness, 1629 . . . . . . . | 244 |
| XV. | Jonson's Patent of 1630 for an increased Pension . . . . . . | 245 |
| XVI. | Warrant for the Administration of Jonson's Goods, 1637 . . . . . . | 249 |

IV. BOOKS IN JONSON'S LIBRARY . . 250

# Contents

## INTRODUCTIONS TO THE PLAYS

|  | PAGE |
|---|---|
| A TALE OF A TUB | 273 |
| THE CASE IS ALTERED | 303 |
| EVERY MAN IN HIS HUMOUR | 329 |
|     Appendix V: The Quarto and the Folio | 355 |
| EVERY MAN OUT OF HIS HUMOUR | 371 |
| CYNTHIA'S REVELS | 391 |
| POETASTER | 413 |

## VOLUME II

### INTRODUCTIONS TO THE PLAYS (*continued*)

| | |
|---|---|
| SEJANUS HIS FALL | 1 |
| EASTWARD HO! | 29 |
| VOLPONE | 47 |
| THE SILENT WOMAN | 67 |
| THE ALCHEMIST | 85 |
|     Appendix VI: Bruno's *Candelaio* | 109 |
| CATILINE HIS CONSPIRACY | 111 |
| BARTHOLOMEW FAIR | 129 |
|     Appendix VII: Lantern Leatherhead and Inigo Jones | 146 |

## Contents

|  | PAGE |
|---|---|
| THE DEVIL IS AN ASS | 149 |
| THE STAPLE OF NEWS | 167 |
| THE NEW INN | 187 |
|     Appendix VIII: *The New Inn* and Fletcher's *Love's Pilgrimage* | 198 |
| THE MAGNETIC LADY | 201 |
| THE SAD SHEPHERD | 211 |
|     Appendix IX: The Additions to *The Spanish Tragedy* | 235 |
| MASQUES AND ENTERTAINMENTS | 247 |
| THE POEMS | 334 |
| THE ENGLISH GRAMMAR | 415 |
| THE DISCOVERIES | 437 |
| INDEX | 453 |

# LIST OF ILLUSTRATIONS

## VOLUME I

PORTRAIT OF BEN JONSON BY GERARD HONTHORST.
Reproduced by Lord Sackville's kind permission from the portrait in the Poets' Parlour at Knole. Portraits of Dryden, Waller, Wycherley, Congreve, and Pope hang with it; and the collection was probably made by Charles Sackville, the sixth Earl of Dorset (1630–1706). A copy of the Jonson portrait is in the National Portrait Gallery. Honthorst was in England in 1628, when he was painting pictures for Charles I at Whitehall. *Frontispiece*

INSCRIPTION IN A GIFT-COPY OF 'VOLPONE' now in the British Museum. *Page 56*

TITLE-PAGES OF JONSON'S COPIES OF PUTTENHAM'S 'ARTE OF ENGLISH POESIE' AND PIGNA'S 'CARMINA', now in the British Museum. *Between pages 264, 265*

## VOLUME II

INIGO JONES'S DESIGN FOR THE QUEEN'S DRESS AS CHLORIS IN 'CHLORIDIA'. Chloris, goddess of the flowers, and her attendant Nymphs, are thus described in Jonson's text: 'their apparell white, embroydered with siluer, trim'd at the shoulders with great leaues of greene, embroydered with gold, falling one vnder the other. And of the same make were their bases, their head-'tires of flowers, mix'd with siluer, and gold, with some sprigs of Ægrets among, and from the top of their dressing, a thinne vayle hanging downe' (*Chloridia*, Quarto, 1630, sig. B 2 verso). Four designs by Inigo Jones are preserved of this dress, as well as the 'fayre drawing' by another hand: these are numbers 94–8 in the Walpole and Malone Societies' Catalogue of *Designs by Inigo Jones for Masques and Plays at Court*, by Percy Simpson and C. F. Bell. The foot-note, in Inigo's hand, is 'the dessigne I con⟨c⟩eaue to bee fitt for the Inue⟨n⟩tion and if it please hir Maʸᵉ to add or alter any thinge I desier to receue hir comand and the dessign againe by this bearer. The collors ar in hir mat choyse but my oppinion is that severall fresh greenes mixt with gould and siller will bee most propper.' *Frontispiece*

xx     *List of Illustrations*

INIGO JONES'S DESIGN FOR A NYMPH IN 'CHLORIDIA'.
The design is described in the note on the frontispiece. This is
the finished drawing by a Court painter. No. 101 in the Walpole
Society's Catalogue. *To face page* 249

INIGO JONES'S DESIGN FOR THE 'FIRST FACE OF
THE SCENE' IN THE MASQUE OF 'OBERON'. 'The first
face of the *Scene* appeared all obscure, and nothing perceiu'd but
a darke Rocke, with trees beyond it; and all wildnesse, that
could be presented: Till, at one corner of the cliffe, aboue the
*Horizon*, the *Moone* began to shew, and rising, a *Satyre* was seene
(by her light) to put forth his head, and call' (Folio, 1616, p. 975).
No. 40 in the Walpole Society's Catalogue.
*Between pages* 284, 285

INIGO JONES'S DESIGN FOR THE PALACE IN THE
MASQUE OF 'OBERON'. 'There the whole *Scene* opened,
and within was discouer'd the *Frontispice* of a bright and glorious
*Palace*, whose gates and walls were transparent' (Folio, 1616,
p. 978). No. 42 in the Walpole Society's Catalogue.
*Between pages* 286, 287

INIGO JONES'S DESIGN FOR THE FIRST SCENE IN
'CHLORIDIA'. 'The Curtaine being drawne vp, the *Scene* is
discouer'd, consisting of pleasant hills, planted with young trees,
and all the lower bankes adorned with flowers. And from some
hollow parts of those hills, Fountaynes came gliding downe, which,
in the farre-off Land-shape, seem'd all to be conuerted to a riuer.
Ouer all, a serene skie, with transparent clouds, giuing a great
lustre to the whole worke, which did imitate the pleasant Spring'
(Quarto, 1630, sig. A 2 verso). No. 83 in the Walpole Society's
Catalogue. *Between pages* 334, 335

The cover-ornament reproduces Jonson's *impresa*, which Drummond describes as 'a Compass with one foot in Center, the other broken, the word. Deest quod duceret orbem' (*Conversations*, xvii. 578-9).

# LIFE OF BEN JONSON

## CHAPTER I

### EARLY LIFE

I

BENJAMIN, or, in the familiar form commonly used by himself and by his contemporaries even in ceremonial verse,[1] and universally adopted by posterity, Ben, Jonson was born in the course of the year 1572,[2] most probably in or near London.[3] Our knowledge of his descent is derived solely from one or two brief but fairly explicit statements reported by Drummond, to the effect that his paternal grandfather, 'a Gentleman',[4] had come up from Carlisle, 'and he thought from Anandale to it', and had entered the service of Henry VIII. He thus inherited—from whichever side of the Border—a strain of Border blood, and that not of the meanest degree, and his biographers have excusably discovered hints of long-silent forays and alarms in the mettlesome brain and blood of Ben. The fortunes of the

---

[1] As in Herrick's *Ode for Jonson*, 'My Ben' (*Hesperides*, 1648, p. 343).

[2] Mr. W. D. Briggs (*Mod. Lang. Notes*, vol. xxxiii, p. 137) has made it probable that he was born on June 11th of this year. His deposition in the Roe trial, May 5, 1610, and his poem 'My Picture left in Scotland', January 19, 1619, show that his birth occurred between May 5, 1572 and January 19, 1573. The *Epigram* 'To my Muse the Lady Digby' (*Underwoods*, xcvii) reads with this:

Witness his action done at Scanderoon
Upon his birthday, the eleventh of June.

But there is good manuscript evidence for the reading 'My [i.e. Jonson's] birthday'. See the critical note to this passage.

[3] Several inferior witnesses state that he was born in Westminster. So Langbaine: Winstanley adds (*Lives of the most Famous English Poets*, 1687, p. 123), 'his Mother living there in *Harts-horn-lane*, near *Charing-Cross*'.

[4] *Convers.*, § xiii. 234. If the grandfather came from Annandale his name was probably 'Johnstone', this family being frequent there and 'Johnson' unknown. Nothing is known of the change; 'Johnson', or as abbreviated by himself 'Jonson', was the only form used by his contemporaries. But he bore the family arms of the Johnstones, 'three spindles or rhombi', as he told Drummond (ibid. § xvii).

family, however, whatever they were under Henry, suffered a speedy collapse in the trying days of Mary ; when the son of the adventurer from Carlisle, Ben's father, 'losed all his estate' (a phrase which suggests that it was not inconsiderable), he himself being further 'cast in prison and forfaitted'; and 'at last turnd Minister'. It is hardly doubtful that the father adopted the Reform doctrines under Edward, suffered for them under Mary, and took orders, finally, under Elizabeth. 'A grave minister of the gospel' was the tradition of him current in Wood's time. His wife we know almost solely from a single anecdote reported by Jonson to Drummond. But we can hardly be wrong in seeing in this Roman matron, with her high disdain for death and for 'churls', and her touch of loud bravery in asserting it, the mother of the man who in a like high Roman fashion sent his challenge to single combat on the Flemish battle-field, and stripped the *opima spolia* from his foe. There are, at least, much stronger grounds for connecting the militant vein in Jonson with the mother, of whom we have this authentic record, than with the father's half-share in a merely presumptive Border-breed.

The 'grave minister of the gospel' died in 1572. One month after his death Benjamin was born. The widow, within two or three years at most, and probably sooner, married a master-bricklayer of Westminster. From the time, at latest, when Ben was 'a little child' in 'long coats', their home was in the neighbourhood of Charing Cross.[1] Of the step-father nothing is certainly known ; but tradition suggests that he was a hard-working yet not very successful craftsman, with considerably more zeal for his craft than for letters, and a decided intention to put his step-son, after some elementary schooling, into the business. Whether from avarice or narrow means, Ben was, at any rate, as he told

---

[1] Fuller, *Worthies*, 1662, 'Westminster', p. 243, art. Jonson : 'Though I cannot with all my industrious inquiry *find him* in his *cradle*, I can *fetch him* from his *long coats*. When a *little child* he lived in *Harts-horn-lane*, near *Charing-cross*, where his Mother married a *Bricklayer* for her Second husband.'

Drummond, 'brought up poorly', and his training in letters would in the ordinary course have ended with the rudiments gathered in 'a private school in St. Martin's Church', where, according to Fuller's researches, he was 'first bred'. But here stepped in a providence wise and kindly, if not, as measured by the result, quite unreservedly 'good', in the person of 'a friend' by whom he was 'put to school' at the great foundation of Westminster, hard by. The 'friend' has commonly, but without convincing reason, been identified with the great antiquary, Camden, then second master of the school. Jonson did not become a Queen's scholar, and may thence be assumed to have been by no means proficient when he entered the school, where Camden was not improbably his master from first to last.[1] To Camden, at any rate, the mature scholar and poet of later days

[1] *Conversations*, § xiii. Drummond's phrase 'putt to school by a friend (his master Cambden)' is unfortunately ambiguous; and may have meant merely that Camden was his master there, not that Camden was the 'friend'. The profound gratitude expressed in the epigram suggests a deeper debt than that of a scholar to one of his form-masters. But the following facts communicated by the kindness of the Rev. Dr. Gow, late Head Master of Westminster, largely remove the difficulty. 1. The Statutes of the School, prepared for the queen, provided only two masters, Head and Second. 2. In 1656-7 one Bagshawe, Second Master, made a complaint against Busby, the then Head, in which he says: 'Ever since the famous Mr. Camden's time (who preceded me both in that place & privilege) the Second Master taught only the third & fourth Forms: & for the instruction of the 1st & 2nd there was constantly an Usher deputed by the Upper Master.' 3. Jonson was not a Queen's scholar.—It would seem from (2) that Camden taught the whole lower school to the Fourth inclusive; and this, together with (3), favours the view that Jonson's language in the epigram means simply that Camden had been his sole or principal teacher, and that he had not proceeded much above the Fourth when he left. Apart from Camden, the only person whose claim to the honour appears to be at all plausible is the distinguished lawyer John Hoskyns, of whom Aubrey reports a pleasant tradition. 'His great Witte quickly made him be taken notice of. Ben Johnson [his junior by six years] called him Father: S$^r$ Benet told me, that one time desiring M$^r$ Johnson to adopt him for his Sonne: "no s$^d$ he I dare not, 'tis honour enough for me to be yo$^r$ Brother. I was your Fathers sonne; and 'twas He that polished me "' (MS. Rawlinson D 727, fol. 93). But this expression suggests a more personal and direct influence than that of one who simply 'put him to school'.—The interesting inscription to Camden discovered by Mr. Simpson in the Chatsworth copy of *Cynthia's Revels*, where Jonson describes himself as 'alumnus olim, aeternum amicus', throws no further light on this point.

declared, in his memorable epigram (xiv), that he owed 'all that I am in arts, all that I know'; and the relation between master and pupil continued till Camden's death to be an example of those hearty and sterling friendships which bound Jonson, as they bind many other men of exacting and difficult temper, to men considerably older, or younger, than themselves.

At Westminster the deep and secure foundations of Jonson's copious learning were, in any case, laid. How much of the imposing superstructure was actually completed there, we cannot know. But he left the school, thanks to the moulding influence of Camden upon a mind of astonishing and precocious vigour, if not already erudite, yet in full possession of all the tools and aptitudes by which the men of the later Renascence supplied their vast appetite for erudition. For thirty years at least after the close of his career at Westminster, amid all the distractions of writing for a livelihood, of lively social intercourse, occasional imprisonment, and frequent feud, he carried on the 'daily readings' of which varied and sometimes tantalizing record remains in the 'Execration upon Vulcan' and the 'Discoveries'.

## II

At the very outset, however, the practice of scholarship had to undergo a rude interruption. From the studies of Westminster, Jonson was 'taken', in his own words, 'and put to ane other Craft', a deliberately ambiguous phrase which Drummond did not venture to ask his formidable guest to explain—adding, however, on hearsay information that he 'thought' it was 'to be a Wright or Bricklayer'. In other words, instead of passing on to one of the Universities— probably Cambridge—as a Westminster boy would ordinarily do,[1] he was removed—perhaps even before reaching

[1] The theory that he actually did enter at Cambridge before being removed to the 'other Craft' rests upon the assertion of Fuller, who declares that he was '*Statutably* admitted into Saint *Johns-colledge*', but

# Early Life

the top of the school[1]—and put into the business of his step-father.

The experience was extremely distasteful, and probably brief. He 'could not endure'[2] the 'other craft', and finally that he there 'continued but *few weeks* for want of further maintenance being fain to return to the trade of his father in law' (*Worthies*, 'Westminster', p. 243). It was hardly worth while to send him to the University for 'a few weeks'; and the legend, when we next meet with it, in Aubrey, has ejected this limitation, and met its hero's consequent need of funds by the expedient of a sympathetic bencher, who, passing the young scholar-bricklayer at work ' on the garden-wall of Lincoln's Inn ... and hearing him repeat some Greek verses out of Homer, discoursing with him and finding him to have a wit extraordinary gave him some exhibition to maintain him at Trinity College Cambridge'. The germ of this statement is also in Fuller, who wrote : ' He helped in the building of the new structure of *Lincolnes-Inn*, when having a *Trowell* in his hand, he had a *book* in his pocket.' Oldys in a MS. note to Langbaine, p. 283, specifies minutely 'in the square where the Chapel stands not far from the old Gate which leads into Chancery Lane '. It is evident that the anomaly of so great a scholar owing nothing to either University tried the credulity even of the next generation, and that the myth-making instinct intervened, as usual, to relieve the strain. But the whole hypothesis is contradicted by Jonson's statement in the text to Drummond, borne out as this is by every other authentic utterance of his which bears upon the matter at all. One of these, also from the *Conversations* (§ xiii, 17 f.) —the assertion that 'he was Master of Arts in both the Universities by their favour, not his studie'—may be understood as asserting either that he had not sought the favour (*studio*), or that he had not obtained it by studies (*studiis*) ; in either case it implies that the degrees were honorary, not won in the ordinary academic course. And it is scarcely credible that an alumnus of either should have penned the lofty apologue to the two 'most equal sisters' without a hint of the vantage-ground he occupied. As it is, Jonson's tone and attitude are those not of one affiliated to either 'sister', but of a coequal 'brother', qualified by a birthright similar to theirs, but not derived from them, to claim their countenance and aid in the pursuit of a common ideal. And the attitude of the Universities towards Jonson in his own time, so far as we know it, was never that of the Alma Mater to a son. It was as a distinguished outsider that he finally received the degree. And in 1601 he had been described by a Cambridge wit, of the very college to which legend assigned him, in terms proper to a townsman who had by sheer dint of brains and hard work won some of the accomplishments of the ' gown ': '*Beniamin Ionson*; The wittiest fellow of a Bricklayer in England. A meere Empyrick, one that getts what he hath by obseruation, and makes only nature priuy to what he indites' (*The Returne from Parnassus*, ed. Macray, ll. 296-300).

[1] George Morley, Bishop of Winchester, who ' knew Jonson well', told Walton that ' he (Jonson) was in the 6º ... forme in Westminster scole'; but he vitiates his testimony by adding ' at which time his father dyed'. See Appendix I, ii.

[2] ' Could not endure.' The phrase was current in Elizabethan English in the colloquial sense 'detested (but continued to put up with)', as

broke away from it. His situation in the interim resembled that of his own Ovid and young Lorenzo, and the subterfuges with which they counter an unpoetic father were doubtless borrowed from his own practice.

Beyond the fact that this unendurable 'other craft' occupied at least some months, weeks, or days after leaving Westminster probably in 1588, and that he cannot have been entirely a novice in stage affairs when, in July 1597, he makes his sudden appearance in Henslowe's employ, the whole period between these events is—with certain reserves —quite problematical, and the research of a century has done little but convert the confident statements of Malone and Gifford into tentative hypotheses. Two facts alone emerge with complete certainty.

After throwing up the bricklaying, he made a temporary diversion into the seat of war in Flanders, apparently as a volunteer.[1] This episode need not be understood as an escape from impossible conditions, for he 'soon' returned. Domestic embarrassments may have made his absence convenient; but in the main it was a piece of adventure pure and simple. He was in the lusty vigour of his

---

well as in the literal: 'found intolerable, and broke away from'. Iago 'cannot endure' the Moor, but aims only at making him 'thank me, love me, and reward me' (*Othello*, II. i. 297, 317).

[1] *Date of the Flemish adventure.* It has commonly been assumed that this happened in 1591-2, the young bricklayer, after a brief experience, running away to 'serve in the wars'. This, however, renders it extremely difficult to understand what Jonson was doing between 1592 and 1597. Did he return to the bricklaying? This would be oddly described by Jonson's phrase to Drummond: 'betook himself to his wonted studies'; nor does one easily imagine a man of his temper, after once tasting blood (in the literal sense) in the field, returning to the trowel. But if his bricklaying was, altogether, only a brief episode of his boyhood in 1589 or 1590, and he now took to his books or to his pen, the persistent description of him as a 'bricklayer' in 1598 (Henslowe) and 1601 (*Return from Parnassus*) is not quite so easy to explain. There is much to be said, so far, for Mr. Fleay's view that Jonson served out his time in the bricklaying (perhaps for five years), the Flemish adventure following in 1596, and that on returning thence he betook himself at once to what were in 1619 'his wonted studies', viz. playmaking and poetry. The young and doughty maker of plays would still be, for malicious persons, the ex-bricklayer. But it is difficult to reconcile this chronology with the known date of his marriage.

early manhood, hardy, mettlesome and full-blooded, eager for exploit and for fame, of athletic build, with no 'mountain belly' yet, but lean and wiry (like Macilente), and already master of the adroit and muscular swordsmanship which a few years later disposed of Gabriel Spencer against heavy odds. To take arms was, for a young fellow of this type in the London of Elizabeth, an obvious resource. Nor, even had Jonson's position and prospects in letters been better than they were, was the division between the sword and the pen so decisive as it became under the more specialized professional conditions of later times. A defined literary class existed as little as a standing army, and Sidney and Ralegh in the higher ranks, Gascoigne and Lodge in the *bourgeoisie*, were only prominent examples of a temper which, during the stirring last decades of the reign, heard the Spartan trumpet across the glades of Arcady, and made songs and romances as they sped through the swirl of Atlantic surges on the sleuth of the Spanish treasure-fleet. Gascoigne's motto *Tam Marti quam Mercurio* might have served them all.

The great struggle in the Netherlands, to be protracted for yet half a century to come, was at the beginning of the nineties passing through one of its more languid phases. The extreme tension of the opening crisis had subsided. Since Zutphen (1586) there had been no considerable battle. To the Captain Hungrys (*Epigr.* cvii) who served for pay and rations this state of affairs might be agreeable enough. To the heroic patriots of the young republic it was not without compensations, for it meant at least that they were successfully holding their own. But to the military adventurer, as such, it was inevitably irritating. Jonson was no Captain Hungry, but neither had he any tincture of the passion for a cause which nerved the Fleming; and he found the general inertia simply tedious. He had come for the fighting, and, circumstances providing no opportunity, he made his own. Even through Drummond's dry and unsympathetic notes we catch a glimpse of the scene: a doughty figure advancing alone 'in the face of both the Campes', to meet an enemy in single combat, killing his man, and even stripping him of his arms and returning in triumph with these *spolia opima*;—a Quixote of the Renascence, if we will, but a Quixote who knew himself and his antagonist, and never allowed pedantry to interfere with business. He referred to this exploit, with dignified reticence, in the epigram 'To true Souldiers' (*Epigr.* cviii). It would seem to have been well known.

Such distractions could not avail for long, however, and Jonson, in his own words already quoted, soon returned and 'betook himself to his wonted studies'. Whatever else may be covered by this phrase, we may assume that the studies included a continuation of the close and critical reading of antique authors of which his earliest published writing bears trace in every line. But we must not think of Jonson's humanism as nourished in the leisured and fastidious seclusion of Horton. He had alienated his step-father, he had no private means, and at some date between 1592 and 1595 he had taken a wife. Putting all other motives for the moment apart, we may assume that from 1596, at latest, his 'studies', whatever else they were, had to be in some degree 'bread-studies', and it is clear that even after his first great success in 1598 the bread was not easily won.

Of Jonson's wife all statistical information is wanting, but a reasonable clue to her character and to the quality of the home is given by Jonson's laconic description of her to Drummond as 'a shrew yet honest'. Neither the five years' separation at a later period, nor the infidelities of his own which he narrated, later still, to the same confidant, in naïve conjunction with this spontaneous tribute to her loyalty, justify any inference in regard to the early years of their married life. Our only other glimpse of her is as the recipient, with her husband, of 'correction' in the London Consistory Court in the spring of 1606, for habitually absenting themselves from service, and also from Communion at their parish church. The incident will be noticed below, but it may be said here that Jonson denies both charges on behalf of his wife. There is thus no ground for supposing that she shared her husband's faith during his Catholic years.

Two children at least were born during these years; they are known to us from their father's epitaphs, not the least beautiful he ever wrote: Mary,[1] 'my first daughter', 'the daughter of (her parents') youth', who died at six months; and Benjamin,[2] 'my first son'—'child of my right hand', 'Ben Jonson his best piece of poetry',—whose death in 1603, at seven, frustrated the 'too-much hope' set upon him.

### III

The London in which Jonson, in his early twenties, thus had to battle for a livelihood, was enormously rich in stimulus and provocation for a mind and eye like his. Since his childhood, and even since his school-days at Westminster, it had grown rapidly in all the attributes of a great capital. Since the fall of Antwerp, in 1576, it had become a chief centre of European commerce in the north, and Gresham's Royal Exchange, still wearing the gloss of novelty, symbolized its advancing status. Professional adepts, medical, metallurgic, commercial, financial, found it worth their while to flock from Italy and France to the English metropolis. Jewish money-lenders came from Venice, the commercial capital of Europe; and Elizabeth's ministers themselves called in foreign experts to exploit the neglected mines. The ground was being prepared for the Jacobean 'projectors' whom Jonson is presently to ridicule, and for those picturesque encounters of commercialism and superstition which furnish forth *The Alchemist*, and are reflected in the balanced conclusions of Bacon's essay on

[1] *Epigr.* xxii. This daughter has been confidently recognized in a burial entry in the register of St. Martin's-in-the-Fields: November 17, 1593: *Seplta fuit Maria Jonson peste.* The date is probable enough, but the name was too common to authorize any conclusion.

[2] *Epigr.* xlv; *Convers.*, § xiii. This first son was therefore born in 1596, giving the latest possible date of the marriage.

'Usury'. The Inns of Court were the nucleus of a society, never before so numerous or so accomplished, of wits and men about town—lawyers, courtiers, young graduates from the Universities—who thronged the aisles of Paul's, indited Senecan blank verse in City garrets, or disconcerted the middle classes by their free living and free talk. And in the capital gathered, too, a crowd of provincials, country squires and their sons, the whole genus Nokes and Stephen, bent on seeing a play, learning to 'take' tobacco, and conversing with the wits. Half the matter of Jonson's future play-making was being enacted daily before his eyes.

And the literature which was being daily produced in this London of the early nineties was no less rich, for this critical onlooker, in provocation and in stimulus. From much that we count among its chief glories he turned away with indifference, or even dislike. The splendid torso of the *Faerie Queene* (1589–96), 'writ in no language' and in Italianate stanzas, can never have been to his mind. As little, the flood of sonnets of the same years, so 'sugared' to a courtlier taste and a more lyrical temperament than his. The whole Petrarchan and Ronsardist tradition left him cold. The languidly elegant pastoral romances of Greene and Lodge, and even the *Arcadia*, now first published (1590), of their master Sidney, did not interest him. The *Apology for Poetry*, on the other hand (published in 1595), appealed to him powerfully, and Sidney's lively diatribe against the romantic drama probably contributed at least to crystallize critical ideas which were presently to animate Jonson to a like assault.

It is likely, indeed, that little of what is to us most memorable in the drama of the nineties was to Jonson's taste. The magnificent expansion in power and depth which it had undergone since Sidney wrote, had been effected with almost complete indifference to the critical ideas of Sidney's school. *Tamburlaine* and *Faustus*, and the crowd of national *Histories* provoked by the triumph of 1588, played as fast and loose with Time and Space as the more childlike romantic plays which Sidney had derided. Whether Shakespeare's brilliant 'prentice-work' touched this critical poet in his susceptible early twenties must be left undetermined; but his obviously sincere lament over the ruin of poetry, on the morrow of *Hamlet* and *Lear*, makes it unlikely (whatever he might say in his posthumous eulogy) that he had felt either the 'Nature' or the 'Art' of *Romeo and Juliet* or *Richard III* ten years before.

But there were not wanting, in this teeming and brilliant literature—even in the drama itself—elements which must have been congenial to him. Jonson's habitual air of one contending with the tide easily blinds us to the fact that in essential respects it was flowing strongly on his side. The taste for realistic satire, drastic and humorous portrayal of manners, with a relish of classical allusion, grew steadily during the decade.[1] When Greene turned from his vague Euphuistic pastorals to tell his own sordid and squalid story in powerful vernacular (1592), with reminiscences of Terence and the Latin dramas of the Prodigal Son, he was complying with this growing current, and reinforcing it. Nashe belabouring Harvey with conscious imitation of the virulence of Humanist controversy foreshadowed Jonson's chastisement of Marston and Dekker through the mouth of Horace. Classical vehicles of literary attack were being introduced; Harington anticipated Jonson in the Epigram, Lodge and Hall in formal Satire. The Jonsonian attitude of *corrector morum* was the characteristic fashion of a 'quick-spirited age' when, as Barnabe Rich said, 'many excellent wittes are endeavouring by their pennes to set upp lightes, & to give the world new eyes to see into deformitie'.[2] Jonson could have wished no better statement of his own aims. His Humour plays, and especially the great 'Comical Satire' of 1599, broke sharply with the traditions of drama, but they formed the crown and culmination of the literature of humorous social satire; and when Jonson dedicated *Every*

[1] Routh, 'London and Popular Literature', *Camb. Lit. Hist.* iv. 317 f.
[2] *The Honestie of this Age*, quoted by Routh, *u. s.*

*Man out of his Humour*, with obvious confidence of their approval, to the Inns of Court, and recalled ' the friendship I had with diuers in your societies ' when he wrote it, he was invoking a bond of common literary sympathies between him and those classically trained wits, which is not likely to have been then first formed.

### IV

Such, in barest outline, was literary London in Jonson's early manhood. It was in this *milieu* that he reached, during the years in which he is invisible to us, the maturity displayed in his first independent work. But our first glimpse of him is in a different region. We find him, in 1597, playing in a strolling company of actors, hardly from pure histrionic zeal.

The stage was now by far the readiest means of livelihood for a poor man with a tincture of letters, and we have seen that Jonson, by 1596, was probably in need of income. Shakespeare, some two months before Jonson's appearance on the strolling stage, had bought New Place out of the profits of his theatrical connexion. Without repeating the familiar history of the beginnings of the London stage, it will suffice to recall that in this summer of 1597 there existed at least three regular theatres—the Theatre (1576)[1], the Curtain (1576), north of the river, and the Rose (1585), on the Bankside. There was also a theatre farther south at Newington Butts (1585); and the Swan, on the Bankside, perhaps already existed. The neighbouring bear-baiting pit, Paris Garden, was occasionally used for dramatic performances. A private house at Blackfriars was also probably by this date used for performances by the Children of the Chapel Royal, the formidable rivals, after 1600, of the men.

These stages were occupied, in 1596, by some three or four Companies, of which the Lord Chamberlain's was the most distinguished and prosperous, and the Lord Admiral's,

[1] The Theatre was probably closed in 1597 (Chambers, *Eliz. Stage*, ii, pp. 397-8).

it is likely, the most frugally managed. These Companies held the London district, and vigorously resented 'intrusion' from the country. But they themselves perambulated the country far and wide, under stress of plague or 'inhibition'; and country troupes, whose numbers and quality we cannot even distantly gauge, spent their whole time in 'strolling', with their wagon, from market-town to market-town, from village-green to village-green.

It was in one of the humbler of these troupes, there is reason to think, that Ben Jonson first entered into direct relations with the stage. Dekker is not to be trusted far when he speaks of Jonson, but his abusive stories and allusions are not to be set aside as inventions because they were malicious. They are not witty nor humorous in themselves; they could hardly have amused the audience unless they were true. 'I ha seene thy shoulders lapt in a Plaiers old cast Cloake, like a Slie knaue as thou art,' says Tucca to Horace in *Satiro-mastix*, 'and when thou ranst mad for the death of Horatio, thou borrowedst a gowne of Roscius the Stager.' And he recurs to the gibe: 'Thou hast forgot how thou amble⟨d⟩st (in a leather pilch) by a play-wagon in the high way, and took'st mad Ieronimoes part, to get seruice among the Mimickes.'[1] These glimpses, concurring as they do in all the essential circumstances, leave little doubt that Jonson had once played the hero's part in Kyd's *Spanish Tragedy* in a strolling company.

But he must have aimed at getting the more important and profitable employment to be had in the London theatres. From the 'play-wagon in the high way' to the furbished-up bear-pit of Paris Garden was no very violent or difficult transition; and another gibe of Dekker's makes it likely that this was the path by which Jonson reached his final important connexion with Henslowe. At Paris Garden he probably, like Dekker's 'Horace', played 'Zulziman',[2] and

---

[1] Quarto, 1602, sigs. D, G3 verso, G 4.
[2] *Satiro-mastix*, 1602, sig. G 3 verso: '*Tuc.* Thou hast been at Parris garden hast not? *Hor.* Yes Captaine, I ha plaide Zulziman there. *Sir Vau.* Then M. Horace you plaide the part of an honest man.'

Henslowe[1] had, since 1595, been the owner of Paris Garden. There the 'strolling actor', with some little rustic reputation, perhaps, for his struttings in Jeronymo's[2] 'old cloak, ruff, and hat', was apparently taken on as a journeyman player, and given a part in a lost play on some Eastern theme—'Zulziman'. Though never a good actor, Jonson had several qualities which would tell with the audience of Paris Garden: a muscular broad-shouldered figure, a loud ranting voice, and probably much swashing energy in action. Even the 'terrible mouth' and the 'face like a rotten russet apple when it is bruised'[3] were meritorious points in the actor of ferocious parts.[4] In the long run, and with a better type of audience and of play, physiognomical advantages might lose their zest. But in the meantime Henslowe had discovered that his journeyman player was a good hand at 'plots', and he was transferred, by pretty rapid steps, to the 'literary' department of the business. Such is a probable, though in some details conjectural, account of the process by which Jonson reached the position in which we find him, in July 1597, of a playwright in Henslowe's employ.

The suggestion that 'Zulziman' is Solyman in Kyd's *Solyman and Perseda* is improbable. Why should Dekker blunt the point of his gibe by a confusion which his audience could only clear up by asking themselves 'What is he hitting at? does he mean Solyman?'

[1] Fleay, *Biog. Chron.* i. 342, who suggests this as the origin of Jonson's connexion with Henslowe.

[2] *Jeronymo's* 'old cloak', &c. Jonson perhaps reverted to this reminiscence, as Mr. Boas suggests, in *Alchemist*, IV. vii. 71.

[3] Small has collected the traits of Jonson's personal appearance as presented 'from the adverse point of view.' in the *Satiro-mastix (Stage Quarrel*, p. 125).

[4] It is probable that he did not play them well. Apart from Dekker's gibes at the failure of the 'poor journeyman player' who could not 'set a good face on't'; apart too from the very definite tradition of his poor quality as an actor, transmitted by Aubrey ('Jonson never was a good Actor, but an excellent Instructor'); the fact remains that he withdrew from the stage as soon as he had won a secure foothold as a writer for it. And in the peculiar irritation with which all his life he played off sarcasms upon 'sporting Kyd' and the too famous Hieronymo (cf. Mr. Boas's *Kyd*, p. lxxxiii f.), sore reminiscence may have had some part. Whether or not he was the author of the *Addicions* their brilliant success never qualified his derision of the old play which they had in effect endowed with a new lease of vigorous life.

The first incident of Jonson's career as a writer for the stage, a somewhat ominous one, cannot be certainly traced to this connexion.[1] Jonson appears to have been employed to finish the fragment of a satiric comedy, *The Isle of Dogs*, left imperfect by Thomas Nashe. Nashe, according to his own pleasant but euphemistic account of the affair in the *Lenten Stuffe*, had, after writing the induction and the first act, conceived such terror of his abortive offspring, 'the infortunate imperfit Embrion of my idle houres', that he fled precipitately into the depths of Norfolk, arriving at Great Yarmouth 'in the latter end of Autumn'. The players, however, were not inclined to lose a piece which must have been brilliant and probably teemed with Rabelaisian piquancies. They accordingly arranged to complete it, without either asking Nashe's consent, as he bitterly but rather unreasonably complains, or 'having the least guesse of my drift or scope'. The principal if not the only hand employed was unquestionably Jonson's. If the master satirist of the age about to dawn misunderstood the drift of the master satirist of the age just over, it was certainly not in the way of giving a harmless or conciliatory turn to a dangerous motive. Jonson was not the man to make the lion he had to personate roar 'like a nightingale' out of concern either for the audience or for his own neck. Nashe even declared that it was this unintelligent supplement which had bred the troublesome consequences that followed both for the players and for his innocent self. The authorities, in any case, drew no distinction between the original fragment and the continuation. On the performance of the completed piece some time before July 28, when the theatres were closed, information was laid before the Privy Council of 'a lewd plaie that was plaied in one of the plaie howses on the Bancke Side, contanynge very seditious and sclandrous matter'. They promptly caused 'some of the Players' to be apprehended and imprisoned in the Marshalsea, 'wherof one... was not only an Actor, but a maker

[1] The entries in Henslowe which seemed to establish this are forgeries.

of parte of the said Plaie', and gave orders for the arrest and examination of the remainder, as well as for a search of Nashe's lodgings and perusal of such papers as should be found there.[1] Nashe's flight to Yarmouth appears to have saved him from arrest. On October 8 the two players, Gabriel Spencer and Robert Shaa, were released, as was also 'Beniamin Iohnson', who is thus identified with the 'maker of part of the plaie' referred to above. The affair, which excited wide attention and comment through the country, seems so far as they were concerned [2] to have ended here; but Nashe had to console himself by praising the Red Herring at Yarmouth (in *Lenten Stuffe*, 1599) for the loss of his wonted means of maintenance, while his enemies freely 'nibbled about his fame'. As for Jonson, his imprisonment was the beginning of a series of troubles with the government, and furnished his assailants in the Stage Quarrel, four years later, with another gibe.[3] Of any further relations between the two men no record remains,[4] nor has Jonson left a single allusion to his brilliant quasi-colleague. But that his first recorded experiment with play-making should have been made in the train of one who used the dramatic form only as a vehicle for exuberant satire is not without significance for the subsequent evolution of Jonsonian comedy, where the fundamentally satiric matter rebels so often successfully against the restraints of dramatic form.

Of this episode the diary of the shrewd manager whose service Jonson had now entered contains no hint. But the references to him, tantalizingly dry and curt, which begin in

[1] From *Acts of the Privy Council*; printed in full in Appendix III, where the warrants for their release are also reproduced.
[2] The current view that he was imprisoned and relieved in prison by Henslowe rests upon a forged entry in the diary. We agree with Mr. McKerrow (*Nashe*, v. 31), that Nashe's account of the matter probably expresses the substantial truth.
[3] '*Tucca* ... When the Stagerites banish thee into the Ile of Dogs, thou turn'st Ban-dog (villanous Guy), & euer since bitest,' &c. (*Satiromastix*, 1602, sig. G 4).
[4] Nashe refers to 'that witty play *The Case is Altered*', in the same treatise which complains of the operations of 'the Players' upon his *Isle of Dogs*.

July, 1597, grow from this time increasingly frequent. On July 28 he borrows four pounds from the manager, a fact which indicates some confidence in his powers on the part of the unsusceptible and far from open-handed man of business. On the same date Henslowe receives 3*s.* 9*d.* 'of Benjamin Jonson's share', no doubt in the proceeds of a performance in which he took part. But before the end of the year, at the latest, he was busy with another play, this time of his own devising. On December 3 Henslowe lent him twenty shillings 'vpon a Bocke w$^{ch}$ he was to writte for vs befor crysmas next ... w$^{ch}$ he showed the plotte vnto the company'.[1] By 1595, besides having collaborated with two others in a lost play for Henslowe, he had written at least two comedies which had been performed elsewhere. By the summer, moreover, at least one tragedy of his had been played, with applause, and his name began to be coupled with those of Marlowe, Kyd, and Shakespeare. It was in the early autumn that Francis Meres issued that naïve valuation of the wit of antiquity and of England which he entitled *Palladis Tamia*. His list of those who 'are our best for Tragedie', and worthy to stand for England, as Aeschylus, Sophocles, and Euripides stood for Greece, closes with the name of 'Beniamin Iohnson'.[2] Clearly, in the early autumn of 1598, for the fairly cultivated section of the playgoing public whose opinions Meres reflects, the quondam player of Jeronymo and Zulziman had likewise become one of the rising stars of the tragic drama.

[1] This 'plot' may be identical with 'bengemens plotte', on the basis of which Henslowe records, on October 28, that Chapman had written 'ii ectes of a tragedie', the tragedy being completed and paid for in full on January 8, 1599. But in view of Jonson's evident fertility in these early years, we must not, with Mr. Fleay, assume this; still less, that the tragedy was the *Fall of Mortimer*, of which the 'plot with the opening verses' still remain.

[2] *Palladis Tamia*, p. 283. The book was entered on the Stationers' Register on September 7.

## CHAPTER II

## THE HUMOUR PLAYS

### I

BUT within a few days after this pronouncement, two events occurred almost simultaneously, one of which placed Jonson at a stride in the foremost rank of English playwrights, while the other came near to closing his career altogether. About the middle of September, 1598, his *Every Man in his Humour*[1] was played by the Lord Chamberlain's Company at the Curtain; Shakespeare himself, to whom, according to a late tradition, its acceptance was due, taking a leading rôle.[2] A few days later (September 22), Jonson quarrelled with an actor of Henslowe's Company, Gabriel Spencer, fought with him in Hoxton Fields beyond Shoreditch,[3] killed him, and was arrested for felony. Jonson himself regarded this exploit with much complacency, declaring that his sword was ten inches shorter than his adversary's, and it is probable that Spencer was, in the final conflict, as he told Drummond, the aggressor.[4] But when put upon his trial at the Old Bailey, in October, he confessed the indictment, and escaped the gallows only by claiming right of clergy; being dismissed with confiscation

---

[1] A letter from T. Matthew to Dudley Carleton, September 20, 1598 (*State Papers* (*Dom.*) *Eliz.*, cclxviii. 61), speaks of it as 'a new play'.

[2] This 'remarkable piece of humanity' was first reported by Rowe, more than a century after its supposed date. That Shakespeare performed in the play is certain, his name heading the list of actors in the Folio.

[3] The formal indictment, discovered by Mr. J. C. Jeafreson in the Middlesex Sessions Rolls, was published by him in the *Athenaeum*, March 6, 1886. See Appendix III. We have two other acounts of the affair: Henslowe's in a letter to Alleyn: 'I haue lost one of my company w^ch hurteth me greatly; that is gabrell for he is slayne in hogesden fylldes by the hands of bengemen Jonson bricklayer' (Dulwich MS. I, 24, No. 25); and Jonson's own, to Drummond (*Convers.*, § xiii). The burial of Spencer is entered in the Register of St. Leonard's, Shoreditch, under September 24.

[4] *Convers.*, § xiii.

# The Humour Plays

of all his goods, and the Tyburn brand on his thumb.[1] There is some indication that other suspicions, less easy to bring home than a felonious assault, were entertained by the authorities. Spies ('two damnd Villans') were set upon him in prison 'to take advantage of him'; warned, however, by his keeper he gave them no handle, and the judges themselves 'could get nothing of him to all their demands, bot I and No'. To what did these 'demands' relate? Not to the charge of felony, for that he confessed, and what more did they want? The explanation is probably to be found in the fact that in the course of his brief confinement he had suddenly adopted the Catholic faith 'by trust of a priest who visited him in prisson'. A prisoner awaiting trial for his life, and only recently released from prison on another count, who voluntarily assumed a form of religion always regarded askance by the authorities, was only rendered the more liable to sinister suspicion by the very absence of obvious motives which commends it to modern sympathies. But all attempts to inculpate the new convert in any treasonable act or intention failed, and he went out of prison, a recusant, a branded felon, and a pauper, but untouched in life and liberty, inspired by a lofty intellectual ambition,[2] and the author of the best example of genuine comedy yet produced in England.

[1] The best evidence that Jonson was innocent of grave offence in the Spencer affair is the paucity and relative mildness of the allusions to it in the satirical diatribes of the Stage Quarrel. Dekker taunts him with his 'good mouth'—the mouth of a good biter; the mouth, too, of a good *reader*—of one, that is, who could save his neck by reading when arraigned for biting: 'thou baitst well, read, *lege*, save thyself and read'. So (in sc. vii), '*Tuc.* Art not famous enough yet, my mad *Horastratus*, for killing a Player, but thou must eate men alive?' (*Satiro-mastix*, 1602, sigs. G 4 and H 2 verso).

[2] *Convers.*, § xiii. The fire that burnt out his library in October, 1623, destroyed, among other things,

      twice-twelve yeares stor'd up humanitie;
With humble Gleanings in Divinitie;
After the Fathers, and those wiser Guides
Whom Faction had not drawne to studie sides.
                *Underwoods*, xliii. 101–4.

These 'gleanings', then, began about 1599. They did not cease when, apparently in 1610, he returned to the Anglican Church; they

The year following the success of *Every Man in his Humour* seems, in any case, to have been one of prosperous activity for its author. Before the close of 1598, his *The Case is Altered*, probably the work of the previous year, but baited for a contemporary audience with a lively introductory caricature of the City pageant-poet Munday, was acted by the Children of the Chapel—the beginning, apparently, of a long and important connexion. It was through the shrill voices of these 'little eyots', whom Shakespeare himself did not disdain to ridicule, that Jonson presently delivered his most elaborate discharges of dramatic satire; and one of the pigmies who had thus come to the support of their Hercules received at his hands, a few years later, the daintiest of his epitaphs (*Epigr.* cxx). With the Admiral's Company, too, his first employers, he again had active relations (perhaps after a temporary coolness due to the Spencer affair) in the latter half of 1599; collaborating with Dekker and others in two tragedies, *Page of Plymouth* and *Robert II King of Scots*, both of which are lost. This evidently involved no breach with the Company which had recently brought his first Humour Comedy on the stage; for in the course of the same year, or at the latest early in 1600, the elaborate 'Comical Satire' which purported to be its sequel and counterpart, *Every Man out of his Humour*, was played by the Chamberlain's men at their newly built theatre, the Globe. There is no reason to suppose that these versatile dealings with the several rival stages of his day indicate that he was attached to any of them by any bond inconsistent with his writing for another, or for any number of others.[1] He was rather in the position of an unattached author in

contributed to bring about the neutral attitude between the rival dogmatisms, which was apparently his later and final temper. 'For any religion as being versed jn both' (*Convers.*, § xix).

[1] See A. H. Thorndike, *The Influence of Beaumont and Fletcher on Shakspere*, pp. 11–12. Professor Thorndike judiciously criticizes the opposite view of Mr. Fleay, *Biog. Chr.* passim. He hardly recognizes sufficiently, however, in Jonson's case, that, though he may never have been formally attached to any company or stage, he certainly for a considerable period wrote exclusively for one, the Chapel Children.

our time, who may have several distinct 'lines' in literature, and publish with as many different firms according to their several specialties. For Henslowe the ex-Jeronymo continued to write romantic tragedy—culminating in *Richard Crookback* or, according to an improbable hypothesis, in the 'additions' to Kyd—as long, apparently, as he wrote it at all. For the Children he wrote, first, the romantic comedy, *The Case is Altered*, then the two dramas of personal satire, *Cynthia's Revels* and *Poetaster*, and the elaborate farce *Epicoene*. For Shakespeare's Company, finally, which had produced his first Humour Comedy, he wrote the second, and then, after an interval of estrangement, the greatest of the mature comedies, *Volpone* and the *Alchemist*, and the two classical tragedies.

These three groups of plays mark ascending gradations in seriousness of artistic purpose and, on the whole, in lasting worth. Of the pieces written for Henslowe not one was included by Jonson in his collected works, while only a single fragment at most—the 'additions' to *The Spanish Tragedy* sometimes ascribed to him—survives at all. Of those written for the Children, *The Case is Altered* was published without his consent, and not recognized by him. The others are applications of drama to personal quarrels of ephemeral interest. But the plays written for the Chamberlain's and King's men were one and all products of his most serious and deliberate art, wrought with titanic labour for the ears of posterity if they failed to touch his contemporaries. They include the three most remarkable of all his plays, two of less fortunate but still imposing power, and one, abortive as a drama but of the most brilliant literary texture—the magnificent perversion of comic method with which, towards the close probably of 1599, he tried the admiration excited by his first great comedy.

## II

*Every Man out of his Humour* was in fact a far more daring violation of precedent and tradition than its predecessor, and the confidence with which Jonson put it forth, coupled with the willingness of Shakespeare's Company to undertake the risk, shows that his first Humour Comedy had won him repute not only with the town at large but with the more exclusive and cultured section of the town to which the second directly and ostentatiously appealed. *Every Man in his Humour* had entertainment enough for all sorts and conditions of men, but in its original form, even more than in the tempered and refined Folio version, it was calculated more peculiarly to touch the vein of the young wits and scholars who thronged the precincts of Temple Bar. They saw grave parents, substantial City merchants, and a variety of solemn humbugs, professional and amateur, beguiled into ridiculous antics by two young university men obviously of their own breed.[1] The spirit of undergraduate fun breathes through this first and most illustrious of Town-and-Gown plays from end to end. It is not surprising that cordial personal relations, even 'friendship', should have existed, as we have seen that they did, between the scholarly playwright and various not undistinguished members of the Inns of Court,[2] some of them old 'Westminsters' and boon companions, like himself. The second Humour play was addressed even more directly to the intellectual part of his audience, and it put their intellectuality to severe tests. This class of hearer, if any, might

---

[1] In the Quarto version, both young Lorenzo and Prospero are much more decidedly academic than their later counterparts, Edward Kno'well and Wellbred.

[2] 'When I wrote this *Poeme* I had friendship with diuers in your Societies; who, as they were great Names in learning, so they were no lesse Examples of liuing' (Dedication of *Every Man out of his Humour*, 'To the ... Innes of Court', 1616). Among them were without doubt John Donne, and his genial 'chamber-fellow' Christopher Brooke, Richard Martin (b. 1570), who afterwards saved Jonson from prosecution for the *Poetaster*, and John Hoskyns (1566–1638), his intellectual 'Father', according to a late tradition already quoted.

be prepared to compound for a story-interest feeble, dispersed, and rather rudimentary, in return for a continuous and sustained brilliance of phrase, and a profusion of characteristic sketches etched in incisive and pungent epigram.  It is plain from the language put (probably by Jonson himself) into the mouth of Balladino (Munday) in *The Case is Altered*, I. i, that a certain cleavage had already shown itself in the audience between the 'gentlemen', who were 'pleased' with new plays where there was 'nothing but humours', and 'the common sort, who cared not for't but looked for good matter, they, and were not edified by such toys'.  For such 'gentle', academic, hearers and readers *Every Man out of his Humour*, with its disquisitions on Humour truly and falsely so called, its defence of the play by the example of the Old Comedy, and its novel application of the satiric 'character' of Theophrastus and Martial to the stage, was obviously calculated.[1]  It would seem, too, that Jonson reckoned rightly, and it was with some reason and fitness that, in 1616, he dedicated this brilliantly accoutred monster of a 'comical satire' to those 'noblest nurseries of humanity and liberty in the Kingdom, the Inns of Court'.

Even with the members of this profession, however, Jonson was soon to exchange sharp recriminations; for his part in which, this magnificent later tribute tacitly offered an honourable amends. Among his fellow playwrights his position was already less secure. His history and circumstances set him apart from them all, and he was not the man to diminish natural isolation by conciliatory manners. The demonic fascination which was soon to win him the warm friendship of men and women far above him in degree was qualified among his equals and rivals by an energy of plain speaking which complied with no man's vanity, and was deterred by no man's ill will. Drummond perhaps did him injustice when he said that Jonson would rather lose

---

[1] 'Of them (i. e. by his friends in the Inns of Court), and then (that I say no more) it was not despis'd' (Dedication to *Every Man out of his Humour*).

his friend than his jest, but Jonson himself declared that 'he would not flatter though he saw Death', and there is little doubt that he would rather have lost his friend than the pleasure of holding an unflattering mirror before his eyes. His relation with his comrades of the theatre was thus from the first one of unstable equilibrium, and his temperament, at once vehement and exacting, 'passionately kind and angry', was of the sort which accentuates every incipient disturbance of a difficult poise.

Agreeable, however, as it might be to the critical Aspers and Cordatos who looked on, the comprehensive castigation of the 'follies' in *Every Man out of his Humour* could not fail to wring some withers. A glaringly indiscreet introduction of the queen into the play, in the original version, also caused widespread resentment. And some incidental sarcasms upon certain grotesque extravagances of speech in the contemporary drama seem to have struck the first spark of that too famous 'Stage Quarrel' which absorbed the energies of the doughty Humour poet, and agitated the whole play-going world, during the next two years.

### III

John Marston, who recognized some of the fantastic mintage of his brain in the fustian speech of Clove (III. iv),[1] and thence assumed that this absurd fop was meant to be a portrait of himself, had some excuse for resentment. He had, since his début, to all appearance, stood closer to Jonson than any other of the younger men: an open admirer, almost a disciple. Though not more than two or three years his junior, he had fallen under the spell of the greater personality, as he was destined, when his anger fit had worn itself out, to fall under it again. A few months before (about August, 1599), in revising the faded old moral-comedy of *Histriomastix* (*c.* 1592), he had sought to

[1] Small (*Quarrel*, p. 45) points out that 'of the thirty-nine words and expressions ridiculed (in Clove's talk) only six can be certainly found in Marston's work'.

remodel the scholastic pedant Chrisoganus into the likeness of the great contemporary chastiser of Ignorance. The portrait was certainly meant to be flattering; to modern eyes, and quite probably to those of contemporaries, it reads like caricature. Marston's bad imitation of Jonson's invective had an air of ridicule. Of vengeance for such a well-meant but irritating act of homage there could be no question; and if there were, Clove would have been a pointless retort. Jonson did, however, permit himself to borrow some articles of Clove's[1] fantastic apparel from his admirer's ample wardrobe of fustian phrase.

This was, no doubt, somewhat rough treatment, and Marston's vanity was stung. He took his revenge in kind by introducing into his next play, *Jack Drum's Entertainment* (about August, 1600), some allusive caricature obviously intended for his quondam friend. Brabant senior, 'the prince of fools, unequalled idiot', wearing a 'perpetual grin', and ridiculously outwitted by a profligate Frenchman, bears intrinsically a hardly closer resemblance to Jonson than Clove bears to Marston. But in his character of a professed gull-hunter, who is 'puffed up with arrogant conceit of his own worth', the specific Jonsonian 'humour' is not unfairly hit off, while the disastrous disillusion which puts him 'out of his humour' is imagined quite in the

---

[1] Small, *Quarrel*, p. 88, conceives Jonson to have 'received this well-intentioned attempt to represent his virtues upon the stage as a personal affront'. He quotes, in support of this, besides Drummond's bitter analysis of Jonson's character, the fact that the name Chrysoganus, 'though noble in origin, would be best known to him as the name of the villain denounced by Cicero in his defence of Roscius'. The suggestion is ingenious, but Jonson was hardly to be thus beguiled by a name. And we agree with M. Castelain (*Rev. Germ.* January, 1907) that it is unreasonable to suppose that he mistook homage, however blundering and however inconvenient, for a personal affront. Jonson's assertion, as reported by Drummond, that the quarrel began with Marston's 'representing him on the stage', is not inconsistent with this interpretation. The decisive correction of the text of the *Conversations* in this place, proposed by Penniman (*War*, p. 40), Small (*Quarrel*, p. 3), and arrived at independently by M. Castelain (*u. s.* p. 136), removes the implication that the act of Marston in which the quarrel originated was the representation of him as 'in his youth given to Venerie'.

spirit of the catastrophes which overtake the humorists of the second Humour play. But Jonson took the measure of his 'Gulls' with more penetration.

There is little doubt that in his next 'Comical Satire', *Cynthia's Revels*, Jonson took cognizance of this attack; little doubt, also, that he used the occasion to retort upon at least one other assailant of whose offence we know nothing. The play was a palpable bid for the queen's favour, and a more diplomatic aspirant would have avoided the indiscretion of dragging his private quarrels into her presence. But such considerations had as little weight with this unknown outsider as they had later with the guest who was turned out of Hampton Court for ridiculing Daniel, or with the famous masque-maker who yet later ridiculed Wither, with impunity, on the same stage. The queen was, for Jonson, simply an enlightened and powerful judge, whose decision (necessarily in his favour) he sought to invoke. But *Cynthia's Revels*, performed most probably in January, 1601, by the Children of the Chapel,[1] was assuredly already on the stocks when the elder Brabant strutted and grinned on the stage of the Children of Paul's. The rivalry of the Companies of Children both with one another and with the Men's Companies was just now at its height, and Jonson's employment of the Chapel boys in itself marked at least strained relations with the Chamberlain's Company. But in one at least of these 'Children',[2] Nathaniel Field, a kidnapped pupil of Mulcaster's at St. Paul's School, Jonson took a personal interest. It may have been a little later that he read Martial and Horace's satires with his 'scholar'. But Field[3] was already, at thirteen, as Jonson

---

[1] Cf. Chambers, *Eliz. Stage*, iii. 364.
[2] Greenstreet papers quoted by Fleay, *History of the Stage*, p. 127. Kidnapping from the London schools for these Chapel stages was a regular practice, which testifies to the efficiency and profitableness of the boy actors. In 1600 Evans, the Master of the Children of the Chapel, and others incurred the censure of the Star Chamber in consequence.
[3] *Convers.*, § xi:

Nid field was his scholar.

publicly declared him in *Bartholomew Fair*,[1] fourteen years later, the best player in the Company. As such he took the leading part in the *Revels*.[2]

To return Marston's blow was, in any case, part of the original purpose of the play. And it can hardly be doubted that Hedon, 'the light voluptuous reveller', and Anaides, his shabby and foul-mouthed comrade, were intended to remind the audience of Marston and his new ally Dekker. They were recognized by his antagonists themselves, and before the year was over both once more returned to the assault. It was rumoured that they were preparing an elaborate revenge; and within a few weeks, at most, of the performance of *Cynthia's Revels*, Jonson, spurred to action, was at work, with a concentrated swiftness he rarely permitted himself, shaping a dramatic weapon which should fall, this time with unmistakable directness and crushing force, upon the two. The result was *Poetaster*, written in fifteen weeks. With all his rapidity, however, it is probable that Marston forestalled him with *What you Will*,[3] where Jonson figures as the satiric poet Lampatho. Marston's triumph was brief. *Poetaster*, which makes no allusion to *What you Will*, must have followed it close, and the sputterings of Marston's anger were lost in the Aristophanic ridicule with which the Humour poet, now thoroughly roused, covered the person and the speech of the unlucky Crispinus. Like *Cynthia's Revels*, *Poetaster* breathes its author's lofty assurance that his cause was the cause of poetry and of letters, and had the approval of all choice and worthy spirits among those in power. The latter conclusion had as yet very little support in facts, and

---

[1] *Barth. Fair*, v. 3 :

    *Cok.* Which is your *Burbage* now?
    *Lan.* What meane you by that, Sir?
    *Cok.* Your best *Actor*. Your *Field*?

[2] Jonson's *Works*, Folio, 1616, p. 270, table of actors.
[3] That *What you Will* was originally produced between *Cynthia's Revels*, which it parodies, and before *Poetaster*, to which it does not allude, has been made highly probable by Small (*Quarrel*, p. 104 f.).

Jonson's attitude justified Dekker's burlesque picture of the 'Humorous poet' venturing on the stage when his play was ended, and exchanging courtesies and compliments with the gallants in the Lords' room, 'to make all the house rise vp in Armes, and to cry "that's Horace, that's he, that's he!"' The two plays certainly made him new enemies; it would seem that *Poetaster* provoked even Shakespeare to a retort in kind;[1] but there is no evidence that they won him any new friends. His vigorous apology[2] for 'Cynthia's' severity to Essex even excited resentful murmurs in the populace, but it is doubtful whether Cynthia took any notice of it, whether it even came directly to her ears. Whether the engaging figures of Maecenas, and Virgil, and the other favoured persons of the Augustan Court stood for contemporaries of Jonson's, will be considered in the Introduction to this play. In any case the noble friends or fellow poets who might be flattered by these portraits, if such they were, did nothing at the moment, with the single exception noticed

---

[1] This is known only from a familiar passage in *Return from Parnassus*, Part II, IV. iii. Jonson's allusion, however, in the Apologetical Dialogue of *Poetaster* (ll. 137–9) lends some support to the surmise:

> Onely amongst them [i. e. the Players], I am sorry for
> Some better natures, by the reste so drawne,
> To run in that vile line.

Kempe, the clown of Shakespeare's company, is there made to say: 'O that *Ben Ionson* is a pestilent fellow, he brought up *Horace* giving the Poets a pill, but our fellow *Shakespeare* hath giuen him a purge that made him bewray his credit.' It seems probable, on the whole, that this 'purge' was given in *Troilus and Cressida*. Mr. Fleay pointed out the resemblance of Ajax, in many satirical traits, to Jonson as his enemies conceived him; and Small (*Stage Quarrel*, p. 167 f.) showed that this character is not derived, like the rest, from either Chapman's *Homer*, Chaucer's *Troilus and Creseyde*, Caxton's *Recuyell*, or common tradition, and may thus be presumed to be drawn from the living original whom it rather grossly caricatures. Jacques, in *As You Like It*, who wants to put on motley in order to speak his mind, and 'through and through Cleanse the foul body of the infected world', recalls the similarly 'armed and resolved hand' with which Asper (not many months earlier) had declared that he would 'Strip the ragged follies of the time Naked as at their birth'. Possibly enough Jonson may be glanced at; but note that Shakespeare gives Jacques the last word. His vindication of satire (which is substantially Jonson's) remains unanswered (II. vii. 83–7). This was clearly no 'purge'.

[2] *Cynthia's Revels*, V. xi. 9 f.

below, to shield the poet from the crowd of fierce and in part powerful resentments excited by the play. The most drastic expression of them was given, a few weeks later, by Dekker, in the *Satiro-mastix*, where the most resonant if not the most stinging cord in the 'lash' (Captain Tucca) was borrowed from Jonson himself. The game of applying the Satirist's scourge to his own back had already been made popular by the anonymous author of *The Whipping of the Satyre*, directed against Marston (who had 'scourged' Villainy in his day) as well as Jonson.[1] But, besides the playwrights, *Poetaster* incidentally offended both soldiers, lawyers, and the body of players at large. Neither Jonson's exploits with the sword, public and private, nor his intimacy with learned members of the Inns of Court, prevented peremptory pressure being put upon him, with the result that he composed as a kind of epilogue, an 'Apological Dialogue';—a manly and sufficient justification, but so much like a repetition of the offence that it rather irritated than soothed the smarting wounds, and, after a single performance, was prohibited. Even when he published the play itself in the following year, Jonson was restrained 'by authority' from coupling with it this unrepentant Apologia. Military swash-bucklers, dull enough to take Captain Tucca for a reflection on the army, were hardly pacified by the blunt concluding intimation that whoever 'is angry for the captain still, is such'. Neither was it a very tangible satisfaction to Templars who resented young Ovid's disparagement of the law, to be confronted with the authentic text of his insulting phrases in the real Ovid. The conclusion of the affair is obscure. But his enemies

[1] *The Whipping of the Satyre*, by W. I. [W. Ingram?] Imprinted at London, for John Flasket (S. R. August 14, 1601). Jonson is here attacked, as 'the Humorist', with two kindred representatives of 'Satyre', the 'Satyrist' (apparently Marston) and the 'Epigramatist'. This produced an anonymous reply (perhaps by Marston): *The Whipper of the Satyre his pennance in a White Sheete* (S. R. November 16). Nicholas Breton tried to throw oil on the waters with his *No Whippinge, nor Trippinge: but a kinde friendly Snippinge* (S. R. September 16). Dekker in the *Satiro-mastix* (last scene) and Jonson in the Apologetical Dialogue, as well as in the last act of the *Poetaster* itself, both allude to the *Whipping*.

were not content with merely suppressing the apology. A prosecution, probably in the Star Chamber, was threatened; and it might have gone hard with the unruly recusant who had, less than two years before, barely escaped the gallows. But the timely intervention of a good friend, a distinguished lawyer and wit of the Middle Temple, with the chief justice averted further consequences. Richard Martin, whose ' facetiousness' was soon to win the favour of James, and who seems indeed to have had Justice Clement's relish for a jest at the cost of solemn dignitaries, undertook to vouch for the 'innocence' of the play and of the author, a service acknowledged by the dedication to him of the Folio version. This indulgence can hardly have mitigated the storm of private wrath; and Jonson not unnaturally felt that his career in the perilous field of comic drama was for the time at an end.

> And, since the *Comick* MVSE
> Hath prou'd so ominous to me, I will trie
> If *Tragœdie* haue a more kind aspect.[1]

In these famous words he announced his withdrawal from the blood-stained arena into the hallowed precincts of a lofty impersonal art. But the old warrior still breathes battle, and there is a kind of inspiration in his lonely song, as he flings a parting gibe at the 'wolf's black jaw' and the 'dull ass's hoof', which will henceforth assail his gates in vain. For a few months he seems to have withdrawn himself literally into a sombre and sullen seclusion, even from his home. In February, 1602, the law student Manningham reported in his Diary that 'Ben Jonson the poet now lives upon one Townesend, and scornes the world'.[2] Jonson might play the misanthrope

---

[1] Apologetical Dialogue, ll. 210–12.
[2] Not, as formerly supposed, Aurelian Townshend, Jonson's later rival in Masque-making. He was now in hopeless poverty (cf. Chambers, *A. T's. Poems and Masks*, p. xiv). The reference is undoubtedly to Sir Robert Townshend, an accomplished patron of letters, to whom Jonson shortly afterwards expressed his grateful affection. A copy of *Sejanus*, quarto, now in the possession of Mr. T. J. Wise, contains the inscription: 'The testimony of my Affection, and Observance to my

as he would, some powerful or hospitable hand intervened to defend or shelter the 'scorner', who, like many other great quarrellers, provoked anger and admiring devotion at once, and often in the same minds.

## IV

From his home he remained absent for five years, but in 1602-3 he exchanged the hospitality of Sir Robert Townshend for that of Esmé Stewart, Lord of Aubigny.[1] D'Aubigny, with his elder brother the Duke of Lennox, belonged to a Scottish family who since the fifteenth century had held the seigneury of Aubigné, in Berry. Born and bred in France, he came to London only at the close of the reign. How Jonson made his acquaintance we are quite ignorant. But this long sojourn, on terms apparently of unbroken cordiality, is strong evidence of Jonson's personal magnetism. It was interrupted only by occasional country visits, sometimes flights from the summer and autumn visitations of the plague. Among his havens at such times was the country house at Connington of Sir Robert Cotton, an old Westminster schoolmate a year or two senior to himself, and already famous for his erudition in the mysteries of ceremonial and precedence, as for the great antiquarian library in his town-house at Westminster.[2]

noble Freind S$^r$ Robert Townseehend w$^{ch}$ I desire may remayne w$^{th}$ him and last beyond Marble.' The signature is unfortunately cut off in binding. Sir R. Townshend was also a patron of Fletcher, whose sprightly verses 'To the perfect Gentleman, Sir R. T.', prefixed to *The Faithful Shepherdess*, seem to imply much familiarity. We are indebted to Mr. Wise's courtesy for the opportunity of access to the *Sejanus* quarto.

[1] *Convers.*, § xiii. '5 yeers he had not bedded with her [his wife], but remained with my lord Aulbanic.' The 'five years' are fixed with much accuracy by Manningham's date February, 1603 (B.M. Harl. MS. 5353, f. 98$^b$), when Jonson 'lived upon' Townshend, and February 7, 1607, when he dated his dedication to *Volpone* 'from my house in the Blackfriars'.

[2] This is attested for a later time and may be assumed for at least the whole of James's reign. 'Beeing asked wher he sawe [the treasonable verses to Felton], he saith at S$^r$ Robert Cottons house at westminster : . . . that, coming in to S$^r$ Robert Cotton's house as he often doth, the paper of these verses liing ther vppon the table after dinner,

The library Jonson certainly used; even from his paralytic bed, long afterwards, he could send to borrow a volume, promising to return it the same day.[1] In the house at Connington, too, Jonson was probably already a frequent guest. It was on occasion of one of these visits, when Jonson had as fellow-guest Sir Robert's and his own master Camden, that he saw the vision of his eldest boy, who, he learned next day, had died at the same hour. The story, perfectly authenticated as it is, is the more interesting, since Jonson was by no means of the neurotic temperament favourable to visionary experiences.[2] These five years of quasi-bachelor existence may be suspected of having witnessed not a few of the discreditable distractions recorded or implied in the Hawthornden confessions. But they did not prevent this time from being, in the main, one of eager study, hard reading, and vigorous writing. Here, in 1604, he put forth against Campion, the blank verse classicist, and Daniel, the champion of romantic stanza, his proof that 'Couplets be the bravest sort of verses'[3]—an Augustan dogma which was still a heresy. Here, also, he made a more direct contribution to English classicism by translating the time-honoured Horatian text-book (or scrap-book) of Poetic Art, with observations, unfortunately lost, from Aristotle.[4] And from the same retreat came forth, at intervals, flashes of bitter gibe, outbursts of honourable praise, and one at least of the rare notes of tenderness, which, with these, were later gathered into the miscellaneous collection of his *Epigrams*.[5]

[he] was asked concerning thos verses, as if himself had been the auther thereof, &c.' (Examination by Attorney-General, 1629, printed in App. III. xii).

[1] The letter is printed for the first time in App. II. 21.
[2] *Convers*, § xiii.
[3] *Convers*., § i: 'Said he had written a discourse of Poesie both against Campion & Daniel ...' His unfinished 'Epick Poeme intitled Heroologia', mentioned in the same place, was 'all in Couplets, for he detesteth all other Rimes'.
[4] Cf. *Execration of Vulcan* (*Underw.* xliii. 89, 90), and note there.
[5] The lines on his eldest son (*Epigr.* xlv). Nearly at the same time he must have written the 'Ode ἀλληγορική' prefixed to his friend Hugh

Nor did his 'scorn for the world' continue long to be incompatible with doing its work and taking its pay. Within three months of the performance of *Poetaster* he was again busy writing for Henslowe, with whom he had, so far as we know, no recent ground of quarrel, and who can hardly have resented his attack upon the great rival Company. On September 25, 1601, Henslowe paid him two pounds for additions to *Jeronymo*, and again on June 22, 1602, no less than ten pounds for further additions to it and in earnest of a book called ' Richard Crookback ', —i.e. Richard III.[1] These were no doubt 'tragedy', but it is not likely that we have to recognize in either those 'fresh strains' with which he meant to 'strike the ear of time'—the 'something come into my thought, that must, and shall be sung, high, and aloof'. The fact that Jonson did not print 'Richard Crookback', any more than the earlier 'tregedies', among his collected works sufficiently proves that it had not engaged the ripened powers of the man of twenty-nine. The extant additions to *Jeronymo* may well seem worthy of all, or more than all, the tragic passion he possessed : but proud as he seems to have been of the amended play, he cannot have assumed thus solemnly the robes of the tragic poet in order merely to add 'salt', of whatever quality, to another man's antiquated dish.

The new trial of the auspices was clearly undertaken with the most resolute determination to extort the difficult 'kindness' of the tragic muse. He chose his subject in a field where he was past master, expended on the execution colossal intellectual labour, and entrusted the performance

Holland's time-serving *Pancharis*. Holland was one of Sir Robert Cotton's associates, and appended to the poem a letter addressed by him to Cotton, explaining its origin and intention.

[1] 'Lent vnto bengemy Johnsone ... in earneste of a Boocke called Richard crookbacke and for new adicyons for Jeronymo the some of x$^l$.' We are not justified in concluding, with Small (*Quarrel*, p. 59), from the magnitude of this sum, that it was full payment, and not earnest, for the play,—exactly what the text tells us it was not. We can, in fact, only conjecture how the money was divided between the unfinished play and the additions, by the presumption that the former had the larger share.

to the Company for which the most serious efforts of his art had hitherto exclusively been composed. He even called in an ally. For the 'second pen' which he later confessed to have had a 'good share' in the composition is most likely to have been that of the only one of his fellow-dramatists who shared his erudition, George Chapman.[1]

[1] 'I would inform you that this book, in all numbers, is not the same with that which was acted on the public stage; wherein a second pen had good share: in place of which I have rather chosen to put weaker, and, no doubt, less pleasing, of mine own, than to defraud so happy a genius of his right by my loathed usurpation' (Jonson, 'To the Readers', prefixed to Quarto, 1605; omitted from Folio). See Introduction to *Sejanus*. In the absence of further evidence no weight can be attached to the claim of an obscure poetaster, Samuel Sheppard, to have 'given personal aid' to Jonson's 'wit' in the *Sejanus* (*The Times Displayed*, p. 22). The claim, first made in 1646, attracted no attention till, in 1874, it found a convinced supporter in Brinsley Nicholson (*Academy*, November 14: *Shakespeare not part-author of Ben Jonson's Sejanus*). Without giving Sheppard the lie, we may conclude that his assertion :
I dictated
To him when as *Sejànus* fall he writ,
refers, as M. Castelain (*B. J.* p. 31, *note*) suggests, to some secretarial service, such as that of dictating Jonson's rough draft—service to which, in the crisis of the Civil War, when Jonson had long been dead and the literary world was scattered, he might well be tempted to give a heightened colour.

## CHAPTER III

### THE NEW REIGN. FROM 'SEJANUS' TO 'CATILINE'

#### I

BUT while *Sejanus* was still slowly growing into shape, the queen died, on March 24, 1603. The accession of a man of pronounced literary pretensions and scholarly tastes to the throne was an event of importance to literature and scholarship in many ways. If James I's example gave an unhappy sanction to pedantry, his genuine love of learning added perceptibly to the general estimation of all those kinds of literature which depend upon the mastery of books. Learning had even begun to organize itself. 'Academies', both literary and scientific, had been familiar for nearly a century in Italy. Isolated and somewhat tentative examples had already appeared in England, and these erudite conclaves, which had incurred Shakespeare's pleasant mockery a dozen years before, were wholly to the new sovereign's mind. The Antiquarian Society had been founded as far back as 1572. There Camden and Speed, Cotton and Carew foregathered, and in the famous library of Cotton House, already a rendezvous of scholars, Jonson and Bacon were equally at home, and may have begun their acquaintance. The generation of great scholars who distinguish this reign beyond all English precedent were not all encouraged by James; and some, like Selden, who misused their learning to support truth against the royal opinion, discovered how far he was from the *magis amica Veritas* of the true scholar. But few of them were wholly unaffected by the scholastic fashions which his example encouraged; folios expanded, quotations multiplied, the phalanxes of authorities grew more serried. Burton's

*Anatomy of Melancholy* (1621) is the first 'book', in the literary sense, which is at the same time monumentally erudite; the texture even of Bacon's *Essays* grows more crowded with quotation and allusion in successive editions.

Of these tendencies of the Jacobean time, *Sejanus*, already well advanced when James succeeded to the throne, was an early symptom. But its completion was retarded by other demands, equally significant of the new age. If James relished the solid banquets of learning, his queen delighted in its elegant diversions. In August, 1603, Jonson was called on to provide an entertainment for the reception of the queen and prince at Althorpe, on their way south from Edinburgh. The performance of *Sejanus* probably after this, and in any case before the close of the year, was far from being equally auspicious. The groundlings 'lookt awry' at its long speeches, and were not placated by their historic authenticity; and the approval of the cultured few did not avail to save it from a fate at their hands which its author compared with the savage doom inflicted on Sejanus himself by the infuriated populace of Rome.[1] Some individuals, too, of sufficient importance to make their resentment disagreeable to the dramatist, but branded as 'dull poet-haters' by his friends, insisted on discovering satirical implications. And it was no doubt hard to believe that the poet who had just used the Court of Augustus as a vehicle for unmeasured personal ridicule of his contemporaries, had portrayed the Court of Tiberius in the guileless spirit of a scholar bent only on the historical

---

[1] In the Dedication to Lord d'Aubigny (1616). The exceptional violence of this popular protest is attested also by the remarkable rally of his scholarly friends to vindicate him from 'the peoples beastly rage'. No less than eight copies of commendatory verses, by Chapman, Hugh Holland, Marston, and others, were prefixed to the Quarto. The picture of the groundlings' attitude is from *Fennors Descriptions*, 1616 ('The Description of a Poet,' sig. B 2), quoted by Gifford:

> With more than humane art it was bedewed,
> Yet to the multitude it nothing shewed;
> They screwed their scurvy iawes, and lookt awry,
> Like hissing snakes adiudging it to die;
> When wits of gentry did applaud the same.

accuracy of his play. In consequence perhaps of pressure from these supposed victims, Jonson was called before the Council to answer for his play. His principal accuser at the Board, according to the most probable interpretation of Drummond's ambiguous words, was the Earl of Northampton,[1] whom he had offended by beating one of his servants. He is said to have charged Jonson with 'popery and treason'. The character of this unprincipled nobleman, the second son of Surrey the poet, was pretty well understood, but the favour he enjoyed with James, and the cool but not unfriendly toleration accorded to him by the astute Cecil, made his enmity dangerous. He was probably, like most other members of the house of Howard, a Catholic, and his policy, so far as he had one, was to secure easier conditions for members of that faith in England. But as he was equally concerned to avoid the suspicion of being one himself, he accompanied his secret machinations in their favour with ostentatiously anti-Catholic activity, and Guy Fawkes, in whose trial he took part, had to suffer for the unfeigned virulence with which he was at this very moment compassing the ruin of Ralegh and Cobham, the arch-enemies of Catholic Spain. To a man of this type, incensed by the beating of his servant, Jonson's known Catholicism offered a ready pretext; nor was he likely to boggle at the task of proving treason in the author of a play which had a traitor for its hero. It is possible indeed that the passages excised from the original version of *Sejanus* contained speeches lending colour to such a charge; and one frank reference to the ingratitude of princes was left standing in the Quarto,[2] which might have served as an easy handle. The issue of this summons is not known. Probably it was not serious. Had Jonson suffered imprisonment or

---

[1] The statement in full is: 'Northampton was his mortall enemie for brauling on a St Georges day one of his attenders, he was called befor ye Councell for his Sejanus & accused both of poperie and treason by him.' Drummond's loose composition makes it by no means absolutely certain that the 'accusation of popery and treason' was grounded on the play, or even made on this occasion at all.
[2] Cf. Introduction to *Sejanus*.

other penalty, he would not have failed to relate it, as he related other things far more unequivocally dishonourable, to his host.

II

An incident of this kind did in fact occur, somewhat more than a year later, and it is reported by Drummond in one of the liveliest bits of the whole *Conversations*. No passage in Jonson's chequered career is better known, or more pleasant to remember. Towards the close of 1604 he had taken part with Chapman and with Marston in writing the comedy of *Eastward Ho*. For some incidental satire upon the Scots, including an amusing but doubtless offensive caricature of James himself, Jonson 'was delated by Sir James Murray to the King, . . . and voluntarily imprisoned himself with' his two collaborators, who had apparently already been arrested for the same offence. Whether the case actually came to trial does not appear, though Drummond speaks loosely of a 'sentence'. But it was rumoured that they 'should then had their ears cutt & noses'. Once more, however, as in the similar emergency provoked by *Poetaster*, some powerful friends of the Muses stepped in,—in particular Suffolk, the lord chamberlain, to whom Chapman in his *Sejanus* poem had returned grateful thanks for an earlier intervention of some kind on his behalf, and Jonson's host d'Aubigny,[1]—and the three culprits were released intact. After their delivery Jonson banqueted 'all his friends', the revered Camden foremost among them, and helpful Mr. Richard Martin, we may surmise, not left out. Of the speeches made over that auspicious table, one only has been reported, and, familiar as it is, it must not be omitted.

At the midst of the Feast his old Mother Dranke to him & shew him a paper which she had (if the Sentence had taken execution), to have mixed jn y^e prisson among his

---

[1] Cf. Chapman's Letter II to Suffolk: 'we heare from the lord Daubeney that his highnes hath remitted one of us wholie to your lo. fauoure.'

drinke, which was full of Lustie strong poison & that she was no churle she told she minded first to have Drunk of it herself.

Of this brief but critical imprisonment we have, however, one other no less vivid glimpse. For it was undoubtedly on this occasion that Jonson and Chapman wrote the much-discussed series of letters in which they severally appeal, with obvious indignation and astonishment at their position, to various powerful persons to be urgent for their release.[1] The letters belong to the interval between May 4 and September 4, 1605. The former is the date of Salisbury's elevation to the title by which Jonson addresses him; the latter, the date of the entry of *Eastward Ho* in the Stationers' Register. Within a few months of the date of his letters we find him not only at liberty, but employed on honourable and even confidential commissions by the two principal persons among those to whom his supplications had been addressed, Suffolk and Salisbury. For the marriage of Suffolk's daughter, the notorious Countess of Essex, he wrote, during the last weeks of 1605, the masque of *Hymenaei* performed on January 6, 1606. His vogue as a writer of Court masques was clearly growing. Notwithstanding his elegant celebrations of the queen's journey into England, he had not been employed for the Court masques of the new king's first Christmas (1603-4). His rival Daniel ('a good honest man, but no poet') had been called in, and had responded with an elementary example of the art of masque-making, which must have provoked Jonson's critical contempt, had he witnessed it. There is reason to suspect that he did witness it, and without concealing his opinion. For in the first days of January, 1604, he, with his good friend Sir John Roe, was 'thrust out' of Court for some kind of unmannerly behaviour by Suffolk himself, as lord chamberlain. But the offence, whatever it was, was soon condoned. The more so, probably, since Jonson had several opportunities, only a

[1] See Appendix II, where the letters are discussed in detail.

few weeks later, of showing his quality as a maker of ceremonial entertainments more decisively than by grimaces or guffaws at a rival's expense. When in March, 1604, James made his long-delayed State entry into the City, Jonson was employed, with Dekker, to provide the speeches. Four days later, when the king opened Parliament, Jonson addressed him in a 'Panegyre' of grave counsel and congratulation. And on the May day following, he furnished the little masque, miscalled by Gifford *The Penates*, with which Sir William Cornwallis regaled the king and queen at his house at Highgate. Their satisfaction is doubtless attested by the fact that Jonson was summoned to provide the Court masque for the following Christmas. The *Masque of Blackness* (1604-5) is the first of a series which continued unbroken, save by his own casual absence, for the remainder of the reign. And two years later, in spite of the fresh entanglements which had intervened, the lord chamberlain himself made amends for that expulsion in the way already described.

### III

It was in a graver matter that Jonson's services were commissioned, towards the end of the following year, by Lord Salisbury. On November 7, 1605, two days after the abortive Gunpowder Plot, he received a warrant from the Privy Council[1] to convey to an unnamed priest 'that offered to do good service to the State', a promise of safe-conduct 'to and from the lords'. How Jonson came to receive this commission is unknown: but as a professing Catholic, and under recent obligations to the clemency of the Council, he might well be credited with both special facilities for communicating with the conspirators and some disposition to use them. It is, however, by no means excluded that he offered his services. He was not in their secrets; their cause was in no sense his; and without

---

[1] Extracted from the lost Register of the Privy Council (Bruce, *Athenaeum*, 22 April, 1865, to whom the discovery of this incident is due).

pressing too literally his asseveration, in the subsequent report to Salisbury, that ' if I had been a priest, I would have put on wings on such an occasion, and have thought it no adventure, where I might have done (besides His Majesty and my country) all Christianity good service ', it is clear that he felt in the matter altogether as a subject and an Englishman, not as a Catholic. The mission, however, proved futile. Armed with his warrant, Jonson went to the chaplain of the Venetian ambassador, who engaged himself, before a witness, to find ' one ' (doubtless a priest) thoroughly informed of the Plot, ' absolute in all numbers ', for the purpose. He had to report, on the following day (November 8),[1] that the chaplain was unable to carry out the engagement, since ' that party will not be found ', and that all his subsequent attempts to get into communication with persons cognizant of the Plot had been met with evasions. The most important result of Jonson's inquiries was his report to Salisbury of the formidable dimensions and compact organization of the Plot which had just escaped success: ' So that, to tell your Lordship plainly my heart, I think they are all so enweaved in it, as it will make 500 gent: less of the Religion within this week, if they carry their understanding about them.' It was doubtless within a few days of this incident that Jonson addressed his congratulatory epigram to Lord Monteagle, the principal agent in the frustration of the Plot:

My countries parents I haue many knowne;
But sauer of my countrey thee alone.[2]

We may probably ascribe to the evidence thus given by Jonson of his sterling loyalty to the government, Catholic as he was, the indulgent treatment which he experienced shortly afterwards, in an encounter, dangerous at such a moment, with the ecclesiastical guardians of the Protestant faith. In April, 1606, he and his wife (as already mentioned)

[1] Letter of Jonson to Salisbury, endorsed by another hand, ' 8 Nov. 1600 ', clearly by an error for ' 1605 ' (*State Papers* (*Domestic*) *James I*, vol. xvi, No. 30). The text is reproduced in Appendix II.
[2] *Epigr.* lx.

were 'presented' at the Consistory Court of London for habitual absence from divine service and from Communion at their parish church. Jonson denied the first part of the charge, affirming that 'bothe he and his wife doe goe ordinarily to Churche & to his owne parishe Churche & so hath don this halfe yeare'—in other words, since the date of the Plot. Politic motives had thus doubtless induced an outward conformity. But to receive the Communion was another matter, and Jonson here had scruples of conscience which he was not the man to waive. He frankly put the matter before the judge, that he had been of another opinion in religion, 'which now upon better advisement he is determined to alter', and requested to have assigned certain learned men to confer with him, 'he promising to conforme him selfe according as they shall advise him & perswade him'. The judge accepted the proposal, and named for the purpose the Dean of St. Paul's, the Archbishop of Canterbury's chaplain, 'with whom he sayethe he hath some acquaintance', and others. The 'conferences' were to take place twice a week, and on the last court-day of the following term the stubborn doubter was to 'certify' to the court 'how he is satisfied and resolved'. We are unfortunately denied any glimpses of these conferences, but they can hardly have been without their humorous aspect. It would seem that Jonson's conscience resisted, for the present, persuasion, and that, having agreed to conform when he was 'persuaded', he in keeping with this proviso declined to conform. To all appearance the court acquiesced. Nothing is known, at least, of any further steps taken to remove his 'difficulties', or bring him back to the fold, and he remained a Catholic, according to his own statement, for five or six years more.

In addition to the charge of neglecting the offices of the Church, a vaguer but more serious accusation had been brought against him in the Consistory Court on the same occasion, that of being 'by fame a seducer of youthe to the popishe Religion'. This Jonson vehemently denied, and called for evidence. None was immediately forthcoming, and the judge thereupon called upon the churchwardens who had presented him to attend in court the next court-day and specify the particulars of their charge. The case was called on several successive (weekly) court-days of May. Nothing is known of the issue. It may be surmised that the churchwardens, failing to discover 'particulars', caused the case to be postponed from week to week. Some powerful influence too may have intervened. The court was plainly disposed to throw the burden of proof upon his accusers.[1]

## IV

The months that followed the discovery of the 'Plot' mark, indeed, in several ways the beginning of a new phase in Jonson's status and prestige. Less by any 'study' of his own than by the evident recognition of his sterling loyalty on the part of a king inclined to be friendly to fellow-scholars, he was now regarded with something more than tolerant eyes by the most powerful persons in the State. He was about to conquer the suffrages of the whole play-going world also, and at a single step to recover the prestige which the later Humour plays had sapped, and *Sejanus*, with all but the scholarly minority, shattered. *The Fox*,[2] in fact, without conceding an inch to unworthy tastes, must have laid as tenacious a grip upon the groundlings as upon the most scholarly relisher of Lucian or Petronius.[3] Some

[1] Our knowledge of these incidents is derived from the original entries in the records of the Consistory Court. Their discovery is due to Mr. F. W. X. Fincham, Superintendent of the Department for Literary Inquiry at Somerset House, who communicated the facts to the Royal Historical Society on April 24, 1921. His paper, 'Notes from Ecclesiastical Records in Somerset House, 1471–1858', was printed in the Society's *Transactions*, 4th Series, vol. iv, pp. 103–39.

[2] The play was probably written during the autumn of 1605; the topical allusions in II. i are more specific than such allusions commonly are, and seem to point clearly to events of the spring and summer of that year (Fleay, *Biog. Chron.* i. 373).

[3] Cf. Jasper Mayne's assertion, in the *Jonsonus Virbius*, 1638, p. 31, that

> When *thy* FOXE had ten times *acted* beene,
> Each *day* was *first*, but that 'twas cheaper seene.

months later, perhaps in the summer of 1606, when the plague was in London, it was presented, successively, before the two Universities, and the occasion appears to have been a signal triumph for the slighted scholar. Two years later he rewarded the 'love and acceptance' shown by the 'two most noble and most equal sisters' to his poem by a dedicatory epistle which is at once an *apologia pro vita sua* and the trumpet of a prophecy. In a prose at once stately, massive, and flexible, like brocade worn by a lithe athlete, he defends himself at the tribunal of these 'most learned arbitresses' from the charges of abusive satire to which his past career, and especially the events of 1605, might seem to render him liable. It is the appeal of a great single-handed champion—a Samson weary with slaughter of the Philistines—to the judgement of his kinsmen of Israel. And it is with the same lofty air of fellowship, of secure alliance in the defence of the temple of the Muses against the profane, that he holds up a scornful mirror to the dramatic degradation of the age—to the 'rotten and base rags, wherwith the Times haue adulterated' the form of Poetry, and declares his will, 'if my MVSES be true to me', to raise up her despised head again, 'restore her to her primitiue habit, feature, and maiesty, and render her worthy to be imbraced, and kist, of all the great and master-spirits of our world'.[1]

If the hope thus eloquently announced was ever fulfilled by Jonson, it was in the very poem which these words ushered in. But *Volpone* was already two years old when he wrote them, and the further fulfilment of the lofty promise tarried. His work as a masque-maker was indeed

[1] No doubt to lament, in 1607-8, over the degradation of poetry was to court the indignant protests of posterity, which recognizes in the first decade of the seventeenth century, if measured by its greatest achievements, the most momentous ten years in the history of the literature of the world. But a few supreme works do not make a literature; and Jonson looked out over the vast welter of writing, now in large part lost; much of it, to judge from the worst of what has survived, incredibly bad to an eye so exacting as Jonson's, though often no doubt, even at the worst, visited with gleams of poetry to which he rarely attained.

# From 'Sejanus' to 'Catiline'

steadily growing in importance as well as in vogue. Each new masque became, in the words of a contemporary, the rage of the hour at Court.[1] And Jonson contrived to keep the poet steadily predominant over the scene-painter, the upholsterer, the milliner, and the jeweller—no slight tribute to his talent and to his tact. The masque of *Hymenaei* for the wedding of Lady Essex (1605) had been followed (1608) by the brilliant *Hue and Cry after Cupid*, for the wedding of Lord Haddington; the rudimentary *Masque of Blackness* of the second Christmas by the rich and splendid *Masque of Beauty*, February, 1608. And a year later came the *Masque of Queens*, surpassing all other Jacobean masques in poetic force and fire. So far, at least, the development of this frail and evanescent genre had consisted in endowing it with nerves of poetry, not with the muscle and marrow of realism. But even so noble a creation as this could hardly suffice to vindicate so lofty a pledge.

On the stage proper, however, he was during these next two years to show the full compass of his dramatic power. *Epicoene* (1609–10),[2] a marvel of constructive technique, grounded on no matter how farcical a base, is by far the most laughable of his plays. It was probably well received by the men of the audience whose withers were not wrung; but Jonson's studies of contemporary folly were too incisively real and too rich in individual traits to escape personal acclamation, and angry protests mingled with the applause. *The Alchemist*, which followed in the autumn

[1] During the preparations for the Haddington wedding masque Donne wrote to his friend Sir Thomas Roe: 'If for custome you will doe a particular office in recompense, deliver this Letter to your Lady now, or when the rage of the Mask is past' (*Letters to Severall Persons of Honour*, 1651, p. 204).

[2] He dedicated the play in the Folio to a literary sailor-friend and boon companion in the Mermaid Literary Club, Sir Francis Stuart, with a veiled reference to the 'certain hatred of some', and to the 'contumely' done him which will be wiped off by Stuart's sentence. Little importance can be attached to the piece of chaff gravely retailed by Drummond (he had doubtless heard it from Jonson), to the effect that when it 'was first acted, there was found Verses after on the stage against him, concluding that that Play was well named the Silent Woman, there was never one man to say Plaudite to it'. How powerfully the illusion of personal intention was created by Jonson's realistically

of 1610, may also have provoked some individual animosity. His 'son' Herrick, in an ode 'Upon M. Ben Johnson', denounced indignantly the 'ignorance' of those

> who once hist
> At thy unequal'd play, the *Alchymist*;
> Oh fie upon 'em![1]

In common with *Epicoene*, it was even 'stayed' from publication for some months after their first entry in the Stationers' Register, and appeared only in 1612. This masterpiece, less recondite and less romantic than *Volpone*, but built with as consummate technique, and full of direct appeal to the business and bosoms of Jacobean London, cannot have missed, even at the outset, the profound effect testified nearly a generation later by Shirley's eulogy.

On these two signal triumphs followed a complete fiasco. *Catiline* (1611) repeated the failure of *Sejanus*; the successes of the intervening years availing nothing, as far as we can see, to temper the general resentment. For even the more refined and educated part of the audience, which had more than once responded to the appeal of his exacting and erudite dramatic work, concurred, this time, in the verdict of the groundlings.[2] Jonson published it the same year elaborated types is well conveyed by Beaumont in his verses on this play:

> Where he that strongly writes, although he meane
> To scourge but vices in a labour'd scene,
> Yet priuate faults shall be so well exprest
> As men do act hem, that each priuate brest,
> That findes these errors in it selfe, shall say,
> He meant me, not my vices, in the play.

[1] *Hesperides*, 1648, p. 173.
[2] This seems to be implied by the motto prefixed to the printed play:
> His non plebecula gaudet:
> Verum equitis quoque, iam migravit ab aure voluptas
> Omnis, ad incertos oculos & gaudia vana.

A curious passage in Gayton's *Pleasant Notes upon Don Quixote*, 1654, p. 271, describing Jonson's demeanour after the failure of one of his plays, applies very closely to this situation, and may perhaps, though the play is called a 'Comœdy', rest upon a confused tradition of it: '... although the only *Laureat* of our stage (having compos'd a Play of excellent worth, but not of equall applause) fell downe upon his knees, and gave thanks, that he had transcended the capacity of the vulgar; yet his protestation against their ignorance, was not sufficient to vindicate the misapplication of the argument; for the judicious part of that Auditory condemn'd it equally with those that did not understand it ...'

with a dedication to Pembroke, who, contrary to 'all noise of opinion', dared 'in these Iig-giuen times to countenance a legitimate Poême'. For three years Jonson offered nothing further to the public stage.

No such disaster checkers the record of the masques with which he now dignified the recurring Christmas festivities of the Court. His unbroken and ever-growing success in this graceful genre is not without an element of pathos. Hercules, out of request for the labours of his club, is eagerly sought for the dainty products of his distaff.

The *Masque of Queens* had been followed on the succeeding Christmas seasons by a series of slighter but even more ingenious and graceful pieces: *Love Freed from Ignorance and Folly*, *Love Restored*, *Mercury Vindicated from the Alchemists*, and the *Golden Age Restored*.[1] For other courtly and royal occasions also his help continued to be called in. With unmistakable zest he responded, in particular, to the summons to devise the elaborate 'Barriers' in which Prince Henry sought to celebrate his investiture as Prince of Wales, and the beautiful *Masque of Oberon* which followed. Nowhere else has the vein of chivalrous romance which undoubtedly ran in Jonson's nature disengaged itself so freely from the obsessions of realism and satire. In the yet more splendid celebration of the wedding of the Princess Elizabeth, in February, 1613, it cannot be doubted that he would have taken a conspicuous part, had he not then been absent from England. In his default, Chapman (who alone, he told Drummond, with Fletcher 'next himself could make a masque'),[2] and Beaumont and Campion, whom qualified opinion would rather seem to have associated with Chapman in this distinction, were employed, respectively, by the Middle Temple and Lincoln's Inn, by the Inner Temple and Gray's Inn, and by the Court.

[1] The last two masques fall in date beyond the limit of the present chapters.
[2] But it may be questioned whether 'Fletcher' is not Drummond's blunder for 'Beaumont'.

## CHAPTER IV

### JONSON'S SOCIETY, 1603-12

#### I

OF Jonson's private life during these years much can be gathered, but very little is precisely known. The years of friction with the authorities, of imprisonment and peril, impending punishment, and unexpected release, which stood out so vividly in Jonson's memory when he told the story of his life at Hawthornden, were followed by years of which he found almost nothing to say. His annals were dull, and to all appearance these years, which in any case saw the crowning achievements of his art and genius, were the happiest of his life. His gigantic faculty of work was being quietly but fruitfully applied, not in drama and masque only, but in the critical labours of a many-sided scholar. The rich collections destroyed by the fire in 1623 must have been in great part the work of these years. The scholar and the dramatist worked side by side; often, as in the Roman tragedies, in collaboration, sometimes in free and independent alliance, as in *The Apology for Bartholomew Fair* which its author prefixed to his Poetic Art founded upon Horace's Poetics. Stage interest probably had some concern, too, in his curious correspondence with Selden, about the same time (1615),[1] upon the purport of the Mosaic prohibition of the wearing of women's garments by men, and of men's by women. Selden, in furnishing him at great length with the Hebrew and Syriac literature of the subject, implies that everything relating to it in the Greek and Latin fathers of the Church was already known to his correspondent. Jonson, on his part, made a contribution, as other friends were doing, to the gigantic work which the hero of El Dorado, baffled in his aims but with his fiery energy still undimmed,

---

[1] *Joannis Seldeni Opera Omnia*, ed. Wilkins, 1726, vol. ii, pp. 1690-6.

was composing in the Tower. Ralegh's *History of the World* appeared in 1614. Jonson had sent him 'a piece of the Punic War', which, as he told Drummond with some resentment, Ralegh, who 'esteemed more of fame than conscience', had 'altered and set in his booke'.[1]

But deep student as Jonson certainly continued to be through these years of his most strenuous original production, he was assuredly never long a recluse. It is precisely to this first decade of James's reign that the famous memories of the Mermaid Tavern in Bread Street most clearly attach themselves. There, from 1603 or 1604 at least, if not the recognized autocrat, he was certainly a leading spirit in the company of 'Right generous, jovial and mercurial Sireniacks', as Coryat[2] called them, who included the best brains then busy for the stage. Two verse epistles, full of gaiety and charm, from Francis Beaumont in the country to Ben in town, give us a lively idea of the genial intimacy that prevailed there. In one of these, recently discovered,[3] he explains that he is not writing to show his wit or learning, or because he has anything new to tell, or 'hoping to be stilde A good Epistler thro the towne', 'but to showe The Love I carrie & methinks do owe To you . . .'

> Know I write not these lines to the end
> To please Ben Johnson but to please my frend.

---

[1] *Conversations*, § xii. 200, 201. Sir Charles Firth has identified the passage as the description of the revolt of the mercenaries against Carthage. See note on the passage in Appendix I.

[2] Coryat in November 1615 addressed a letter from Agra to about twenty-five friends in England, members of 'the right worshipfull Fraternitie of Sirenical Gentlemen, that meet the first Fridaie of euery Moneth, at the signe of the Mere-Maide in Bread-streete in London'. They include, beside Jonson, Donne, Sir Robert Cotton, Christopher Brooke, Sir Richard Martin, Inigo Jones, but doubtless also Beaumont and Shakespeare.

[3] Quoted by W. G. P. in *Times Lit. Suppt.*, September 15, 1921, from an old commonplace-book. The letter (twenty lines as quoted) contains an interesting new allusion to Shakespeare at the height of his career:

> heere I would let slippe
> (If I had any in mee) schollershippe
> And from all learning keep these lines as cleere [MS. deere]
> As Shakespeares best are, which our heires shall heere.

The other letter is famous. It was in 1606 or 1607 that Beaumont, detained in the country by an unfinished play, wistfully dreamed, amid his pastoral hayfields and harvest-ale, of the 'full Mermaid wine', and the 'things' done and spoken there—

> Words that have been
> So nimble, and so full of subtle flame,
> As if that every one from whom they came
> Had meant to put his whole wit in a jest
> And had resolved to live a fool the rest
> Of his dull life;—[1]

and protested that all his own wit flowed from Ben's, and that he had no good but in his company. Sarcastic outsiders put the matter less kindly, ascribed Ben's wit, such as it was, to his vast potations, and declared that all his plays were 'drawn' at the Mermaid first.[2] To the years between 1602 and 1610, too, we must assign Jonson's famous wit-combats with Shakespeare, of which Fuller[3] reported a tradition too vivid and too intrinsically probable to be dismissed. Yet it is doubtful whether Fuller's account does justice to the magnetism of Jonson. He judged from hearsay, and his report is to be qualified by the first-hand witness of the Beaumonts and the Herricks who had come under his spell. If, as Fuller says, 'his parts were not so ready to run of themselves as able to answer the spur', if 'he would sit silent in a learned company, and sink in (besides wine) their several humours into his observation', he clearly had the quality which makes the silences and slownesses of men of

---

[1] *Master Francis Beaumont's Letter to Ben Jonson, written before he and M. Fletcher came to London, &c.* The sarcastic reference to 'Sutcliffe's wit', as Mr. Fleay points out, makes it probable that the letter was written in or shortly after 1606, when Sutcliffe issued three tracts (*Biog. Chron.*, i. 170).

[2] Jasper Mayne in *Jonsonus Virbius*, 1638, p. 30.

[3] Fuller, *Worthies*, 1662, 'Warwick-Shire', p. 126, 'Many were the *wit-combates* betwixt him and *Ben Johnson*, which two I behold like a *Spanish great Gallion*, and an *English man of War*; Master *Johnson* (like the former) was built far higher in Learning; *Solid*, but *Slow* in his performances. *Shake-spear* with the *English-man of War*, lesser in *bulk*, but lighter in *sailing*, could turn with all tides, tack about and take advantage of all winds, by the quickness of his Wit and Invention.'

strong personality as alluring as eloquence, and their mere presence a fertilizing source of wit in other men.

Whether his great antagonist in those half-legendary wit-combats was allured or repelled, whether he was on intimate or distant terms with Jonson, whether they were close friends as well as fellow-dramatists who worked for rival companies on radically different principles, are questions which Jonson's biographer cannot avoid, but can answer only with surmise. The complete silence of authentic tradition fortifies, but does not compel, the more negative conclusion.

But the Mermaid was far from being the only resort in which Jonson in these years was a welcome and even honoured guest. He was certainly intimate with several men of his own or similar standing, who can only occasionally have crossed its threshold. John Donne, to whom Jonson, so difficult a critic of other men's experiments in epigram, humbly submitted his own,[1] and whom he thought 'the first poet in the world in some things', did not love the company of lesser poets; his passionate temperament, whatever depths of profligacy it lured him to explore, was not without its haughty reserves; his Bohemianism was, like Jaques's melancholy, his own. To Jonson he was a loyal friend, and Jonson honoured his judgement and revered his counsel even when he demurred to it. An extant letter (App. II, xi) shows us Jonson smarting under certain calumnious 'whisperings', and bent, against Donne's advice, upon publicly repelling them, 'the proper justice that every clear man owes to his innocency'. None of Jonson's friendships stimulates our curiosity and interest more than this.

An intimacy of a different kind, which excites our interest hardly less, and baffles it more completely, connected both poets with the distinguished civic family of Roe. To Sir John and also to William Roe, Jonson addressed, at various

---

[1] *Epigr.* xcvi:
>  Who shall doubt, DONNE, where I a *Poet* be
>  When I dare send my *Epigrames* to thee?

times, the most heartily affectionate of all his epigrams. In 1616, according to a recently discovered record (printed in Appendix III), Jonson appeared as witness in a lawsuit arising out of William Roe's university career. Sir John was something of a scholar as well as a brave soldier, and an 'infinite spender'. He was honoured by Jonson with a copy of a treasured volume, Casaubon's *Persius*; was severely wounded in the Netherlands in 1605, but recovered and finally died of the plague in Jonson's arms;[1] Jonson furnishing the cost of the funeral to the extent of £20, 'which was given him back'. It was this friend who shared Jonson's ejection from Hampton Court at the performance of a masque, and wrote him an epigram on the event in the spirited key of—

> Forget we were thrust out; It is but thus,
> God threatens Kings, Kings Lords, as Lords doe us.[2]

## II

But one of the two ejected spectators had speedily found his way back into the precincts of the Court as poet. And it is plain that the barrier normally interposed between the

---

[1] *Epigr.* xxxii refers to his wound. Jonson's inscription in the *Persius* is worth noticing as an indication of his estimate both of Roe and of Persius, as well as, incidentally, of himself: ' D. Joanni Roe, Amico Probatissimo, Hunc amorem et delicias Suas, Satiricorum doctissimum, Persium, cum doctissimo Commentario Sacravit Ben. Jonsonius . . .' The other details from *Convers.*, § xii.

With a third brother, Sir Thomas, Jonson was doubtless on less intimate terms, but they can hardly have been unacquainted. Sir Thomas Roe was by far the most distinguished man of a capable family. Still well remembered as the first official resident at the Court of the Mogul (1614) and as the author of a fascinating account of his adventures there, he had been a comrade of Donne in his secular days and was to become the trusted confidant ('honest Tom') of the fugitive Queen of Bohemia. The description of him placed on record by the Court of the Company before his appointment as a 'man of a pregnant understanding, well-spoken, learned, industrious and of a comely personage', may be taken to express, with whatever heightening, the generic character of the Roe brothers.

Sir Thomas Roe's account of his embassy is now edited in a readily accessible form. Many of Donne's letters to him, addressed 'dear Tom', are extant (*D. N. B.* sub nomine).

[2] *The Poems of John Donne*, ed. Grierson, i. 414.

Court society and the professional persons who catered for its amusement was in his case easily relaxed or overcome. Still in the prime of manhood, his rugged and irregular features, scarred and blotched as they were with disease, conveyed an impression of formidable and aggressive power; but their harshness was tempered by a brilliant eye, sensitive and speaking lips, and a finely moulded brow, shadowed by waving clusters of short black curls. With little interest in women, and a very imperfect apprehension of their finer qualities, Jonson had in extraordinary measure the virility which attracts many women more surely than tenderness. It is certain that he found among the ladies of distinguished family who surrounded the queen, and who took part with her in the stately diversions he devised, some who admitted him to friendship, if not to more intimate relations still. Of such an episode, and one of which the memory and the aroma lingered long, the graceful lyrics in which he celebrated 'Charis' appear to be the record.[1] 'Charis' was probably the lady who played Venus ('See the chariot at hand here of love, wherein my lady rideth!') in the masque, hitherto known as the *Hue and Cry after Cupid*, performed at Lord Haddington's marriage in 1608. The identity of 'Charis' can only be guessed at; but we know that eight years later Jonson put two, perhaps the finest, stanzas ('Do but look on her eyes') into a play,[2] that eleven years later 'I'll taste as lightly as the bee' was one of the commonplaces of his repetition at Hawthornden, and that fourteen or fifteen years later he wrote a proem to the series, still 'celebrating', at fifty, her who 'shall make the old man young'.

If 'Charis' inspired his choicest verses of love, Jonson enjoyed with several other women of rank an intercourse in which there was more of friendship than of patronage. In a number of noble families literature was a traditional interest or occupation, and the society of men of letters willingly cultivated. Chief among them were those in

---

[1] *Underwoods*, ii.   [2] *The Devil is an Ass*, II. vi.

which ran the blood of the Sidneys and the Haringtons. Lucy Harington, Countess of Bedford, above all, made her country house at Twickenham a little court of literature—as near an approach to the French *salon* as the English seventeenth century ever achieved. To Donne she was 'the Countess' *par excellence,* not without reason; to Drayton also, and to Jonson, she showed herself a generous friend, and Jonson's epistles and epigrams to her disclose the rare quality of friendship which admits both of familiarity and of reverence.[1]  Two ladies of the Sidney family not unworthily rivalled the Countess of Bedford:—Sidney's daughter, the Countess of Rutland, and his niece, wife of Sir Robert Wroth. In both friendships the husbands played a secondary or even hostile part. Lady Rutland—a 'widowed wife', in a peculiarly poignant sense—was herself a poet, and one, in Jonson's opinion, 'nothing inferior to her Father', if we may trust the Hawthornden conversations, which contain little flattery. Addressing herself, he heightened the same comparison into shameless hyperbole.[2] Jonson enjoyed her hospitalities on a familiar footing, and two picturesque scenes, of which they were the occasion, stood out in his memory and are not easily obliterated from ours.[3]  One, when he read Overbury's *The Wife* aloud at her request, and with so rare a grace that Overbury charged him with intending an unlawful suit, while the lady herself kept certain lines of his reading always in her remembrance; the other, when Rutland suddenly entered as she sat at table with Jonson, and angrily rebuked her for 'keeping table to poets'. Lady Wroth's literary proclivities were even more pronounced. Her pastoral romance *Urania* (1621) gracefully continued the Arcadian and Sidneian tradition. Jonson 'exscribed' some of her fluent sonnets and addressed to her a well-written if not very poetical sonnet of his own

---

[1] *Epigrs.* lxxxiv and lxxvi. The letter already mentioned from Jonson to Donne (App. II, xi) probably refers to his friendship with the Countess, and to some calumny of which it had been the occasion.
[2] *Convers.*, § xii; *Epigr.* lxxix.
[3] *Convers.*, §§ xii; xiv. 357-60.

(*Underwoods*, xxviii). Between 1606, when Sir Robert Wroth succeeded to his father's estates, and 1614, when he died, Jonson was on a familiar footing with both husband and wife, and assuredly knew at first hand the rural hospitalities which they dispensed at Durance, and which he describes with so unmistakable a relish, and with so much genuine and unsought charm, in the epistle to Wroth.[1]

With two, at least, of the male scions of the Sidney family, Sir Robert Sidney and the Earl of Pembroke, son of Sir Philip's sister, Jonson was on similarly friendly terms. At the ancestral mansion of Penshurst he enjoyed a hospitality which imposed none of the indignities to which men of letters were liable in some other noble houses; there

> comes no guest, but is allow'd to eate,
> Without his feare, and of thy lords owne meate: ...
> And I not faine to sit (as some, this day,
> At great mens tables) and yet dine away.[2]

The Earl of Pembroke (to whom he had so confidently dedicated *Catiline* as well as, a little later, his *Epigrams*) was accustomed to send him £20 (equivalent to nearly £150 now)[3] every New Year's Day, to buy new books, and the 'penance' playfully imposed upon the poet by the countess, for approving her husband's assertion that 'women be men's shadows',[4] throws an attractive light upon his personal relations with them.

---

[1] *Forest*, iii, 'To Sir Robert Wroth'. The frank and comrade-like tone of this epistle to 'my Wroth' does not harmonize very well with Jonson's assertion (*Convers.*, § xiv) that Lady Wroth was 'unworthily maried on a Iealous husband'. But it is surely incredible that Jonson should have written thus had he himself, as Mr. Fleay suspects, been the occasion of Wroth's jealousy. This gratuitous suggestion rests, however, on no more tangible grounds than the fact that Jonson's poems to 'Celia' occur in the *Forest* near the epistle to Wroth, and that Mr. Fleay believes 'Celia' to stand for Lady Wroth.

[2] *Forest*, ii, 'To Penshurst'.

[3] *Convers.*, § xiii.

[4] *Convers.*, § xiv. Jonson's 'proof' is given in the *Forest*, vii. A French Latinist, Aneau, had already 'justified' this satiric commonplace, and Jonson did little more than translate, though with more than his usual neatness, Aneau's epigram. Whatever his regard for individual women, it probably represents not unfairly his opinion of the sex at large.

But Jonson's occupations during these sojourns in country houses were not exclusively literary. At Polesworth, at any rate, the seat of Sir Henry Goodyere in Warwickshire, where he was perhaps introduced by Donne, he witnessed the sport in which Goodyere was as keen a connoisseur as in books and friends. If Jonson did not hawk himself, he learned 'why wise-men hawking follow', and rewarded his host with a pleasant comparison between the hawk and the satirist.[1] Wroth, too, was a devoted sportsman, who hunted hare, partridge, and stags in their season, and 'gave his gladder guests the sight'.

With a large number of other persons of rank or distinction the *Epigrams* and the *Forest* show that Jonson had, by 1612, at least a formal acquaintance. That his intercourse with his five years' host, d'Aubigny, did not end with his removal in 1607, on d'Aubigny's marriage, to his own house in Blackfriars, is shown by his fine epistle, some months later, to the young wife (*Forest*, xiii). At the Universities, which had spontaneously recognized his rank and where *Volpone* had been performed with signal applause, he had warm wellwishers, as his reception at Oxford in 1619 was to show; but the evidence of his intercourse with either Oxford or Cambridge between these visits is very meagre. When James visited Cambridge in March, 1614–15, Robert Lane, president of St. John's College, requested Jonson 'to penne a dyttye' for the reception.[2] At Oxford, Sir Henry Savile, the stateliest figure in the then academic world, was still presiding over the fortunes of Merton, as well as of Eton, when Jonson addressed to him his striking epigram (xcv). But it is doubtful whether the most Tacitean of English dramatists had other than slight occasional relations with the translator of Tacitus.

With another Scotsman of distinction and influence at Court he seems to have been on a friendly footing. Sir

[1] *Epigr.* lxxxv.
[2] Cf. the St. John's College Magazine, *The Eagle*, vols. xvi, p. 237, and xxv, p. 134.

To his Loving Father, & worthy Friend
Mr. John Florio:

The ayde of his Muses.

Ben: Jonson seales this testimony
of Friendship, & Loue.

Inscription in a gift-copy of 'Volpone' now in the British Museum

Robert Aytoun, gentleman of the bedchamber and secretary to the queen, was, Aubrey tells us,[1] 'acquainted with all the wits of his time in England', and was something of a wit himself. Well versed in French and Italian, he wrote courtly love-songs which Burns thought it worth while to rewrite in dialect, but hardly improved. Jonson he 'loved dearly', if we may trust the *Conversations* (§ xi); and they had apparently a further tie, not shared by most of the wits, in scholarship.

Without doubt there was a very decided reverse to this picture of growing honour and extending friendships. Jonson was a generous but a difficult friend; he paid willing homage to intellect and learning in whatever station, but bore fools with undisguised impatience, whatever their rank. And he demanded recognition for himself with a fearless assurance which sometimes strained the rigorous code of seventeenth-century etiquette. With the Court, in particular, Jonson's relations were decidedly chequered. With the great dignitaries, Suffolk and Salisbury, he was now reconciled, and he requited their not unimportant favours with literary tributes which have done some service to their fame.[2] But it is probable that their estimate of the value of these and other services differed appreciably from his own. Salisbury, he remarked bitterly to Drummond, 'never cared for any man longer than he can make use of him'.[3] And his pointed praise of the even-handed hospitality of Penshurst may well have been prompted by recollection of the scene at Salisbury's otherwise managed table,[4] which he described to the same reporter.

---

[1] Aubrey says that Aytoun was 'a great acquaintance of Mr. Tho: Hobbes of Malmesbury, whom Mr. Hobbes told me he made use of (together with Ben Johnson) for an Aristarchus, when he drew up his Epte dedicatory for his translation of Thucydides' (Aubrey MS. 6, fol. 116).

[2] *Epigrams* xliii, lxiii, lxiv, and lxvii.

[3] *Convers.*, § xiv. 353-4. Drummond wrote 'longer *nor*', but this is his provincialism.

[4] *Convers.*, § xiii, 317-21. 'Being at the end of my Lord Salisburie's table with Inigo Jones, and demanded by my Lord why he was not glad, "My lord, said he, you promised I should dine with you, but I doe not", for

In this case Jonson had some reason to resent his treatment, however unconventional his mode of protest. The guest at the bottom of the board whose scowl attracted the notice and inquiry of his host at the high table was no nonentity, and his reply, 'My lord, you promised I should dine with you, but I doe not', though doubtless received with derisive laughter by the company, was as dignified and cogent as it was bold. Clearly the man who understood courtly usage in this democratic sense was not likely to show excessive deference to the well-born witlings and criticasters, the 'Lords Ignorant' and 'Courtlings' and 'Court-parrots' and 'Court-worms', who, like Hotspur's perfumed popinjay, presumed on their superiority to the rough strong man. The strong man wrote of them with an intensity of scornful phrase such as Pope used to brand the silken and milk-white effeminacy of 'Sporus'. It was not, perhaps, necessary to be a Shakespeare to score momentary triumphs over the solid but slow-moving intellect of Ben. But there can have been no lasting peace between the autocrat of the Mermaid and the 'chamber-critics' who dined and supped 'at Madams table', and 'made all wit goe high, or low', at their own valuation;[1] or who 'set up new wits still' to 'pluck down' his. Ben Jonson, in these circles, must have endured some of the humiliations, and achieved also the condign revenge, of his great namesake in his classical affair with Lord Chesterfield. For the niceties of feminine etiquette he had little regard, and if women did not admire his masculine power the less because it was often blunt and unceremonious, he was singularly exempt from a corresponding illusion in their case; and the marked and painted Court beauty attracted with peculiar readiness the cynical regard which for him— a few chosen women friends set apart—habitually disrobed

he had none of his meat; he esteemed only that his meat which was of his own dish.' Cunningham suggests that this probably occurred on one of the two festive occasions at Theobald's for which Jonson provided an 'Entertainment', i.e. either on July 24, 1606, or May 22, 1607.

[1] Cf. *Epigr.* lxxi, 'On Court Parrat'; lxxii, 'To Court-ling.'

womankind of even ordinary grace and virtue. 'I', he says,

> Have eaten with the Beauties, and the Wits, . . .
> And came so nigh to know
> Whether their faces were their owne, or no.[1]

For the most part the welter of personal antagonism, quarrel, and intrigue which lies behind these diatribes escapes our scrutiny. But in one case at least the woman at whom he levels his scorn in these years can be identified. What Jonson's special quarrel with Cecily Bulstrode was, we do not know. Certainly few men in his day, or in any day, have assailed a woman with the foul-mouthed ferocity of his lines to 'The Court Pucell' (*Underwoods*, xlix). The erotic verses addressed to her by one of her intimates (probably either Donne or Roe)[2] sufficiently attest her character. But Jonson impatiently flings aside the dignity of just rebuke (which indeed he had little title to administer), in order to outdo her in ribald abuse. It is not Juvenal denouncing Messalina, or Knox rebuking Mary, that the spectacle recalls, but Pope hitching into rhyme his acrid and shameless gibes at Lady Mary Wortley Montagu.

### III

Jonson's relations with the Court were not the less difficult and precarious because his position there was that of an artist whose services, though not easily dispensed with, were needed only on rare occasions, and were moreover of a kind peculiarly exposed to the jealousies of colleagues and rivals. The masque, as a joint product of several categories of artists—poet, scene-painter, architect, musician, the devisers of dresses and dances—surpassed even modern opera in its capabilities as a hotbed of professional intrigue. Jonson, who from first to last stood for the supremacy of the literary element in the masque, had to contend not only with the professional pride of the representatives of

---

[1] *Underwoods*, xiii. 33–6.
[2] See *The Poems of John Donne*, ed. Grierson, i. 410.

other arts but with the insatiable appetite of Court audiences for spectacle and pageantry. With some of his fellow-artists, as Thomas Giles, the ingenious maker of dances, he was on cordial terms; with one, at least, the musician Alphonso Ferrabosco, on terms of affectionate friendship. Ferrabosco, who was of English birth though of Italian parentage, was one of the distinguished band of composers who made the early decades of the seventeenth century the golden age of English song. His equally distinguished father had exercised his invention, in friendly emulation with Byrd, upon the gem of Elizabethan anonymous lyrics, 'I saw my lady weep';[1] the son found music for all the songs of Jonson's earlier masques, as well as for the 'Celia' in *Volpone*, and Jonson rewarded his help with the heartiest acknowledgement in prose and verse.[2] Notoriously different, even in these early years of their joint career, were Jonson's relations with the architect Inigo Jones. The two men had much in common, but their community was not of the kind that makes for concord. Each, with a vast equipment of knowledge, ideas, and inventive capacity in his special domain, had his full measure of the masterful arrogance of genius. Inigo had returned from Italy steeped in the neo-classicism of Palladio, and eager to graft upon the half-Gothic luxuriance of Elizabethan art its severer and more disciplined technique. His talents had already won him powerful patrons at other European Courts, and the sister of one of these, Christian IV of Denmark, was now Queen of England. From the first he enjoyed the marked favour of Anne, and from 1604–5 to her death, and long afterwards, his invention and versatile craftsmanship left their mark upon each season's festivities. In the *Masque of Blackness*, which gave the first example of the developed Jacobean masque, the new *régisseur* and the new masque-poet for

---

[1] Peacham, *The Compleat Gentleman*, 1622, p. 101.
[2] Cf. the tributes appended to *Hymenaei* and to the *Masque of Queens*, and the two epigrams (cxxx, cxxxi) to Ferrabosco, prefixed severally to his *Book of Ayres* and to his *Lesson for 1, 2, and 3 Viols*, both published 1609.

the first time met in collaboration. The cause and occasion of the original rupture between them cannot be clearly made out. It is evident that the two artists entertained radically divergent notions of the importance of their several functions in the masque. The equilibrium between them, however long maintained, was therefore eminently unstable. For Jones, as for most of the spectators, the life of masques lay in show; whence the conclusion modestly drawn by Daniel in his preface to *Tethys' Festival* readily followed, that in them 'the art and invention of the Architect gives the greatest grace, and is of most importance'. For Jonson, on the contrary, the 'show', however elaborate, furnished by the architect was only 'the bodily part' which the poet's invention and verse had to animate.[1] His statements of the shares of the several artists, in the notes to the published masques, cannot be called unjust or grudging towards Inigo, but they convey the impression that he is tacitly rebutting much larger claims[2] on his colleague's part. No conclusion can be drawn from the fact that some of these statements were excised, and others retained, in the Folio. However hostile his attitude towards Jones may by that time have become, he might well be willing to retain statements already published which defined his opponent's pretensions. On the other hand, we cannot argue hostility from the omission of such statements in the *Love Freed from Ignorance and Folly* and the *Oberon*, or the omission of the former reference to Jones in *Hymenaei*; for the address to his undoubted friend Ferrabosco is also omitted. But two of the Epigrams tell a different story. We can hardly mistake the person aimed at in the lines to 'Mime' (cxv), and on 'The Town's Honest Man' (cxxix), nor the deep-seated long accumulated malignity which discharges itself, with calculated

---

[1] Commentary on *Masque of Blackness* (Folio, 1616, p. 895).
[2] Cf. the close of the comment on the *Masque of Queens* (ib. p. 946) and the defiant flourish of the *Haddington Masque*: 'The deuice and act of the scene. M. YNIGO IONES his, with additions of the Trophæes. For the inuention of the whole and the verses, Assertor qui dicat esse meos, Imponet plagiario pudorem' (ib. p. 942).

irony, in both. The two men were, then, before the publication of the Folio, and probably by 1612, bitter enemies at heart. For more than two years after this latter date, owing first to Jonson's, then to Inigo's, absence from England, they never met; and absence may have tempered their feud. They in any case resumed collaboration; but the gusto with which Jonson, in 1619, recounted the insults he had levelled at Jones shows that the fire first kindled about 1612, which blazed out so fiercely in 1631, only smouldered during the intervening years.[1]

In spite, then, of our almost complete ignorance of definite events in Jonson's life, apart from the annals of his literary output, during these years of his intellectual prime, we can construct a tolerably distinct picture of his social *milieu* between his thirtieth and fortieth year, and of his demeanour in and towards it. A personality of immense force, which stamps with ineffaceable character every line he wrote, but was neither very supple nor very sensitive, he exercised over both men and women a charm which always contained the germs of repulsion. His strength, though capable of delicacy, and even of tenderness, and pouring itself out without stint in praise of what was strong in others, passed readily, when confronted by ignorance and pretension, into a ferocity which knew neither chivalry nor mercy. No man of his time probably had heartier friends and bitterer enemies, nor more of either. And the diversity of his attachments is as remarkable as their number. Jonson's towering egoism was not that of a narrow nature. He was poorly endowed with the sympathetic imagination which crosses the frontier of alien souls. But he had in a high degree the genial versatility of the full-blooded temperament; he touched life and character at many points, knew

---

[1] The whole matter is excellently discussed by Brotanek, *Die engl. Maskenspiele*, p. 243 f. Brotanek ascribes their first quarrel to Jones's resentment at the omission in the Folio of some of the published references to him—due he thinks merely to want of space. He would thus date their quarrel in 1616. But the Epigrams referred to in the text leave little doubt that they had quarrelled before the publication of the Folio.

the austere discipline of the schools and the riotous abandonment of the tavern; he had Camden for his master and Venetia Digby for his 'Muse', and could yet indulge in a boisterous freak of stercoraceous humour like the 'Famous Voyage'[1]—deliberately printed in his collected works,—of which the great Samuel's midnight 'frisk' with his 'gay dogs' is a decorous shadow.

[1] *Epigr.* cxxxiii.

## CHAPTER V

## LATER MATURITY

I

THE year 1612-13 has no claim to be regarded as a turning-point in Jonson's career, but circumstances have made it a valuable landmark for his biographer. By 1612, it is probable, he had begun to prepare the definitive edition of his works, in folio. It marks Jonson's critical self-consciousness—in contrast with Shakespeare's lofty unconcern—that already, in his fortieth year, while still in the heyday of his powers, he deliberately and with the minutest care brought his literary output into the shape by which he wished it to be finally judged.

But the volume was not published until 1616. Mr. Simpson (*Every Man in his Humour*, p. xxxii f.) has shown that the delay may be sufficiently explained by the fact that Jonson's printer was engaged during the intervening years in printing Ralegh's *History of the World*. These years were also a time of lean harvests with Jonson himself. He produced no play between *Catiline* (1611) and *Bartholomew Fair* (1614), and no masque between *Love Restored*, Twelfth Night, 1612, and *A Challenge at Tilt*, December, 1613. During a great part of the interval Jonson himself was absent from the country, and thus took no part either in the obsequies of Prince Henry (who died on November 6, 1612) or in the wedding festivities of the Princess Elizabeth, celebrated with extraordinary splendour in February, 1613. Jonson had apparently not visited the Continent since his Flemish campaign of some twenty years before.

This visit, like the first, is known to us chiefly from one or two reminiscences touched with characteristic bravado which fastened on the memory of the laird of Hawthornden.

On the recommendation, a late tradition asserts, of Camden Jonson, his former pupil, was invited by Sir Walter Ralegh, then and for nearly ten years past a prisoner in the Tower, to act as tutor, on a foreign tour, to his son. It was hardly a happy choice which singled out Jonson to play Mentor to a notorious young scapegrace among the distractions of Paris. His eminence as a scholar was unquestioned; and Ralegh was indebted to him, among others of the 'best wits in England', as already noticed, for some help in his *History of the World*. He was now, moreover, once more a Protestant; and if Ralegh had heard how the zealous convert 'drank out the cup in token of complete reconciliation', he is not unlikely to have relished this unequivocal demonstration against the Church of the Inquisition and Philip II. But Ben's genial redundance in the cup was a dangerous trait. He was, moreover, imperfectly versed in French, in which his pupil seems to have had some colloquial skill. In his attempts to apply a salutary discipline to his charge, he was thus heavily handicapped. It is needless to repeat the story of young Ralegh's exploit in the streets of Paris; a dangerous insult to the Catholic religion which might well have cost the lives of both. Happily Jonson found occasion twice at least to put off the rôle of the pedagogue which he played so imperfectly, and resume his more natural function as a scholar and critic.

The first of these occasions was a theological Debate between Protestant and Catholic champions, held in a private house in Paris on September 4, 1612, and witnessed by Jonson. A certain 'S. E.' later published a summary of the discussion,[1] from which we learn that a certain M. Knevet, a Catholic, coming to Paris during the sojourn there of a doughty Protestant minister, Daniel Featley,[2] was 'put in

---

[1] Included in *The Relation of a Conference touching the Reall Presence*, by L. I., Douay, 1635.

[2] Featley had been young Ralegh's tutor at Oxford, and left an unfavourable report of him. Was Ralegh present at the disputation, and did it suggest the profane turn which he gave to the exhibition of the drunken Ben?

mind that he was mistaken in the matter of religion', in particular, it would seem, on the doctrine of the Real Presence. Knevet thereupon told his brother, 'an honest gentleman living in Paris', that he would like to hear the case argued. On the following day, accordingly, a formal 'disputation' on the Real Presence, of a kind then familiar, took place in Knevet's chamber between Featley as 'opponent' and Smith, later Bishop of Chalcedon, as 'respondent'. Featley had with him John Pory, a member of James's first Parliament; and among those present, clearly by invitation, was 'M. *Ben Iohnson*'. A report of the proceedings was subsequently issued, certified as accurate by both Pory and Jonson. Jonson's words, appended to Pory's, are:

> I professe, that all things in this Narration deliuered and quoted out of D. *Smiths Autographie*, are true out of my Examination. And of the rest I remember the most, or all; neither can I suspect any part.
> B. I.'

Jonson listened, then, as an invited guest, to a debate between spokesmen of the faith he had recently resumed, and of that which he had previously held 'for twelve years'; and it is plain that his certificate of the accuracy of the report was accepted by the Protestant champion, Featley, who published it with the report itself in his *Grand Sacrilege of the Church of Rome*, 1630.[1]

The argument, to judge from the specimens given, appears to have been, on both sides, a peculiarly tasteless and futile example of scholastic logic, and no conclusion can be drawn from the fact that Jonson heard it and certified the accuracy of a report as to the grounds either of his previous abandonment of Protestantism or of his recent return to it. But the trust evidently reposed in him by the Protestants goes to confirm the conviction, supported by all we know of him besides, that his return to Protestantism now, when his

[1] W. D. Briggs, 'On certain Incidents in Ben Jonson's Life' (*Mod. Philology*, xi. 279 f.).

worldly interest concurred with it, was as sincere as his former acceptance of Catholicism at the peril of his life.

The date of the Disputation shows that Jonson left England, at latest, at the end of August, 1612. We know that he was again in London by June 29, 1613, the date of the burning of the Globe Theatre, which he tells us in the 'Execration of Vulcan' that he 'saw'. It is possible, of course, that Jonson paid two visits to Paris, one at the time of the Debate, the other in 1613 when, according to Drummond's report, he was there with young Ralegh. But this is most unlikely in itself, and his complete silence in connexion with a national event so considerable as the marriage of the princess in February confirms the conclusion that he was then absent from the country.

Of the circumstances which brought him into contact with the Cardinal Duperron nothing is known, and our knowledge of their intercourse is confined to Drummond's tantalizingly laconic report of a single interview, which not improbably brought it to an abrupt end. Jacques Davy Duperron was, in 1613, approaching the close of a long and highly prosperous career. The son of a Huguenot refugee, he had rapidly discovered that full scope for his brilliant and supple intellect was only to be found in the Catholic Church. Here his advance was rapid. Eloquent, persuasive, and adroit to the highest degree, a master of dialectic and of policy, he established his sway not only over the weak Henri III, but over the shrewd and politic Béarnois himself, whose acceptance of the Roman faith, as the only basis of peace, was mainly his work. In the Conference at Fontainebleau, in 1600, between Catholics and Calvinists, he was chosen to champion the Catholic faith, and scored a rhetorical if not a moral triumph over Duplessis and Mornay. At Rome he twice procured the success of the French candidate in the election of popes. As a preacher, a wit, and a scholar, he had a high repute. While still a young man he had been chosen to pronounce the funeral *éloge* of Ronsard. His oration is a classical piece of obituary eloquence. His bons mots were famous.[1] He threw off fluent copies of verse,—satires, ballads, translations from Virgil and Horace—all long since forgotten. Yet in his own day, his 'free translation' from Virgil—portions of the First and Fourth Books of the *Aeneid*—acquired at least a momentary notoriety, and not in his own country alone. A copy sent by him, apparently in 1612, to his countryman and controversial antagonist, Casaubon, in England, aroused the interest of James, who expressed through Casaubon a desire to receive a copy for himself. Duperron's reply went astray, was surreptitiously printed, translated into English, and published in London.[2] In it, after excusing himself for the delay and thanking Casaubon for showing the king a former letter, and procuring for him some part of the royal favour, he proceeds: 'As for the Translation of Virgil's Verse, whereof you say his Majesty desired a Copy, that being lost, which before I sent to you, I must defer for some days the performance of this duty, for that I have caused it to be printed again with an addition of one part of the Fourth.' He will presently, he adds, send a copy for Casaubon to present to the king in his name.[3]

When, a few months later, Jonson met Duperron,— probably introduced by Casaubon, and at the cardinal's house—it was natural that the cardinal should bring out the translations which had won so flattering a notice from the English king, to receive the plaudits of his learned subject. The result, to a great ecclesiastic, wit, and courtier, whose career had been a series of intellectual and social triumphs, must have been highly disconcerting. 'He told

[1] Cf. *Perroniana et Thuana, ou Pensées judicieuses et bonmots du card. Perron* . . . Colon, 1594.
[2] *A Letter written from Paris by lord Card. of Perron to M. Casaubon in England, translated out of French.* 1612.
[3] The subsequent relations, not here in question, between the king and the cardinal, were less amicable. Du Perron in 1614 delivered an oration on behalf of the Lords Spiritual, in opposition to a motion of the third Estate, to the effect that neither temporal nor spiritual power can release a subject from its allegiance to the monarch. To this James wrote a reply in the name of offended divine right, and the cardinal retorted.

Cardinal de Perron . . . who shew him his translations of Virgil, that they were naught.'[1] This frankness was yet more shocking to French notions of politeness than to ours, and his distinguished French biographer finds it scarcely credible.[2] But it is hard to believe that this was not substantially what Jonson said. He was not morose, and it was no peevish willingness to wound that prompted him. The cardinal's work, described in the published title-page as 'une traduction libre', was not likely to conciliate a scholar whose own foible was rather a wooden literalness, and to invite his approval of a translation executed on the wrong principle was to call out all that formidable passion for holding up a glass before the eyes of faulty men which made him wish, as he told Drummond, for the chance of preaching one sermon to the king; 'for he would not flatter though he saw Death'. Circumstances had now actually given him the chance of preaching to the cardinal, and he used it in the same spirit, —stripping him of the literary *spolia opima* as he had once stripped his unlucky Spanish opponent of his material arms, and relating the feat afterwards with a like touch of conscious bravado to his Scottish host.

## II

Before the end of June, 1613, at latest, Jonson had returned home, and parted with his pupil—'I think not in cold blood', says Walton credibly enough. On June 29 he was in London, and witnessed the swift destruction of the Globe by fire, during the performance of *Henry VIII*.[3] He appears to have resumed at once his ordinary activities. *Bartholomew Fair*, played in October, 1614, must have occupied much of his time during the preceding months of that year. After a great popular success with the audience of the Hope, it was given, the next day, apparently with no less acceptance, at Whitehall.

*Bartholomew Fair* may be said, in effect, to have rehabili-

---
[1] *Convers.*, § iv.    [2] P. Féret, *Cardinal Du Perron*, 1877.
[3] 'Execration upon Vulcan', *Und.* xliii, l. 135.

tated the author of *Catiline*, as the *Fox* had rehabilitated the no less discredited author of *Sejanus*. A picture of the great London Fair, drawn with Jonson's incomparable wealth of realism, was likely to captivate just those elements of the audience which had revolted at the erudite *longueurs* of his second Roman tragedy. It marked, however, an undoubted relaxation of the sinews of Jonson's dramatic technique; a return from the organized and coherent intricacy of *Volpone* and the *Alchemist* towards the loose multiplicity of *Every Man out of his Humour* or *Cynthia's Revels*.[1] But it marked no decline of genius. Such a decline, however, can hardly be ignored in *The Devil is an Ass*,[2] which followed two years later; an experiment in the antiquated devilry which had once made the fortune of *Dr. Faustus*, and which the author of *Every Man in his Humour* had begun his career by renouncing. The vein of comic invention here ran palpably thin. The enduring dramatic work of Jonson was in fact substantially done. Once more, however, and more strikingly than ever, the vein of light and delicate fancy which yielded the Court masques showed that it was still untouched by exhaustion or decay. On the first Christmas after his return the ordinary festivities of the season were merged in the celebration of a great Court wedding, the most splendid and the most infamous in the history of the reign. On December 26 Lady Frances Howard was married to the Earl of Somerset. The so-called *Squires' Masque*, by Campion, was performed in the evening. The wedding festivities continued till Twelfth Night, when the Gentlemen of Gray's Inn presented the

[1] Jonson's 'Apologie' or defence of the play in his lost Art of Poetry (Drum., *Convers.*, § v) probably attempted some kind of justification of its glaring disregard of classical structure. But it cannot have satisfied his stricter critical conscience; and Chetwood (in *Memoirs of the Life and Writings of Ben Jonson Esq.*, 1756) reports a saying of his, apparently authentic, to this effect: 'This Comedy had prodigious success, and, as *Ben* himself, in a Letter to a Friend, says, "so unmerited, that, for the Time to come, he would feed the Swine with the Husks, or Chaff of Wit, since the good Grain they had no Relish for".'

[2] On the objection apparently taken to the satire in this play, and the king's intervention, see the Introduction.

*Masque of Flowers*, the work of three of their number. Jonson, so far as is known, contributed only the slight *Challenge at Tilt*, the homely *Irish Masque*, and a copy of verses addressed to 'Virtuous Somerset'. We may regret that Jonson, who had joined, innocently enough, in celebrating the first marriage of the countess as a child of ten, should have consented to take any part in this second act of her career. But it is to be remembered that, though her reputation was already sinister, her full guilt was not yet known. The studied vagueness with which Jonson described both entertainments in the Folio makes his judgement upon the whole sordid drama sufficiently clear. The verses to Somerset he did not print, and they would probably have remained unknown had they not been preserved in manuscript in a copy of the Folio. With the following Christmas season, however, begins a series of masques which, at least in felicitous ingenuity of invention, marks Jonson's highest achievement in this kind. *Mercury Vindicated from the Alchemists* (1614-15), *The Golden Age Restored* (1615-16), *The Vision of Delight* and *Lovers made Men* (1616-17), and *Pleasure Reconciled to Virtue* (1617-18) are distinguished by happy artistry and easy command of the most varied resources. They belong to the moment of happy poise in the growth of the Jonsonian masque, when it had put off its early stiffness of design, but as yet showed no sign of succumbing to the disintegrating attractions of comedy, personal satire, and topical allusion. It is not surprising that at the festivities of the following Christmas, 1618-19, when Jonson was absent in the north, the masque, by another hand, was 'not so approved of the King as in former times', and that Jonson's absence was 'regretted'.[1]

---

[1] Drummond to Jonson, January 17, 1619. Gifford supposed this letter to have been written in 1620, after Jonson's return, and is followed by Professor Gregory Smith (*Ben Jonson*, p. 170). But its date is fixed by the contents. Drummond says he is sending Jonson the 'Epigram which you desired'. This Epigram was the Latin original of the 'Madrigale' which Jonson, as parting gift to his host, sent him with a cordial inscription two days later (January 19). Jonson evidently wrote from Edinburgh, a few days before departing southwards.

During the remainder of the reign his masques continue to hold the first place in the esteem of the Court. On every Twelfth Night from 1621 to 1625 his services were called in. With the *Masque of Gipsies*, thrice performed during the summer of 1621, at Burley, Belvoir, and Windsor, Jonson reached the summit of his popularity as a masque writer. Its, to us, often unsavoury realism probably contributed to the result. In the ensuing masques the realistic elements, without submerging the rest, as here, grew steadily in importance. In *Time Vindicated* (1622-3) he launched a caustic satire upon a fellow-assailant of the time's abuses, George Wither; and in *Neptune's Triumph* and *The Fortunate Isles* essayed the more delicate and hazardous task of playing upon the abortive project of the Spanish Marriage. With *The Fortunate Isles*, save for a brief renewal five years later, the history of the Jonsonian masque abruptly closes, but for reasons that had no connexion with any decline of power.

In drama, on the other hand, the author of *The Alchemist* might well be concluded to have now written himself out. For nine years following *The Devil is an Ass*, no new play of his was brought upon the stage. There are few signs that he even concerned himself in any way with dramatic affairs. During the two years 1619 and 1620 he seems to have sent nothing at all to press. 'Marry,' says the printer in the *News from the New World* (January, 1621), after an allusion to his visit to Edinburgh, 'he has been restive they say ever since, for we have had nothing from him, he has set out nothing I am sure.' The two great documents for his life and work during the interval between *The Devil is an Ass* and *The Staple of News*, the *Conversations with Drummond* (1619) and the 'Execration upon Vulcan' (1623), rather indicate that the drama had fallen into the second line of his interests and activities, and that, without having expressly renounced it, his labours in this kind were at most fitful. Jonson's literary talk at Hawthornden did not often, if we may trust Drummond, turn upon the popular stage.

His host was a keen student of the drama, and zealous collector of plays in quarto. Yet in 1619, three years after Shakespeare's death, he learnt nothing from Jonson that he thought worth reporting, about him or his work, but two offhand criticisms; of Fletcher, of Middleton, only a passing word; of Massinger and Webster, nothing whatever. This might be 'envy'. But even his own plays Jonson hardly mentions save as occasions of trouble with the government and slender profit to himself. They had not brought him, he says, £200 in all—and he scarcely touches on dramatic theory or practice at all. We owe to Drummond, however, the knowledge of his guest's abandoned project of an English *Amphitryon* (§ xvi). The one dramatic inspiration which Scotland brought him, of a 'fisher or pastoral play' with its 'scene on Loch Lomond', remained a dream. His living interest now attaches unmistakably to non-dramatic poetry. He is at work upon an epic poem of 'the Worthies of this Country roused by fame'; his keenest remarks on literary technique relate to verse structure, the demerits of long lines, stanzas, and sonnets, the superiority of the couplet, the true nature of epigram, and the like; while the pieces he loved to recite, 'the commonplaces of his repetition', were not purple patches from the plays, his own or other, but satires, epigrams, songs; bits of Spenser, Wotton, and Donne.

The second document, the 'Execration upon Vulcan', gives us a yet more valuable, because first-hand glimpse of his preoccupations nearly five years later (November, 1623). That tragi-comic elegy commemorates among his lost writings the 'Parcels of a play'. He was, then, once more occupied with drama at the date of the fire. But the rest of the work recorded is remote from drama, and in the main from poetry: an epic on Proserpine, his 'journey into Scotland sung', a prose history of the reign of Henry V, the scholar's notes of twenty-four years' reading in the classics, with 'his humble gleanings in divinity'; finally, an English Grammar. It would be idle to speculate upon the precise character of these lost pieces; but the mere record of all this lost or projected work suffices to show that Jonson's range of interest and enterprise at fifty reached farther in several directions than we should gather from his extant writings. None of them is more to be regretted than the Epic on 'the Worthies of this Country' called Heroologia, 'all in couplets, for he detesteth all other rimes'. Its manner and spirit, if not its substance, may be guessed from the occasional heroic passages of the masques, such as Merlin's prophecy ('all in couplets', too) of the great worthies of the English throne (*Prince Henry's Barriers*), and perhaps the scene of the restoration of the worthies of song—Chaucer, Gower, Lydgate, Spenser—in *The Golden Age Restored*. Arthur, whose story he thought unmatched as the ground of a Heroic poem, cannot have been wanting in his own.[1] The *Discovery* of his Scottish journey, 'with all the adventures', excited the interest of James, and was to have contained not only accounts of scenery (Loch Lomond, an early trace of romantic interest), but antiquarian inscriptions and notices of municipal and academic institutions.[2] It would clearly have been a sociological as well as literary document of importance, like *The Excursion*. The history of Henry V ('eight of his nine years') besides the 'material succours lent' by his antiquarian friends, Selden, Carew, and Cotton, may be surmised to have borne witness in style and composition to his declared and characteristic admiration of Tacitus.[3]

To these works which the fire found incomplete, or still unprinted, if ready for the press, must be added one which had already been entered in the Stationers' Register, on October 2, 1623, his translation of Barclay's vigorously written Latin romance of *Argenis*.[4] Barclay had enjoyed

---

[1] *Convers.*, § x.
[2] Letter to Drummond, May 10, 1619. It appears from Drummond's letter of July 1, enclosing a map of Loch Lomond, that he had previously supplied Jonson, in a lost letter, with these particulars. See Appendix II, xv.
[3] *Convers.*, § ix, and passim.
[4] This translation is actually specified in the first draft of the 'Execra-

James's favour in England, and his veiled allegory of contemporary European politics won a celebrity out of proportion to its merits.[1] Jonson's translation had been commissioned by the king in the previous year, and must have occupied even so doughty a translator a large part of the intervening months.

### III

Our detailed knowledge of Jonson's occupations and projects in these years is due mainly, it will be seen, to two events, the Scottish journey and the fire, which in different ways induced him to communicate himself with unusual freedom. His journey to the north, if less familiar to us in detail than some other journeys of the time, stands easily first in literary and personal significance. Even before the accession of James had made London the social capital of Scotland, 'the road to England' was probably more frequented than the road out of it. But apart from the rapidly multiplying trade relations, and the public and private messengers who, as the queen drew near her end, pursued and crossed one another's path between the English and Scottish Courts, pleasure-touring in the modern sense was already beginning; and the leisured and well-to-do persons who could undertake it were to be found mostly in the southern kingdom. Camden's great work had contributed to make educated Englishmen more keenly aware of the vast treasures of antiquarian interest still visible in all parts of England, and Fynes Moryson, the itinerarist

tion' preserved in the Harley MS. 4955, fol. 44 verso, 'Three bookes, not amisse, Reveald (if some can iudge) of Argenis, For our owne Ladyes'.

[1] The vogue of *Argenis* at this date may be judged from Chamberlain's remark to Carleton (*Dom. State Papers*, 1622, May 11) that its price had risen from 5*s*. to 14*s*.; and from his conviction that Jonson 'will not be able to equal the original'. Charles I, after his accession, revived the project, and an English version by Sir Robert Le Grys and Thomas May was published in 1629. It is not known whether Jonson had declined to do his work again, as he well might. More probably perhaps, in view of his distant relations with the Court in those years, he was not asked.

*par excellence* of his time, recommended the *Britannia* to intending tourists as a guide, supplementing it with a sketch of his own Scotch tour and suggestions for a continuation in Ireland and Wales. Even the players of London, though their frequent travels rarely took them farther north than Leicester or Shrewsbury, had at least once, in 1599, sought the doubtful suffrages of an Edinburgh audience. Nothing is definitely known of the occasion of Jonson's tour. Gossip invested it, long before it actually came off, with the air of an athletic feat undertaken 'for profit', in the manner of Taylor the Water-poet.[1] In spite of the 'mountain belly' and the incipient grey hair, Jonson was still a robust man, in the prime of life, and the four-hundred-mile walk through England in summer time, at his own pace, may well have presented itself to him as a far from disagreeable method of economy. In the Scottish capital, his name and fame, authenticated as they now were by the imposing edition of his 'works', were as current as in London; an evidence of enlightenment which doubtless had its share in inspiring his later eulogy of Edinburgh as 'Britain's other eye'; and it may be conjectured that if Jonson's tour was not actually the result of an invitation, the rumour of his coming evoked encouraging intimations of the welcome which awaited him there, and which he in fact received.

Jonson's personal ties with Scotsmen of distinction were indeed unusually numerous, and even lend some support to the surmise that he was recognized as something of a Scot himself, in virtue of the Annandale grandfather. Not to speak of the king, who took a kindly interest in his journey, his five years' intimacy with d'Aubigny, as his guest, gave him an important link with another branch of the Stuart family, of which Esmé's elder brother, the Duke of Lennox, was head. His cordial relations with Sir Robert

---

[1] 'Ben Jonson is going on foot to Edinburgh and back, for his profit,' it was reported in a news-letter from London (*State Papers, Domestic, James I*, xcii. 62).

Aytoun may also have counted for something. Of the slender band of Scottish men of letters, however, one, and that the most influential and the best known, Sir William Alexander, certainly took no part in furthering Jonson's welcome; he bore him a grudge, Jonson thought, as the enemy of Drayton, and had openly 'neglected' him. Another friend both of Drayton and of Alexander, however, and the most considerable poet then living in Scotland, took the lead in his entertainment and has left us the most enduring memorial of the visit of his redoubtable guest.

For Scotland, then, Jonson set out in the course of the summer of 1618, adding momentarily to the gaiety of the literary world by the pedestrian method of his journey. Of the facetiae occasioned, in great wits and small, by this exploit few specimens have survived. ' I love not ', said Francis Bacon to him, 'to see Poesy go on other feet than poetical dactylus and spondaeus.'[1] This kindly jest affords our only glimpse of Jonson's personal relations with the greatest of the very few contemporaries for whom he entertained an unqualified admiration. He took the then usual route to Scotland, by the North Road, through Yorkshire and Northumberland; all we know of his journey, however, in the absence of the lost Itinerary, is that at Darlington he replaced his worn-out shoes with a new pair, which he expected to last as far as the same place on his way home.[2]

At Edinburgh, where he probably arrived early in August, he was warmly received. Taylor the Water-poet, who had come on foot, too,—malicious gossip said, in order to ridicule Jonson—testifies to the hospitable attentions paid him by the most distinguished circles.[3] 'I found my long approoued and assured good friend ... at one Master *Iohn*

---

[1] *Convers.*, § xiii. 88 f. Drummond's Scottish orthography is not retained. A piece of chaff in rhyme, doubtless occasioned by the journey, will be found in *Ungathered Verse*, No. xlvii.

[2] Some verses, ascribed to him in W. Gray's *Chorographia, or A Survey of Newcastle upon Tyne 1649*, on St. Nicholas' Church there, indicate that the tradition of his passing through the town thirty years before was still alive.

[3] Taylor had travelled by the west country route, and explored the

Stuarts house ... I left him, as well, as I hope neuer to see him in a worse estate : for he is among Noblemen and Gentlemen that knowe his true worth, and their owne honours, where with much respectiue loue he is worthily entertained.'[1] Of these noble and gentle acquaintances a few only are known to us by name ; the Fentons, Nisbets, Scots, Levingstones, Wriths,[2] to whom he sent cordial messages after his departure. The most distinct among them to us is that of Sir John Scot of Scotstarvet, ' a busy man in foul weather' according to contemporary repute, who was rapidly building up a fortune and estate by shrewd practice in the law, but who was also scholar of St. Andrews, a connoisseur and collector of Latin verse, and a correspondent of other scholars. In September, 1618, Jonson was staying at Leith with Mr. John Stuart,[3] probably the most important man in the town ; and here, on the 18th, the Water-poet found his 'long approoued and assured good friend', and received from him, on taking leave, as he tells us in his *Penniless Pilgrimage*, a gold piece of twenty-two shillings to drink his health in England.  Public honours were not wanting. On September 20th the Edinburgh Town Council authorized the admission of ' Benjamyn Jonsoun inglisman ' as a ' burges and gildbrother in communi forma '. In October they entertained him to dinner, at a cost to the City Treasury of £221. 6s. 4d. (Scots).[4] All these distinctions and acquaintanceships, however, are insignificant for us compared to a single, probably the closing, episode of his Highlands as far as Braemar and Badenoch before he met Jonson at Leith.

[1] *The Pennyles Pilgrimage*, 1618, sig. F 2 verso.

[2] Professor Masson (*Register of the Privy Council of Scotland*, vol. xi, Introduction, p. clxvi) gives all that can now be gathered about these persons (cf. App. II, Letters xii and xiv).

[3] Masson identifies him, no doubt rightly, with the Water-bailie and Shipper of the name at Leith, owner of the ship called *The Post of Leith*, which was occasionally hired from him for government service (*Register, u. s.*).

[4] *Town Council Register*, under September 18 and October 16, 1618. The Dean of Gild's accounts indicate the liberal provision made for their guest's gilded and engrossed ' burgess ticket '. See Appendix III.

sojourn; the visit paid to Sir John Scot's brother-in-law, William Drummond of Hawthornden.

Drummond was the most considerable of the little group of Scotsmen who sought to make southern English the vehicle of literature in Scotland. Well-to-do and independent, he had travelled extensively and collected a good library in several languages. Few Elizabethan poets can have been as well read as he in French and Italian, extensive as the literary importation from these literatures confessedly was; and his own manner, which owes more to study and discipline than to talent, has more of the chiselled elegance of the Ronsardists than of the hardihood of the Elizabethans.[1] He had a picturesque fancy and a good ear, and the best of his sonnets fully match that second class of Elizabethan sonnets which is excelled only by Shakespeare's and the best of Sidney's, Spenser's, and Drayton's. But he had little passion, and though he keenly relished intellectual exercise, and the signs of it in others, had not himself any considerable intellectual power. At the time of Jonson's visit, he had been before the literary world some five years, having published his *Tears on the Death of Maeliades* in commemoration of Prince Henry in 1613. In 1616 had followed his *Poems, Amorous, Funerall, Divine, Pastorall*, mainly a memorial of a lost mistress; in 1617 he joined in celebrating the tardy first visit of the king to his native country with *Forth Feasting*. A prose *Characters of several Authors*, jotted down apparently for his private use between 1613 and 1616, somewhat in the fashion of his later notes of Jonson's talk, gives us an indication of his independent opinion of English poets some years before he met Jonson. He measures them by Petrarch; gives the palm, for different excellences, as poets of Love, to Sidney, Alexander, Daniel, Donne—'among the Anacreontic Lyrics second to none, and far from all second',—and, with

---

[1] How intimate Drummond's French studies were, and how much he owed to them, has been shown for the first time by Professor L. E. Kastner in his articles in the *Mod. Lang. Rev.*, 1909-10, and later in his excellent edition of Drummond's Works.

more qualification, Drayton. Shakespeare and Spenser are barely mentioned, Jonson not at all. At Drummond's home, then, above the glen of Hawthornden, seven or eight miles south of Edinburgh, Jonson spent two or three weeks at or shortly after Christmas. By January 17 the visit was over. The so-called 'Conversations' deserve the name hardly more than *Bishop Blougram's Apology* or *Prince Hohenstiel-Schwangau*, so completely does the one mind dominate the record. The grouping of topics further impairs the conversational form. Hardly anywhere can we detect that Drummond gave a lead or asked a question. Boswell freely reports his own share in discussion, even when it sets off Johnson to his own disadvantage; Eckermann retails his own speeches, even when he has to enlighten his great friend. But both men put themselves forward only as accessories, or even foils, to the full-length figure they are absorbed in portraying. Both Boswell and Eckermann show genius in their portrait-painting, and in both this gift goes along with an unreserved love and admiration for their hero. Drummond admires with many reserves, and his portrait, though it has more shady features, cannot be compared with theirs in critical, far less in artistic, power. If Jonson stands out in these casual pages, it is because his personality permeated his talk, and communicated itself even to a collection of notes of it, mechanically arranged under headings. Drummond's apparent self-effacement is the result less of modesty than of the fact that, in his intercourse with Jonson, there was probably little self to efface. He sat, like Gigadibs, secretly critical if outwardly subdued, while his formidable guest rolled him out his mind. Twice he sets down judgements upon himself or his writings. 'He said to me I was too good and simple'; 'his censure of my verses were that they were all good . . . save that they smelled too much of the schooles.' The psychological, like the physical, contrast between the two was enormous, and the personality of Jonson, imposing itself by massiveness of conviction and trenchancy of judgement upon the slightlierbuilt nature of his host, exerted its usual ascendancy, with less than its usual charm. A sensitive, temperate, and reserved man, whose best hours had been spent at

> that sweet and solitary place
> Where from the vulgar I estranged live,

in lonely efforts to capture a lyric garb of Petrarchan elegance for the memories of a lost love, he listened with unwilling and querulous homage to the highly seasoned talk of the great Elizabethan; noting for future record, as the bottles of canary disappeared, that drink was 'one of the elements in which he liveth'.

Jonson's visit to Drummond ended towards the middle of January, but he remained in or near Edinburgh till the 25th. On the 17th Drummond wrote him a note, warm in expression if somewhat formal in tone, enclosing an epigram which he had wished for, and offering his service, 'if there be any other thing in this country unto which my power can reach; there is nothing I wish more than to be in the calendar of them who love you'. On the 19th Jonson replied in terms strikingly effusive, and even affectionate, enclosing two poems, the 'Lover's Dust' and the 'Picture of Myself', which Drummond on receiving them copied at the close of his notes of Jonson's talk. The picture of himself drawn by Jonson certainly did not flatter his physical person; it may have suggested to Drummond the addition of the still less indulgent portrait of his character.[1]

Though composed with irritation, this prose portrait, by one who had for weeks watched and listened to Jonson *tête à tête*, is not to be lightly set aside. A too fastidious criticism doubtless blinded Drummond to some of Jonson's greater qualities, but it sharpened his perception of others. He has emphasized what his discreet and cautious and orderly mind found distressing and uncomfortable; and the things that distressed him included failings very incident to genius,—the oppressive 'phantasy', 'ever mastering his

---

[1] The correspondence is given at large in Appendix II, xii f.

reason, a general disease in many Poets'; the great vehemence of temper, 'passionately kind and angry, careless either to gain or keep'; the intellectual frankness, 'vindicative, but if he be well answered, at himself'. This demonic, Carlylean Ben, flashing out in uncalculated violences of laughter and wrath, and hurried across the confines of cool intelligence by bursts of despotic imagination, is a different and a less familiar, but hardly a less worthy presentation than Fuller's picture of the solid but unwieldy scholar whom the nimble versatility of Shakespeare, in the wit-combats of the Mermaid, took, he thought, so much at a disadvantage.

From Leith, where he had again perhaps been the guest of John Stuart, Jonson on January 25 turned his steps finally homewards, apparently by the route he had come.[1] The weeks at Hawthornden had not been spent wholly in talk and drink, and Jonson carried with him rough sketches for various pieces of writing, in prose and verse, which he promised Drummond to send him, rough as they were, should he die by the way. In London the 'regretted' masque-writer was warmly welcomed by the king, who showed keen interest in his proposed Scottish poem. Cordial letters to and from Drummond followed. Jonson's requests for further local information to be used in his Scottish poem have been already mentioned. On July 1 Drummond supplements this with a list of *Impresas* and *Emblems* worked by Queen Mary, 'mother to our sacred

---

[1] His saying about his boots, as reported by Drummond shortly after his departure from Leith, certainly points to this. But it may be noted (1) that the MS. verses of Inigo Jones 'to his false friend Mr Ben Johnson' perhaps indicate that he entered London by way of Hammersmith,

> I never went to Scotland, nor did meete
> thee at returne my selfe alone or with
> my friends but soe far of as Hamersmith.
> (Harl. MS. 6057, fol. 30.)

(2) that at Pemberton, near Wigan, near the west coast route, is a tavern, the 'Ben Jonson'.—But these indications amount to very little. What is in any case probable is that his journey was not without some genuine 'adventures' which may have caused a detour.

Sovereign', in the embroidery of a Bed of State. Drummond was probably more interested in these things than Jonson, but the talk at Hawthornden had occasionally glanced at them, and Jonson had furnished an *impresa* for Prince Henry (*Convers.*, § xvii).

## IV

The memorable journey to Scotland was followed after a short interval by another, of which we know much less, to Oxford. An old Westminster, ten years his junior, Richard Corbet, was then senior Student of Christ Church, and Jonson stayed with him. It seems likely that this visit was the occasion rather than the result of the somewhat tardy proposal of the University to induct him formally into the degree of Master of Arts; this having long before been conferred upon him, on the recommendation of his friend Lord Pembroke, and perhaps a little also in acknowledgement of the splendid dedication of *The Fox*.[1] The proposal was made to Convocation in a letter from the Chancellor on July 17, Jonson being described as a man of distinguished learning in humane letters; and the ceremony took place two days later,[2] in full Convocation. It was a tribute, rare in the history of the University before or since, to a great scholar poet who owed nothing to Universities. Its nearest parallel was probably the day, two hundred and fifty years later, on which Oxford crowded the Sheldonian to see Robert Browning receive, and confer, a similar honour. Only one other incident throws a glimpse of light upon this Oxford visit. Corbet, a genial soul and a gay and witty poet, doubtless contributed more than Drummond had done to the glory of the talk; but he did not record it.

---

[1] A marginal note to the lines attributed to Chapman ('An Invective wrighten by M$^r$ George Chapman against M$^r$ Ben: Johnson', Ashmolean MS. 38, pp. 16–18) states: 'W$^m$ then Lord Chamberlayne and Earle of Pemb. made him M$^r$ of Arts w$^{th}$ his Letter.'

[2] See Appendix III, where the record of Convocation is printed for the first time.

The two poets had, however, an added personal tie in Corbet's father. Vincent Corbet had died in hale old age in the previous April. Jonson's beautiful epitaph was written with the son's before him, and some little time after his death—not improbably, therefore, during this Oxford visit. Its finely felt and simple lines make clear that the quiet strength of the old gardener of Twickenham had impressed and captivated this 'contemner and scorner of others', who had yet so quick a vein of 'tenderness for children', and of 'worship' for the 'reverend head'. The tough fibre which so long

> Had wrestled with Diseases strong,
> That though they did possesse each limb,
> Yet he broke them, e're they could him,

had its part no doubt in inspiring Ben's warm regard; but the doughty somewhat loud-voiced corrector of men was accessible too to the charm of 'a life that knew nor noise nor strife', and humbled himself before one whose 'very manners taught t' amend'. There were not many of his contemporaries of whom Jonson would have written,

> Much from him I professe I wonne,
> And more, and more, I should have done . . .

as he wrote of Vincent Corbet.[1]

## V

The Edinburgh and Oxford honours mark the status which Jonson had now won in the educated English world, and which, in spite of all later reverses of favour, health, and fortune, he never lost. The Ishmael of the Stage Quarrel now stood beyond question at the head of English letters. The years between the publication of his works in 1616 and the close of the reign were the heyday of his personal dictatorship in the literary world. His stage disasters were lost sight of in the halo which surrounded his undoubted

[1] *Underwoods*, xii.

triumphs; and his withdrawal from active concern with the stage, instead of impairing his hold upon the general memory, probably contributed to confirm his prestige. He stood apart from the struggling throng as a past-master who had indisputably 'arrived', and who did not endanger that vantage-ground by encountering the risks of fiasco which even in his best days every new play of his involved. The choice spirits of the London world of letters rallied about him, not merely, as in the days of Beaumont, as one of a band of fellow wits and jesters, but as the recognized chief of a body of sworn liegemen, the 'father' of the 'tribe of Ben'. The old wit-contests of the Mermaid—genially renewed, perhaps, in that traditional last banquet with Drayton and Shakespeare at New Place[1] in the spring of 1616—belonged to the past. But they had worthy successors in the 'lyric feasts' at the Sun, the Dog, the Triple Tun, and, above all, at the Old Devil tavern. Situated close to the City side of Temple Bar in the very heart of the legal and literary quarter, this hostelry, under the guidance of its notable host, Simon Wadloe ('brave duke Wadloe, king of skinkers', as he was variously called [2]), became in the later years of James the most famous of the haunts of wit and letters. The upper chamber of this tavern, known as the 'Apollo', in which Jonson and his coterie forgathered, remained, in the eighteenth century, a speaking monument of these symposia, while to the days of Pope and Addison at least the tradition of them lingered in the neighbouring coffee-houses, spiced with a few sayings of Ben himself. On the walls of the 'Apollo', Pope and Addison may have read in faded gold letters on a black ground the laws which the Elizabethan 'censor morum' laid down for the convivialities of his 'little senate', conveyed in a Latin which, for nervous force and idiomatic elegance, neither the Roman nor the English 'Cato' could have bettered. If their feasts were Bacchanalia, as one joyous

---

[1] Reported in the diary of the Stratford vicar, John Ward.
[2] *Staple of News*, II. v.

messmate declared,[1] they were Bacchanalia over which not Bacchus but the 'boon Delphic god' himself presided; and the grosser excesses of riot yielded to the nobler intoxication of music and poetry, diffused by a commanding and genial personality, whose every verse 'outdid the meat, outdid the frolic wine', and whose careless *obiter dicta* begat poems in the sensitive and ardent brains that heard.[2] Doubtless, too, there were times when Jonson's robust egoism got the better of his wit, when he told and retold the stale glories and hardships of his famous 'Journey', and when hearers less devoted or more critical than Herrick rather endured than enjoyed.[3] 'Select women' were not excluded; there was even a corner reserved for 'lovers to quarrel' and 'sigh' in. How far this privilege was used by women of character may be doubtful. But Pennyboy junior, in *The Staple of News*, takes the Princess Pecunia to 'dine in Apollo' without demur; and the 'two Gentlewomen, call'd the *Graces*' ('They were euer three in *Poetry*';—'This was truth, Sir'),[4] with whom Madrigal had supped there, doubtless had their counterparts among the actual guests.

Evidences of the royal goodwill, too, became, from 1610 onwards, more frequent and significant. In February of that year James granted him a pension of 100 marks yearly. A year later, when Jonson's friend, Edmond Bolton, was petitioning for an Academy of letters, Jonson would naturally be thought of as a probable candidate.[5] In 1618, when

[1] Marmion, *A Fine Companion* 1633, II. v.
[2] Herrick, *Ode for Ben Jonson* (*Hesperides*, 1648, p. 342).
[3] Cf. the lines addressed by Inigo Jones 'to his false freind Mr. Ben Johnson' (Harl. MS. 6057, fol. 30), where he describes himself as having 'heard you tell the tedious story' of the Scottish journey,

> Of all you in that trafficke suffered though
> I was as tyrd as thou couldst bee to goe.

[4] *Staple of News*, III. iii.
[5] The 'Academ Roial' or 'College of Honour' was discussed from 1617 to James's death, when the project fell through. Jonson's name is included in the list of eighty-four members in a MS. of Bolton, dated 1626. See E. M. Portal, 'The Academ Roial of James I' (*Proceedings of the British Academy*, vol. vii).

his friend Selden had incurred the anger of the king by writing the history of Tithes [1] in the spirit of a scholar, not of a partisan, Jonson intervened with equal courage and success. Such facts naturally enhanced his literary reputation in quarters less accessible to a purely literary appeal. The London Livery companies, when they had occasion to address the king, began to apply to Jonson for appropriate formulas. 'Dyers, clothdressers with their shuttles, and Hamburgians', wrote Gerrard to Dudley Carleton, June 14, 1616, 'were presented to the King, and spake such language as Ben Jonson put in their mouths.' His relations with the king are wholly honourable to him, and not discreditable to James. The king's favours were apt to compromise the dignity of the recipients. Jonson's dignity, when he stood by it, was not easily compromised; and we read with amusement in a contemporary letter of 1621 that 'Ben Jonson' was not knighted, but escaped it narrowly, 'for that his Majestie would have done it, had not been means made (himself not unwilling) to avoid it'.[2] More to the purpose was his nomination to the office of Master of the Revels; but as it was to fall to him only by reversion, on the deaths of Sir George Buc and Sir John Astley, his prospect of the appointment was, for a man verging on fifty, speculative, and proved in fact illusory. Nor can his selection for the privilege, already mentioned, of translating the *Argenis*, have been altogether welcome, distinguished honour as it was certainly intended to be. The son of a

---

[1] Selden's own account is given in his *Vindiciæ Maris Clausi*, ch. vi (*Opera*, ed. Wilkins, II. ii. 1422). He was summoned to come with the offending book to Theobalds. 'Me tunc aulae alienissimum ... incomitatum Theoboldas ire noluere viri doctissimi, summi, mihique amicissimi ... Edwardus Heywardus a Reiffham in agro Norfolciensi, armiger, ... & Benjaminus Jonsonius, poetarum ille facile princeps. Illuc igitur curru simul pergimus, medio Decembri aut circiter, ubi cum regem quidem, ob scriptum illud de decimis satis infensum me audivissem, procuravit Jonsonus illustri heroi, Georgio tunc Buchinghamiae marchioni ... in pretio habitus, ut ille me amicius coram rege sisteret, eumque in causam meam placaret.'

[2] Letter of Joseph Mead to Sir Martin Stuteville, dated September 15, 1621 (Harl. MS. 389, fol. 118).

devoted adherent of Mary, and himself a scholar of brilliant capacity, Barclay, though a Catholic, had, as already stated, been warmly received by James, to whom the flowing Latinity and the intricate political allegory of the *Argenis* were equally acceptable. But the hours spent in this task may have contributed among other things to keep the unnamed play unfinished and in manuscript until the fatal day of the fire, and thus have postponed the return to the stage which Jonson in effect made, in the beginning of 1626, with *The Staple of News*.

## CHAPTER VI

## RETURN TO THE STAGE

### I

NATHANIEL BUTTER, who in 1622 issued one of the first periodical News sheets, long counted as the founder of English journalism. He has the additional title of having thereby created a new source of comic humours, which modern drama has put to somewhat rare, but occasionally distinguished, use. The newspaper had to pass through a long process of development and become a far more complex and highly articulated creation, before it was ripe for the art of Sheridan, Freytag, Ibsen, and Mr. Bernard Shaw. But in its crude first beginnings it could already furnish thoroughly congenial food to the comedy of Jonson. Infantine as were its processes, it had already learnt to practise with barefaced grossness some of the tricks of the trade, and as a piece of organized imposture the News office or 'Staple' could easily match such established institutions as the alchemists' laboratory and the booths of Bartholomew Fair. Jonson had once fleshed his sword on the 'Staple' men in a masque: he now dissected them in the ampler and more legitimate medium of comedy with unmistakable gusto and with unclouded power. Performed by the great Company which had brought out almost all the masterpieces of his prime, *The Staple of News* might well appear to herald a further succession of triumphs. It was in reality not a beginning, but an end; the last brilliant effort of a genius verging on complete decay, and soon to be capable only of fitful moments of power. And far from opening a period of new prosperity for its author, its appearance nearly coincided with events, public and private, which wrought a sudden and in the main disastrous change in his situation, and make the remaining twelve years of his life only at infrequent intervals cheering to contemplate.

In March, 1625, the death of James had removed a personal influence which on the whole told powerfully in Jonson's favour. His momentary arrest, a few months later, to be noticed below, on the charge of having written a poem in praise of Buckingham's assassin Felton, perhaps marked the change in his position. But even during the last year of the reign, Court influences hostile or indifferent to Jonson had subjected him to some real or apparent slights. During the early summer of 1624, while the fortunes of Prince Charles in Spain still hung in suspense, he appears to have been treated with marked coolness. In particular he was not taken into the secret of the preparations for celebrating the prince's return; a neglect which the author of *Neptune's Triumph* had reason to resent, not the less because this masque, where the splendours of that return were so brilliantly, but illusively, anticipated, had never in fact been performed. He had now to hear that Inigo was in authority, to 'guide the motions' and—as he wrote, with a savage stab at the degraded tastes which found scope when his controlling presence was withdrawn—' direct the *bears*'.[1] It is not easy to resent such slights with dignity; yet the bitterness with which he reflects upon them in the 'Letter to one who' in these months 'asked to be Sealed of the Tribe of Ben', does not pass the limit. For the moment the blow was suspended. Jonson was called in to provide the masque for the Twelfth Night of 1625, and skilfully turned to account for Henrietta Maria the literary 'baked meats' he had prepared for the Infanta. Nevertheless, the influences and atmosphere of the new Court were on the whole unfavourable to him. The young queen herself, with the fastidious disdain of her French breeding, heightened

---

[1] *Underwoods*, xlvii: 'An Epistle answering to one that asked to be Sealed of the Tribe of Ben.' That Jones is referred to was first shown by Brotanek (*Die engl. Maskenspiele*, p. 251), on the basis of two letters of Mead and Chamberlain, June 5 and 14, 1623 (*Court and Times of James I*, ii. 403).

by the delicacy of a *précieuse* for all things English, was not likely to be captivated by this 'tun of man', outwardly the most ruggedly English personage, without doubt, in the entire Court circle. The romantic speeches of Lovel in *The New Inn* are perhaps to be taken as designed to conciliate the 'Platonic' chivalry which she made fashionable at Court. But they were probably too loftily conceived for her understanding, even had they, after the disastrous performance, reached her ear. The new king, too, was a man of finer sensibilities than his father, without his keen intellect or his passion for erudition and debate; and neither circumstance made for a continuance of the mutual attraction which had drawn the 'lettered prince' to the chief of contemporary English men of letters. Charles did not, says Clarendon, 'love very confident men'. To a man of his delicate and effeminate temperament, acutely resentful of breaches of etiquette and decorum, and shrinking from excesses of every kind, the full-blooded ultra-masculine self-sufficiency and self-assertiveness of Jonson would hardly have been attractive even in an equal. To the ingenious artistry of the Jonsonian masque he was himself artist enough to respond,[1] and he rewarded it now and then in bursts of magnificent generosity; but even favourable observers, like Clarendon, found that he 'paused too long in giving'. Nor was he generous by nature. His kindliness was fitful and impulsive, and long intervals of keenly felt neglect were not effaced by an occasional lavish act.

Other old and firm friends, of Jonson's own class, died within a year or two of James: among them his old master Camden. And to this loss of friends was added, early in the new reign, the yet graver burden of loss of health. Struck down with paralysis in 1628, he appears henceforth to have been confined to his chamber, and finally to his bed. 'Disease, the enemy', as he wrote in grim pathetic phrases

[1] Charles had, as prince, repeatedly summoned Jonson and 'the Players at the Blackfriars' to attend at Whitehall, evidently for the purpose of a Court performance. Cf. the Messenger's bill for his expenses on two of these journeys, App. III.

to the lord treasurer, three years later,[1]—disease had laid siege to him, and it held him in close blockade for the rest of his life. Enforced inaction exaggerated the existing disproportion of his ample figure. The scholar's stoop and the toper's obesity grew upon him together, producing a drooping rotundity which he playfully told the painter Borlase could be faithfully represented on canvas by 'one great blot'.[2] On the other hand, his formidable presence probably gained something of venerable dignity when, in the course of the thirties, his mane of short black curls became white. Among other privileges dependent on health, this stroke must have closed his personal participation in the glories of the Club. 'Apollo from his shrine can no more divine', and though he continued to wield from his pallet an authority as potent over select minds, the lustre of the meetings was fatally impaired to the English world at large. The disappearance of his unmistakable person from the streets of London meant, not oblivion certainly, but his quiet relegation, in the general mind, to the age gone by, whose glories perhaps even gained lustre in retrospect, but were definitely over. His name was famous, but people were apt to forget that the man who bore it was still alive. In September, 1632, for instance, it was possible for a purveyor of London news to be surprised at the announcement, for the following term, of a new play (*The Magnetic Lady*) by 'Ben Jonson, who I thought had been dead'.[3]

And both disasters were aggravated by a serious diminution in his pecuniary resources, due indeed in part directly to the first. If we may accept the implication of the same 'Epistle Mendicant', it amounted, even in the first year of the reign, to actual want.[4] Jonson, with all his Stoic hardihood,

---

[1] *To the Rt. Hon. the High Treasurer of England, An Epistle Mendicant*, MDCXXXI (*Underwoods*, lxxi).
[2] *Underwoods*, lii: 'The Poet to the Painter.'
[3] Letter from Pory to Sir T. Puckering, September 20, 1632, Harl. MS. 7000, fol. 336.
[4]    *Want*, with the rest of his conceal'd compeeres,
       Have cast a trench about mee, now five yeares.
                    'Epistle Mendicant', 5–6 (*Und.* lxxi).

was neither thrifty nor provident; he lived much in taverns, ate and drank freely, and stood much upon the quality of the cooking and the wine. A loss of income found him without resources. The changed disposition at the Court made itself felt already at the first Christmas of the reign. For nearly twenty years Jonson, when in England, had been called on for a Court masque. In 1618-19 his absence had been regretted. In 1625-6 his aid was not asked. For the first five winters of the new reign he wrote no masque for the Court. Nor, so far as is known, was he called in, during these years, to dignify in this way the festivities of noble houses, as so frequently during the later years of James.

II

It was under these pathetic conditions that Jonson, driven, we can hardly doubt, by sheer stress of need, prepared, in the spring or summer of 1628, to try the fortunes of the stage again. While *The New Inn* was still on the stocks, a timely and not inconsiderable relief came from a somewhat unexpected quarter. Upon the death of the City chronologer, Thomas Middleton, in September, the City appointed Jonson his successor. Calculation rather than magnanimity may have dictated this honour done to the old London poet, whose power of covering with ridicule the social and commercial enterprise of its citizens—even of honourable liverymen like Butter—was obviously so far from exhaustion. The City chronologer, holding office and receiving pay subject to the good pleasure of the City fathers, might be assumed to have given effective pledges of good behaviour. And, in effect, Jonson's remaining plays show a remarkable abstention from topics offensive to the City. In *The New Inn* and the revived and adapted *Tale of a Tub*—not to speak of the problematic *Sad Shepherd*—he even abandons his familiar London itself, and transports us to a country hostelry or a suburban hamlet, while the satire of *The*

*Magnetic Lady*, though its scene is laid in London, leaves the withers of the City, on the whole, unwrung.

The new historiographer was scarcely appointed when he was called, in a way equally unwelcome and unexpected, to throw light upon a grave event in recent history. On August 23 the Duke of Buckingham had been stabbed by Felton. Some verses addressed to Felton, and apparently approving of this act, were ascribed by rumour to Jonson. On October 26 he was accordingly examined by the attorney-general, Sir Robert Heath. In his deposition, which is extant (*State Papers, Domestic, Charles I*, cxix. 33), Jonson admits having seen the verses at Sir Robert Cotton's, 'lying on the table after dinner', but denies all knowledge of their authorship save that he has heard it ascribed to one Zouch Townly, a Student of Christ Church, and an acquaintance of his own.[1] A still more dangerous report that he had given Townly a dagger he easily explains: Zouch, then 'a scholler & a divine', 'took a liking to' the dagger, which Jonson ordinarily wore upon his person; Jonson, supping with him shortly after, made him a present of it. It is clear that Jonson was completely exonerated: any doubt would be dispelled by the marked favour shown him only three months later by the king, the one man in the kingdom who deeply resented Buckingham's assassination.

He was soon to invite the decision of a less patient tribunal upon a weaker case. For his next play was an example of the hazards involved in the effort to break new ground, with declining powers and 'a brain, unhurt indeed, but set round with pain'. *The New Inn*, now complete, was performed on January 19, 1629, and proved the most disastrous of all Jonson's dramatic ventures. He petulantly charged both actors and audience with gross injustice towards the play. But in spite of some splendid passages—chosen with unerring instinct by Lamb—we cannot seriously blame the impatience of the audience with a plot so mon-

[1] For full text see App. III.

strous and so dull. Unfortunately, however, it prevented their hearing the Epilogue, that subdued cry of the weary Titan, bending under his burden and knowing that he cannot long hold out, but heroic to the last. With all his sense of failing power Jonson could not anticipate so complete a fiasco. Instantly his pathetic humility vanished, the sick brain forgot its weariness, and London presently listened, with mingled exasperation, derision, and pity, to the impassioned arrogance of the 'Ode to Himself'. The author of a rejected play reviling the rejecters is necessarily at a disadvantage, and all the fire and occasional splendour of Jonson's invective could not make his action dignified. The rejoinders and vindications which this defiant challenge called forth remain an eloquent witness to the imposing reputation which the author of *Volpone* and *The Alchemist*, in spite of all, still enjoyed. Feltham's retort is a not unfair rebuke to a great man who had tried to capture fortune by violence; and his survey of Jonson's achievements, though grudging, allows that he had 'hit the white' as often as not. Randolph's and Cleveland's are the tributes of adoring disciples to a blameless master; Carew's, the finely tempered plea of a friend for the right to discriminate and prefer. The damning of *The New Inn* was capable of being interpreted as an involuntary tribute to the poet of *The Alchemist*, who had there fallen so grievously below himself. The disaster had, however, the incidental effect of recalling the attention of the Court to the suffering poet. He was not indeed absolutely neglected; on the very day of the disaster, the Chapter of Westminster had sent 'to Mr. Beniamin Jhonson in his sickness and want' a gift of five pounds.[1] And a pointed reference, in one of the unspoken Epilogues, to the rarity of such attentions—'Had he liu'd the care of King, and Queene',—doubtless reached Charles's ears; the announcement at the close of the 'Ode to Himself' that he meant to sing the glories of 'his sweet reign' may have enforced the appeal to his impulsive

[1] See Appendix III, xiii.

but untrustworthy generosity. For the epoch of his personal government was about to begin, and the services of a favourable historian were not to be despised. He in any case sent the chronologer a gift, far in excess of what the occasion demanded, of £100, receiving a grateful epigram in acknowledgement.[1] Other courtly effusions followed, during this and the following years; consolation on the death of one infant, congratulations on the birth of another, addresses to Charles on his anniversary day; performances which do not, on the whole, lead us to regret that the task of writing the history of the 'sweet reign' was reserved for other pens. Charles, on his part, added new marks of consideration. Jonson appealed towards the close of 1629 for a commutation of his pension of a hundred marks (£66 13s. 4d.) to a hundred pounds. Charles not only complied, but added the further bounty of an annual 'terse' of canary from the cellars of Whitehall, during the term of his natural life.[2] The treasurer's warrant formally conveying these grants is dated March 26, 1630. The Household appears to have at first refused to supply the wine, incurring thereby an epigram of frank but good-humoured remonstrance from the 'old bard'.[3]

There followed a triumph of another kind, apparently far more significant than rise of pension or grants of wine, but which proved to be the beginning of a new series of disasters graver than the old. Towards the close of 1630 Jonson was once more called upon to produce, in conjunction with his old comrade and rival, Inigo Jones, a masque for the ensuing Christmas season. On January 9, 1631, a Sunday night, *Love's Triumph through Callipolis*, and at Shrovetide, its counterpart, *Chloridia*, were given 'with great splendour' in Whitehall. His old cunning asserted itself once more,

---

[1] *Underwoods*, lxii.
[2] This, as indicated on a previous page, sufficiently shows that Jonson was completely exonerated from the suspicion of complicity with Felton which had led to his examination in October, 1628. The text of the grant is given in App. III.
[3] *Underwoods*, lxviii.

little impaired, and he might well dream that the spacious days and festive nights of James were to be renewed. But no success could restore his old prestige. Five years of silence and absence had relaxed his hold upon the memory of a Whitehall audience; his vigorous presence—it was in these years that scholarly friends found his face like the portraits of Menander [1]—no longer, save with a little circle of intimates and disciples, supported his name and fame; the masques he sent in from his paralytic bed were in some sense, from the Court point of view, tentative and experimental. Inigo, on the other hand, had during these years succeeded in making himself an indispensable and at the same time an authoritative person at Court. His equally masterful will was united with a much readier tact than Jonson often condescended to exercise, and his extraordinary gifts and acquisitions as an artist were displayed in those arts of painting and architecture in which Charles himself was an accomplished connoisseur. Inigo in short stood, in 1631, with Charles where Jonson, ten years before, had stood with James. He had complied—not too willingly one surmises—with the royal command to invent a masque in conjunction with Jonson. In any case, he was by no means prepared to yield his accustomed priority to the bedridden absentee who had supplied the copy, and who had even constructed the plot only in close consultation with himself. It would seem, in effect, that Inigo's invention has entered much more intimately into these masques than into any of their predecessors from Jonson's hand, and Jonson himself admitted this in conceding to Jones a place on the title-page of the *Love's Triumph through Callipolis,* when published shortly after the performance. This, however, was not enough. Jonson put his own name, as a matter of course, first. Jones angrily

---

[1] I. C. in his 'Ode to Ben Jonson upon his Ode to himselfe' prefixed to the collection of the Horatian *Art of Poetry* and minor poems issued in duodecimo in 1640. 'Thou art as whole *Menander,* and dost looke like the old *Greek,*' with a note, '*Ben Jonson* is said to be very like the picture we have of *Menander,* taken from an ancient Medall'.

resented the audacity, and the old quarrel flamed out afresh, with a ferocity quickened on Jonson's side by the bitterness of conscious decline. From his sick room in Westminster,[1] he discharged the 'Expostulation with Inigo Jones' and two other fulminations ('An epigram of Inigo Jones'; 'To Inigo Marquis Would-be'), which are hardly redeemed from vulgar truculence by an occasional flash of intellectual scorn. Friends reported that Inigo stood in 'fear' of his 'sharp verse', and was plotting to give Jonson at any rate good reason to punish him. Inigo could afford to make light of the attack, but whether out of fear or not, he did, in effect, inflict upon his assailant a heavy and damaging blow. At the following Christmas season, 1631-2, Jonson's services, at Inigo's direct urgency, were dispensed with, and Aurelian Townshend, a third-rate poet about the Court, was called on for a masque in his stead. Through the later months of 1631 his situation, between poverty and disease, had steadily grown worse. The 'Epistle Mendicant' to Treasurer Weston, already noticed, was written during these months. Five years of sickness and want had almost choked the springs of poetry. His Muse was

> block'd up and straightned, narrow'd in,
> Fix'd to the bed, and boords, unlike to win
> Health, or scarce breath, as she had never bin,

so that she 'not peeps out, one of hundred dayes!' His silence was to be brought painfully home to him in another way. In November the City passed an order to withhold payment of his wages as chronologer 'until he present some fruit of his labours'. There is, in fact, no sign that he ever concerned himself with the duties, doubtless uncongenial, attached to the office he had accepted. He wrote, nevertheless, cavalierly enough, of the 'chanderly pension' which the City had withdrawn.[2]

[1] The precise date of his removal from the City cannot be determined; but he was already of Westminster when examined, in October, 1628, by the attorney-general.
[2] Letter to the Earl of Newcastle, printed in Appendix II.

## III

It was under these unpromising circumstances that Jonson once more turned to his old, now almost desperate, resource, the stage. He had printed *The New Inn* in the spring, soon after the quarrel, with a title-page in which the unquenched anger stirred in him by the performance still visibly glows and glares. He had also begun to pass through the press the still unfinished plays of his maturity—*Bartholomew Fair*, *The Devil is an Ass*, *The Staple of News*—for the second volume of his works. The process was slow, and Jonson wrote impatiently to his staunchest friend at this time, the Duke of Newcastle, of the 'lewd printer' whose fault it was 'that I can send your lordship no more of my book. . . . My printer and I shall afford subject enough for a tragic-comedy; for with his delays and vexation I am become almost blind.' The printing was, in any case, suspended long before it was complete, whether through the printer's fault or, as seems equally probable, because Jonson himself never completed the final revision which the bulk of the second volume, as we have it, has palpably not undergone. But failing powers can hardly be held responsible for the neglect. The riches and resource of Jonson's intellect are nowhere more astonishing than in the birth, under these grim conditions, of a comedy so far from contemptible, when all is said, as *The Magnetic Lady*, licensed on October 12 to the King's Men, and played by them shortly afterwards at Blackfriars. It attained at least the relative success of not being indignantly rejected like *The New Inn*. But even his 'sons' owned, as Howell in a letter to him pleasantly puts it, that the divine madman of *The Alchemist* was 'not so mad' when he wrote *The Magnetic Lady*.[1] As for his enemies, old and new, they used their chance and played their game, excusably perhaps when we consider what they had undergone, but

---

[1] *Familiar Letters*, l. v. 16.

none the less ignobly. In the ribald verses of Alexander Gill we have a glimpse of the scene; the fashionable audience which frequented the Blackfriars Theatre, 'silks and plush, and all the wit', and Nat Butter and Inigo in conspicuous positions, venting themselves in ostentatious guffaws. The wretched feud with Inigo reached its culminating moment a few months later, when Jonson prepared to deal with him by the dramatic method he had long ago used to punish the assaults of Dekker and Marston. Taking up, it is probable, an old play of his early days, *A Tale of a Tub*, he put into it the unmistakable caricature of Vitruvius Hoop. Even in the heyday of his early prime his ridicule of 'Crispinus' and 'Demetrius' had done little for his fame, and he had been glad to withdraw from the arena into a sullen privacy, safe from the hoofs and jaws of the herd he had aspired to correct and inform. The present blow was aimed with equal violence, but less skill, at a far more formidable antagonist; and Inigo, securely entrenched in the favour of Whitehall, parried it with contemptuous ease. On his application the scenes intended to ridicule him were struck out of the play by order of the lord chamberlain. In this mutilated form *A Tale of a Tub* was licensed, on May 7, to the Queen's Men, and presumably played by them on the public stage. Nothing is known of this performance, but it must have amounted to a tolerable success, since a repetition was ordered at Whitehall, and actually took place, in January, 1634. Although the homely and rustic piece—'inficeto inficetior rure'—was 'not liked' by the Court, its performance there at all was, under the circumstances, a triumph for Jonson and a defeat for Inigo. And it is probable that Charles's fluctuating sympathies had in reality undergone a change in Jonson's favour, the cause of which we can surmise. On his way to Scotland, in May of the previous year, Charles dined at Welbeck as the guest of Jonson's most powerful and loyal friend, the Duke of Newcastle. For this occasion the duke, who had received, during the spring, repeated applications for help from Jonson, desired him to prepare an entertainment. *The King's Entertainment at Welbeck*, which resulted, has no claim to rank with the better masques of Jonson, but it was skilfully contrived as a frame to the brilliant shows which made this festivity a byword for magnificence. And discount as we may the natural exaltation of the duchess's narrative, it is plain that the king was greatly pleased. For the very next year he arranged another progress to the North, in which the queen would accompany him, expressly intimating to the duke his desire for a second 'Welcome' like the first in his Nottinghamshire home. Jonson was naturally once more called in, and finished the *Love's Welcome at Bolsover*, with which the long record of his masques and entertainments ends. In this piece, with characteristic hardihood, he tried to compensate himself for the forced omission of Vitruvius Hoop from *A Tale of a Tub*. He was on friendly ground, where he himself had a much firmer footing than Inigo enjoyed at Whitehall; but to confront the king and queen with this unmistakable and amusing caricature of his successful rival, ' Coronel Iniquo Vitruvius', was a perilous freedom. It is certain, however, that it was not seriously resented. For in the ensuing autumn Charles gave Jonson an unequivocal sign of restored goodwill, by intervening on his behalf with the dissatisfied City authorities who had three years before refused to pay Jonson's salary until he did some work. Their reason remained as good or better than ever; but in deference to the king's request, the City, on September 18, 1634, ordered the pension of 100 nobles to be continued and the arrears to be paid. There is probably significance in their choice of terms. It was a 'pension' that they paid, 'a fee or wages' that they had refused to pay. With the resumption of payment, the expectation of work to be done was tacitly dropped. The office became a recognized sinecure, and as such Jonson continued to enjoy it to the end.

With the performance of *A Tale of a Tub* in the

January of 1634, and the Bolsover *Welcome* in July, Jonson's career as a man of letters practically ends. He sent a copy of verses to the king at the beginning of 1633, and these may not be the latest: one or two of the epistles to friends, too, may belong to the same years: but for the two years preceding his death, he appears to have been completely silent.

## CHAPTER VII

## THE LAST PHASE: JONSON AND HIS FRIENDS

### I

THE outward history of this final phase of Jonson's life is not alluring either to the biographer or to the reader. An old poet, struggling with disease and want, wringing plays and entertainments from a jaded and reluctant brain, heard with derision or indifference by the public, carrying on with futile violence a miserable quarrel, soliciting the king's bounty and provoking his rebuffs,—it is a picture more pitiful than heroic. But we are fortunately able to add from various indirect sources a good deal of refining and humanizing detail which perceptibly modifies this impression.

The sick chamber in Westminster ('in the house under which you passe as you goe out of the Churchyard into the old Palace'[1]) where Jonson spent most of these twelve years, and where he died, had, during the whole of this time, a better claim than any other spot to be the focus of learning and letters in London. The 'well-furnished library' to which Selden had once resorted for the scholiast on Euripides had been seriously impoverished, if not gutted, by the fire of 1623; it had often been 'devoured', as he told Drummond, and therefore often replenished, before; and he certainly in these years had many books about him. Howell, who about 1634 saved him from a second fire,[2] tells us of his large collection of grammars, to which he himself added a Welsh Grammar at Jonson's application. He 'read daily', as he had always done; and

[1] So the house was described by Aubrey. His uncle Danver had known Jonson.
[2] *Familiar Letters, u.s.* The letter is dated June 27, 1629, but Howell's dates are well known to have no authority, and this one is disproved by an allusion to *The Magnetic Lady.*

perhaps, when the distractions in the 'Old Devil' and elsewhere were no longer available, more than ever. Out of these 'daily readings' 'flowed', to use his own modest phrase, the collection of reflections and criticisms which he entitled *Discoveries*.

The *Discoveries*, as we have them, certainly belong to this later phase of his life; James is dead, Bacon is dead. They are, for these recluse years, what the 'stored up humanity and humble gleanings in divinity' were for the years before the fire. He still 'gleans' and 'stores up' with undiminished diligence; and the most autocratic of dramatists and critics modestly transcribes from Heinsius pages on the theory of drama. More often without translating he follows the general lines of a discussion, taking over, for instance, Quintilian's requisites of good style, and supplying modern comment and illustration in his own unmistakable idiom. But in a great proportion of these pregnant jottings we have to recognize, not the kind of laborious compilation from many sources which the successful hunting down of these sources is liable to suggest, but the spontaneous outflow of a brain charged with classical memories, and largely Latin in its stylistic instincts and proclivities. So that even when he is writing of his contemporaries, of Shakespeare, of Bacon, he writes what Seneca might have written of them, and a Roman writer's phrases about his own contemporaries come unsought to his pen. Pliny regards his time as an age of decadence, genius is stricken with decay and all things go backwards; yet he has profound confidence in the eternal fecundity of Nature, and repudiates the servile following of antiquity. But this temper, in both its aspects, was Jonson's also, and he can without affectation express both his despondence and his security in language which had served to formulate these emotions in the age of Nero.[1]

The criticism of style which the *Discoveries* show to have much occupied Jonson's thoughts during these years

[1] *Discoveries*, 1640, p. 89.

# Jonson and his Friends

touched closely upon another study, never strange to him but particularly active in his later life, the grammatical analysis of speech. Of this philological interest of his, a fragmentary memorial survives in the *English Grammar*. At a time when a fine excess was the hall-mark of poetic expression, Jonson, alone among his fellow-poets, applied the scholar's ἀκρίβεια to decide the right use of words. What was still more unusual, he had in him a germ (never matured, it is true) of historical philology. As became the friend of Camden and Selden, he was curious about local, and also about foreign, forms of speech. He studied English dialects; he had a collection of foreign grammars. The first version of the *Grammar* perished in the fire. The extant *Grammar* may probably be dated in the early thirties. There are various indications that his philological interests were particularly active in 1633-4. He was occupied at least in revising and supplementing the dialect colloquies of *A Tale of a Tub*. He may have been elaborating the choicer rustic speech of *The Sad Shepherd*. It was now that, as we have seen, he was importuning Howell for Davies's *Welsh Grammar*, which his friend ultimately, with difficulty, procured.[1] And the poet who, called upon to design a 'Welcome' for Charles at Welbeck, put it into the mouth of 'Accidence' in a cassock of black buckram painted with the Parts of Speech, may be shrewdly suspected of having been recently concerned with the *English Grammar* when the summons came. This interest is perhaps reflected in the Yorkshire dialect of his servant-disciple Brome's *Northern Lass* (1632).

## II

These and other literary occupations, however, did not prevent Jonson's life from being, at least until the last two years before his death, an eminently social one. 'His

---

[1] Howell's *Familiar Letters*, I. v. 16, 26. The book, with Howell's inscription to Jonson, is still extant in the Pepys Library at Cambridge. It bears the title: *Cambro-Brytannicae Cymraecaeque Linguae Institutiones*, 1592 (cf. App. IV).

conversation' (i.e. the society he frequented) 'was very good and with men of most note'; so Clarendon, who as an intimate younger friend had the best means of knowing, and who judged rather as a lawyer and a man of the world than as a man of letters, wrote some years after Jonson's death.[1] Lord Falkland wrote to the same effect in his memorial verses:

> To him how daily *flockt*, what *reverence* gave,
> All that had *wit*, or would be thought to have, . . .
> How the wise too, did with mere *wits* agree,
> As *Pembroke, Portland*, and grave *Aubigny*;
> Nor thought the rigid'st senator a shame
> To contribute to so deserved a fame![2]

—words which the noble sincerity of the writer's character forbids us seriously to discount. The position of Jonson in these later years is in fact by no means adequately described as that of a literary dictator. This he undoubtedly was; but the boundless homage paid to him with perfect sincerity in this capacity is not easily justified by the intrinsic literary value of his work. In precisely those excellences which were most sought and delighted in by the coming poets of the day he was singularly poor. In swiftness and reach of fancy, in sweet and intricate music, the venerated 'Father' was no match for most of his 'sons'. But they were not mistaken in recognizing his supremacy, even if its precise nature evaded their terms. A temperament of immense expansive and contagious force, a character of imposing weight, these demonic or titanic traits added apparent significance as well as real momentum to what he spoke or wrote, made his wit appear wittier, and his wisdom yet more wise. Jonson cannot for us be counted among

---

[1] While still a law student, he tells us, his 'chief acquaintance were Ben Jonson, John Selden, . . . Sir Kenelm Digby, . . . Thomas Carew, and some other of eminent faculties in their several ways. He [Jonson] had for many years an extraordinary kindness for Mr. Hyde, till he found he betook himself to business, which he believed ought never to be preferred to his company.' Hyde was eighteen in 1626; this friendship will therefore have begun nearly at the time of Jonson's stroke.

[2] 'An Eglogue on the Death of Ben Jonson' in *Jonsonus Virbius*, p. 6.

the great sages to whom we go for counsel, as men go or have gone to Goethe or to Vergil, in the supreme or the minor crises of life. But in his own day the comparison with the Apolline oracle was not beside the mark. 'Thy *Scænes* are *precepts*,' wrote an admirer; 'every verse doth give Counsel, and teach us not to *laugh*, but *live*.'[1] Few kings have received 'praise' from a subject so like the counsel of an independent authority as Jonson's 'Panegyre' to James. Latin dignity, Elizabethan pithiness, the disciplined sobriety of the schools, and the peremptory style of a naturally authoritative mind, concurred in giving a certain oracular quality to the typical Jonsonian sentence, whether conveyed in private epistle or over the tavern supper-table. Ancient wisdom, too, often supplied or inspired the substance of the counsel, as in the letter to Savile, or the advice on the schooling of boys; but the antique matter was welded into the very texture of a modern English brain. 'They prefer him to Euripides,' wrote a French observer, Saint-Amant, who visited London and its stage in 1631;[2] and both the comparison and the preference rested in part upon the impressiveness of the antique 'sentence' in its Jonsonian mould and setting.

By far the greater number of these intimates of his later years were men much younger than himself. This was no doubt a natural circumstance in the old age of a man of genial temper, whose contemporaries have passed away. Jonson, though he died at sixty-four, did in fact outlive most of his former comrades. Chapman had died in 1634; Drayton, Donne, and Cotton, in 1631.[3] But mere dearth of older companionship cannot account for the extraordinary intimacy of Jonson's relations with the *élite* of the younger

---

[1] Richard West, in *Jonsonus Virbius*, p. 56.
[2] Quoted by Jusserand, *Hist. du Peuple anglais*, ii, 773.
[3] At some date between Jonson's paralytic attack and this year the old poet testified that disease and want had not touched his scholar's passion for accurate knowledge, by the undated letter (printed in Appendix IV) in which he asks the loan of 'some booke that would determinately satisfy mee, of the true site & distance betwixt *Bauli* or *Portus Baiarum* and *Villa Augusta*'. (Cf. App. II, xxi.)

generation. The friendship of ripe genius with brilliant youth has never been rare, and is of perennial charm. But there is nothing in literary history quite like the institution of the 'Tribe of Ben'. It was based upon no common literary formula or program, like the Cénacles of later Romanticism, or the 'Pléiade' and 'Areopagus' of earlier classicism; it imposed no vow of fidelity to the ideas or ideals of the master. Its bond was the magnetism of the dominating personality, a bond which no doubt exercised a subtle influence upon the writing of the younger men, yet chiefly in the way of critical control and intellectual discipline. In this respect it resembled the influence exercised by Boileau's disciplinary criticism over the creative work of Molière and Racine. Its potency was yet more signally shown in the almost total absence, during Jonson's later years, of pronounced and declared reaction from his ways. The clamorous disapproval and derision which greeted some of his later plays did not come from the men who were making literature; they rallied in his defence; or if they gently criticized, it was in the name of the greater things he himself had done before. Even Suckling, the least idolatrous of his 'sons', whose easy gaiety in lyric and drama was more in the vein of his time than Jonson's severe technique, uttered his pleasantries about Ben's laboured wit, in the *Session of the Poets*, only in the year of Jonson's death. A greater than Suckling had already sounded the first note of a poetical revolution of immeasurably vaster scope and depth; but Milton, though no disciple, knew no better entertainment for cheerful moods than 'Jonson's learned sock'. Even *Comus* is, with all its profound and deliberate divergences, an implicit tribute to the master of masque-makers.

### III

Of the history of this informal society little is recorded. Its discussions and repartees, its songs and stories, survive for us only in an eloquent allusive phrase or two at most;

the door of the temple is opened for a moment, and the burly voice of the laurelled 'Apollo' is heard outdoing the frolic wine with the overplus of his wit. But the individual figures which compose Jonson's entourage are, in great part, very clear to us; even their special dealings with Jonson are sometimes, for the after world, the most luminous moment of their lives. The Sidneys and Haringtons of his early maturity have vanished; but in their place appear the names, no less instinct with sterling English quality, of Cary, Cavendish, Digby, Weston. Falkland (Lucius Cary) was the loftiest in character, and certainly not the least devoted, of the 'sons'. His friendship with Moryson heightened the glamour of chivalrous idealism which gathers for us about both; and both comrade and master helped to enshrine the dead friend in worthy verse; Falkland in those 'Anniversaries', one of which, full of praise for Jonson, he sent to his 'noble Father'; the other, in the Pindaric ode which 'he sung ere he went himself to rest',[1] an old man's tribute, unequal, laboured, but here and there finely felt, to the glory and grace of youth. Falkland's letter enclosing his lines is delightful in its mingled gaiety and reverence. His later homage to the dead master, which was given the place of honour in the Memorial Verses, is also one of the finest in temper, if hardly the most accomplished in technique. In William Cavendish, made Earl of Newcastle in 1628, the noble harmony of Falkland's personality is replaced by a romantic prodigality and exuberance. He had his full share of the virtuosities which were to make a later generation of his family illustrious. He wrote plays and poems, the best that were written by any one in his time, his ardent second wife declared; he made a great reputation later as a theorist on horse-training, and his passion for riding and fencing called forth tributes from Jonson which may have given occasion for their friendship;[2] in recitations, too, he was a connoisseur, loved to hear Jonson read aloud, and used in later days to

---

[1] 'A Pindaric Ode on the death of Sir H. Moryson', *Underwoods*, lxx.
[2] *Underwoods*, liii, lix.

tell the same eager reporter that he had heard no other read well. But the virtuoso *par excellence* among these associates was Sir Kenelm Digby, man of fashion, man of affairs, wit, dashing soldier, fantastic dabbler in speculation and experiment, and capable civil servant, the victor of Scanderoon, commentator on the *Faerie Queene*, and critic of *Religio Medici*; 'skilled in six tongues, and learned in all the arts'. We have Jonson's word for it that he loved Jonson's verses 'next to *Spenser*'s noble booke'; and it was probably Digby who prepared for the press the manuscript material of the 1640 Folio. In a pleasant epigram the old poet imagines Sir Kenelm receiving his poetic salutations from the hands of Lady Venetia, his wife, and carrying them off to the Treasury Board, where they find admiring 'allowance'.[1] With the Lady Digby Jonson's bond was still closer. He called her his 'Muse', and more than any woman of these later years, with perhaps one exception, she replaced for him the Lady Rutlands and Lady Bedfords of his earlier time. Her death, in 1633, elicited from Jonson by far the most elaborate and not the least moving of his elegies ('Eupheme').

> Twere time that I dy'd too, now she is dead,
> Who was my *Muse*, and life of all I sey'd.[2]

To the Westons, father and son, Jonson stood less close. But in the elder, Lord Portland, he honoured the vigilant official ('that waking man! that Eye of State!') learned in the 'arts of life', and none the worse for not being a master of the fine arts, like Inigo. Jonson addressed him repeatedly in complimentary or in 'mendicant' epistles, both alike dignified and honourable to both sides.[3] The younger Weston was not a 'son' of Jonson's, and was much abroad on diplomatic missions; but his marriage, in 1633, with the daughter of Jonson's five years' host d'Aubigny (later Duke

---

[1] 'An Epigram, To my Muse, the Lady Digby, on Her Husband, Sir Kenelm Digby', *Underwoods*, lxxviii.

[2] *Underwoods*, lxxxiv, ll. 205-6.

[3] *Underwoods*, lxxi, lxxiii, lxxvii.

of Lennox) gave him a new title to his interest, hardly borne out by the honest dullness of the Ode in which he celebrated these nuptials. This matter-of-fact recital is a useful document for seventeenth-century wedding ceremonies, but leaves the bride one of the shadowiest figures in Jonson's entourage. It was otherwise with the young wife of another noble friend. Lady Jane Pawlett, Marchioness of Winchester, lives in the vivid and pathetic elegies in which she was independently commemorated by Jonson and Milton.

But Jonson's closer intimacies were naturally to be found among his literary fellows. Specific literary influence he did not always exercise; but the atmosphere of literature and the fellowship of poetry were dominant wherever Jonson was. James Howell, for instance, his neighbour in Westminster, though a 'son', was in no sense a disciple. His wide accomplishment, supple intelligence, and practical aptitudes made him, nevertheless, a very serviceable friend. He hears a good story, and retails it to Jonson as a possible plot for a new play; Jonson is in want of a rare book, Howell searches the London bookshops till he finds it. And the same watchful friend, who seems to have saved him from a second fire, did his best, less successfully, to temper other conflagrations. The bitter diatribes against Inigo encountered his courteous but energetic protests, enforced with a hint that Ben had 'lost some ground at court by it; and, as I hear from a good hand, the King, who hath so great a judgement in poetry (as in all things else), is not well pleased therewith'. To the number of the friends who could venture rebuke belongs also Thomas Carew,—with Robert Herrick the most brilliant of all the 'sons'. Like Howell, both were at the beginning of the reign no longer young; and their attitude towards the old man could not be exactly that of the flock of neophytes, who came to learn their business, or to procure his profitable public recognition of their 'virtue'. Herrick, who had certainly been a member of the society before Jonson's illness (he was thirty-four in 1625), carried away to his exile under Dartmoor in 1629 his memory of those matchless 'lyric feasts', which nowhere live so vividly as in the vibrating memory they left in the magnificent temperament of this born singer.

Carew, a Court official, doubtless remained in touch to the last. We have a glimpse of him at Ben's supper-table no less vivid than that which Herrick has left of him at the board of the Dog or the Triple Tun; no glorious reveller, however, intoxicated with the overplus of Jonsonian wit, but a critical and fastidious listener, whispering in his neighbour's ear a sarcasm upon the overplus of Jonson's self-laudation.[1] Yet Jonson exercised self-restraint in his art if not in his potations, and it was precisely his critical severity that told upon Carew, and kept the intellectual artist in him from being submerged in the amorous voluptuary. And in the *Coelum Britannicum* of 1634 he showed, in addition, that faculty of executing pleasant variations, touched to modern and satirical issues, on the material of classic myth, which makes a large part of the charm of Jonson's better masques. The appearance of the *Coelum Britannicum* and of *Comus* within a few months of one another is a remarkable though wholly undesigned tribute to the great master of the masque. In the first a brilliant disciple played upon the master's instrument with new vivacity but to the same purpose; in the second an alien but still youthful and plastic genius seized it for a passing moment and compelled it to convey the passion of his Puritan austerity and of his ravishing sense of beauty. Neither work would have been possible without Jonson.

But Jonson's fame rested pre-eminently upon his plays, and it was the past master of comedy, rather than the writer of lyrics and of masques, whose prestige attracted most of the men of letters who gathered about him in these later years. They were almost all considerably younger than Carew and Herrick; young men of twenty or thereabouts at the beginning of the reign, for whom the chequered history of Jonson's long struggle with embattled Ignorance had

[1] Howell, *Familiar Letters*, ii. 13.

become a vague legendary background to the glories of *Volpone* and *The Alchemist*. Thomas Nabbes, Thomas Randolph, Jasper Mayne, Shakerley Marmion, Joseph Rutter, Richard Brome, and, several years younger than these, William Cartwright, all approached the stage with a bias more or less pronounced towards Jonsonian procedure or design. Brome, the servant-apprentice of his later craft, as young Field had been the 'scholer' of his prime, remained his most devoted disciple. The verses with which Jonson winged his 'Dick's' *Northern Lass* (1632) and his 'Joseph's' *Shepherd's Holiday* (1635) are characteristic expressions of the generous recognition, masterful self-assertion, and vivacious criticism, which made the old master's nervous talk so piquant and bracing as it was clearly felt to be.

Our knowledge of Jonson's literary and personal relationships in these last years is thus by no means slight.[1] But outside this inner circle of facts fairly luminous to us, we must recognize a penumbra of countless obscure connexions of which only one here and there can now be vaguely discerned.[2] Jonson, the dictator of letters, the oracle, the man with powerful friends at Court, was certainly the object, or

[1] There is a picture of Ben in the manuscript poems of Michael Oldisworth, of Wotton-under-Edge, put together in 1644, in an *Iter Australe*, 1632, from London to Southampton; the poet starts with a friend from Westminster.

    Behind the Abbey lives a man of fame;
With awe and reverence wee repeat his name,
*Ben Johnson*: him we saw, and thought to heare
From him some flashes and fantastique Guere;
But hee spake nothing lesse. His whole Discourse
Was how Mankinde grew daily worse and worse,
How God was disregarded, how Men went
Downe even to Hell, and neuer did repent,
With many such sadd Tales; as hee would teach
Vs Scholars, how herafter Wee should preach.
Great wearer of the baies, looke to thy lines,
Lest they chance to bee challeng'd by Divines:
Some future Times will, by a grosse Mistake,
*Johnson* a Bishop, not a Poët make.

We are indebted to Mr. P. J. Dobell, the owner of the manuscript, for this quotation.

[2] Some hitherto obscure or unknown specimens of these occasional expressions of friendship or piety will be found in the 'Ungathered Verses' below.

the victim, of constant applications, consultations, flatteries, dedications, books sent for his approval by old acquaintances or young aspirants. Our vision of Ben in his last decade is incomplete unless we stipple in around the clear profile this background of half-lit shade. As a clue to a host of not very dissimilar letters which have vanished, we may recall one, by chance preserved; in which one Joseph Webbe, on January 28, 1629, sends to 'his deare and loving frend M[r] Benj. Jonson' ('eldest son of our Brittain Muses') a little treatise on pentameter and hexameter.[1]

## IV

It is in the midst of occupations and companionships such as these that we have our last glimpses of Jonson. From November, 1635, when his only remaining son died, to his own death, two years later, we have no certain information about him. The silence that falls about the close of this famous life helps us to guess at the circumstances in which these years were spent. It was impossible for him to become obscure; but physical infirmities and money troubles steadily grew, diminishing his power of work and occasions of friendly contact with the world. Considerable as his nominal income was, and numerous as were his wealthy friends, it is certain that he died almost penniless and in debt.[2] Whether there was also mental decline, and in what degree, must remain undetermined. One friendly witness hints at failure of mind. But Falkland in his elegy makes Meliboeus expressly state that

> Not long before his death our woods he meant
> To visit and descend from Thames to Trent:
> Mete with thy elegy his pastoral—

lines which may not decisively prove that *The Sad Shepherd* was the work of his closing months. but certainly

---

[1] British Museum, Sloane MS. 1466, ff. 203–10; quoted by Briggs, *Mod. Phil.* xi. Jonson's 'ansere', originally appended, is unfortunately lost.

[2] This is officially certified in the Act Book of the Dean and Chapter of Westminster anno 1637, fol. 53, printed in Appendix III.

show that a new pastoral poem was expected almost to the last by those who knew him best, and that this expectation was not regarded as in any way unreasonable. If the 'pastoral' thus planned among the woods by Trent really was the *Sad Shepherd* fragment, where the elegant conventions of pastoralism are braced and invigorated by the genial naturalism of Robin Hood, the rugged old poet's most consummate and sustained lyric effort was his last. That the least lyric personality among all the poets of his time should pass away with such a swan-song is no doubt startling. But the seeds of song were planted deep in the stubborn soil of his brain, and that they could yield him this golden sheaf at the last is not wholly beyond belief.

Another less authentic but still probable tradition of these last months discloses for a moment the rarer Jonson of reticent but vehement piety. His old friend George Morley, afterwards Bishop of Winchester, told Walton that in the poet's long retirement and sickness he had visited him and found him 'much afflicted that he had profaned the Scriptures in his plays and lamented it with horror'. Long before, in the great preface to *Volpone* he had 'trembled to think towards the least profaneness'. That haughty virginal self-vindication was the temper of a man in the strength of his prime. This lowly self-abasement was the temper of the death-bed. Both were equally sincere.

He died on August 6, 1637.[1] Three days later he was followed from his house in Westminster to his grave in the Abbey by a throng which included 'all or the greatest part of the nobilitie and gentry then in the town'.[2] Neglected as his later days had been, the passing of Ben was, for the entire English world of letters, the passing of its king—a king who had perhaps ceased to govern, but who still reigned. Poets and kings, Jonson was fond of saying, were equal rarities, and he even complimented James in an epigram

[1] Apparently intestate. Cf. the entry in the Act Book printed in App. III.
[2] Sir Edward Walker, Garter, 17 Aug. 1637 (quoted *N. & Q.*, 1st ser., vi. 405.)

on combining both functions. Truer poets than James had sat on the throne of his predecessors. But no earlier British poet had so truly reigned, or been commemorated at his passing, with honours so signal, on purely literary grounds, as Jonson. The mourning for Sidney was the nearest earlier parallel. But Sidney was a courtier and a soldier, as well as a poet, and he had just been cut off in his prime by a heroic death in the field. For some months, however, the illustrious gathering at his funeral remained the only public testimony in Jonson's honour. Preparations were set on foot for a volume of memorial poems, but some of the contributors found that so great an argument needed prolonged consideration,—'not that the Gentlemens affections were lesse readie to grieve, but their judgements to write', if we may adopt the apology which 'the printer' thought it necessary to offer to 'the Reader' when, in March, 1638, the volume *Jonsonus Virbius* at length appeared.

Jonson's good friend, Brian Duppa, then Dean of Christ Church, appears to have done good service as editor. It is no doubt easy to cavil at defects both of omission and of commission. The collection, of thirty-three pieces, is on the whole remarkable rather for hearty feeling than for poetic force or felicity. There is little in it of the lofty critical appreciation which the funeral *éloge* in skilful hands permits.. But such pieces as Falkland's, Godolphin's,[1] Cartwright's, Mayne's, contain much that is striking and memorable. And almost all the pieces testify, in whatever halting and blundering accents, to the radiating and mastering force of Jonson's personality. These literary souls of very varied calibre had 'felt' him, unmistakably, —and he, unlike Byron, had 'taught' them not a little to boot. There are some strange omissions in the list of contributors, due possibly to editorial neglect or oversight.

[1] The unsigned piece, 'The Muses fairest light', commonly ascribed to Cleveland as well as the following poem which bears his initials, has been shown by Mr. Drinkwater (*Times Lit. Supplement*, Oct. 25, 1923) to be probably by Sidney Godolphin. It is found in a MS. volume of Godolphin's poems made by his nephew.

Neither Carew nor Herrick joined in the chorus of singers, not one of whom could for a moment be measured for strength of poetic sinew with themselves. A greater than they, who had lately immortalized an obscure college contemporary in consummate verse, would perhaps not have been unwilling to pay his meed of haughty and frugal praise to the older Humanist poet. But *Lycidas* itself marks with sufficient emphasis the gulf which now divided Milton from the throng of courtly poets who called Jonson father; and the fierce onslaught upon the dissolute clergy would have in itself made him impossible to courtly Dean Duppa. He had at disposal, too, a sufficient crowd of young Oxford graduates and enthusiastic cavaliers eager to do honour to the 'first of poets'.

If the literary monument was less splendid than it might have been, the material monument in the Abbey which had been contemplated and subscribed for remained a dream. The 'men of wit and learning' who formed the plan were probably, as in the case of *Virbius*, ill organized; divided counsels perhaps delayed decision; and finally, before anything was decided, the gathering political storm swept the interests and pieties of literature into an oblivion from which they only emerged, gravely denuded and transformed, at the Restoration. The monument and statue were abandoned, and the money returned to the subscribers. Where it should have stood, a square flag of blue marble was alone to be seen, rudely inscribed with the legend: 'O rare Ben Jonson.'[1] John Young, who, according to Aubrey, 'walking there when the grave was covering, gave the fellow eighteen pence to cutt it', deserves the humble but secure niche in the Jonsonian gallery which he has won at that modest cost.

---

[1] The flag has now disappeared owing to repaving. Its exact site, in the north aisle of the nave, is indicated in Stanley's *Memorials of Westminster* (ed. 1868, p. 238).—It will suffice to mention here the somewhat analogous fate of Jonson's skull. F. Buckland in his *Curiosities of Natural History*, 3rd series, ii. 181-9, describes his examination of it. He finally placed it in the coffin of the famous surgeon John Hunter, where it now presumably rests.

## 118  *Last Phase: Jonson and his Friends*

That brief vernacular ejaculation, so naïvely human in its contrast with the sententious Latin epitaphs around, conveys the impression made by Jonson upon his age more vividly than any formal obituary.  Jonson figures in our current analysis as the staunch asserter of classic tradition, instructed reason, and enlightened common sense, against the imaginative individualism of Elizabethan romancers.  But the Jacobean world saw in this doughty champion of unpopular traditions the most incisive individual personality, the most commanding personal force which had, within its memory, mingled in the world of letters.  For it, he was not the assertor of commonplace, but the 'rare', the incomparable, the unique, Ben Jonson.

## CHAPTER VIII

### FINAL APPRECIATION

#### I

AND modern criticism, on the whole, endorses this impression. The personality of Jonson detaches itself from the crowd of his literary contemporaries with a distinctness by no means wholly due to the fact that our knowledge of it happens to be unusually full and clear. The relatively abundant witness which he has left of himself in contemporary literature is itself a result of something potent and distinctive in the *ethos* of the man, which attracted curiosity and interest in circles very remote from his own, and made him throughout his career an object of devoted friendships and discipleships, of bitter enmities and envies, of understanding eulogy, and tell-tale gibe. Almost every sentence he wrote, however derivative in substance, carries an unmistakable relish of the man,—is, in greater or less degree, a document of the Jonsonian temperament and the Jonsonian will. Even the half-translated or paraphrased *Discoveries* bear the individual stamp of his mind, and eminent critics have excusably taken them to be yet more original than they are. He was distinguished among his great contemporaries by his scornful repudiation of the literary affectations and eccentricities of the time in the name of classical plainness and massive common sense. But he also satisfied in a rare degree a more difficult classical ideal, by putting his matter of common sense, his *communia*, in a way of his own. For the things he had to say were, in general, 'common' things. He was no adventurous explorer in the unknown solitudes of the human soul; he broke for the first time into no strange and silent sea. No despotic compulsion of thought led him up into the godlike heights, or out into the barren wildernesses, of speculation; no rare exaltation or ethereal delicacy of passion estranged him from the mass of men. The incongruities, even contradictions, which our analysis

120                    *Final Appreciation*

detects in his nature never, so far as we can see, issued in those inner conflicts which thrust men into wonder and self-questioning, experiment and research, discovery and development.  His masterful self-confidence saved him from the faltering stroke of the artist who doubts his powers, but it also precluded him from some heights and depths which men of aspiring humility achieve.  Hence his work is, in a rare degree, of a piece; we can distinguish its phases and its kinds; but the note of Jonsonian personality is singularly continuous; the apprentice challenging the veterans of Spain and the old poet inditing an Ode to Himself are the same; of the extraordinary power of inner growth, which astonishes us in a Dante, a Shakespeare, a Goethe, there is little trace in Jonson.  In some very obvious senses, then, 'rare' Ben Jonson is not one of the rarer spirits, but a man built of somewhat common materials, and on no very exalted lines.

Wherein then does his 'rarity' consist?  Obviously it was in part only a relative and conditioned rarity.  His contemporaries found him singular because his unmistakable genius was not in fact made on the common Elizabethan or Jacobean pattern.  Had he been born two generations later, and written for that England of Dryden to which he seemed the greatest of English dramatists, he would have found himself in a society at some points more intellectually akin than his own.  Even in the eighteenth century he might have been almost as much at home at the Literary Club, laying mind to mind with his great namesake, as in the wit-combats with Shakespeare or Beaumont at the Mermaid. His limitations, like his powers, were not those most characteristic of his time, and their singularity invested them, not in his own eyes only, with a certain glamour of distinction; while their very nature tended to exempt him from more commonplace failings, and to throw his exemption into yet more proud relief.  He was arrogantly conscious of his merit, but he was not vain; he thought too highly of learning, but there was nothing in him of the sciolist; he believed too implicitly in the potency of labour and deliberate art, but he was incapable of the slipshod volubility of 'the gentlemen who write with ease'.

## II

Yet it is clear that with all his aggressive singularity and aloofness, Jonson was not really alien to his time. He shared to the full in the eager tumult of contemporary men of letters, contended in the same arena for the same prizes, worked under the same conditions for the same audiences. Nay, in some aspects he was the most completely 'of his age' among them all. Few of them had grown up, as he had, in the very heart of Elizabethan England, or knew as intimately as he did every corner and alley of crowded, reeking, picturesque London. With the Court and with men of position and influence in the country at large, he enjoyed more numerous and intimate relations than any of them. No other man of his time has comparable claims to have been, not its supreme creative genius, certainly, but its most salient and indispensable personality.

Such a history, and such a position, imply much more than the inevitable bond of kinship with his time which compels the most original mind to oppose or disown his age in terms of the thought and language it provides. And it is clear that the cleavage between his work and the mass of contemporary production was by no means so deep and wide as his frequent air of aggressive isolation would suggest. To contrast Jonson as a thoroughbred neo-classic with the 'romantic' Elizabethans is a very imperfect way of representing his relation to his fellow-dramatists. In some respects he was rather ultra-Elizabethan, pursuing artistic effects cognate to theirs with a more conscious purpose and a more powerful will. He shared to the full, on the stage as in the ordinary, the robust appetite which calls for a plentiful diet. The Goethean stage-manager's recipe for catching the ear of the populace, 'Make sure that plenty of things happen', was at least as valid in London as at Weimar, and it had no better example in those days than in the packed and crowded plots of Jonson. No kind or degree of profusion was foreign to his art, or uncongenial to his mind, provided its constituent elements were clearly presented, sharply distinguished, and logically arranged. Plautus, catering for 'the English of the ancient world', doubled the plots of Menander; Jonson, like Shakespeare a few years earlier, employed his prentice hand in doubling a plot of Plautus; and his later art repudiated only the incoherence, not the intricacy, of *The Case is Altered*.

More than this, a great part of the matter of the Jonsonian drama is common ground. Marston and Dekker, Nashe, Middleton, Fletcher, Beaumont, Shakespeare himself, and scores of others, whatever their other divergences from him and from one another, are Jonson's fellows and comrades at one point,—the drastic and humorous representation of the life of Elizabethan England. Fantastic comedy, romantic tragedy, 'Tales and Tempests', and the native 'History' with its 'three rusty swords', lay beyond his proper sphere; but no vital difference of method divides Eastcheap from Bartholomew Fair. Only, while almost all the others had the strongholds of their art in those un-Jonsonian haunts of tragedy and romance, this drastic and humorous presentation of Elizabethan England is the proper domain of the Jonsonian drama. He is at home there, and there only, whatever excursions he may make into Roman tragedy or poetic Pastoral.

Yet even when he is treading this common ground Jonson's step cannot for a moment be mistaken for any other. His drastic and humorous presentation of Elizabethan England is distinctive in temper, distinctive in method. And a great part of that distinctiveness is explained by the fact that doubled with Jonson the dramatist were two other Jonsons, no less inseparably parts of himself,—the scholar and the satirist. Each of them set his stamp upon the Jonsonian drama; each gravely limited its range; but each also provided one of the conditions of the intense and concentrated power which at its highest it attains.

## III

Take, first, the scholar. Jonson's scholarship was critical, not pedantic. The Renascence drama teems with the lumber of pseudo-classical imitation. Jonson's bears witness in every line to a reverence for antiquity which, like all his other reverences, stopped short of idolatry; the reasoned and reflective reverence of one who knew that 'to all the observations of the ancients we have our own experience, which if we will use and apply, we have the better means to pronounce'.[1] We have to do, in Jonson, almost always with reinterpretation or adaptation of classical tradition, not with either blank acceptance or out-and-out revolt; and the result is a dramatic type sharply marked off from every school of 'classical', as well as contemporary, drama, though intimately related, in different ways, to both. The unities of Time, Place, and Action in his hands are not felt as restraints, and they never compel him to the absurdities which Corneille did not escape. If they preclude him from Shakespeare's freedom of expansion and evolution, they provoke him to the invention of plots, in his greatest plays, at once complex and highly organized to an unsurpassed degree,—magnificent evasions of the bondage they seemed to impose.

In *Volpone* and its two successors, there is no question of any attenuation of the natural range and wealth of the action. The pieces employed in the game were as numerous and as varied, and their evolutions as complex, as in any drama of any school, but the game was played with a rigour and precision of strategy altogether new under such conditions. Nothing at once so prodigal in invention and so severely controlled had yet been seen on any stage as the steady upbuilding of the fabric of delusion, story upon story, in *Epicoene*, and the wonderful duels between past masters of rascality, late in league, which so long suspend the catastrophe of *Volpone* and *The Alchemist*.

---

[1] *Discov.*, 1640, p. 89: 'Non nimium credendum antiquitati.'

In some other respects Jonson's erudite inspirations were less perfectly moulded to the service of drama. His inventions often smelt of the lamp; he repudiated the romantic marvels of the popular stage, but a piece of learned symbolism never appealed to him in vain. Nowhere is Jonson less Elizabethan than in the Aristophanic allegory of the *Poetaster* or *The Staple of News*; nor does he in compensation approach the poetic splendour of *The Birds* or *The Clouds* themselves. It is only in the purely fantastic masque that this vein of Jonsonian invention finds free and beautiful utterance. In Jonson's style and diction, on the other hand, the scholar and the dramatist co-operated to admirable purpose. A comparison of the original and revised texts of *Every Man in his Humour* shows by what sedulous self-criticism Jonson reached the mature manner of which the 'hypercritical' Edmund Bolton wrote in 1618: ' I never tasted *English* more to my liking, nor more smart, and put to the height of Use in Poetry, then in that vital, judicious, and most practicable Language of *Benjamin Jonson*'s Poems.' More than any of his contemporaries Jonson gave English comedy a language which would have served Molière.

But the work both of the dramatist and the scholar was qualified by what may be compendiously called the bias of the satirist. Jonson's satire was the native speech of one who, like his own Asper or Crites, was impassioned for intellectual perfection, and saw his ideal ignored or violated on every side. Jonson did not count all men fools or knaves, but few men who had not some knavery or folly in their composition caught his eye or stirred his dramatic imagination. Hence the dearth in his comedy of pure humour, of innocent laughter, of sheer fun. He could pay noble tribute to the men he revered, to a Camden, a Bacon, a Shakespeare; he could describe in language of almost Miltonic magnificence his hope 'that he himself might one day raise the despised head of poetry again . . .'[1] But his

---
[1] Dedication of *Volpone*.

own grip as a dramatist is almost solely upon the characters that offend these ideals. His good or simply blameless people are almost all without dramatic colour. His good or blameless women above all : whether they be abstractions like Arete, or denizens of Venetian palace or London shop, like Celia and Bridget. He cannot create the women who, like Rosalind or Molière's Dorine, make us forget to ask whether they are 'good' because they are above all delightful and human.

But within the limits thus drawn by his flagellant scorn Jonson is genuinely creative, and the satirist's mastery of the whole gamut of contemporary folly and crime provided a wealth of characteristic detail which gave his boldest imaginings a veracious air. Bobadill in the lighter vein, Face and Subtle in the graver, are triumphs of an imagination at once erudite and resourceful, working upon the data of Elizabethan camouflage and Jacobean rascality. In the more exotic figures of Volpone and Mammon the colossal energy of Jonson's visualization of the utmost reach of human greed and cunning becomes poetic and sublime.

## IV

Firmly rooted, then, as Jonson was in the life and mentality of his time, he yet effected his imposing work in drama along lines and with aims and inspirations which mark it sharply off from the characteristic productions of his predecessors and contemporaries. The immense force and the brilliant workmanship which he put into his plays deeply impressed the next two generations. But posterity has tended even to over-accentuate the deficiencies which attended, and were often only the corollary of, his strong qualities. An indefatigable champion of 'art', he was gravely wanting in the sense of beauty, and his satisfaction in the logical neatness of a well-made action blinded him to the loveliness which Shakespeare elicited from wild and fantastic plots. His realism had no room for romance:

subtleties of character escaped his brilliant analysis of human infirmities. Simplicity and nature become in his hands foolish or insipid, and untaught innocence and mellow cultivation, feminine tenderness and masculine strength, alike lack charm. In all the finer lights and shades of soul painting Jonson is not so much inferior to the rest as out of the competition altogether. Souls, as he understood them, or at least as they interested and engaged his art, have no chiaroscuro, and no perspective; no problematic possibilities, no dimly descried background, no conflicting moods. The only background is the face that cowers behind the mask; the only problem, whether a man will finally outwit or be outwitted. We must not seek in the hard, categorical veracity of Jonson's art, the kind of truth by which supreme artists like Dante or Shakespeare in interpreting a country and an age interpret also universal humanity.

## V

It is not surprising that, outside England, Jonson has excited little interest. It has availed him little in the Latin countries to have championed classic art against native provincialism; his European culture, which might have conciliated at least a scholarly fame, was conveyed in a form exceptionally rich in the qualities which estrange so much of our art and literature. Years of life in London, at the culminating moment of Jonson's fame, had tempered the Gallic bias in Saint-Évremond when he put Jonson on a level, in his own kind, with Molière.[1] Distinguished work has been done upon him by scholars, in America, Germany, and France, in our time; but he has remained, and is likely to remain, a name even to the educated world.

In England itself his fame has persisted with singular

[1] *De la comédie anglaise.* The value of this praise is discounted by the fact that he regarded all the tragedies of Jonson's time, except his, as 'undigested heaps of matter'. On Shadwell too, Jonson's chief follower in the Restoration period, he bestowed unexpected praise, to the annoyance of Dryden, who complained that he had given 'to some of our coarsest poets a reputation abroad they never had at home'.

tenacity. But it is founded even now less upon enjoyment or admiration for his work than on the unforgettable image which has come down to us of 'Ben', the most familiarly known to us, beyond comparison, of all the Elizabethans. Jonson, apart from all questions of merit or demerit, is *there*, a personal force even more than a creative power. He taught us little, but we still feel him, as their generations felt the no less massive personalities of Samuel Johnson and Thomas Carlyle. Like every strong man, he stood for more than he knew, and when he seemed most isolated was fighting battles other than his own. The generation of which he was the lifelong critic and corrector was itself undergoing a momentous change of temper and outlook, which these clashing currents of Jonson's life and art symbolize and reflect. Only some nine years younger than Shakespeare, Jonson belongs to an England which had grown older by at least twice as many in that swiftly maturing time. In Shakespeare, whatever premonitions we may seem to catch of the perplexed and sombre age to come, the sanguine and sunny temper of the Elizabethans prevails. In Jonson the sanguine temper is not extinct; it still glows in the splendid confidence of that resolve to restore to her pristine majesty the 'despised' and 'adulterated' form of Poetry; but the very scorn for contemporary achievement—on the morrow of *Lear* and *Macbeth*—thus implied, anticipates the austere negations of that Puritan spirit which in its grosser embodiments he did his best to cover with ridicule.

Like Bacon, Jonson mediates between the age of Shakespeare and the age of Milton. Bacon unites the genial audacity of the Elizabethans with the systematic thought of Hobbes; and Jonson, akin on his lower poetic plane to Shakespeare in realistic power, while still animated by the Elizabethan riot of profusion and vitality, anticipates on the other side, if on the same lower plane, the self-consciousness, the intellectual severity, the curious and erudite elaboration, of the author of *Paradise Lost*.

# APPENDIX I

## CONTEMPORARY NOTES AND RECORDS

### I

### BEN JONSON'S CONVERSATIONS WITH WILLIAM DRUMMOND OF HAWTHORNDEN

Among the contemporary records of Jonson the memoranda made by William Drummond during the visit to Hawthornden are unique. Drummond appears to have jotted down these 'Certain Informations & Maners of Ben Johnsons' day by day, just as they occurred, and to have summed up his impressions afterwards in a brief final note of characterization. They were first printed in an abridged form in *The Works of William Drummond, of Hawthornden. Consisting of Those which were formerly Printed, and Those which were design'd for the Press. Now Published from the Author's Original Copies. Edinburgh: Printed by James Watson, in Craig's-Close, 1711.* The editors were Bishop John Sage and Thomas Ruddiman. They prefixed a life of Drummond, which contains the following account by Sage of the *Conversations*:

> He had great Intimacy and Correspondence with the Two Famous *English* Poets *Michael Drayton* and *Ben Johnson*: The First, in an Elogy on the *English* Poets, makes very honourable Mention of him; the other came to *Scotland* on Foot in the Year 1619. on Purpose to visit him, and stay'd some Three or Four Weeks with him at *Hawthornden*. In their Conversation there was a deal of Learning, Wit and Innocent Mirth. The Heads of the Conversation is still remaining under our Author's own Hand. 'Tis true, they were very frank and free together: *Ben Johnson* is very liberal of his Censures upon Ancient Authors. He does not miss himself, and gives large accounts of his own Wildness and Extravagancies; and for his Cotemporaries, the *English* Poets, he's very severe on them, and never spares them, when he can in the least attack them. And this is no extraordinary Thing; for *Scaliger, Perron, Menage &c.* have done the like: . . . I have published among our Author's other Tracts, some of the most remarkable Passages of their Conversation, for the Use and Benefit of the curious Reader (P. viii).

Accordingly, on pp. 224–6 there is a section entitled '*Heads of a Conversation betwixt the Famous Poet* Ben Johnson, *and* William Drummond of Hawthornden, January, 1619'. The 'Heads' are arranged and classified, but the gain in coherence detracts from the natural effect. In the original the desultory character of the jottings, the repetitions, and even the errors are a convincing proof of their authenticity. At one point in the summary a connecting link was supplied very unhappily. Drummond records (l. 50) the isolated remark 'That Shakſperr wanted Arte', and in a later and entirely distinct passage (ll. 208–10) 'Sheakſpear jn a play brought jn a number of men ſaying they had ſuffered Shipwrack jn Bohemia, wher y$^r$ is no Sea neer by ſome 100 Miles'. In the 1711 abstract this appears as follows: 'He said, *Shakſpear* wanted Art and ſometimes Senſe; for in one of his Plays he brought in a Number of Men. . . .' The sentence in this altered shape played a part in the extinct controversy about Jonson's envy of Shakespeare. In two passages at least the Folio helps us to correct the transcript—'his Country' for 'this Country' in l. 2, and 'Heart of Scotland' for 'part of Scotland' in l. 407.

Drummond's original manuscript of the *Conversations* appears to have perished. The outer leaf is preserved in the ninth volume of the *Hawthornden Manuscripts*, now in the Library of the Society of Antiquaries of Scotland; it is headed:

> Informations & Manners
> [of Ben Jonſon] to W. D: 1619.

The words 'of Ben Jonſon' are struck out in the manuscript. Eight lines of irrelevant doggrel follow, and then there is a sub-heading:

> Informations be Ben Jonſton
> to W. D. when he cam to
> Scotland upon foot 1619.

But a transcript was made by the Edinburgh antiquary and physician, Sir Robert Sibbald (1641–1722); it is preserved among the Sibbald manuscripts in the National Library of Scotland. The manuscript is a collection of Sibbald's Adversaria, MS. 33. 3. 19, and the Drummond transcript begins on folio 25 verso and ends on folio 31. It is clear that Sibbald attempted to make an exact copy. It was printed by David Laing in the volume of collected papers of the Society of Antiquaries of Scotland, *Archaeologia Scotica*, issued in 1833, vol. iv, part ii, pp. 241–70. His paper to the Society is dated January 9, 1832. Laing reissued it in a slightly revised form as a separate publication for the old Shakespeare Society in 1842; and Cunningham reprinted this text in his revision of Gifford's *Jonson*, thus making the record accessible for the first time to the general public.

Laing's account of the Sibbald transcript is as follows: 'The volume has no date, but was probably anterior to 1710, when Sibbald was in his seventieth year. It is transcribed with his own hand; and the volume containing it was purchased after his death, with the rest of his MSS., for the Faculty of Advocates, in 1723.

He might either have been a personal acquaintance of Sir William Drummond,'—the poet's son, who died in 1713,—'or have obtained the use of the original papers through his friend Bishop Sage, who contributed to the publication of Drummond's Works in 1711.'

Laing's text of the *Conversations* may be described as fairly accurate in the main, but he did some editorial tinkering: he suppressed a sentence which shocked his morals; he stuck in modern punctuation, and he made an occasional slip. The most serious, perhaps, is the distortion of Jonson's most important pronouncement on the heroic couplet (l. 384), which Laing prints thus:

That of S. Joh. Davies, 'Some loved running verses', *plus mihi complacet.*

In the original 'That of S. John Davies' is an unfinished note standing in a line by itself and having no connexion with the following line. 'Some loved running verses' is a statement of Jonson's, not a quotation from Davies; the quotation marks are absurd. And the extraordinary word 'complacet' is a misquotation of the epitaph on Lucan 'Plus mihi comma placet', which Jonson applied to English verse with the interpretation, 'I prefer the stopped line'.

An edition of the *Conversations* with introduction and notes by Mr. Philip Sidney appeared in 1900. Its inaccuracies are pilloried in the edition of Dr. R. F. Patterson. They include such errors as omitting the 'not' in l. 59, taking over a misreading of the 1711 Folio, which describes Donne's poem of the 'Lost Chaine' as the 'Lost Ochadine' (l. 118), and making Jonson's poem on Lady Bedford's 'Bucke' a poem on her 'luck' (l. 93). Dr. Patterson's edition, published by Messrs. Blackie in 1923, is fully annotated, and makes a distinct advance upon its predecessors, but his incisive criticism of their shortcomings loses something of its edge when his own text is critically examined. While keeping the old spelling, he modernizes two features of the manuscript without warning the reader: he uses modern capitals and modern punctuation. He corrects some (though not all) of the errors of fact which he finds in the text. Thus, 'Sir Edward Wotton' (l. 123), 'ninth worthy' (l. 191), and 'Earle of Worfter' (l. 232) are corrected to 'Sir Henry Wotton', 'Tenth Worthy', and 'Earle of Leister': but who made these errors? Sibbald, or Drummond himself? There can hardly be ground for doubting that Sibbald faithfully copied his original, and to rewrite the manuscript in this fashion is to perpetuate a perverse form of textual error. Besides, where is the process to stop? The list of Drummond's inaccuracies and confusions is a lengthy one, and an editor who ruthlessly corrected them all would plunge into a quicksand of emendation. Of Dr. Patterson's purely textual conjectures we have adopted only one, which had occurred to us independently, the verb 'to quintessence' in l. 623—Jonson's boast that he knew more Greek and Latin than all the poets in England 'and quintefsence⟨th⟩ their braines': it is merely an example of ἁπλογραφία. The two new emendations which Dr. Patterson proposes are 'The epigrame of Martial XI in Verpum' for 'the Epigrame of Martial Vin Verpum' (l. 610), which is ingenious but credits Drummond with an accuracy of reference belied by his constant blunders in citing the classics, and 'Feraboscos Pauane with his letter' for 'Paraboſtes Pariane with his Letter' (l. 92), which is both misleading and superfluous. The latter is the title of a poem which Jonson was fond of repeating—a 'common place of his repetition', says Drummond. Dr. Patterson explains that 'Feraboscos Pauane' was a dance by Ferrabosco with words by Jonson. But he fails to explain how anybody could dance a pavan 'with', or to, 'a letter', or how a poet could repeat a pavan. The reference is to some amusing verses of the Italian poet Parabosco, published at Venice in 1553; Drummond made a copy of them.

The edition by Mr. G. B. Harrison in the series of the Bodley Head Quartos, 1923, in which the *Conversations* are appended to the *Discoveries*, follows the manuscript more closely than any earlier edition; indeed it professes to be an exact reprint. But it is disfigured by serious errors: for example, 'things' for 'Rimes' (l. 5), 'Virgilium Veneris' (l. 68), 'the faſhion of yͤ Greeks & latine verſes in cunning' for 'in running' (l. 114), 'He can get Horoſcopes' for 'can fet' (l. 306), 'all Engliſh' for 'ill Engliſh' (l. 546), and 'Borrowlands' for 'Borrow lawes' (l. 644).

The present edition keeps close to the form of the manuscript. A few words necessary to the sense of a passage have been inserted within conical brackets; and a few corrections have been made in the arrangement of the paragraphs. The most important of the latter class is in the thirteenth section at lines 286-7—the explanation why Jonson originally quarrelled with Marston. The manuscript reads: 'the beginning of yᵐ', i.e. of the quarrels, 'were that Marston represented him jn the ſtage jn his youth given to Venerie.' We are convinced that Dr. J. H. Penniman is right in conjecturing that a full stop should be placed after the words 'jn the ſtage' and a new paragraph should be marked before 'jn his youth given to Venerie'. Drummond's habit of beginning a number of his sentences without a capital letter and writing his paragraphs without an inset probably misled Sibbald, especially if the words 'represented him jn the ſtage' happened to come at or near the end of a line in the original manuscript.

## Informations be Ben Johnſton to W. D. when he came to Scotland upon foot

### 1619

Certain Informations and maners of Ben Johnſons to W. Drumond

1 that he had ane jntention to perfect ane Epick Poeme jntitled Heroologia of the Worthies of his Country, rowſed by fame, and was to dedicate it to his Country, it is all jn Couplets, for he deteſteth all other Rimes, ſaid he had written a diſcourſe of Poeſie both againſt Campion & Daniel eſpecially this Laſt, wher he proves couplets to be the braveſt ſort of Verſes, eſpecially when they are broken, like Hexameters and that croſse Rimes and Stanzaes (becaus the pūrpoſe would lead him beyond 8 lines to conclude) were all forced.

2 He recommended to my reading Qūintilian (who (he ſaid) would tell me the faūlts of my Verſes as if he had Lived with me) and Horace, Plinius 2dus Epiſtles, Tacitus, Jūvenall, Martiall, whoſe Epigrame Vitam quæ faciunt Beatiorem etc: he heth tranſlated

Cenſure of Sidney
3 his Cenſure of the Engliſh Poets was this, that Sidney did not keep a Decorūm jn making every one ſpeak as well as himſelf.

Spencer
Spencers ſtanzaes pleaſed him not, nor his matter, the meaning of which Allegorie he had delivered jn Papers to S$^{ir}$ Walter Raughlie.

Sam: Daniel
Samuel Daniel was a good honeſt Man, had no children, bot no poet.

that Michael Draytons Polya⟨l⟩bion (if ⟨he⟩ had performed what he promiſed to writte the deads of all ye

---
*Title*: *in the MS. headed* Ben Ionsiana.
2 his *1711*: this *MS.*     3 dedicate] dedidicate *MS.*
6 Campion] Champion *MS. originally.*
10 pūrpose] *Sibbald writes* u *sometimes with a cross-stroke.*
24 bot no] *Apparently Sibbald began to write* both, *and altered the* h *to* n.

|  |  |  |
|---|---|---|
|  | Worthies) had been excellent his Long Verses pleased him not. |  |
| Silvester | that Silvesters translation of Du Bartas was not well done, and that he wrote his Verses befor it err he understood to conferr. | 30 |
|  | nor that of Fairfax his. |  |
| of ye translation Homer & Virgill | that the translations of Homer and Virgill jn Long Alexandrines were but Prose. |  |
|  | that John Haringtones Ariosto, under all translations was the worst. | 35 |
| Harington | that when Sir John Harrington desyred him to tell the Truth of his Epigrames, he answered him that he loved not the Truth, for they were Narrations and not Epigrames. | 40 |
| Warner | that Warner since the Kings comming to England ⟨ha⟩d marrd all his Albions England. |  |
| Donne | that Dones Anniversarie was profane and full of Blasphemies |  |
|  | that he told Mr Donne, if it had been written of ye Virgin Marie it had been something to which he answered that he described the Idea of a Woman and not as she was.  that Done for not keeping of accent deserved hanging. | 45 |
| of Shakspear | That Shaksperr wanted Arte | 50 |
| of Sharpham, Day & Dicker | that Sharpham, Day, Dicker were all Rogues and that Minshew was one. |  |
| Minshew |  |  |
| Abram Francis | That Abram Francis jn his English Hexameters was a Foole |  |
| of Fletcher & Chapman | That next himself only Fletcher and Chapman could make a Mask. | 55 |
|  | 4     His judgement of Stranger Poets was |  |
| of Bartas | that he thought not Bartas a Poet but a Verser, becaufe he wrote not Fiction. |  |
| of Petrarch, | he cursed petrarch for redacting Verses to Sonnets, | 60 |

42 had] *The MS. is torn at this point.*
46 something] *After this word there is a slight tear in the MS.*
48, 49 *Sibbald originally omitted* that Done . . . hanging *and then inserted it afterwards; he went on from* not as she was *to the statement about Fletcher and Chapman (l. 55–6); then he copied ll. 50–4, but numbered these paragraphs,* 5, 1, 2, 3, 4 *to correct the misplacement.*

which he ſaid were like that Tirrants bed, wher some who were too ſhort were racked, others too long cūt ſhort.

*of Guarini*  that Guarini jn his Paſtor Fido keept not decorum jn making ſhepherds ſpeek as well as himſelf coūld.

*of Lucan*  that Lucan taken jn parts was Good divided, read alltogidder merited not the name of a Poet

*of Bonefonius*  that Bonefonius Vigilium Veneris was excellent

*of Cardinall Perron*  that he told Cardinal deperron at his being jn France anno 1613 who ſhew him in his tranſlations of Virgill that they were naūght.

*of Ronsard*  that the beſt pieces of Ronſard were his Odes.

all this was to no purpoſe, for he neither doeth underſtand French nor Italianne/

*of Horace*  he read his tranſlation of that ode of Horace

Beatūs ille qui procūl Negotijs etc:

& admired jt.

*of Petroniᵒ*  of ane Epigrame of Petronius

fœda et brevis eſt veneris voluptas

Concluding it was better to lie ſtill and Kiſſe then pante.

to me he read the Preface of his arte of Poeſie, ūpon Horace Arte of poeſie, wher he heth ane apologie of a Play of his St Bartholomees faire, by Criticus is underſtood Done.   ther is ane Epigrame of Sir Edward Herberts befor it, the ⟨tranſlation⟩ he ſaid he had done jn my Lord Aubanies Hoūſe 10 yeers ſince anno 1604.

The moſt common place of his repetition was a dialogue Paſtoral betueen a ſhepherd & ſhipherdeſſe about ſinging

---

63 ſhort] *The ſ is a correction in the MS.*
74 Italianne] *The stroke after this word has usually been read as* s.
76, 77 *One line in the MS.*
80 Kiſſe] *The K and the first ſ are corrections.*
81 pante] *The word has been partly scratched out:* p *and* nte *are clear, but after the* p *is a long downstroke as if the scribe began to write a second* p. *The reading is doubtful.*
86 the *ends a line in the MS.: Sibbald has omitted a word.*

an other Paraboſtes Pariane with his Letter,
that Epigrame of Goūt, my Lady Bedfoords Bucke
his verſes of Drinking, drinke to me bot with thyne
Eyes,                                                                  95
ſwell me a Bowle etc, his verſes of a Kiſse

> bot Kiſse me once and Faith I will begone
> and I will touch as Harmeleſse as the Bee
> that doeth bot taſte the flower and flee away.

that is but half a one,                                        100
what ſould be done but once, ſhould be done long.
he read a Satyre of a Lady come from the Bath.
Verſes on the Pūcelle of the Coūrt Miſtriſs Boulſtred,
whose Epitaph Done made.
a Satyre telling there was no abuſes to writte a Satyre  105
of and ⟨in⟩ which he repeateth all the abūſes jn
England and the world.
he jnſiſted in that of Martialis
vitam quæ faciūnt Beatiorem

*Cenſur of lauthor⟨n⟩de ns⟩ verſes*

6 his cenſure of my verſes was that they were all good, 110
eſpeciallie my Epitaph of the Prince ſave that they
ſmelled too much of yͤ ſchooles and were not after the
Fancie of yͤ tyme. for a child ſayes he may writte
after the faſhion of yͤ Greeks & latine verſes jn running. yett that he wiſhed to pleaſe the King, that  115
piece of Forth-Feaſting had been his owne.

7 he eſteemeth John Done the firſt poet jn the World
jn ſome things his verſes of the Loſt Chaine, he heth
by Heart & that paſsage of the calme, that duſt
and feathers doe not ſtirr, all was ſo quiet. affirmeth  120
Done to have written all his beſt pieces err he was
25 years old.
Sir Edward Wottons verſes of a happie lyfe he hath
by Heart, and a peice of Chapmans tranſlation of ye
13 of the Iliads, which he thinketh well done.

95 Eyes,] Eyes., *MS.*
100, 101 *as prose in the MS.*
106 and *ends a line in the MS.*
115 King,] King. *MS.*

That Done said to him he wrott that Epitaph on Prince Henry
    Look to me Fath
to match Sir Ed: Herbert jn obfcurenefse
he hath by Heart fome verfes of Spenfers Calender about
wyne between Coline & percye.

8 the Conceit of Dones tranfformation or μετεμψυχοσις was that he fought the foūle of that Aple which Eva pūlled, and therafter made it the foule of a Bitch, then of a fheewolf & fo of a woman. his generall pūrpofe was to have brought jn all the bodies of the Hereticks from ye foūle of Cain & at laft left it jn ye body of Calvin. of this he never wrotte but one fheet, & now fince he was made Doctor repenteth highlie & feeketh to deftroy all his poems.

9 that petroniūs, Plinius Secundus, Tacitus fpeke beft Latine, that Quintilianes 6. 7. 8. bookes, were not only to be read but altogither digefted. Jūvenal, Perfe, Horace, Martiall for delight & fo was Pindar. for Health Hippocrates.
of their Nation Hookers Ecclefiafticall hiftorie (whofe children are now beggars) for church matters. Seldens titles of honour for Antiquities here & ane book of the Gods of ye Gentiles whofe Names are in the fcripture of Seldens.
Tacitus he faid wrott the fecrets of the Councill and Senate, as Suetoniūs did thofe of the Cabinet and Coūrte.

10 for a Heroik poeme he faid ther was no fuch Groūnd as King Arthurs fiction & yt S. P. Sidney had ane jntention to have tranfform'd all his Arcadia to ye ftories of King Arthure.

xi his acqūaintance & Behaviour with Poets Living with him.
Daniel was at Jealoufies with him.
Drayton feared him, and he efteemed not of him,
that Francis Beamont loved too much himfelf & his own verfes
yt S<sup>r</sup> John Roe loved him & when they two were ufhered by my Lord Suffolk from a Mafk, Roe wrott a moral epiftle to him, which began that next to plays the Court and the State were the beft. God threateneth Kings, Kings Lords & Lords do us
He beate Marfton and took his piftoll from him.

---

132 of a fheewolf] of of a fheewolf *MS.*    138 fpeke] fpoke *MS. originally.*
152–160 *written continuously in the MS.*
160 He beate] *So in MS.*; *the* He *written over a word* f..d (? said), *the* ate *of* beate *written over a word originally ending in* s.

Sir W. Alexander was not half-Kinde unto him & neglected him becaūſe a friend to Drayton.
that Sir R. Aiton loved him dearly,
Nid field was his Schollar & he had read to him the Satyres of Horace & ſome Epigrames of Martiall.
that Markham (who added his Engliſh Arcadia) was not of the number of the Faithfull .j. Poets and but a baſe fellow
that ſuch were Day and Midleton.
that Chapman and Fletcher were loved of him,
Overbury was first his friend. then turn'd his mortall enimie.
12 Particulars of the actions of other Poets and apothegmes.
That the Iriſh having Robd Spenſers goods & burnt his houſe & a litle child new born, he and his wyfe eſcaped, & after he died for lake of bread jn King ſtreet and refuſed 20 pieces ſent to him by my Lord of Eſsex & ſaid he was ſorrie he had no time to ſpend them.
that jn yt paper S. W Raughly had of ye Allegories of his Fayrie Queen by ye Blating beaſt the Pūritans were ūnderſtood by ye falſe Dūeſſa the Q of Scots.
That Southwell was hanged yett ſo he had written that piece of his ye burning babe he woūld have been content to deſtroy many of his.
Franc: Beaūmont died err he was 30 years of age,
Sr John Roe was ane jnfinit Spender & uſed to Say when he had no more to ſpende he coūld die. he died jn his armes of the peſt & he furniſhed his charges 20 lb, which was given him back.
That Drayton was chalenged for jntitling one book Mortimuriados
That S. J. Davies played jn ane Epigrame on Drayton, who jn a Sonnet concluded his Miſtriſs might been the ninth worthy & ſaid he uſed a phraſe like Dametas jn Arcadia, who ſaid for wit his miſtreſſe might be a Gyant.
Dones Grandfather on the mother ſide was Heywood the Epigrammatiſt.

161-170 *written continuously in the MS.*
161 Kinde unto him] *written as if one word because the* unto *has been crushed into the space between the other two words. Sibbald perhaps began to write* to.
179 Dūeſſa] *The* D *is a correction, perhaps written over a* Q. *Sibbald beginning to write* Queen.
180 he had] ha had *MS.*     183-4, 195-6 *written continuously in the MS.*

that Done himſelf for not being ūnderſtood would periſh.

That Sʳ W. Raughlye eſteemed more of fame than conſcience/ The beſt wits of England were Employed for making of his hiſtorie.

Ben himſelf had written a peice to him of ye punick warre which he altered and ſet in his booke.

S. W. heth written the lyfe of Queen Elizabeth, of which ther is copies extant

Sir P. Sidney had tranſlated ſome of the Pſalmes, which went abroad under the name of ye Counteſse of Pembrock.

Marſton wrott his Father jn Lawes preachings & his Father jn Law his Commedies.

Sheakſpear jn a play brought jn a number of men ſaying they had ſuffered Shipwrack jn Bohemia, wher yʳ is no Sea neer by ſome 100 Miles.

Daniel wrott civill warres & yett hath not one batle jn all his Book.

The Counteſs of Rūtland was nothing jnferior to her Father S. P. Sidney jn Poeſie. Sir Th: Overbūrie was in love with her, and cauſed Ben to read his wyffe to her, which he with ane excellent grace did & praiſed the Aūthor. that the Morne Therafter he diſcorded with Overbūrie, who woūld have him to jntend a ſūte yt was unlawfull. the lines my Lady Keepd jn remembrance he comes to near, who comes to be denied.

Beamont wrot that Elegie on the death of the Counteſs of Rutland, and jn effect her huſband wanted the half of his. jn his travells.

Owen is a pure Pedantiqūe Schoolmaſter ſweeping his living from the Poſteriors of litle children, and hath no thinge good in him, his Epigrames being bare narrations.

Chapman hath tranſlated Mūſæus jn his verſes like his Homer Fleſher and Beaumont ten yeers ſince hath written the Fathfull Shipheardesses a Tragicomedie well·done.

Dyer died ūnmaried.

S. P. Sidney was no pleaſant man jn countenance, his face

213 jnferior] *The firſt* 1 *is a correction: apparently Sibbald began to make a second* f. Father] Father. *MS.*
223 pure] poor *1711* 224 thinge] *The* e *is a correction.*
228 Shipheardesses] *Originally in the MS.* Shipheards, *which accounts for the plural of the text.*

being fpoilled with Pimples & of high blood & Long, that My
Lord lifle now earle of Worfter his eldeft fon refembleth him.
13 of his owne lyfe, education, birth, actions
His Grandfather came from Carlifle & he thought from
Anandale to it, he ferved King Henry 8 & was a Gentleman
his father Lofed all his eftate under Queen Marie, having been
caft jn prifson and forfaitted, at last turn'd Minifter So he was
a Minifters fon, he himfelf was Posthūmoūs born a moneth
after his fathers deceafe, brought up poorly, putt to fchool by a
friend (his mafter Cambden) after taken from it, and put to
ane other Craft (I thinke was to be a Wright or Bricklayer)
which he coūld not endure, then went he to ye low Countries
būt returning foone he betook himfelf to his wonted ftudies.
In his fervuce in the Low Countries, he had jn the face of both
the Campes Killed ane Enimie & taken opima fpolia from
him, and fince his comming to England being appealed to the
fields he had Killed his adverfarie, which had hurt him jn the
arme & whose fword was 10 Inches Longer than his, for the
which he was Emprifsoned and almoft at the Gallowes.  then
took he his Religion by truft of a prieft who Vifited him jn
Prifson.   therafter he was 12 yeares a Papift
He was Mafter of Arts jn both ye Univerfities by y$^r$ favour not
his ftūdie.
he maried a wyfe who was a fhrew yet honeft, 5 yeers he had
not bedded w$^t$ her but remained w$^t$ my Lord Aulbanie.
jn the tyme of his clofe Imprifsonment under Queen Elifabeth
his judges coūld gett nothing of him to all y$^r$ demands bot I
and No, they placed two damn'd Villans to catch advantage of
him, w$^t$ him, but he was advertifed by his Keeper, of the Spies
he hath ane Epigrame.
When the King came jn England, at that tyme the Peft was jn
London, he being jn the Coūntry at S$^r$ Robert Cottons hoūfe
with old Cambden, he saw jn a vifion his eldeft fone (y$^n$ a child
and at London) appear unto him w$^t$ ye Marke of a bloodie
crofse on his forehead as if it had been cutted w$^t$ a fūord, at
which amazed he prayed ūnto God, and jn ye morning he
came to M$^r$. Cambdens chamber to tell him, who perfuaded

251 12] *The first numeral is a correction.*   258 No,] No *MS.*
263 (y$^n$] y$^n$ *MS.*

him it was but ane appreehenſion of his fantaſie at which he ſould not be disjected(.) jn ye mean tyme comes yr letters from his wife of ye death of yt Boy jn ye plague. he appeared to him he ſaid of a Manlie ſhape & of yt Grouth that he thinks he ſhall be at the reſurrection.

he was delated by Sr James Murray to the King for writting ſomething against the Scots jn a play Eaſtward hoe & voluntarily Impriſſonned himſelf wt Chapman and Marſton, who had written it amongſt ym. the report was that they ſhoūld then had their ears cūtt & noſes. after yr delivery he banqūeted all his friends, yr was Camden Selden and others. at the midſt of the Feaſt his old Mother Dranke to him & ſhew him a paper which ſhe had (if the Sentence had taken execution) to have mixed jn ye Priſson among his drinke, which was fūll of Lūstie ſtrong poiſon & that ſhe was no chūrle ſhe told ſhe minded firſt to have Drunk of it herſelf.

he had many quarrells with Marſton beat him & took his Piſtol from him, wrote his Poetaſter on him the beginning of ym were that Marſton repreſented him jn the ſtage

jn his youth given to Venerie. he thought the ūſe of a maide, nothing jn compariſon to ye wantoneſs of a wyfe & would never haue ane other Miſtreſs. he ſaid two accidents ſtrange befell him, one that a man made his own wyfe to Coūrt him, whom he enjoyed two yeares erre he knew of it, & one day finding them by chance Was paſsingly delighted with it, one other lay diverſe tymes with a woman, who ſhew him all that he wiſhed except the laſt act, which ſhe woūld neuer agree unto.

S. W. Raulighe ſent him Governour wt his ſon anno 1613 to France. this Yoūth being knaviſhly jnclyned, among other paſtimes (as the ſetting of the favour of Damoſells on a Cod piece) caūſed him to be Drunken & dead drunk, ſo that he knew not wher he was, therafter laid him on a Carr which he made to be Drawen by Pioners through the ſtreets, at every corner ſhowing his Governoūr ſtreetched out & telling them that was a more Lively jmage of ye Crucifix then any they had, at which Sporte young Raughlies mother delyghted much

---

286, 287 stage. / jn *J. H. Penniman, marking a new paragraph* : stage jn *MS*.
292 Was] *The* W *is a correction written large to hide the original letter.*
294 unto] *Originally* to.        297 (as] as *MS*.

(saying his father young was so jnclyned) though the father abhorred it. 305

He can set Horoscopes, but trusts not jn y^m, he with ye consent of a friend Cousened a lady, with whom he had made ane apointment to meet ane old Astrologer jn the suburbs, which she Keeped & it was himself disguysed jn a Longe Gowne & a whyte beard at the light of ⟨a⟩ Dimm burning Candle up jn a litle Cabjnet reached unto by a Ledder. 310

every first day of the new year he had 20lb sent him from the Earl of Pembrok to buy bookes.

after he was reconciled with the Chūrch & left of to be a recūsant at his first communion jn token of trūe Reconciliation, he drank out all the full cup of wyne. 315

being at ye end of my Lord Salisburie's table with Inigo Jones & demanded by my Lord, why he was not glad My Lord said he yow promised I should dine with yow, bot I doe not, for he had none of his meate, he esteamed only yt his meate which was of his owne dish. 320

he heth consumed a whole night jn lying looking to his great toe, about which he hath seen tartars & turks Romans and Carthaginions feight in his jmagination.

Northampton was his mortall enimie for brauling on a S^t Georges day one of his attenders, he was called befor ye Coūncell for his Sejanus & accused both of popperie and treason by him. 325

Sundry tymes he heth devoured his bookes .j. sold y^m all for Necessity.

he heth a minde to be a churchman, & so he might have favour to make one Sermon to the King, he careth not what y^rafter sould befall him, for he would not flatter though he saw Death. 330

at his hither comming S^r Francis Bacon said to him, he loved not to sie poesy goe on other feet y^n poetical dactil^9 & spondæ^9. 335

⟨14⟩ His Narrations of great ones

He never esteemed of a man for the name of a Lord.

Queen Elizabeth never saw her self after she became old jn a

---

316, 317 wyne. / being *marking a new paragraph* : wyne, being *MS*.
321 was] was was *MS. with a word struck out.*   owne] *The reading is a doubtful correction in the MS.* : wyne *originally.*   323 toe] *The e is a correction.*
325 brauling] *The* u *has one minim.*   334 poesy] poesy. *MS*.

trūe Glafs. they painted her & fometymes would vermilion her nofe, fhe had allwayes about Chriflmafs evens fet dice, that threw fixes or five, & fhe knew not they were other, to make her win & efteame her felf fortūnate. that fhe had a Membrana on her which made her uncapable of man, though for her delight fhe tryed many, at the comming over of Monfieur, ther was a French Chirurgion who took jn hand to cut it, yett fear ftayed her & his death. King Philip had jntention by difpenfation of ye Pope to have maried her.

S$^r$ P. Sidneyes mother Liceflers fifter after fhe had ye litle pox never fhew her felf jn Court y$^r$after bot Mafked:

The Earl of Licefter Gave a botle of liquor to his Lady which he willed her to ūfe jn any faintnefs which fhe after his returne from court not knowing it was Poifon gave him and fo he died Salifbury never cared for any man longer nor he coūld make ūfe of him.

My Lord Lifles daughter my Lady wroth is unworthily maried on a Jealous hūsband.

Ben one day being at table with my Lady Rūtland, her hufband comming jn, accufed her that fhe keept table to poets, of which fhe wrott a letter to him which he anfwered My Lord jntercepted the letter, but never chalenged him.

My Lord Chancelor of England wringeth his fpeeches from the ftrings of his band & other Councellours from ye pyking of y$^r$ teeth.

Pembrok and his Lady difcourfing the Earl faid the Woemen were mens fhadowes, and fhe maintained y$^m$, both appealing to Johnfon, he affirmed it true, for which my Lady gave a pennance to prove it jn Verfe, hence his Epigrame

Effex wrotte that Epiftle or preface before the tranflation of y$^e$ laft part of Tacitus which is A B. the laft book ye Gentleman durft not tranflate for ye evill it containes of ye Jewes.

the King faid Sir P. Sidney was no poet neither did he fee ever any verfes jn England to ye Scullors

it were good that the half of the Preachers of England were Plain ignorants for that either jn their fermons they flatter, or ftrive to fhow their owne Eloquence.

362 Councellours] *The second* o *is doubtful.*
372-3 Scullors. / it *marking a new paragraph* : Scullors it *MS.*

⟨15⟩ his opinion of Verses
   that he wrott all his first jn prose, for so his master Cambden had Learned him.
   That Verses stood by sense without either Colour's or accent, which yett other tymes he denied. 380
   A Great many Epigrams were ill, becaufe they expressed jn the end, what sould have been understood, by what was said that of S. John Davies.
   some loved running Verses plus mihi com⟨m⟩a placet
   he jmitated the description of a night from Bonifonius his Vigilium Veneris 385
   he scorned such verses as could be transponed
      wher is the man yt never yett did hear
      of faire Penelope Ulisses Queene—
      of faire Penelope Ulisses Queen 390
      wher is the man yt never yett did hear
16 of his workes.
   that the half of his comedies were not jn Print, he heth a Pastorall jntitled the May Lord, his own name is Alkin Ethra the Countess of Bedfoords Mogibell overberry, the old 395 Countesse of Suffolk ane jnchanteress other names are given to somersets Lady, Pemb⟨r⟩ook the Countess of Rutland, Lady Wroth.
   In his first storie Alkin commeth jn mending his broken pipe. contrary to all other pastoralls, he bringeth the Clownes 400 making Mirth and foolish Sports
   he heth jntention to writt a fisher or Pastorall play & sett the stage of it jn the Lowmond Lake.
   that Epithalamium that wants a name jn his Printed Workes was made at the Earl of Essex Mariage. 405
   he is to writt his foot pilgrimage hither & to call it a discoverie jn a poem he calleth Edinborough the hart of Scotland Britaines other eye.
   a play of his upon which he was accused the Divell is ane ass, according to Comedia Vetus, jn England the divell was 410

394 his] *This word is a correction.*
396 Suffolk] Suffolk. *MS.*   397 Pembrook] Lady Pembrook *F. G. Fleay conj.*
405–6 Mariage. / he *marking a new paragraph* : Mariage, he *MS.*
406–7 discoverie / jn *making a new paragraph* : discoverie jn *MS.*
407 hart] Heart *1711* : part *MS.*

brought jn either wt one Vice or other, the Play done the divel caried away the Vice, he brings jn ye divel fo overcome wt ye wickednes of this age that ⟨he⟩ thought himfelf ane ass⟨.⟩ παρεργως is discourfed of the Dūke of Drown land. the King defyred him to conceal it.

he heth commented & tranflated Horace Art of Poefie, it is jn Dialogue wayes by Criticus he ūnderftandeth Dr. Done.

The old book yt goes about (the art of English Poefie) was done 20 yeers fince & Keept Long in wrytte as a fecret.

he had ane jntention to have made a play like Plaut9 Amphitrio but left it of, for that he could never find two fo like others that he could perfuade the fpectators they were one

17 Of his Jeafts and Apothegms

at what tyme Henry the 4t turn'd Catholick, pafquill had jn his hand a booke & was afked by Morphoriūs what it was, he told him it was Gramer, Why doe ye ftudie Gramer being fo old afked Morphorius, becaufe anfwered he I have found a Pofitive that heth no fuperlative, and a fuperlative that wants a pofitive, the King of Spain is Rex Catholicus & is not Catholicifsimus & the French King Chriftianifsimus yett is not Chriftianūs.

when they drank on him he cited yt of plinie that they had call'd him ad prandium non ad pœnam et notam.

& faid of that Panagyrift who wrott Panagyriques in acroftics, Windowes crofses, that he was homo Miferrimæ patientiæ, he fcorned Anagrams & had ever jn his mouth

        turpe eft, difficiles amare Nugas.

        et ftūltus labor eft ineptiarụ

a Cook who was of ane Evill lyfe, when a minifter told him he would to hell, afkt what torment was yr, being anfwered fyre, fire (said he) that is my Play fellow.

a Lord playing at Tenis & having afked those jn the Gallerie whither a ftrock was chafe or Lofse, a Brother of my Lord Northumberlands anfwered it was lofs. the Lord demanded

---

411 Vice *D. Laing*: Voice *MS*.
417-18 Done. / The *marking a new paragraph* : Done. The *MS*.
418 about (the] about. (the *MS*. *apparently, and after* Poefie *a small bracket below the line, turned the wrong way*.
425 tyme] *The letters* me *are a correction*.

if he did fay it  I fay it faid he, what are yow.  I have played
your worth faid ye Lord, ye know not the Worth of a Gentleman
replyed the other.  & it proved fo for err he died, he was greater
then the other.  ane other Englifh Lord loffed all his Game,
if he had feen a face that liked him not he ftroke his Balls at y$^t$  450
Gallerie.

ane English man who had maintained democritus opinion of
atomes, being old wrott a book to his fon (who was not then
Six years of age) jn which he left him argūments to maintain
and anfwer objections, for all that was jn his book, only if they  455
objected obfcuritie againft his book he bid him anfwer that his
father above all names jn the world hated moft the name of
Lucifer, and all open writters were Luciferi.

Butlar excommunicat from his table all reporters of Long
Poems, wilfull difpūters, tedious difcourfers, the beft banquets  460
were thofe, wher they miftered no Mufitians to chafe tym

the greateft fport he faw jn france, was the picture of our faviour
with ye apoftles eating ye Pafcall Lamb yt was all Larded.

at a fupper wher a Gentlewoman had Given him unfavory
wild-foul & yrafter to wafh fweet water, he commendet her that  465
fhee gave him fueet water, becaufe her flefh ftinked.

he faid to Prince Charles of Inigo Jones, that when he wanted
words to exprefs the greateft Villaine jn ye world he would call
him ane Inigo.

Jones having accufed him for naming him behind his back  470
a foole he denied it but fayes he. I faid he was ane arrant
knave & I avouch it.

one who fired a Tobacco pipe with a ballet the next day having
a fore head, fwoare he had a great finging jn his heade & he
thought it was the ballet.  a Poet fhould deteft a Ballet maker.  475

He faw a picture painted by a bad painter of Eafter, Haman
& Afsuerus, Haman coūrting Efther jn a Bed after the fafhion
of oūrs, was only feen by one Leg, afsuerus back was turned
with this Verfe over him & wilt thou Haman be fo malitious
as to lye wt myne own wyfe jn myne houfe     480
he himfelf being once fo taken the Good man faid, I would
not believe yee would abufe my houfe fo

450 he ftroke] *Over these words* in ftroken *is written in the MS.*
461 chafe] cherifh *MS. originally, imperfectly corrected* to chafh.
478 Leg,] Legs *MS.*      480 myne houfe] *Originally* my houfe.

# 146 *Contemporary Notes and Records*

In a Profound Contemplation a ſtudent of Oxeford ran over a Man jn the fields & walked 12 Miles ere he knew what he was doing

one who wore ſide hair, being aſked of ane other who was Bald, why he ſuffered his haire to grow ſo long, anſwered it was to ſie if his haire would grow to feed, yt he might ſow of it on Bald Pates.

a painter who could paint nothing but a Roſe, when ane Innkeeper had adviſed wt him about ane Enſing, ſaid that a horſe was a good one. ſo was a Hare, but a Roſe was above y$^m$ all

a litle man drinking prince Henries Health, between two tall Fellowes ſaid he made up the H.

Sir Henry Wotton, befor his Majeſties going to England, being Diſguiſed at Lieth, on ſunday when all the reſt were at Chūrch. being interūpted of his Occupation, by ane other Wenche who came jn at the Door, cryed out Pox on the, for thou haſt hindered the procreation of a Chyld & betrayed himſelf.

a Juſtice of peace would have comanded a Captaine to ſit firſt, at a table becaūſe ſayes he, I ame a Jūſtice of Peace, the other drawing his ſuord comanded him for ſayeth he I ame a Jūſtice of War.

what is that, that the more yow cut of it, groweth ſtill y$^e$ longer? a ditch.

he uſed to ſay that they who delight to fill men extraordinarie full jn their own hoūſes, loved to have their meate againe.

a Certain puritain Miniſter, would not give the Comunion ſave unto 13 at once (imitating as he thought our maſter) now when they were ſett & one bethikinge himſelf that ſome of y$^m$ muſt repreſent Jūdas, that it ſould not be he returned & ſo did all y$^e$ reſt underſtanding his thought.

a Gentlewoman fell jn ſuch a Phantaſie or Phrenſie w$^t$ one M$^r$ Dod a Puritan preacher yt ſhe requeeſted her huſband that for the procreation of ane Angel or Saint he might lye wt her, which having obtained it was bot ane ordinarie birth.

Scaliger writtes ane Epjſtle to Caſawbone wher he ſcorns the

---
491 adviſed] *the* v *is written over a second* d *which it is intended to cancel.*
494 ſaid] ſaid *MS.*     504 cut *Laing*: out *MS.*
516 obtained] *An* e *is written above the* i, *and runs into it.*     it] its *MS.*
517 Epiſtle] *So the MS. apparently*: *the word is a correction.*     ſcorns] *A correction, perhaps of* ſpurns.

Englifhe fpeak of Latine for He thought he had fpeken
Englifh to him.
A Gentleman reading a Poem yt began with  520
>Wher is that man that never yet did hear
of fair Penelope, Ulifses Queene.
calling his Cook afked if he had ever hard of her, who anfūering
no, demonftrate to him
>Lo ther the man that never yet did hear  525
of fair Penelope Ulifses Queene
a waiting woman having cockered w$^t$ Mufkadel and eggs her
Mifterefse page, for a fhee meeting jn the dark, his miftrefs
jnvaded of whom fhe woūld of fūch boldness have a reason.
faith Lady faid hee I have no reason. fave that fuch was the  530
good Pleafure of Mūfcadel and eggs.
a Judge comming a long a Hall, and being ftopped by a throng
cried Dominum cognofcite veftrūm, one of y$^m$ y$^r$ faid they
woūld if he durft fay the beginning of yt verfe (for he had
a fair wyfe).  535
>Actæon ego fum
cryed he, and went on
a Packet of letters which had fallen over Boord was devored
of a Fifh, that was tane at flūfhing, and the letters were fafely
delivered to him to whom they were written at London  540
he fcorned that fimplicitie of Cardan, about the peeble ftone
of Dover, which he thought had yt vertue keeped, betweene
ones teeth as to fave him from being fick.
A fchollar expert jn Latine and Greke but Nothing jn the
Englifh faid of Hott broath, that he woūld make the danger  545
of it. for it coūld not be ill Englifh yt was good Latine facere
periculᶻ
a tranflatour of the Emperours lyves, tranflated Antoniūs Piūs,
Antonie Pye.
The word Harlott was taken from Arlotte, who was the mother  550
of William the Conqūeroūr, a Rogūe from the Latine erro, by
putting a G to it.

518 fpeak] fpeaking *MS. originally.*   535 wyfe)] wyfe *MS.*
536 fum] um *is written with four minims.*
550 Harlott] *the* ar *is a correction.*
551-2 by putting] by putting, by putting *MS.*

L 2

S$^r$ Geflaine Piercy afked the Major of Plimmouth, whither it was his own Beard or the Towns Beard that he came to wellcome my Lord with, for he thought it was fo long, that he thought every one of the Town had eked fome part to it.
That he ftroke at S$^r$ Hierofme Bowes Breast, and afked him, if he was within.
an epitaph was made upon one who had a Long Beard.

> here Lyes a Man at a Beards end etc.

He faid to the King his mafter M. G. Buchanan, had corrupted his eare when yoūng & learned him to fing Verfes, when he foūld have read them.
S$^r$ Francis Walfingham faid of our King when he was Ambaffadour jn Scotland, hic nunqūam regnabit fūper nos of all his Playes he never Gained 2 hundreth pounds.
He had oft this Verfe, though he fcorned it

> fo long as we may, let us enjoy this breath
> for nought doth kill a man fo foon, as death.

one Mafter Gryfe told the King of a man who being confūmed occupied his wyfe with a Dildoe, and fhe never knew of it till on day he all flepperie had ther left his.
Heywood the Epigrammatift being apparelled jn Velvet by Qūeen Mary with his Cap on jn the prefence, jn fpight of all the Gentlemen, till the Qūeen her felf afked him what he meaned, and then he afked her if he was Heywood, for she had made him fo brave that he almoft had mifknowen himfelf.
His Imprefsa was a Compafs with one foot jn Center, the other Broken, the word. Deeft qūod duceret orbem.
Efsex after his brothers death M$^r$ D'Evreux jn France at Tilt had a black fhield void, the word Par nulla figura dolori. ane other tyme, when the Qūeen was offended at him. a Diamond with its own afhes, with which it is Cutt, about it the word Dum Formas Mjnūjs.
he gave the Prince Fax gloria mentis honeftæ.
He faid to me that I was too good and fimple, and that oft a mans modeftie, made a fool of his witt.
His armes were three fpindles or Rhombi, his own word about y$^m$ percunctabor or perfcrūtator.

570 Gryfe] Guyfe *MS. originally* : *the second letter is blotted by the correction.*
582 a] a. *MS.*    584 Mjnūjs] *The* M *and the second* j *are corrections.*

His Epitaph by a companion written is
> here Lyes Benjamin Johnſon dead
> and hath no more wit than ⟨a⟩ gooſe jn his head,
> that as he was wont, ſo doth he ſtill
> live by his wit, and evermore will.

ane other
> here lyes honeſt Ben
> that had not a beard on his chen.

18 Miſcellanies
John Stow had monſtrous obſervations jn his Chronicle and was of his craft a Tailour. he and I walking alone he aſked two Criples what they would have to take him to their order.
jn his Sejanus he hath tranſlated a whole oration of Tacitus.
The firſt foūr bookes of Tacit$^9$ ignorantly done jn Engliſhe.
J. Selden liveth on his owne, is the Law book of ye Judges of England, the braveſt man jn all Languages, his booke titles of honour, written to his chamber fellow Heyward.
Tailor was ſent along here to ſcorn him.
Cambden wrot that book remaines of Bretagne.
Joseph Hall the Herbenger to Dones Anniverſarie
the Epigrame of Martial Vin Verpum he Vantes to expone.
Lucan, Sidney, Gūarini make every man ſpeak as well as themſelves, forgetting decorūm, for Dametas ſometymes ſpeaks Grave ſentences, Lucan taken jn parts excellent; altogidder naught.
He difſūaded me from Poetrie, for that ſhe had beggered him, when he might have been a rich lawer, Phyſitian or Marchant.
Qūeſtioned about Engliſh, them, they, thoſe. they is ſtill the Nominative, thoſe accuſative, them Newter, collective, not them men them trees, but them by it ſelf referrd to Many.
which, who, be relatives, not that.
flouds, Hilles, he would have Maſculines.
he was better Verſed & knew more jn Greek and Latin, than all the Poets jn England and quintefſence⟨th⟩ their braines.
He made Much of that Epiſtle of Plinīus, wher ad prandiụ non ad notam is & yt other of Marcellinūs who plinie made to be removed from the table, & of the Groſse Turbat.

610 Vin] *Perhaps* V (= Book V) in: XI in *R. F. Patterson conj.*
623 quinteſſenceth *R. F. Patterson conj. (and independently P. Simpson).*

one wrote ane Epigrame to his father & vanted he had flain ten. the qūantity of decem being falfe, an other anfwered the Epigrame telling that decem was falfe. S. J. Davies Epigrame of the Whoores C. compared to a Coūle. of all ftiles he loved moft to be named honeft, and hath of that ane hundreth letters fo naming him
he had this oft
> thy flattering Picture Phrenee is lyke the
> only jn this that ye both painted be.

In his merry humor, he was wont to name himfelf the Poet he went from Lieth homeward the 25 of Janūary 1619 jn a pair of fhoes, which he told lafted him fince he came from Darnton, which he minded to take back that farr againe they were appearing like Coriats, the firft two dayes he was all excoriate.

if he died by the Way, he promifed to fend me his papers of this Country, Hewen as they were.

I have to fend him defcriptions of Edinbrough Borrow lawes, of the Lowmond.

that piece of the Pūcelle of the Court, was ftollen out of his pocket by a Gentleman who drank him droūfie & given Miftrefs Boūlftraid, which brought him great difpleafur.

19 he sent to me this Madrigal

> on a lovers duft, made fand for ane Houre Glafse
> Doe but confider this fmall dūst here running jn ye Glafse
> > by atomes moved
> could thoū believe that this the bodie ever was
> > of one that loved?
> and, jn his Miftrefse flaming Playing like the Flye,
> > turn'd to Cinders by her eye?
> > > Yes, and jn death, as lyfe ūnbleft
> > > to haue it expreft
> > Even afhes of lovers find no reft.

and this which is (as he faid) a picture of himfelfe.

> I doūbt that love is rather deafe than blinde
> > for elfe it could not bee
> > > that fhee,

630 C.] *This letter is a correction.*
644 Edinbrough *R. F. Patterson*: Edinbrough, *MS.*     663 fhee,] fhee. *MS.*

whom I adore fo much fhoūld fo flight mee,
and caſt my fute behinde.

I' am fure my Langūage to her is as fweet
and all my clofes meet
jn numbers of as fubtile feete,
as makes the yoūngeſt hee
that fits jn fhadow of Apollos tree.

Ô, but my confcioūs feares
that flye my thoūghts betweene,
prompt mee, that fhee hath feene
my hundred of Gray haires,
told Six and forty yeares,
read fo much Waſte as fhe cannot embrace
my Mountaine belly and my rockye face.
and all thefe through her eies, have ſtop'd her eares.

Janūary 19 .1619.

He is a great lover and praifer of himfelf, a contemner and Scorner of others, given rather to lofse a friend, than a Jeſt, jealous of every word and action of thofe about him (efpeciallie after drink) which is one of the Elements jn which he liveth) a difsembler of ill parts which raigne jn him, a bragger of fome good that he wanteth, thinketh nothing well bot what either he himfelf, or fome of his friends and Countrymen hath faid or done. he is pafsionately kynde and angry, carelefse either to gaine or keep, Vindicative, būt if he be well anfwered, at himfelf.

for any religion as being verfed jn both.
jnterpreteth beſt fayings and deeds often to the worſt:
opprefsed with fantafie, which hath ever maſtered his reafon, a generall difeafe jn many poets. his jnventions are fmooth and eafie, but above all he excelleth jn a tranſlation.

when his Play of a Silent woman was firſt acted, ther was found Verfes after on the ſtage againſt him, concluding that, that play was well named the Silent Woman. ther was never one man to fay plaūdite to it

Finis

674 haires,] haires. *MS.*
692 ever maſtered] over-mastered *1711.*

## NOTES

### i

**2.** *Heroologia.* Merlin's description of Richard I, the Black Prince, and Henry V, written in heroic couplets, in *The Speeches at Prince Henry's Barriers* (1610), and the description of Boadicea, with references to Spenser, Tacitus, and Dion Cassius, in *The Masque of Queens celebrated from the House of Fame*, give clear hints how Jonson would have treated the subject.

**6.** *Campion and Daniel.* The former published in 1602 his *Obseruations in the Art of English Poesie*, ' Wherein it is demonstratiuely prooued, and by example confirmed, that the English toong will receiue eight seuerall kinds' of rhymeless verse. Daniel replied in 1603 with *A Defence of Ryme*, ' Wherein is demonstratiuely proued, that *Ryme* is the fittest Harmonie of wordes that comportes with our Language'. Cf. *Und.* xxix.

For Jonson's advocacy of the couplet, see also section xv. 384, ' Some loved running verses, plus mihi comma placet '. Daniel held that ' those continuall cadences of couplets vsed in long & continued Poemes, are very tyresome, & vnpleasing', and preferred ' sometimes to beguile the eare, with a running out, and passing ouer the Ryme' (sig. H 6). Jonson's comment on Drummond's verses is quoted in vi. 113, 114, ' a child may writte after the fashion of the Greeks & latine verses in running '.

### ii

**15.** *Vitam* . . . Jonson ' insisted in' this translation (v. 108). It is printed in *The Underwood*, x.

### iii

**18.** *did not keep a Decorum.* Repeated of Sidney, Guarini, and Lucan, iv. 64, xviii. 611–13. See *Alch.* v. v. 160 note.

**20.** *nor his matter*. This opinion is toned down, or at any rate made clearer, in the *Discoveries*: ' *Spencer*, in affecting the Ancients writ no Language: Yet I would have him read for his matter; but as *Virgil* read *Ennius*' (Folio, p. 116). Drummond is not always an accurate reporter, and may have missed the subtle distinction here.

**22.** *to S*$^{ir}$ *Walter Raughlie.* The ' Letter of the Authors' to Raleigh ' expounding his whole intention in the course of' the *Faerie Queene* was appended to the 1590 edition of Books I–III; but this is a general exposition of the allegory. Jonson seems to refer to something more explicit, such as the references in xii. 177. The ' papers' of the present passage there become ' that paper'.

**24.** *no poet.* Exactly echoing the reference to Daniel and his patroness Lucy, Countess of Bedford, in *The Forest*, xii. 68–9 ;

> Who, though shee haue a better verser got,
> (Or *Poet*, in the court account) then I.

Jonson carefully observed the distinction, as old as Quintilian, between a 'rhymer' or 'verser ' and a ' poet ': see *infra*, iv. 58, and *C.R.* II. i, ' a rimer, and that's a thought better then a poet'. Drayton in the ' Epistle to Henry Reynolds ' (*The Battaile of Agincourt*, &c., 1627, p. 207), notes Daniel's reputation

To be too much *Historian* in verse;
His rimes were smooth, his meeters well did close,
But yet his maner better fitted prose.

25. *Polyabion.* Apparently Drummond wrote 'Polyalbion', from a confusion about the Worthies of England. The first part of *Polyolbion*, consisting of eighteen songs, appeared in 1613. Drayton was corresponding with Drummond during Jonson's visit to Scotland; in November 1618 he enclosed a letter to Drummond in a letter to Andrew Hart, the Edinburgh publisher, negotiating for a Scottish edition of the work, and Drummond replied sympathetically on December 20.

27. *Long Verses.* Also objected to *infra*, l. 33.

29. *Silvesters .. Du Bartas.* This version was first published in full in 1605. Jonson had prefixed commendatory verses, afterwards printed as *Epigram* cxxxii; in these he admitted his own ignorance of French and his inability to judge the translation.

32. *Fairfax.* His *Godfrey of Bulloigne ... Done into English heroicall verse* was published in 1600.

33. *translations of Homer.* Ten *books of Homers Iliades, translated out of French, By Arthur Hall Esquire*, 1581, and Chapman's *Seauen Bookes of the Iliades of Homere, Prince of Poets*, 1598, were both in fourteeners. But in *Achilles Shield*, 1598, excerpted from the eighteenth book of the *Iliad*, Chapman used the heroic couplet ; and similarly his later translations, the *Odyssey* (1614?, 1615), *Hero and Leander* (1616), *Hesiod* (1618), and the *Homeric Hymns* (c. 1624), are in heroic couplets. But he prefaced his translation of *Achilles Shield*, 1598, with a sharp comment on the critics of his Homer :—'Let the length of the verse neuer discourage your endeuours : for talke our quidditicall Italianistes of what proportion so euer their strooting lips affect ; vnlesse it be in these cooplets, into which I haue hastely translated this Shield, they shall neuer doe *Homer* so much right, in any octaues, canzons, canzonets, or with whatsoeuer fustian Epigraphes they shall entitle their measures.' The exception in favour of the couplet is interesting, and Chapman must have been startled to find that the criticism of his metre was not confined to Italianists.

*Virgill.* Thomas Phaer translated nine books of the *Aeneid* into fourteen-syllable rhyming ballad metre. Seven were issued in 1558 ; the fuller work in 1562. In 1584 Thomas Twyne completed the translation.

35. *Haringtones Ariosto,* ' in English heroicall verse', was published in 1591. His freedom in translating offended Jonson. So probably did his defence of 'polysyllable meeter' in his preface.

38. *Epigrames.* A printed collection of these had appeared in 1615. The collection of 1618, *The Most Elegant and Witty Epigrams of Sir Iohn Harrington, Knight, Digested into foure Bookes : Three whereof neuer before published*, opens with some lines that read like a reply to Jonson, though the point of the criticism is different :

*Against* MOMVS.

1 *That his Poetrie shall be no fictions, but meere truths.*

Scant wrate I sixteene lines, but I had newes,
*Momus* had found one fault, past all excuse,
That of *Epistle* I the name abuse.
No gentle *Momus*, that is none abuse,

Without I call that *Gospel* that ensues,
But read to carpe, as still hath been thine vse:
Fret out thine heart to search, seek, sift and pry,
Thy heart shall hardly giue my pen the ly.

39–40. *Narrations and not Epigrames.* So Owen's *Epigrams* are 'bare narrations' (xii. 225). For further criticism of the epigram see xv. 381–2.

41. *Warner.* Warner published *Albion's England* in sections. The first (1586) brought the history down to the Norman Conquest; the second (1589) to Henry VII; the third (1592) to Elizabeth. He reissued and enlarged these in 1596 and 1602. Jonson's criticism is levelled at *A Continuance of Albions England, by the first Authour, W. W.*, 1606, and a fuller edition 'with the most chiefe Alterations and Accidents there hapning, vnto, and in the happie Raigne of our now most Soueraigne Lord King Iames' (1612).

43. *Dones Anniverſarie.* The two 'Anniversaries', *An Anatomy of the World* and *The Progres of the Soule*, commemorating the fifteen-year-old Elizabeth Drury, were first published in 1611 and 1612. The poem gave offence to various patrons and friends of the poet, including Lady Bedford, and Donne defends himself in his *Letters* substantially as he did to Jonson: 'Since I never saw the Gentlewoman, I cannot be understood to have bound my self to have spoken just truths, but I would not be thought to have gone about to praise her, or any other in rime; except I took such a person, as might be capable of all I could say. If any of those Ladies think that Mistris *Drewry* was not so, let that Lady make her self fit for all those praises in the book, and they shall be hers' (*Letters*, 1651, p. 239).

48. *for not keeping of accent.* Donne completely broke with the verse conventions of his time, and the violence he did to rhythm was part of his revolt. Jonson, loyally accepting critical laws, was naturally repelled, with the result that his dislike ranged him with those who failed to understand the principle. On the other hand, his tribute to Donne as 'the first poet in the world in some things' (vii. 117–18) is his finest example of critical insight.

50. *Shakſperr wanted Arte.* An exact illustration of Jonson's meaning is the attack on the romantic plays of Shakespeare in the induction to *Bartholomew Fair*: *The Winter's Tale* and *The Tempest* are 'drolleries', and the poet by introducing dances 'mixes his head with other mens heeles' and confuses two types of art.

51. *Sharpham.* 'Edward Sharpham of the Middle Temple, Gentleman,' published two plays, *Cupids Whirligig* and *The Fleire*, in 1607.

*Day.* John Day wrote for the stage from 1598 to his death, about 1640. His delicate dramatic poem, *The Parliament of Bees*, was published posthumously.

*Dicker.* Dekker, the 'Demetrius' of *Poetaster.*

52. *Minſhew.* Abraham Fraunce appears to have shared Jonson's opinion. In a note gratuitously added to 'The third day' of *The Countesse of Pembrokes Yuychurch*, 1591, sig. H 2, he attacks a critic of his *Lawiers Logike* who censured him for abridging the record of 'Saunders case in *Plowden* . . . Better might hee haue reprehended the misprysion of the Printer, whoe *Pag.* 74, should haue left out *Higgs*, and put in *Mynſhew*, the very liuing image of Syr *Philip Sydneys Damætas*.' The passage in *The Lawiers Logike*, 1588, is on page 74 :— '. . . I have put qualitie before quantitie. For it were absurd to aske wheather *Higs*

of *Balkot*, or *Shepheard* of *Tugford*, were the falser knaue, vnlesse it were first graunted that they were both false knaues.'

53. *Abram Francis*, or Fraunce, stuck steadily to hexameters, and usually announced the fact on his title-pages: thus *The Countesse of Pembrokes Yuychurch. Conteining the affectionate life, and vnfortunate death of Phillis and Amyntas: That in a Pastorall*; *This in a Funerall: both in English Hexameters*.

55. *Fletcher and Chapman*. Chapman's only known attempt was *The memorable Masque of the two honourable Houses or Innes of Court; the Middle Temple, and Lyncolnes Inne*, 1613. It was printed with an 'applicable Argument' explaining Chapman's carefully wrought 'device'. Jonson would approve of it. No masques of Fletcher's are known, except the slight sketches inserted in *The False One*, III. vii, and *The Nice Valour*, II. i, which are negligible. Mr. E. K. Chambers suggests (*Elizabethan Stage*, i, p. 171) that Jonson meant 'The Triumph of Time' in *Four Plays, or Morall Representations*, 'which is practically a mask'. But it is more likely that the reference is to Beaumont, whose *Masque of the Inner Temple and Grayes Inne* was acted at Whitehall on February 20, 1613, and published in quarto. He also wrote the masque inserted in Act I, Scene ii, of *The Maid's Tragedy*, and he has been credited with the authorship of the masque in *The Tempest*. Drummond must have misreported here as in xii. 227–8.

The point of the remark—whatever confusion there may be in Drummond's report of it—is that Daniel and Campion could not write masques. The critical manifesto with which Jonson opened *Hymenaei* should be read in this connexion; he himself is in the classical tradition, but he is content that 'fastidious *stomachs* should leaue my full tables, and enioy at home, their cleane emptie trenchers, fittest for such ayrie tasts: where perhaps a few *Italian* herbs, pick'd vp, and made into a *sallade*, may find sweeter acceptance, than all, the most nourishing, and sound meates of the world'.

iv

58–9. *becaufe he wrote not Fiction.* Compare the objection to epigrams which were only 'narrations' (iii. 39–40), and the Horatian maxim expressed in the second prologue to *Epicoene*,

> For he knowes, *Poet* neuer credit gain'd
> By writing truths, but things (like truths) well fain'd.

61. *that Tirrants bed.* Campion had applied the image of Procrustes' bed to rhyming quatrains generally (*Obseruations in the Art of English Poesie*, 1602, p. 6); and Sir Sidney Lee (*Athenaeum*, 9 July 1904) has traced back this criticism of the sonnet to Stefano Guazzo's *Dialoghi Piaceuoli*, 1587, p. 197, where it is attributed to Signor Claudio Tolomei. Jonson no doubt used the image independently. His own sonnets, five in number, are quite undistinguished: see the Court-prologue to the *Staple of News* and *Underwoods*, xxviii, for specimens in the Petrarchan form, and *Epigram* lvi, *Underwoods*, lxviii, and *Ungathered Verse*, ii, for specimens in the English form.

64. *Guarini.* Cf. xviii. 611, and *Volp.* III. iv. 86.

66. *Lucan.* Repeated xviii. 613. A judicious toning down of the 'religion to the diuine *Lucan*', 'whose admirable verses I can neuer be wearie to transcribe' in the notes illustrating the witchcraft of *The Masque of Queens*. The criticism may have been suggested by Quin-

tilian's dictum that Lucan was 'magis oratoribus quam poetis imitandus' (*Inst. Orat.* V. i. 90).
68. *Bonefonius.* Cf. xv. 385.
69. *Cardinal deperron.* See the *Life*, pp. 67-9, *supra*.

v

75-9. The translation of Horace and the supposed epigram of Petronius were printed in *The Underwood*, lxxxv, lxxxviii: Drummond misquotes the opening line of the latter.
81. *pante.* If, as seems probable, this is the reading, Dr. Patterson confirms it from Juvenal, *Sat.* iii. 134.
82. *Preface of his arte of Poefie.* See the Quarto dedication of *Sejanus*, 1605, where Jonson spoke of his intention to publish this preface, together with his translation of Horace's *Ars Poetica*, 'shortly'. He had evidently expanded this critical introduction after writing *Bartholomew Fair* in 1614. The preface was written in dialogue (see xvi. 416-17). The concluding words of this paragraph must refer to the translation.
87. *Lord Aubanies.* Cf. xiii. 255. *Sejanus* was dedicated to Lord Aubigny in the Folio.
89-90. *a dialogue Pafloral.* Printed in *Und.* iii with the title 'The Musicall strife; In a Pastorall Dialogue'.
92. *Paraboftes Pariane.* In the Drummond MSS., vol. viii, is an Italian poem near the end of the volume entitled 'Parabosco in his lettere amorose sendeth this Madrigal to on of his mistresses:

Donna, un tempo di voi l' ira soffersi,
E sì di cor vi amai,
che lietissimamente il tempo persi:
ma hor forza è ch' io dica,
che siete più crudel che tigre od orsa
perchè mi traffigete anche la borsa.
questa è quella fatica,
questi sono que' guai,
e questo è quel martire,
che non si può soffrire;
e nel suo regno Amore
non ha di questo più crudel dolore.'

Apparently Jonson had translated this. It appeared in *Il Terzo Libro delle Lettere Amorose, di M. Girolamo Parabosco*, Venice, 1553, p. 33. We cannot explain the word 'Pariane'. Drummond's statement in iv. 73-4 that Jonson did not understand Italian seems to need some qualification.
93. *Epigrame of Goūt.* Epigram cxviii, 'On Gut'.
*my Lady Bedfoords Bucke.* Epigram lxxxiv, 'To Lucy Countesse of Bedford'.
94. *drinke to me.* The *Forest*, ix, 'To Celia'.
96. *fwell me a Bowle.* In *Poetaster*, III. i.
*of a Kifse.* The seventh of the 'Charis' group of poems, *Und.* ii.
102. *Satyre of a Lady.* Lost.
103. *Verfes on the Pūcelle.* *Und.* xlix.
105. *a Satyre.* Lost.
108. *that of Martialls.* *Und.* xc, already noticed by Drummond, ii. 15.

vi

111. *Epitaph of the Prince.* *Teares on the Death of Meliades*, 1613.
114-15. *in running.* Cf. i. 6 note.
116. *Forth-Feafting.* *Forth Feasting. A Panegyricke to the Kings Most Excellent Majestie* appeared in 1617.

vii

118. *the Loſt Chaine*. *Elegie* xi, 'The Bracelet. Vpon the losse of his Mistresses Chaine, for which he made satisfaction' (ed. Grierson, *Poems*, p. 96).

119. *the calme*. In *Letters to seuerall Personages* (ibid. p. 178).

121-2. *err he was 25 years old*. Cf. Walton in the *Life of John Donne*, 1640, sig. B 4 (of his poems), 'most of them, being written before the twentieth yeare of his age'.

122. *Edward* should be 'Henry'. Collier found a transcript of this poem in Jonson's handwriting among the Dulwich MSS. (MS. I, fol. 259), and printed it in his *Memoirs of Edward Alleyn*, p. 53. The text differs from that of the printed copies, and is here reproduced from the original:

> How happy is he borne, or taught,
>   That ſerueth not anothers will!
>   Whoſe armor is his honeſt thought,
>   And ſilly truth his higheſt ſkill.
> Whoſe paſſions not his Maſters are,
>   Whoſe ſoule is ſtill prepar'd for death,
>   Vntied vnto the world, w$^{th}$ care
>   Of princes grace, or vulgar breath.
> Who hath his life from rumors free'd,
>   Whoſe conſcience is his ſtrong retreate,
>   Whose ſtate can neyther flatterers feed,
>   Nor ruine make accuſers great.
> Who envie'th none, Whome chance doth rayſe;
>   Or Vice: Who neuer vnderstood
>   How ſwordes giue ſleighter wounds, ȳ prayſe;
>   Nor rules of ſtate, but rules of good.
> Who God doth late, and early pray
>   More of his grace, then guifts to lend;
>   And entertaynes the harmeleſſe day
>   W$^{th}$ a well⸗choſen booke, or freind.
> This man is free from ſeruile bandes
>   Of hope to riſe, or feare to fall;
>   Lord of himſelfe, though not of landes:
>   And hauing nothing, yet hath all./

125. *Epitaph on Prince Henry*. Donne's *Elegie* first appeared in the anthology edited by Joshua Sylvester, *Lachrymæ Lachrymarum, or The Spirit of Teares, Distilled from the vn-tymely Death of the incomparable Prince Panaretus*, the third edition, 1613, sigg. E-E 2 verso. As Herbert was a 'Metaphysical', Donne's effort to outbid him in obscure conceit was rather cruel; Donne could have known his follower's work only in manuscript, for Herbert's poems were not printed till 1665.

129. *Coline* should be 'Cuddie'. The passage is in the October 'Æglogue' of *The Shepheardes Calender*, 1579, fol. 42:

> Who euer casts to compasse weightye prise,
> And thinks to throwe out thondring words of threate:
> Let powre in lauish cups and thriftie bitts of meate,
> For *Bacchus* fruit is frend to *Phoebus* wise.
> And when with Wine the braine begins to sweate,
> The nombers flowe as fast as spring doth ryse.

Thou kenst not *Percie* howe the ryme should rage
O if my temples were distain'd with wine,
And girt in girlonds of wilde Yuie twine,
How I could reare the Muse on stately stage,
And teache her tread aloft in buskin fine,
With queint *Bellona* in her equipage.

### viii

130. *Dones tranfformation.* The poem *Infinitati Sacrum, 16 Augusti 1601. Metempsycosis. Poëma Satyricon*, first printed in the *Poems* of 1633; only the introductory part of the poem was written. This fragment shows in stanzas vi and vii that the final resting-place of the heretic soul was to be in the body of Queen Elizabeth. Professor Grierson notes that the date of composition was six months after the death of Essex; and that in this very year Jonson had noticed in *Cynthia's Revels* the 'black and enuious slanders hourely breath'd against her, for her diuine iustice on ACTEON' (I. i). Donne was still Catholic in his sympathies when he wrote this poem.

Professor's Grierson's conclusion that Jonson was recalling the poem inaccurately, though giving the substance of what Donne had told him, and that 'probably Donne mystified him on purpose', is not a satisfactory explanation of the discrepancy. May not Donne have changed his plan? A satire of this kind on Elizabeth would be highly dangerous, even if cautiously circulated in private. Further there is a contradiction, which Professor Grierson does not notice, in the preliminary Epistle. As printed in 1633, the Epistle ends by promising to relate all the passages of the Soule 'from her first making when shee was that aple which Eve eate, to this time when shee is *hee*, whose life you shall finde in the end of this booke'. 'Hee' was altered to 'shee' in the 1635 text to suit the allusion to Elizabeth. Four manuscripts also have the inconsistent reading. Probably the substitution of Calvin was an afterthought. Jonson, as a Catholic in 1601, would sympathize with this idea. It is evident that the panegyrist of Cynthia knew nothing of the other version; and if he had, he would have strongly disapproved of it. Jonson's statement that Donne wrote only 'one sheet' shows that the fragment which has come down to us is all that Donne committed to writing.

μετεμψχοσις. Doubtless Drummond's spelling. The word was so pronounced, even in the correct form μετεμψύχωσις, at that date, because of the accent. Cf. Jonson's *Time Vindicated* (Folio, p. 96):

I envie not the 'Αποθέωσις,

where the Folio prints the long vowel but shortens it in the scansion.

136–7. *feeketh to deftroy all his poems.* Walton, in the life of Donne prefixed to the *Sermons* of 1640, says more guardedly, 'It is a truth, that in his penitentiall yeares, viewing some of those pieces loosely scattered in his youth, he wisht they had been abortive, or so short-liv'd, that he had witnessed their funerals'.

### ix

141. *Pindar.* Jonson carefully studied the metrical structure of the Pindaric Ode, but the only direct echo of Pindar in his writings is to be found in the opening lines of *Volpone*.

*for Health Hippocrates.* Not, as Coleridge supposed, a joke of Jonson's which Drummond failed to understand. Hippocrates was a recognized authority on medicine down to the eighteenth century.

142-3. *whose children are now beggars.* The Appendix to Walton's *Life of Hooker*, ed. 1670, p. 113, contradicts this statement, and Walton appears to write from some personal knowledge of the family.

143. *Seldens titles of honour.* See *Und.* xiv.

144. *Gods of ye Gentiles.* De Diis Syris Syntagmata Duo, 1617. Cunningham notes that Jonson's copy of this with his manuscript notes was sold at Bright's sale for £1 12*s*.

x

148-9. *King Arthurs fiction.* Drayton's comment in *Polyolbion*, Song III, is to the same effect:

So, almost through the world his fame flew from this Realme;
That iustlie I may charge those ancient *Bards* of wrong,
So idly to neglect his glorie in their Song.
For some aboundant braine, ô there had been a storie
Beyond the \* Blind-mans might to haue inhanc't our glorie.

\* *Homer.*

(Ed. 1613, p. 48.)

Milton and Dryden were similarly attracted to the theme.

xi

152. *Daniel .. at Iealoufies.* Similarly in *The Forest*, xii. 70, Jonson says of the 'better verser', who has supplanted him with Lady Bedford,

And, who doth me (though I not him) enuy.

153. *Drayton feared him.* Cf. xi. 161-2, and *Ungathered Verse*, xxx. 1, 2, 'The Vision of Ben. Ionson, on the Muses of his Friend, M. Drayton':

It hath beene question'd, MICHAEL, if I bee
A Friend at all; or, if at all, to thee.

154. *Francis Beaumont.* A severe comment on the author of the famous verse-letter about the Mermaid. Jonson had replied in *Epig.* lv:

How I doe loue thee BEAVMONT, and thy *Muse*,
That vnto me dost such religion vse!

155. *Sʳ John Roe.* See further in xii. 184-7, and Appendix III, iv. Professor Grierson, in *The Poems of John Donne*, i, pp. 414-15, has printed the moral epistle. It first appeared in the 1635 edition of Donne, with the heading '*To Ben. Ionson, 6 Jan. 1603*' (old style). Two MSS. of Donne, the O'Flaherty MS. at Harvard and Lansdowne MS. 740 in the British Museum, also have this date. Drummond as usual quotes laxly, jotting down the lines from memory. The poem begins:

The State and mens affaires are the best playes
Next yours.

The reference to their being 'ushered' from the masque is in lines 11 and 12

Forget we were thrust out; It is but thus,
God threatens Kings, Kings Lords, as Lords doe us.

The occasion was the performance of the Scots' masque at Hampton Court on Twelfth Night, 6 January 1604. Jonson and Rowe evidently showed some open contempt for the performance.

Suffolk was appointed Lord Chamberlain on 4 May 1603, and Jonson acclaimed the appointment in *Epig.* lxvii. He had befriended Jonson and Chapman in the trouble over *Sejanus*, so the *Epigram* was probably written immediately after the appointment.

160. *Marſton.* Repeated in xiii. 284-5. More *spolia opima!*

161. *Sir W. Alexander*, the author of four *Monarchicke Tragedies* on classical themes, afterwards created Earl of Stirling. He brought Drummond and Drayton into correspondence with one another, and Drayton paid a high tribute to him in his verse 'Epistle to Henry Reynolds', concluding his survey of English poetry from Chaucer thus :

> So *Scotland* sent vs hither, for our owne,
> That man, whose name I euer would haue knowne,
> To stand by mine, that most ingenious knight,
> My *Alexander*, to whom in his right,
> I want extreamely, yet in speaking thus
> I doe but shew the loue, that was twixt vs,
> And not his numbers which were braue and hie,
> So like his mind, was his clear Poesie,
> And my deare *Drummond* to whom much I owe
> For his much loue, and proud I was to know,
> His poesie, for which two worthy men,
> I *Menstry* still shall loue, and *Hawthorne-den.*
> (*Elegies* appended to *The Battaile of Agincourt*, 1627, pp. 207–8.)

163. *Sir R. Aiton*, secretary to Queen Anne, died 1638. Aubrey's notes on Hobbes associate Ayton with Jonson. In Aubrey MS. 9, fol. 50, a 'Catalogue' of Hobbes's 'learned familiar Friends & Acquaintance' includes Jonson and 'Ayton, Scoto-Britannus, a Good Poet & Critique, & good scholar . . . he desired Ben: Johnson and this Gent. to give their judgement ⟨on⟩ his style of his translation of Thucidides'.

164. *Nid* or Nathan *Field*, the actor and playwright. He acted in the first performances of *Cynthia's Revels*, *Pœtaster*, *Epicoene*, and *Bartholomew Fair*, and he prefixed verse-tributes to the Quartos of *Volpone* and *Catiline*.

*he*, Field, *had read to him*, Jonson. Cf. *Epig.* ci. 20–2, 'Inuiting a Friend to Supper':

> How so ere, my man
> Shall reade a piece of VIRGIL, TACITVS,
> LIVIE, or of some better booke to vs.

In the mock-dedication and in the address 'To the Reader', prefixed to *A Woman is a Weather-cocke*, 1612, Field refers to his knowledge of Latin and quotes Juvenal; and in Act I. i he translates Persius :

> I loue that Poet,
> That gaue vs reading, not to seeke our selues
> Beyond our selues.

166. *Markham.* Gervase Markham, who published in 1607 *The English Arcadia, Alluding his beginning from Sir Philip Sydnes ending*, and in 1613 *The Second and Last Part of the First Booke of the English Arcadia. Making a compleate End of the First History.*

167. *j.* = 'i', or in modern usage, 'i. e.'

168. *Day*, already denounced in iii. 51.

*Midleton.* Thomas Middleton, the dramatist. There is no record of any personal relations between him and Jonson, but Jonson sneered at *A Game at Chesse* as a 'poor' play in *S. of N.*, III. ii. 210.

169. *Chapman.* Jonson and he were close friends till the end of Chapman's life, when in his last sickness he penned an 'Invective' against Jonson (preserved in Ashmole MS. 38, pp. 16–18, of the Bodleian).

*Fletcher*. Cf. the tribute of Richard Brome, Jonson's old 'servant', prefixed to the first folio of *Beaumont and Fletcher*, 1647, sig. g :—

> *I knew him in his strength; even then, when* He
> *That was the Master of his Art and Me*
> *Most knowing* Johnson (*proud to call him* Sonne)
> *In friendly Envy swore, He had out-done*
> His very Selfe.

170. *Overbury*. Cf. *Epig*. cxiii. A reason for the change of feeling is given in xii. 214–18; see the note on that passage.

### xii

172–6. The story of the burnt child and of Spenser's dying of hunger is incredible. As Professor de Sélincourt points out, in the interval between Spenser's escape from Kilcolman and his journey with official dispatches to London—between October and the end of December 1598—he wrote a carefully considered statement of 'certayne poynts to be considered of in the recovery of the Realme of Ireland'. But contemporaries believed the story. Collier in his life of Spenser quoted from B.M. Royal MS. 17 B. xv an account by John Lane, similar to Jonson's. Phineas Fletcher in *The Purple Island*, 1633, Canto I, stanza 20, addressing Spenser and referring to Essex, wrote :

> And had not that great *Hart*, (whose honour'd head
> Ah lies full low) piti'd thy wofull plight ;
> There hadst thou lien unwept, unburied,
> Unblest, nor grac't with any common rite.

Peacham in *The Truth of our Times*, 1638, pp. 37–8, states that Essex sent £20 'either to relieve or bury him'. Essex did defray the cost of the funeral, and it may be noted that the funeral charges of Sir John Roe, which Jonson paid, were also £20 (xii. 186).

177. *paper*. Cf. iii. 21, 22.

178. *the Puritans*. The Blatant Beast is primarily a type of scandal (*F. Q.* vi. vi. 2, xii. 28), but as with all Spenser's allegorical figures it has new phases: the iconoclasm of attacking a monastery and a church (ibid., stanzas 23–5) is perhaps responsible for the suggestion that the beast typifies the Puritans.

179. *the Q of Scots*. Duessa again is a type of Falsehood, depicted on the religious side as Catholicism and on the political side as Queen Mary. This last phase is clear in Book v. ix, st. 38–50. In November 1596 Robert Bowes, the English ambassador in Scotland, transmitted to Burleigh the protest of King James and his request that Spenser might be punished.

180. *Southwell* the priest, brutally executed on February 21, 1595. Jonson's praise of the 'Burning Babe' is the most striking tribute paid to Southwell by a contemporary. Is Addison's remark in the *Spectator*, Essay No. 70, on *Chevy Chase*, that '*Ben. Johnson* used to say he had rather have been the Author of it than of all his Works', a distorted reflection of this criticism?

183. *err he was 30*. Beaumont matriculated at Oxford on February 4, 1597, 'ætat. 12', and died on March 6, 1616, in his thirty-second year.

184. *Sʳ John Roe*. See xi. 155.

188–9. *Mortimuriados*. In 1596 Drayton published *Mortimeriados. The Lamentable ciuell warres of Edward the second and the Barrons*. He recast it in 1603 as *The Barrons Wars in the raigne of Edward the second* with this explanation of the change of title, '*Grammaticasters* haue quarreld at the title of *Mortimeriados*, as if it had beene a sin against *Syntaxis* to haue inscribed it in the second case, but not theyr idle reproofe hath made me now abstaine from fronting it by the name of *Mortimer* at all, but the same better aduise which hath caused me to alter the whole'.

190. *S. J. Davies*. Drayton's sonnet, to the effect that his mistress was the Tenth Worthy—not the Ninth—appeared in *Ideas Mirrour*, 1594, 'Amour 8'. Sir John Davies's 25th *Epigramme*, '*In Decium*', attacks him for it :

> Audacious painters haue nine worthies made,
> But Poet *Decius* more audacious farre
> Making his mistris march with men of warre,
> With title of tenth worthy doth her lade.
> Me thinks that gull did vse his tearmes as fit
> Which tearm'd his loue a giant for her wit.

192. *Dametas in Arcadia*. Untraced, and probably an error. In xviii. 612-13 Jonson complains that 'Dametas sometymes speaks Graue sentences'. But Drummond seems to have confused Dametas with the gull cited in the preceding note, or the sense is that he, in saying his mistress was a giant, talked in the sententious style of Dametas.

197. *more of fame than confcience*. Cf. *Catiline*, Chorus after Act II, 'studie conscience, aboue fame'.

198. *The beſt wits* . . . Professor C. H. Firth has elucidated this statement in his paper on *Sir Walter Raleigh's History of the World* (printed in *Proceedings of the British Academy*, vol. viii). He notes (p. 3) that 'some of the incidents in the history of Carthage recounted in the second part of the *History of the World* are treated at disproportionate length, notably one episode which was likely to attract a dramatist, viz. the revolt of the mercenaries against Carthage'. (The reference is ii. 371-6, 386-93.) 'The account of this episode was so little connected with the rest of the *History* that it was detached from it in 1647, and printed separately as "A Notable and Memorable story of the cruel war between the Carthaginians and their own Mercenaries". Considering that Jonson based one of his plays on Tacitus, and another on Sallust and Cicero, there is nothing unreasonable in supposing that an episode in Polybius might have seemed to him a fitting subject for a drama. The story seemed to Flaubert a good foundation for a novel. The alterations made by Raleigh in Jonson's contribution were, I suppose, the insertion of the discussion on mercenaries in general, and that on the habit of employing two generals of one army' (p. 390).

The only other claimant to the honour of helping Ralegh is, as Professor Firth also notes, Robert Burhill, D.D. His widow told Aubrey that her husband had helped, and that 'all or the greatest part of the drudgery of his booke, for criticisms, chronology, and reading of Greeke and Hebrew authors, was performed by him for Sir Walter Ralegh' (*Brief Lives*, ed. Clark, ii, p. 194).

Jonson's lines prefixed to the frontispiece of the *History* were reprinted in *Und.* xxiv.

202. *lyfe of Queen Elizabeth*. A lost work.

204. *Pſalmes*. They 'went abroad' in manuscript till 1823, when they were published from a transcript made by John Davies of Hereford. The first forty-three are by Sidney. Donne knew of the double

authorship and eulogized the work of 'this *Moses* and this *Miriam*' in his *Divine Poems* (*Works*, ed. Grierson, i, pp. 348–50).

206. *Marston . . . his Father jn Lawe.* The Rev. William Wilkes, chaplain to James I and Rector of Barford St. Martin in Wiltshire (identified by Gifford in vol. i, p. cvi). Wood says he was a favourite preacher of the king's.

209. *Shipwrack jn Bohemia.* Shakespeare took his geography from Greene's *Pandosto*, in which the King of Sicily 'prouided a nauie of ships, and sayled into *Bohemia*' (1588, sig. A 3 verso).

211. *civill warres.* The First Foure Bookes *of the ciuile wars between the two houses of Lancaster and Yorke* appeared in 1595; the remaining Books followed in 1599, 1601, and 1609.

*hath not one batle.* Battles are described in Books III, IV, VI, and VIII.

213. *The Countefs of Rutland . . .* So Jonson had sung of her in ceremonial verse, *Epigr.* lxxix, *Forest*, xii, but there is a ring of sincerity in the praise of her here quoted from a private conversation six years after her death.

214. *Overbūrie.* See xi. 170. 'His Wyffe' was the poem printed in 1614 as *A Wife Now the Widdow of Sir Thomas Ouerburye*; on sig. C verso is the stanza,

>    Womens *Behauiour* is a surer barre
>    Than is their *No* : *That* fairely doth deny
>    Without *denying, thereby* kept they are
>    Safe eu'n from *Hope*; in part to blame is shee,
>      Which hath *without consent* bin only tride;
>      He comes too *neere*, that comes *to be denide*.

The poem remained in manuscript until after Overbury's death. The statement in the text is perplexing, for the poem is moral in tone and preaches chastity: Overbury's father even asserted that it was written in order to dissuade Somerset from marrying so vicious a woman as the divorced Countess of Essex.

220. *that Elegie*, printed, according to Dyce, in the miscellanies prefixed to various editions of Overbury's *Wife and Characters* with an epistle *Ad Comitissam Rutlandiae*. The elegy elucidates Jonson's reference to her husband, Roger, fifth Earl of Rutland:

>                . . . the chief
>    Blessing of women, marriage, was to thee
>    Nought but a sacrament of misery;
>    For whom thou hadst, if we may trust to fame,
>    Could nothing change about thee but thy name.

See Dyce's *Beaumont and Fletcher*, xi, pp. 505-11. Cunningham is clearly right in suggesting that Lady Rutland is the 'widow'd wife' addressed in *Underwoods*, l. Her husband's resentment of her intimate relations with Jonson is recorded in xiv. 357-60. Beaumont was evidently another of the poets to whom she 'keept table'.

223. *Owen.* He wrote eleven books of epigrams, issued in 1606, 1607, 1612, and probably in 1613. They afterwards in collected form enjoyed a great vogue on the Continent. John Vicars issued the first English translation in 1619.

225. *bare narrations,* like Harington's (iii. 39).

226. *Mūfæus.* In *The Divine Poem of Musæus*, 1616, a close rendering of the Greek poem.

*like his Homer,* i. e. in heroic couplets, like his *Odyssey*, but unlike his *Iliad.* Cf. iii. 33 note.

227-8. *the Fathfull Shipheardesses.* 'Ten yeers since' is fairly correct; the first performance was probably in the winter of 1609–10. The attribution to Beaumont and Fletcher is found only in this passage; it is refuted by the fact that both Beaumont and Jonson prefixed complimentary verses to the First Quarto—Beaumont heading his 'To my Friend Master John Fletcher, upon his Faithful Shepherdess', and Jonson heading his 'To the worthy Authour, Master John Fletcher'. It is impossible that he should have credited Beaumont with the part authorship. Drummond made a similar error about Fletcher in iii. 55. It is clear that from time to time his recollection of the conversations was not accurate.

230. *S. P. Sidney.* Jonson was born in 1572, Sidney died in 1586. Jonson might have seen him as a Westminster schoolboy. Again Drummond's reporting is in question. Mr. Philip Sidney, in his edition of the *Conversations*, 1906, objects that 'Sir Philip's portraits reveal him as having had a clear, rather effeminate skin, free from blemishes'. But Jonson must have made the statement; this could not have been a confused recollection of Drummond's.

232. *Worſter* should be Leicester. *Earle of Worſter his eldeſt ſon* means 'Earl of Worcester's eldest son'; Sir Philip had no son.

### xiii

234-5. *he thought from Anandale.* The guarded wording is noticeable: see the *Life of Jonson*, pp. 1, 2. But the presumption is confirmed by the heraldry of xvii. 588, which shows that Jonson used the armorial bearings of the Johnstones of Annandale. The vivid epithet in his lines prefixed to Holland's *Pancharis* (U. V. vi. 72), '*Tweedes* blacke-springing fountaine', is also indirect evidence of his interest in the Lowlands.

237. *Miniſter.* See p. 2, *supra*.

239-40. *a friend.* Probably John Hoskins: see p. 3, *supra*, and Aubrey's notes, p. 179, *infra*. The words in parenthesis, *his maſter Cambden*, are probably to be taken as a nominative absolute, 'his master being Camden'.

241. *a Wright or Bricklayer.* Jonson had been reticent on the point; his enemies were not. When he killed Gabriel Spenser in the duel, Henslowe comments 'slayen . . . by the hands of bengemen Jonson bricklayer' (*Henslowe Papers*, ed. Greg, p. 48); Dekker salutes him in *Satiro-mastix* (1602, sigg. C 4 verso, H 2) as 'poore lyme & hayre-rascall' and 'foule-fisted Morter-treader'; and when *Pleasure Reconciled to Virtue* was considered dull at Court on Twelfth Night, 1618, Nathaniel Brent wrote to Carleton, 'The maske on 12th night is not comended of any. ye poet is growen so dul yt his devise is not worth ye relating, much lesse ye copiing out. divers thinke fit he should returne to his ould trade of brick laying againe' (*Domestic State Papers, Chas. I*, xcv. 12).

247. *his adverſarie.* Gabriel Spenser: see p. 18.

252. *Maſter of Arts.* See pp. 4, 5 *n*.

255. *Aulbanie.* See v. 87.

260. *ane Epigrame.* *Epig.* lix.

262. *at . . . Cottons houſe*, at Connington in Huntingdonshire.

263. *his eldeſt ſone.* Touchingly commemorated in *Epig.* xlv.

273. *Sr James Murray*, knighted on August 5, 1603. In 1610 he was one of the gentlemen of the Privy Chamber in ordinary to Prince Henry (Nichols, *Progresses of James I*, ii, p. 44). He may have been personally gibed at in *Eastward Hoe*, IV. i, in the dialogue :—' 1. Gen. I

ken the man weel, hee's one of my thirty pound Knights. 2. *Gen.* No no, this is he that stole his knighthood o' the grand day, for *foure pound*, giuing to a Page, all the money in 's purse I wot well.'

275. *w<sup>t</sup> Chapman and Marſton.* Discussed on pp. 190–3.

284. Partly repeated from xi. 160.

286. The MS. reads 'represented him jn the stage jn his youth given to Venerie'. The convincing readjustment of the text was made by Dr. J. H. Penniman in *The War of the Theatres*, p. 40. This disposes of Fleay's grotesque suggestion that Monsieur John fo' de King in the anonymous play of *Jack Drum* is Marston's caricature of Jonson. For any one to depict Jonson as a Frenchman gabbling broken English would be imbecile.

295. With Drummond's narrative here compare Oldys's MS. notes to Langbaine (in the British Museum copy). They add a new detail in the reference to Camden. It should be remembered that the *Conversations* were not printed until 1711, and then only in an abridged form. Oldys writes: 'Mr. Cambden recommended him to S<sup>r</sup> Walter Ralegh who trusted him with the Care and Instruction of his eldest son Walter a gay young spark who could not brook Ben's rigorous Treatment but perceiving one foible in his Disposition made use of that to throw off the Yoak of his Government and this was an unlucky habit Ben had contracted, thro his love of jovial company, of being overtaken with liquor w<sup>ch</sup> Sir Walter of all vices did most abominate & has most exclaimd against. One day when Ben had taken a plentifull Dose and was faln into a sound sleep young Ralegh got a great Basket and a Couple of Men who laid Ben in it, then with a Pole carried him between their shoulders to S<sup>r</sup> Walter Ralegh telling him their young Master had sent home his Tutor. This I have from a MSS. Memorandum Book written in the time of the Civil War by Mr. W. Oldisworth who was Secretary I think to Philip E. of Pembroke. Yet in the year 1614 when S<sup>r</sup> Walter published his Hist. of the World there was a good Understanding between him & Ben. For the verses which explain the grand Frontispiece before that History were written by Jonson and are reprinted in his Underwoods where the Poem is calld The Mind of the Frontispiece to a Book but he names not the Book.'

*his ſon.* Walter, who matriculated at Corpus Christi College, Oxford, in 1607 and took his degree in 1610. He was killed in the Guiana expedition in 1618.

304. *his father* ... As Charles Chester found to his cost (Aubrey, *Brief Lives*, ed. Clark, ii, p. 184).

313. *Earl of Pembrok.* It is significant that Jonson dedicated to him his *Catiline* because he 'thought it the best' he had done in tragedy, and his *Epigrams*, 'the ripest of my studies'.

316. *drank out all the full cup.* In token of robust faith. The Reformation practice of extending the cup to the laity no doubt at first produced similar scenes elsewhere. The form of the communion cup was necessarily changed, especially in the reign of Elizabeth, from the slighter chalices previously in use. The Rev. J. E. Vaux (*Church Folklore*, 1894, p. 64) notes that communicants in those days did not take a sip of the sacramental wine, and he notices the church plate given to the Minsterley Church near Shrewsbury by Lady Thynne in 1691; it included two large flagons and two chalices containing about three pints each, and this though the church was only a private chapel to the hall and probably had not more than twenty communicants.

319. *dine with yow, bot I doe not.* Contrast *The Forest*, ii. 61-6. Did Ben recall his favourite Martial?—' Cur sine te ceno cum tecum, Pontice, cenem?' (III. lx).

325. *Northampton.* Henry Howard, Earl of Northampton (1540-1614), was a noted intriguer. Brought up as a papist, he changed his religion four times, reverting to Catholicism on his death-bed. He corresponded with Mary of Scotland, and was pensioned by Spain. But he posed as an anti-Catholic, sitting on a commission appointed in 1604 to expel Jesuits and seminary priests from England and attacking Garnet at his trial in 1606. His attack on Jonson was made during this Protestant phase. Cunningham aptly notes that Lady Bacon warned her sons Antony and Francis against him as a 'dangerous intelligencing man, and no doubt a subtle papist inwardly, a very instrument of the Spanish papist'.

325-6. *on a S$^t$ Georges day.* Fleay (*Biog. Chron.* i, p. 371) suggests the year 1605, when Northampton was made Knight of the Garter.

333. *Bacon.* Cf. *Und.* li, and the sympathetic comment written after Bacon's death in the *Discoveries* (Folio, p. 102).

xiv

337. *for the name of a Lord.* So, of Bacon, in the passage just cited, 'My conceit of his Person was never increased toward him, by his place, or honours'.

338. *Queen Elizabeth.* Cf. Chettle's account of her in *Englandes Mourning Garment*, 1603, sig. E 2, . . . 'so farre was she from all nicenes, that I haue heard it credibly reported, and know it by many instances to be true, that she neuer could abide to gaze in a mirror or looking glasse: no not to behold one, while her head was tyred and adornd, but simply trusted to her attendant Ladies for the comelinesse of her attyre: and that this is true, *Thenot* I am the rather perswaded, for that when I was yong, almost thirtie yeeres agoe, courting it now and than: I haue seene the Ladies make great shift to hide away their looking glasses if her Maiestie had past by their lodgings'.

342. *ſhe had a Membrana* . . . Mary Queen of Scots told Elizabeth in 1586 of this scandal, and gave the Countess of Shrewsbury as her authority; the letter is printed in Murdin's *State Papers*, p. 559. Osborne, *Traditional Memoirs on the Reign of Queen Elizabeth*, 1658, p. 61, alludes to it. In *Letters . . . by Eminent Persons . . . from the Originals in the Bodleian Library*, 1813, ii, pp. 138-40, T. Carte refers to the notes of Du Plessis Mornay on the *History of Tuanus* (vol. vii, ed. Carte, 1733, c. vi, p. 97), and quotes a letter from Saint-Aldegonde of the Queen at the last moment breaking off the marriage with the Duke of Anjou. 'Disoit la Lettre que comme la Reyne eut la plume en la main pour signer, tremblant de colere elle l'avoit jettée; et tournée vers les Seigneurs de son Conseil, elle leur avoit dit, "Malheureux, étes vous si aveugles, que vous ne voyez qu'apres ma mort vous vous entrecouperez la gorge, et ne sçavez vous pas que me mariant, je ne la feray pas longue". Ce qu'on interpretoit de quelque defaut naturel connu de peu.' Carte says, 'This incapacity was ascribed to poison given her, which affected her womb: and though she got over it, she was in a dangerous state of body for several years, so that every body despaired of her recovery (as I find in the Letters of Messrs. de Noailles, the French Embrs. in England in Q. Mary's time) till almost the very end of her sister's reign'. De Silva, the Spanish ambassador, satisfied himself that the charges were groundless (Froude, *History*, 1870, xi, p. 2).

344. *comming over of Monſieur.* The Duke d'Alençon in 1579.
348. *S*ʳ *P. Sidneyes mother.* Peter Cunningham quotes Greville's *Life of Sidney*, 1652, '... shee chose rather to hide her self from the curious eyes of a delicate time, than come up on the stage of the world with any manner of disparagement, the mischance of sicknesse having cast such a kind of veile over her excellent beauty ...' (ed. Nowell Smith, p. 5).
350. *Earl of Liceſter.* He died suddenly on September 4, 1588. Bliss in a note to Wood's *Athenae Oxonienses*, ii, pp. 74-5, shows on the evidence of a contemporary manuscript that the Countess was charged with poisoning Leicester to enable her to marry Christopher Blount.
353. *Saliſbury never cared for any man.* F. Cunningham quotes Bacon's letter to Buckingham of August 12, 1616, advising him to 'countenance, and encourage and advance able men and virtuous men and meriting men in all kinds, degrees, and professions. For in the time of the Cecils, the father and the son, able men were by design and of purpose suppressed' (Spedding, *Life and Letters of Bacon*, vi, pp. 6, 7).
355. *Lady wroth.* Jonson dedicated *The Alchemist*, and addressed *Epigram* ciii, to her. He sang the praises of Sir Robert in *The Forest*, iii. But '*is ... maried*' should be '*was ... maried*'; Sir Robert died in 1614.
357. *Lady Rūtland.* See xii. 213 fol.
361. *Lord Chancelor.* Bacon, who held the office from March 7, 1617, till his fall in 1621. Apparently a nervous twitching or twisting of the strings of the bands is meant; it is an interesting revelation of one whose mastery of his subject, as attested in the famous tribute in the *Discoveries* (Folio, p. 101), would suggest absolute self-possession. The toothpick was affected by courtiers ('A great man, Ile warrant: I know by the picking on's Teeth'—*Winter's Tale*, IV. iii. 781-2), and its use was a mark of careless ease.
367. *his Epigrame.* See *The Forest*, vii, 'Song. That Women are but Mens shaddowes', a translation from Aneau's *Picta Poesis*, 1552, fol. 58; it was copied in Whitney's *Emblems*, 1580, p. 218, *Mulier vmbra viri*. Cunningham thought the anecdote in the text refuted by the fact that the 'Song' is a translation, but emblem books were fashionable, the verses in Aneau may have prompted the debate, and Jonson may have been commanded to translate them.
368. *Eſſex.* Jonson includes him in 'Scriptorum Catalogus' of the Tudor age in the *Discoveries* (Folio, p. 102), 'The Earle of *Essex*, noble and high', where he is grouped with Ralegh. In Edmund Bolton's *Hypercritica*, printed from MS. in 1724, we read, 'That Tractate which goeth under the name of the Earl of *Essex* his Apology, was thought by some to be Mr *Antony Bacon's*: but as it bears that E. name, so do I also think that it was the Earl's own, as also his Advices for Travel to *Roger* Earl of *Rutland*; then which nothing almost can be more honourably utter'd, nor more to the Writer's Praise, so far as belongs to a noble *English* Oratour' (p. 234); again, 'And of such works the late Earl of *Essex* under the letters *A.B.* (for Fames (*sic*) gives it him,) in an Epistle before the translated *Tacitus* of his Friend Sir *Henry Savil*' (p. 242).
In Savile's *The Ende of Nero and the Beginning of Galba ... Agricola*, 1591—'the last part of Tacitus', because chronologically later than the period of the *Annals*—the address of 'A. B. To the Reader' follows the dedication to Elizabeth. It is repeated in Savile's part of the composite volume, Grenewey's *Annals* and Savile's *Ende of Galba*, 1598 and 1604.

371. *no poet.* But James wrote an elegiac sonnet on Sidney's death. 'The Scullor' is John Taylor, 'the King's Majesty's water-Poet', as he styled himself. Cunningham suggests that Jonson was joking, and that Drummond did not see the joke. But James rather liked doggerel, and a passage in the *Discoveries* (Folio, p. 97) treats this kind of comparative estimate seriously. 'But a man cannot imagine that thing so foolish, or rude, but will find, and enjoy an Admirer; at least, a Reader, or *Spectator.* The Puppets are seene now in despight of the Players: *Heath's Epigrams*, and the *Skullers Poems* have their applause'; and he adds, ' if it were put to the question of the Water-rimers workes, against *Spencers*; I doubt not, but they would find more *Suffrages*'.

### xv

377. *firſt in proſe.* As Virgil did, according to Suetonius (*Life*, ch. 23). For examples of Jonson's practice see notes on *S. of N.*, I. v. 36-62, III. ii. 238-48, iv. 45-68.

379. *Colour's*, style and ornament; *accent*, metre. Cf. Horace's ' tragicus color' (*A. P.* 236).

383. *that of S. John Davies.* This line is misplaced; it should follow ' transposed ' in l. 386. The mistake is probably Drummond's.

384. *running Verſes.* See i. 7, and note.

*plus mihi comma placet.* From the epitaph on Lucan, found in the manuscripts of the *Pharsalia*.

385. *Bonifonius.* Cf. iv. 68. The poem is lost.

388-9. The opening couplet of Sir J. Davies's *Orchestra*, 1596. 'Faire' should be 'chaste'. Repeated with more point at xvii. 521-6.

### xvi

393. *half of his comedies.* We know the names of only five:—*A Tale of a Tub* (the Elizabethan version), *Hot Anger soon Cold*, written with Chettle and Porter in 1598, *The Case is Altered*, 1598, *Bartholomew Fair*, 1614, and *The Devil is an Ass*, 1616.

394. *the May Lord.* Discussed in the introduction to *The Sad Shepherd*. *Alkin.* In *The Sad Shepherd* 'Alken' is 'The Sage Shepherd'.

399. *first ſtorie.* Cf. *The Sad Shepherd*, II. viii. 35, and the discussion in our introduction of Dr. Greg's theory that *The May Lord* was written as a series of eclogues or pastoral tales.

400. *contrary to all other paſtoralls.* Cf. the prologue to *The Sad Shepherd*, 31-8:

> But here's an Heresie of late let fall;
> That Mirth by no meanes fits a Pastorall;
> Such say so, who can make none, he presumes:
> Else, there's no Scene, more properly assumes
> The Sock. For whence can sport in kind arise,
> But from the Rurall Routs and Families?
> Safe on this ground then, wee not feare to day,
> To tempt your laughter by our rustick Play.

402. *a fiſher or Paſtorall play.* Not written; but the suggestion is interesting as showing Jonson's desire to break new ground in drama. Phineas Fletcher's *Sicelides A Piscatory*, not printed till 1631, had been acted at King's College, Cambridge, in March, 1615; it was written for presentation before King James, though he did not see it.

403. *Lowmond Lake.* Writing to Drummond from London on May

10, 1619, Jonson 'earnestly sollicits' him to keep his promise of sending 'some things concerning the Loch of Lomond', and Drummond replies on July 1, 'In my last I sent you a description of *Lough Lomond* with a map of *Inchmerinoch*, which may by your Book be made most famous' (Appendix II. xiv, xv). Already in *The Masque of Beauty*, 1608, Jonson, setting his scene on a floating island, noted 'To giue authoritie to this part of our fiction' that Pliny had discussed this natural phenomenon, and that Cardan in '*lib. 1. de rerum vari. & cap. 7.* reports one to be in his time knowne, in the Lake of *Loumond*, in *Scotland*'.

404. *that Epithalamiūm.* Printed in the Folio as *Hymenæi, Or the Solemnities of Masque and Barriers at a Marriage*. But the Quarto edition of 1606 had stated that it was composed 'To the auspicious celebrating of the Marriage-vnion, betweene Robert, Earle of Essex, and the Lady Frances, second Daughter to the most noble Earle of Suffolke'.

406. *a difcoverie.* Written, and lost in Jonson's fire. In the 'Execration upon Vulcan' (*Und.* xliii, 94–5) he records amongst his losses

> my journey into *Scotland* song,
> With all th' adventures.

408. *Britaines other eye.* Perhaps suggested by the appeal to the Spartans to spare Athens in Plutarch, *Praecepta Gerendae Reipublicae*, vi, μὴ ποιήσατε ἑτερόφθαλμον τὴν Ἑλλάδα. Cf. Milton, *Par. Regain'd*, IV. 240, '*Athens* the eye of *Greece*'.

409. *upon which he was accufed.* Nothing is known of this accusation for *The Devil is an Ass*; evidently it was for the satire on Fitz-Dottrell, the Norfolk squire who aspired to be 'the Duke of Drounland'. Drummond is cryptic about it: but presumably Παρέργως from πάρεργον, 'a by-work, a secondary business, a thing beside the main purpose', implies that the satire was incidental. Fleay confidently, but unconvincingly, identified Fitz-Dottrell with Coke.

410. *Comedia Vetus*, i. e. old English Comedy, not as in the induction to *Every Man out of his Humour*, where the play is hailed by Cordatus as 'strange, and of a particular kind by its selfe, somewhat like *Vetus Comœdia*', i.e. the Comedy of the ancients.

411. *wᵗ one Vice or other.* Jonson is wrong, historically, about the Vice; in the earlier interludes this character was, as the name implies, the opponent of goodness as personified in some other character and the corrupter of mankind. The Vice and the Devil appear together in eight extant plays—*Perseverance, Mankynd, Mary Magdalene, Nigromansir, Juventus, Like will to Like, The Conflict of Conscience,* and *Money*; but only in *Mankynd, Mary Magdalene, Juventus,* and *Like will to Like* does the Vice attend on the Devil. In *Wisdom* and *The Disobedient Child*, the Devil appears without the Vice; in most of the interludes the Vice appears without the Devil. But in Jonson's day the original significance was lost, and the Vice had sunk to the level of a clown: Puttenham can talk of 'buffons or vices in plays' (*The Arte of English Poesie*, 1589, II. ix, p. 69).

For the Devil carrying off the Vice, see *D. is an A.* v. vi. 74–7, and note.

416. *tranflated Horace.* Cf. v. 82–3.

418. *the art of English Poefie.* Puttenham's work was published anonymously in 1589: '20 yeers since' should be '30'; was this a scribal error? The internal evidence collected by Dr. Arber suggests 1585 for the probable date of composition. Jonson's own copy of the work is among the Granville books in the British Museum.

xvii

A number of these 'Jeasts and Apothegms', as David Laing pointed out, were drawn up by Drummond for a collection of his own, entitled *Democritie A Labyrinth of Delight or Worke preparatiue for the apologie of Democritus*, preserved among the Hawthornden MSS. in the library of the Society of Antiquaries of Scotland, vol. viii, part ii, ff. 3–5. Drummond was apt to leave out the point of Jonson's jokes; an attempt to restore it is made in some of the following notes. Thus the joke on the opening lines of Davies's *Orchestra*, refuted by the cook who had never heard of Penelope (ll. 521 foll.), is significant only if we know who the gentleman was: Jonson must have told his name, but Drummond, by missing it, makes the story flat.

425–32. The Pasquil and Marforius literature, admitting originally attacks on cardinals and even on the Pope, lent itself later to Protestant polemic, but we have not traced the source of this particular sarcasm. Drummond quotes it also in his *Democritie*.

430. *Rex Catholicus*. The title given to Ferdinand of Aragon (1479–1516) for expelling the Moors.

431. *Chriſtianiſsimus*, bestowed on the kings of France in 1469.

433. *plinie*. Pliny, *Epistles*, II. vi—a favourite quotation repeated in xviii. 624–5, but incorrectly quoted in both passages: the quotation should be 'Ad cenam, non ad notam'. The original refers to a vulgar personage in high life who made distinctions between the treatment of his guests at the dinner table; he gave poorer food and wine to those of lower rank. As Drummond says later that Jonson 'made Much of that Epistle', he may have quoted it to Lord Salisbury when he underwent the similar humiliation recorded in xiii. 317–21.

435–7. Quoted in the Hawthornden MS., fol. 5, with the introductory comment 'one said of an author who excelled in acrostickes and eteostickes'. The Martial quotation (II. lxxxvi. 9, 10) was also used by Drummond in his 'Character of a perfect Anagram' (*Works*, 1711, p. 230)—'One will say, it is a frivolous Art, upon which that of *Martial* is current . . .' Cf. *Und*. xliii. 35, 'Or pomp'd for those hard trifles *Anagrams*' (and the context). Jonson twice committed this literary sin: mildly in 'Juno' and 'Unio' in *Hymenaei*, and flagrantly in *The Speeches at Prince Henry's Barriers*, l. 20, in which he extracted 'claimes Arthurs seat' out of 'Charles Iames Stuart'.

440–2. In the Hawthornden MS., fol. 4, in the form 'A Cooke when he was told that he must to Hell for his wickednesse, asked what torment was there and being told fire said that was his daylie Playfellow'. The joke was utilized in the play of *The Bloody Brother, or Rollo, Duke of Normandy*, 'By B. J. F.', II. ii (1639, sig. D 4, a portion of the play which has been attributed to Jonson), where Latorche has plotted with the servants to poison Otto, and the Pantler and the Cook comment afterwards:

> *Pant.* But 'tis a damnd sinne. *Cook.* O, never feare that. The fire's my play-fellow, and now I am resolvd, boyes.

444. *chaſe*. 'Applied to the second impact on the floor (or in a gallery) of a ball which the opponent has failed or declined to return; the value of which is determined by the nearness of the spot of impact to the end wall. If the opponent, on sides being changed . . ., can "better" this stroke (i. e. cause his ball to rebound nearer the wall) he wins and scores it; if not, it is scored by the first player; until it is so decided, the "chase" is a stroke in abeyance.'—*N. E. D.*

444-5. *a Brother of my Lord Northumberlands.* Perhaps the Sir Jocelyn Percy celebrated below, ll. 553-6. The reference to his inferior status later is no doubt due to the losses of the family for the alleged complicity of the ninth Earl of Northumberland in the Gunpowder Plot. (See Fonblanque, *Annals of the House of Percy,* ii, pp. 298-9.)

452-8. Quoted in the MS., fol. 5. The reference is to Nicolaus Hill's *Philosophia Epicurea, Democratiana, Theophrastica, proposita simpliciter, non edocta,* 1601, at which Jonson has a fling in *Epigram* cxxxiii. 128. It is dedicated 'Filiolo meo Laurentio Hill', and possible objections to the work are answered in this fashion: 'Obijcienti ... Pueri mei ἄνοιαν respondeo istam dedicationem dehinc excitaturam in illo desideria forsan profundioris cognitionis, & abstrusiorum literarum. / Obijcienti Infantuli mei officiosam conditionem, respondeo debere meam ætatem aliquid ei seriū, cuius ætatula mille millenis ioculis me exhilarauit.' And finally—'Obijcienti Obscuritatem, respondeo damnatissimum esse luciferi nomen'.

459. *Butlar.* Probably William Butler (1535-1618), 'Medicorum omnium quos præsens ætas vidit facile Princeps', to quote his epitaph in Great St. Mary's, Cambridge.

461. *miſtered,* needed.

*no Muſitians.* Mr. Gregory Smith (*Ben Jonson,* p. 279) compares the fifteenth rule of the *Leges Convivales,* 'Fidicen, nisi arcessitus, non venito'.

462-3. In the Hawthornden MS., fol. 4, which states that the picture was 'in Paris'.

464-6. On the same leaf as the preceding, introduced with the statement 'B. J. told mee'.

467-9. On folio 5 of the MS.: 'Jonſon said to prince charles ...'

469. *ane Inigo.* Cf. the satire of Inigo Jones as '*Iniquo Vitruvius*' in *Love's Welcome at Bolsover.* Lord Pembroke, Jonson's patron, scribbled 'Iniquity Jones' as a marginal note in his copy of Inigo Jones's *Stonehenge* (Nichols, *Progresses of James I,* ii, p. 155 n.).

473-5. In the Hawthornden MS., fol. 4, in the form—'One who had fired a Pipe of Tobacco with a ballet sweare he felt the singing of it in his head thereafter the space of two Dayes'. It was an old joke of Chapman's in *All Fooles,* 1605, sig. I:

       My Boy once lighted
A pipe of Cane *Tabacco* with a peece
Of a vild Ballad, and I'll sweare I had
A singing in my head a whole weeke after.

'Ballet' or 'ballad' is used here in the old sense of a song.

475. *a Poet ſhould deteſt a Ballet maker.* Cf. the gibe in *Neptune's Triumph* (Folio, p. 108) that the masque had waited till they had done with 'th' abortive, and extemporall dinne Of balladry'.

486-9. On folio 3 of the MS. Cf. *S. of N.* III. ii. 190-1:

A *Precept* for the wearing of long haire,
To runne to seed, to sow bald pates withall.

490-2. A variant of the story told in the Scholia on Horace's *Ars Poetica,* 19-21, about the painter of a cypress tree and a shipwrecked sailor, who wanted a picture of the wreck to carry about as a beggar. Jonson alludes to this jest in *S. of N.,* IV. ii. 90; *S. S.,* prol., 61-2.

496. *Diſguiſed at Leith.* Sir Henry Wotton, a year before Elizabeth's death, was sent by the Duke of Florence to warn James I of a plot to assassinate him. Wotton disguised himselfe as 'Octavio Baldi', and

travelled to Scotland from Norway. See Pearsall Smith, *The Life and Letters of Sir Henry Wotton*, i, pp. 40–2.

514. *M{{r}} Dod.* Presumably John Dod, the Puritan divine, Fellow of Jesus College, Cambridge, who died in 1645.

517. *Scaliger.* See Joseph Scaliger's *Opuscula*, 1612, p. 311. Jonson's copy is in the Dyce Library at South Kensington, and the passage is marked: 'Anglorum vero etiam doctissimi tam prave Latina efferunt ut in hac urbe cum quidam ex ea gente per quadrantem horae integrum apud me verba fecisset, neque ego magis eum intelligerem quam si Turcice locutus fuisset, ego hominem rogaverim excusatum me habere quod Anglice non bene intelligerem.'

*Caſawbone* should be Stephanus Ubertus.

521–6. Already quoted in xv. 388–9.

527. *Muſkadel and eggs.* A well-known provocative: cf. *N. I.* III. i. 197.

532–7. A variant of the anecdote in Antony Copley's *Wits, Fits, and Fancies* (second edition, 1614, p. 98), 'A Gentleman whom the world stronglye supposed to be a Cuckold, hauing occasion amongst other Gentlemen to talke of the duties of seruants: said *Dominum Cognoscite vestrum*, I pray you sir said one of the gentlemen how doth that verse begin? why reply'd he *Acteon ego sum*'. Aubrey (MS. 6, fol. 28) fastens the story on Chief Justice Coke (whose wife was supposed to be unfaithful), and attributes the capping quotation to Henry Cuff, 'Secretary to y{{e}} E. of Essex', when disputing with Coke. 'Cuff was a smart man an(d) a great Scholar and baffeld him.' The quotation is from Ovid, *Metamorphoses*, III. 230.

538. *a Packet of letters.* With this piece of news cf. the entry in the *Stationers' Register* on September 13, 1626, 'The booke ffish, Conteyning three printed treatises, which was found in the Codfishes belly at Cambridge the 23{{th}} of June being Midsomer Day 1626'.

541. *Cardan.* Girolamo Cardano, the great Milanese doctor, visited London in 1552, and was consulted about the health of Edward VI.

541–2. *the peeble ſtone of Dover.* There appears to be no reference to this in Cardano's medical works.

545. *make the danger.* 'Risk it.' A phrase affected by Fletcher, who has it three times. Cf. *The Loyal Subject*, III. iv, 'make danger, Try what they are, try'; *The Humorous Lieutenant*, IV. ii, 'Yet Ile make danger, Colonel'; and *The Wild-goose Chase*, I. ii, '*Mi.* You must now put on boldness, there's no avoiding it . . . *Bel.* I shall make danger sure'. If the Latin origin is an objection, why did Jonson himself adopt *facere religionem*, 'make religion', in *Cynthia's Revels*, V. xi, and *facere fidem*, 'make credit', in *The Silent Woman*, V. i?

549. *Antonie Pie.* Lord Berners in *The Golden Boke of Marcus Aurelius*, 1535, treats 'Of the byrth and lygnage of Marke aurele Anthony Emperour' in ch. i, and refers to the 'consulles Fuluie Cato and Enee Patrocle'.

550. *from Arlotte.* Put forward by Lambarde, 1570–6, as a conjectural etymology. It was long accepted, in spite of the fact that the term was originally applied to men. See Dekker, *The Honest Whore*, Part II, ed. 1630, sig. G 4, and Cartwright, *The Ordinary*, III. i.

551. *Rogūe from . . . erro.* This looks suspiciously like an etymology of Jonson's own. The accepted etymon was 'rogo': see Lambarde, *Eirenarcha*, 1599, p. 427, 'The word *Rogue* is but a late Guest in our Lawe: . . . and it seemeth to be fetched from the Latine *Rogator*, an asker, or Beggar', and Minsheu.

553. *Sʳ Geſlaine Piercy.* Sir Jocelyn Percy, seventh son of Henry, eighth Earl of Northumberland, who died in 1631. The Hawthornden MS. has the anecdote on folio 3, followed overleaf by another anecdote not recorded in the text, though it may well have come from Jonson: 'In the stage when an actor had come up and walked a while then said and what does now that melancholie lord your Brother? S. G. p. answered I left him taking Tobacco and Wine.'

557. *That he ſtroke.* 'He' is Sir Jocelyn. The Hawthornden MS. (folio 4) has 'S. G. P. beate once vpon S. J. B. brest and asked if Sʳ Jerosme was within'. Jonson used the joke in his plays: see *D. is an A.* I. v. 2, 'Friend *Manly*, who's within here? fixed?' with a stage-direction in the margin, '*Wittipol knocks his friend o' the brest*'. Gifford added a similar note to the parallel passage in *The New Inn*, I. vi. 80, '*Ho.* What say you, Sir? where are you? are you within?' Plautus has a similar idea in the *Miles Gloriosus*, 202, 'Pectus digitis pulsat: cor credo evocatumst foras'.

559–60. Laing recovered the complete text from the Hawthornden MS., in which it followed appropriately on Sir J. Percy's witticism to the Mayor of Plymouth:

> epitaph of a long bearde
> At a bear(d)es end heere lies a Man
> The odds tween them was scarce a spane
> liuing with his wombe it did meet
> And now Dead it couers his feet.

562. *to ſing Verses.* Professor W. L. Renwick illustrates from Ronsard: 'Je te veux aussi bien advertir de hautement prononcer tes vers quand tu les feras, ou *plustost les chanter quelque voix que puisses avoir*; car cela est bien une des principales parties, que tu dois le plus curieusement observer' (*Abrégé de l'Art Poëtique François*, ed. Blanchemain, vol. vii, p. 332). The *Conversations* record some remarkable instances of Jonson's frankness to the great, but nothing quite so startling as this.

568. *ſo long as we may . . .* Untraced.

570. *Maſter Gryſe.* No doubt the Robert Gryse (or Le Grys) who was knighted on August 16, 1628, and that year issued a translation of *Argenis*, made and published by the command of King Charles. The dedication to the King speaks of the author 'being so long bred vnder your Royall Father, my first and most gracious Master'.

577. *ſo brave that he almoſt had miſknowen himſelf.* Applied to Awdrey dressed in Lady Tub's clothes in *A Tale of a Tub*, V. iv. 23–4.

> But she was so disguis'd, so Lady-like;
> I thinke she did not know her selfe the while!

578. *Impreſsa*, a miniature symbolic picture epigrammatically interpreted by a motto. It was fashionable at Court, especially for tournaments or jousts. Camden, Daniel, and Drummond all wrote on this subject.

579. *Deest quod duceret orbem.* Ovid, describing the two legs of the compass, has 'altera pars staret, pars altera duceret orbem' (*Met.* viii. 249).

580. *Mʳ D'Evreux.* Walter Devereux, killed at the siege of Rouen on September 8, 1591. These impresas of Essex are noticed by Camden in his *Remaines*, 1614, pp. 219, 228; and the first of them also in Henry Peacham's emblem-book *Minerua Britanna, or a Garden of Heroical Deuices*, 1612, p. 81.

585. *Fax gloria.* . . . Cf. Sir C. Cornwallis, *The Life and Daath of . . . Henry Prince of Wales*, 1641, p. 87 ; 'his Highnesse Motto, *Fax mentis honestæ Gloria*' is described as being along with armorial bearings on his 'Herse' in the Abbey. It is from Silius Italicus, vi. 332.

588. *His armes were three spindles or Rhombi.* The heraldry is rather vague, but J. A. Symonds, with the help of Mr. R. R. Stodart, elucidated it sufficiently to establish Jonson's connexion with the Annandale Johnstones (Symonds, *Ben Jonson*, pp. 2, 3). Jonson himself said cautiously that 'he thought' his grandfather came from Annandale to Carlisle (see xiii. 234–5, above). The 'three spindles or Rhombi' give the clue. The shield of the Johnstones of Annandale was originally a saltire and a chief, the latter charged with three cushions. Burke in his *General Armoury*, 1842, blazons one coat of Johnson 'Or, three fusils in fesse, sable'. The heraldic fusil is in rhombus form, and in old Scotch heraldry the cushion was presented in the form of a lozenge—not, as now, in the form of a rectangle. Jonson's coat was therefore that of his Annandale forbears—three cushions, depicted lozenge-wise. Further than this we cannot go. We do not know the point at which Jonson's line branched off from the main line of the Johnstones of Annandale; nor do we know its mark of cadency—whether it was the addition of a bordure, as with the Johnstones of Benholme; or by engrailing or otherwise altering the saltire, as with the Johnstones of Hilton; or by placing some small charge on the saltire, like the cinquefoil of the Johnstones of Elphinstone. No seal of Ben Jonson is known to exist, and his grandfather's Christian name is unknown, so that we have no final clue. But it seems certain that he was of Border blood.[1]

589. *percunctabor or perscrūtator.* This is still more hazy. Jonson's 'word' or motto, which he inscribed in his books, was 'Tanquam explorator' (see Aubrey's *Notes*, 52, below). Was Drummond trying to recall this?

590. *His Epitaph.* Recorded in the Hawthornden MS. (fol. 3), as 'B. Jonsons his Epitaph. / told to mee by himselfe. not made by him.' In line 2 the MS. reads 'a Goosse', and in line 3 'yet as he was wont'.

596–7. The scanty beard is commemorated by Dekker in *Satiro-mastix*, 1602:—'thou thin bearded Hermaphrodite' (sig. C 4 verso); 'thou hast such a terrible mouth, that thy beard's afraide to peepe out' (sig. L 4). See variations on this theme in Archdeacon Plume's *Notes* below (pp. 184–5).

xviii

599. *monstrous observations*, e. g. his careful records of a whale and porpoises appearing in the Thames, or of lions whelping in the Tower. Jonson ridicules this in *Volpone*, II. i, in the character of Sir Politic Would-be.

601. *to take him to their order.* Stow was very poor at the end of his life ; the King granted him Letters Patent in May, 1603, and in February and October, 1604, giving him licence to ask and take benevolence (*Calendar of Domestic State Papers, James I, 1603–10*, vi, No. 82).

602. *a whole oration.* The speech of Cremutius Cordus in *Sejanus*, iii. 407–60, from Tacitus, *Annals*, iv. 34–5.

603. *first four bookes.* R. Grenewey's translation, *The annales of Cornelius Tacitus. The description of Germanie*, published in 1598, and four times reprinted. Jonson notes in his preface to the 1605 Quarto

[1] The Editors wish to acknowledge the help of Mr. F. P. Barnard in their attempt to solve this problem.

of *Sejanus* that he has used the original texts of his authorities, 'the Authors themselves being all in the learned *Tongues*, saue one, with whose English side I haue had little to doe'.

605–6. *titles of honour.* Cf. ix. 143, above.

606. *his chamber fellow Heyward.* Selden dedicated both editions of the work, 1614 and 1631, to Edward Heyward, described in the first edition as 'my most beloved friend, and Chamberfellow'. Jonson celebrated him in the complimentary poem which he prefixed to the work and which was reprinted in *Underwoods*, xiv.

> He, thou hast giu'n it to,
> Thy learned Chamber-fellow, knowes to do
> It true respects. He will, not only, love,
> Embrace, and cherish; but, he can approve
> And estimate thy paines: as hauing wrought
> In the rich Mines of knowledge; . . .
>     O, how I doe count
> Amongst my commings in (and see it mount)
> The gaine of two such friendships; *Heyward* and
> *Selden*, two *Names*, that so much understand:
> On whome, I could take vp (and nere abuse
> The credit) what would furnish a tenth *Muse*.

In the same poem is a striking tribute to 'the bravest man in all Languages':

> The Matter of your prayse
> Flowes in vpon me: Nothing but the round
> Large claspe of *Nature*, such a wit can bound.
> *Monarch* in *Letters*! 'Mongst thy *Titles* showne
> Of others *Honors*; thus, enioy thine owne.

607. *Tailor.* John Taylor, the Water-poet, walked to Scotland at the same time as Jonson. Taylor denied the accusation, but it evidently obtained currency. In *The Penyles Pilgrimage*, 1618, sig. A 3, he published the following address:

'*To all my louing Aduenturers, by what name or title so euer, my generall salutation.*

'Reader, these Trauailes of mine into *Scotland*, were not vndertaken, neither in imitation, or emulation of any man, but onely deuised by my selfe, on purpose to make triall of my friends, both in this Kingdome of *England*, and that of *Scotland*, and because I would be an eye witnesse of diuers things which I had heard of that Country; and whereas many shallow-brain'd Critickes, doe lay an aspersion on me, that I was set on by others, or that I did vndergoe this proiect, either in malice, or mockage of Maister *Beniamin Ionson*, I vow by the faith of a Christian, that their imaginations are all wide, for he is a Gentleman, to whom I am so much obliged for many vndeserued courtesies that I haue receiued from him, and from others by his fauour, that I durst neuer to be so impudent or ingratefull, as either to suffer any mans perswasions, or mine owne instigation, to incite me, to make so bad a requitall, for so much goodnesse formerly receiued.'

The two men met, as Taylor describes on sig. F 3 verso:

'Now the day before I came from *Edinbrough*, I went to *Leeth*, where I found my long approoued and assured good friend Master *Beniamin Iohnson*, at one Master *Iohn Stuarts* house: I thanke him for his great kindnesse towards mee: for at my taking leaue of him, hee gaue mee a piece of golde of two and twentie shillings to drinke his health in England. And withall, willed mee to remember his kinde commendations to all his friendes: So with a friendly farewell, I left him, as well, as I hope neuer to see him in a worse estate: for hee is amongst Noble-men and Gentle-men that knowes his true worth, and their owne honours, where with much respectiue loue hee is worthily entertained.'

608. Camden's *Remaines of a greater worke concerning Britaine* was published in 1605, with no other clue to the authorship than a dedication signed 'M. N.', the last letters of his Christian name and surname.

609. The second Anniversary of Donne's *Progresse of the Soule* is prefaced by a poem entitled 'The Harbinger to the *Progresse*'. Mr. E. K. Chambers further suggests that a similar poem preceding 'The first Anniversary', 'To the praise of the dead, and the ANATOMIE', is by Hall.

610. *Vin Verpum.* Another of Drummond's inaccurate references: Jonson had evidently discussed Martial's Epigram XI. xciv, with the refrain 'verpe poeta'. The concluding couplet on this Jew runs:

Ecce negas iurasque mihi per templa Tonantis.
non credo: iura, verpe, per Anchialum.

Jonson's friend, Selden, had tried his hand at an emendation: in *De Successionibus in Bona Defuncti*, Prolegomena, 1636, following up a suggestion of Joseph Scaliger that the last word was probably a corruption of a Hebrew oath, he proposed 'iura, verpe, iperan chi olam'— יפרע חי עולם—'*id est, ulciscatur, aut vindictam sumat is, qui vivit in æternum*'. Perhaps Jonson had attempted to convey this to Drummond. Dr. Patterson ingeniously conjectures that we should read 'XI in Verpum'. Did Drummond inaccurately set down 'V' (i.e. Book V), and Sibbald run 'V in' into one word?

611. Sidney and Guarini have been already condemned (iii. 16, iv. 64); and Lucan's failure in the total effect (iv. 66).

615. *He difsūaded me from Poetrie.* Cf. the 'Censura de Poetis' in the *Discoveries* (Folio, p. 97): '*Poetry* in this latter Age, hath prov'd but a meane *Mistresse*, to such as have wholly addicted themselves to her; or given their names up to her family. They who have but saluted her on the by; and now and then tendred their visits, shee hath done much for, and advanced in the way of their owne professions (both the *Law*, and the *Gospel*), beyond all they could have hoped, or done for themselves, without her favour.'

623. *quintefsenceth their braines.* Dr. Patterson has anticipated our conjecture, suggested to us by Drummond's use of this rare verb in *Irene* (*Works*, 1711, p. 170), 'for Quintessencing and Alembicking thee, and using thee as *Alchymists* do gold '.

624. *Epiftle of Plinius.* Already noted xvii. 433.

625. *yt other of Marcellinūs.* Drummond's ignorance of the classics betrays itself again: probably Jonson had told him the anecdote of Catullus Messalinus recorded by Pliny, *Ep.* IV. xxii. At a dinner party given by the Emperor Nerva, the talk falling on Messalinus, a blind man famous for his brutality and a useful tool to Domitian, Nerva asked, 'Quid putamus passurum fuisse si viveret?' and got the answer, 'Nobis-cum cenaret'.

626. *the Grofse Turbat,* i.e. the fourth *Satire* of Juvenal.

627. *one wrote.* Campion on Barnaby Barnes; Drummond has completely blunted the point of the epigram. Barnes had boasted of

killing 'dēcem Gallos' in the French campaign of 1591. It appeared in *Thomæ Campiani Poemata*, 1595, sig. F 5 verso:

In Barnum

> Mortales decem tela inter Gallica cæsos,
> Marte tuo perhibes, in numero vitiũ est.
> Mortales nullos si dicere Barne volebas,
> Seruassent versus & numerum atq̃ fidem.

The epigram was famous. Nashe referred to it in *Haue with you to Saffron-Walden*, 1596, sig. R 2 (*Works*, ed. McKerrow, iii, p. 110): 'One of the best Articles against Barnes I haue ouer-slipt, which is, that he is in Print for a Braggart in that vniuersall applauded Latine Poem of Master *Campions*; where, in an Epigram entituled *In Barnum*, beginning thus,

> Mortales decem tela inter Gallica cæsos,

he shewes how hee bragd when he was in *France* he slue ten men, when (fearfull cowbaby) he neuer heard peice shot off but hee fell flat on his face. To this effect it is, though the words somwhat varie.' John Heath, in his *Two Centuries of Epigrammes*, 1610, sig. C 4 verso, made an ingenious attempt at an English adaptation with the help of the words 'nine' and 'none'.

EPIGRAM LXIII<br>In Syllam è bello reducem.

> *I* Question'd Sylla, *being all alone,*
> *What store he slew in warre; he answer'd nine:*
> *Had he said none, as the trueth was that time,*
> *So had the tale beene true, and eke the rime.*

629. *S. J. Davies Epigrame.* The eighth epigram, '*In Katam*'.

634. *thy flattering Picture.* Donne's epigram on 'Phryne' (ed. Grierson, i, p. 77). The text reads 'you' for 'ye' in l. 2.

639. *Darnton.* Darlington in Durham.

640. *like Coriats.* As in the engraved title-page of Coryat's *Crudities*, 1611: a trophy of his travel-worn clothes, including his boots, is pictured in one compartment. Henry Peacham also celebrated them in Latin and English verse (ibid., sig. K 4). They were hung up in the church at Odcombe.

644. *Edinbrough Borrow lawes.* Jonson wrote to Drummond on May 10, 1619, for information 'touching the Government of *Edinburgh*'. Drummond replied on July 1, sending the information. (See Appendix II, xiv, xv.) For the *Lowmond* see l. 403, above, and note.

646. *That piece of the Pucelle.* *Underwoods*, xlix. See v. 103, 104, above.

xix

These two lyrics (*Underwoods*, viii and ix) were printed in the 1711 Folio of Drummond's *Works*, p. 155, from Jonson's autograph, the first headed with the inscription:

To the Honouring Respect,<br>Born<br>To the Friendship contracted with<br>The Right Virtuous and Learned,<br>Mr. William Drummond,<br>And the Perpetuating the same by all Offices of Love<br>Hereafter,

I *Benjamin Johnson*,
Whom he hath honoured with the Leave to be call'd His,
Have with mine own Hand, to satisfy his Request,
Written this Imperfect Song,
On a *Lover's Dust, made Sand for an Hour-Glass.*
The second lyric is introduced thus :
Yet that Love when it is at full, may admit Heaping,
Receive another ; and this a Picture of my self.

The poems are dated in the Drummond Folio '*January* 19. 1619'. The texts agree except that in l. 26 the Folio, by an evident misreading, has ' My *Hundreds* of Gray Hairs '.

681. *given rather to loſse a friend, than a Jeſt.* Satirically applied by Jonson to himself in *Poetaster*, IV. iii ; ' Tucca' is describing ' Horace' : ' hee will pen all hee knowes. A sharpe thornie-tooth'd *satyricall* rascall, flie him ; hee carries hay in his horne : he will sooner lose his best friend, then his least iest.'

## II

## JOHN AUBREY'S NOTES ON BEN JONSON

Mr. Benjamin Johnſon Poet Laureat.

Aubrey MS. 6, fol. 108.

I remember when I was a Scholar at Trin: Coll: Oxōn. 1646 I heard Mr Ralph Bathurst [now Deane of Welles] say that Ben: Johnſon was a Warwyckshire * man. 'Tis agreed, that his father was a Miniſter, and by his Epiſtle dd of Every man . . . . . . to
5 Mr W. Camden, that he was a Weſtminſter Scholer ; & yt Mr W. Camdē was his Schoolmaſter. His mother, after his fathers death, maried a Bricklayer, & 'tis grally ſayd that he wrought ſome time with his father in lawe, & pticularly on the Garden-wall
 a knight
of Lincolns Inne next to Chancery lane, and that . . . . . . . . .
10 a Bencher walking thro & hearing him repeat ſome Greeke verſes out of Homer, diſcourſing wth him & finding him to have a Witt extraordinary, gave him ſome Exhibition to maintaine him at
¶ † Trinity College in Cambridge, where he was † . . . . . . . . . . . .
Then he went into the Lowe-countreys and spent ſome time not
15 very long in the armie, not to ye diſgrace of ⟨ ⟩ as you may find

⟨*⟩ from old parſon Hill of Stretton Hereff. 1646.

*From Aubrey MS. 6 in Bodley, fol. 108. Note added later at the top of the left-hand margin*—' He killed Mr . . . . . Marlow ye Poet on Bunhill, comeing from the Green-curtain playhouſe—frō Sr Ed. Shirburn.'    3-8] *A laurel wreath in the margin, lowering the note intended for* l. 3 *to* ll. 8-10.    14-15 not very long *interlined.*    armie] *Originally* War.    not to ye diſgrace of *interlined and left unfinished at the end of a line.*

in his Epigrames. Then he came over into England, and acted and wrote at *The Green curtaine* but both ill, a kind of nurfery or obfcure Play houfe, somewhere in y^e Suburbes (I thinke frō J. Greenhill. towards Shoreditch, or Clarkenwell) Then he undertooke againe to write a Playe and did hitt it admirably well, viz : Every man ......... w^ch was his firſt good one. Serjeant Jo: *Hoskins* of Herefordshire, was his *Father*—I remember his Sonne [S^r Bennet Hofkins Baronet, who was fomething Poeticall in his youth] told me, that when he defired to be adopted his Son : *No*, fayd he, *'tis honour enough for me to be your Brother ; I am your fathers son: 'twas he, that polifhed me : I doe acknowledge it.* He was (or rather had been) of a cleare & faire skin his habit was very plaine. I have heard M^r Lacy the Player say, that he was wont to weare a coate like a coach-mans coate, with slitts under the arme-pitts. he would many times exceed in drinke : Canarie was his beloved liquour : then he would tumble home to bed ; and when he had thoroughly perspired then to studie. I have seen his studyeing chaire, w^ch was of strawe, such as old woemen ufed ; and as Aulus Gellius is drawen in. When I was an Oxōn: B^p: Skinner [of Oxford] who lay at our coll: was wont to fay that he underſtood an Author as well as any man in England. He mentions in his Epigrames, a Sonne that he had, and his Epitaph. Long fince in King James time I have heard my uncle Dāvers say who knew him) that he lived without temple Barre at a Combe makers shop about the Eleph: & Caſtle. in his later time he lived in Weſt- minſter in the houfe under w^ch you paſſe, as you goe out of the Church yard into the old Palace ; where he dyed : he lies buryed in the north aifle, in the path of square stones, y^e rest is lozenge oppofite to the Scutcheon of *Robertus de* * *Ros* with this Inscrip- tion only on him in a pavement square blew marble about 14 inches square O RARE BENN: IONSON, w^ch was donne at the chardge of Jack Young afterwards Knighted, who walking there

---

17 but both ill *interlined*.  19–25] *Note added in margin—*' W.' [i. e. Wood] 'in hiſt Hiſt. sayes he was borne in Weſtminſter that (at riper yeares) after he had ſtudied at Cambridge) he came of his owne accord to Oxōn, and there entred himfelfe in Ch. Ch. and tooke his Masters degree in Oxford (soe con- ferred on him) Anno 1619. / lib. 2. p. 273.'   21 Jo: *added in interline*. 27 & faire *interlined*.   43 the path ... is lozenge *interlined*.   *44] *The coat is tricked in the margin*—*argent, three water-bougots gules*.   45 pavement square] square *is interlined*.   blew] *originally* of blew.   46 IONSON] *Originally* IOHNSON.   47 afterwards Knighted *interlined*.

N 2

when the grave was covering gave the fellow eighteen pence to cutt it.

50 'Twas an ingeniose remarque of my Lady Hoskins, that B. J. never writes of Love. or if he does, does it not naturally.

His Motto before his (bought) Bookes was *Tanquam Explorator*. I remember 'tis in Seneca's Epīes. / He was a Favourite of y*e* L*d* Chancellor Egerton, as appeares by severall verses to him. In
55 one, he begges his Lop. to doe a friend of his a favour.

Aubrey MS. 8, folios 54, 55.

### Ben Johnson.

lyes buryed in the north aisle of W. abbey just opposite to the Scutcheon of *Robertus de Ros.* under the middle walke or path of square stones on one of w*ch* is wrote o rare Ben Jonson. King
60 James made him write against the Puritans, who becan to be troublesome in his time.

A Grace by     Ben: Johnson.     extempore.
                                  before King James.

Our King and Queen the Lord-God blesse,
The Paltzgrave, and the Lady Besse,
65 And God blesse every living thing,
That lives, and breath's, and loves the King.
God blesse the Councill of Estate
And Buckingham the fortunate.
God blesse them all, and keepe them safe:
70 And God blesse me, and God blesse *Raph*.

The K. was mighty enquisitive to know who this Raph was; Ben told him 'twas the Drawer at the Swanne-taverne by Charing-crosse who drew him good Canarie. for this Drollery his Mat*ie* gave him an hundred poundes./

75 Ben. Johnson had one eie lower, than tother, and bigger. like Clun the Player. perhaps he begott Clun. He tooke a Catalogue
                                      Dialect
from M*r* Lacy (the Player) of the Yorkshire *words*—'twas his Hint for Clownery, to his Comœdy called,—The Tale of a Tub. This I had from M*r* Lacy./

52 before] before before *in MS.*    59 middle *interlined.* or path *interlined.*    60 Jonson] *originally* Johnson. *After* Jonson *Aubrey originally added* 4 yds from the pillar.    62–70 *The margin quotes an extract from the dedication to Camden of* 'Every Man in his Humour'—since I am none of those ... present things.

Aubrey MS. 8, fol. 15.

B. Jonſon had 50$^{\text{li}}$ p annū for . . . yeares together to keepe off S$^r$ 80
W. Wiſeman of Eſſex from being Sheriff; at laſt K. James prickt
him, & Ben: came to his Ma$^{ti}$. & told him he had prickt him to the
heart. & then explayned himſelfe, innuendo S$^r$ W. W. being
prickt Sheriff : & gott him ſtruck off.

v. None-ſuch-Charles. when B. J. was dyeing. K. Ch: ſent him 85
but x$^{li}$.

Q T. Shadwell p Notes of B. J. from y$^e$ D. of N-caſtle. & alſo
v. his Execration of Vulcan.

Q Th. Henſhawe [as alſo de Saxis in Hiberniâ]

Q my L$^d$ Clifford—of the Gentlemen y$^t$ cutt the graſſe under 90
Ben Jonſons feet, of whom he ſayd *Ungratefull man ! I ſhewed him Juvenal.*

87 B. J. from *interlined.*     91 Ben Jonſons] *Originally* Bens.

## Note by Isaac Walton, communicated to Aubrey.

ffor yo$^r$ ffriends quæ, this :

I only knew Ben Johnſon : but my lord of Winton knew him
very well, and ſays he was in the 6º—that is the vpermoſt fforme
in weſtminſter ſcole. at which time, his father dyed, and his
mother marryed a brickelayer who made him (much againſt his 5
will) to help him in his trade. but in a ſhort time, his ſcole
maiſter m$^r$ Camden got him in better imployment, which was to
atend or acompany a ſon of S$^r$. Walter Raulyes in his trauills.
within a ſhort time after their returne, they parted (I think not in
Cold bloud) and with a loue ſutable to what they had in their 10
trauills (not to be comended). and then, Ben began to ſet vp for
himſelfe in the trade by which he got his ſubſiſtance and fame.
of which I nede not giue any acount. he got in time to haue a
100$^{ti}$ a yeare from the king, alſo a pention from the Cittie, and
the like from many of the nobilitie, and ſom of the gentry. w$^{ch}$ 15
was well pay'd for loue or fere of his raling in verſe, or proſe, or
boeth. my lord of Winton told me, he told him, he was (in his
long retyrement, and ſicknes, when he ſaw him, which was often)
much aflickted, that hee had profain'd the ſcripture, in his playes ;

In Aubrey MS. 6, fol. 107. 11 (not to be comended), 12 and, 17 lord
*added in interline.*

and lamented it with horror: yet, that in that time of his long retyrement his pentions (fo much as Came In) was giuen to a woman that gouern'd him. with whome he liud and dyed nere the Abie in weft minfter.) and that nether he nor fhe tooke much Care for next weike: and wood be fure not to want Wine: of w^ch he vfually tooke too much before he went to bed, if not oftner and foner. my lord tells me, he knowes not, but thinks he was borne in weftminfter. the queftion may be put to m^r wood very eafily vpon what grounds he is pofitiue as to his being borne their; he is a friendly man, and will refolue it. fo much for braue Ben. yo^u will not think the reft fo tedyus, as I doe this.

\* \* \* \* \* \*

Nou^er 22  
80
J. W.

This Account I rec^d from M^r Ifaac Walton [who wrote D^r Jo: Donnes life &c.] Decemb. 2. 1680. he being then eighty-feaven yeares of age. This is his owne handwriting./

22 that gouern'd him *added in interline.*  32–4 *Aubrey's note.*

## NOTES ON AUBREY.

There is a reference to Jonson in Aubrey's notes on Shakespeare (MS. 6, fol. 109) that Shakespeare 'was an Actor at one of the Playhoufes and did act exceedingly well: now B. Johnfon was never a good Actor, but an excellent Inftructor. ... Ben Johnson and he did gather Humours of men dayly where ever they came.'

2. M^r *Ralph Bathurst* (1620–1704), president of Trinity College, Oxford—Aubrey's college—and dean of Wells.

4. *Every man . . . .* Sic: it should be *Every Man in his Humour*, but Aubrey could not remember whether it was this play or *Every Man out of his Humour*.

12–13. *at Trinity College.* Probably a confusion due to the fact that Old Westminsters went to Trinity. Aubrey's marginal 'query' shows that he was hazy about the statement; and he failed to verify it.

16. *in his Epigrames.* *Epig.* cvii, 'To True Souldiers'.

17. *The Green curtaine.* The name should be 'The Curtain', derived from an adjacent 'curtain' or outer wall of an old fortification abutting on the old London Wall. Curtain Road, Shoreditch, preserves the name. *Every Man in his Humour* was acted there.

21. *his firft good one.* So Dryden (*Essay of Dramatic Poesy*, ed. W. P. Ker, p. 81), speaking of *Philaster* as the first success of Beaumont and Fletcher, adds 'before that, they had written two or three very unsuccessfully, as the like is reported of Ben Johnson, before he writ *Every Man in his Humour*'.

21. *Serjeant Jo: Hoskins.* Probably the 'friend' of the *Drummond Conversations*, xiii. 240. Aubrey repeated this statement almost verbally in Bodley MS. Rawlinson, D. 727, fol. 93 verso (quoted on p. 3).

28. M^r *Lacy*, the dramatist, who died in 1681.

32–3. *his studyeing chaire.* Cf. Edward Phillips, Milton's nephew, *Mysteries of Love and Eloquence*; or, *the Arts of Wooing and Complimenting*, 1685, p. 174, ' *Q.* Why is *Ben Johnson's Chair* at Robert Wilson's *Tiplinghouse in the Strand? A.* To signifie that Poets in these hard times, though they should invoke the nine Muses, may still want nine pence to purchase a pint of Canary.' The 1656 edition of *Wit and Drollery* contained at page 79 a feeble poem entitled ' *Verses written over the Chair of* Ben: Johnson, *now remaining at* Robert Wilsons, *at the Signe of* Johnson's *head in the Strand*.'

33–4. *Aulus Gellius.* In the *Noctes Atticae*, 1644, ' Lugd. Batavorum Apud Hieronymum de Vogel', is an engraved title-page, with Aulus Gellius composing as he sits in a chair, the hatching of which and the rolled top suggest wicker-work; but two knobs above at either end show that it is a wooden chair.

36–7. *in his Epigrames. Epig.* xlv, ' On my first Sonne '.

46. *O rare Ben: Ionson.* Gifford in a final note to *Bartholomew Fair* quotes the tradition that this cry—or epiphonema, as he calls it—was first raised over the success of that play. Oldys in a MS. note to Langbaine, p. 287, is the original authority for the story : ' what old Mr. Clud told me of the Inscription on his Tomb-stone arising from the popular applause of this Play after his solemn Cataline had been coldly received by the Audience.'

47. *Jack Young.* Probably the John Younge de Escot, of Great Milton, Oxfordshire, whom Shaw doubtfully records as knighted on January 24, 1685.

52. *Tanquam Explorator.* From Seneca, *Ep.* 2, § 5.

54. *severall verses. Epig.* lxxiv, ' To Thomas Lord Chancelor ' ; *Und.* xxxi, xxxii.

62–70. Printed in the section of *Ungathered Verse*, xlvii. See below, § iv, ' Memorandums of the Immortal Ben ', 23.

76. *Clun.* He played Falstaff and Iago, and was murdered on August 2, 1664, ' near Tatnam Court, as he was riding to his country-house at Kentish Town '—as his ' Elegy ' informs us.

78. *The Tale of a Tub.* Aubrey must have confused this play, the scene of which is laid in ' Finsbury-hundred ', with *The Sad Shepherd*.

80–1. S^r *W. Wiseman* knighted in July, 1604 (W. A. Shaw, *The Knights of England*, ii. p. 135).

85. *None-such-Charles.* An anonymous work, *The None-such Charles his Character* : *Extracted, Out of divers Originall Transactions, Dispatches and the Notes of severall Publick Ministers, and Councellours of State as wel at home as abroad,* was ' Published by Authority ' in 1651, and professes on p. 170 to quote Ben Jonson on Charles :—' Now men may see, how much reason *Ben. Jonson* had, when as, lying sicke in his bed, very poore, and that after much importunity of Courtiers, ten pounds were sent to him by the King, after the receit of which, *Ben.* threw them through the glasse windowes, saying, *this mans soule was not fit to live in an alley*.' Gifford quotes a more picturesque working up of this from Shiels, ' His majesty has sent me ten guineas because I am poor, and live in an alley : go and tell him that his soul lives in an alley '.

87. *p.* Apparently an abbreviation for ' pour '.

184    *Notes on Aubrey*

89. *Th. Henshawe* (1618-1700), scientific writer and editor of Skinner's *Etymologicon Linguae Anglicanae*, 1671.

90-2. Told in a slightly different form by the Hon. R. Boyle, in *Some Considerations Touching the Style Of the H. Scriptures*, 1661, Epistle Dedicatory, sig. a 3 . . . . 'Ben. *Johnson* passionately complaining to a learned Acquaintance of mine, that a Man of the long Robe, whom his Wit had rais'd to great Dignities and Power, had Refus'd to grant him some very valuable thing he had Begg'd of him, concluded with saying with an upbrading Tone and Gesture to my Friend ; *Why the ungratefull Wretch knows very well, that before he came to Preferment, I was the Man that made him Relish* Horace '.

*Isaac Walton's Note.* Walton is not accurate. Thus Jonson's father did not die when the boy was at Westminster; Jonson was a posthumous child. Camden got Jonson the tutorship in 1612, and not ' in short time ' after his leaving school. The statement that Jonson was in the sixth form at Westminster does not fit in with the record, as far as it can now be ascertained, of his schooldays. ' My lord of Winton ', who is quoted as the authority for the statement, was George Morley, who was appointed to the see of Winchester in 1662 and died in 1684. He was a younger contemporary of Jonson, & was not at school with him.

21-2. *a woman.* Some quite untrustworthy ancedotes of Jonson preserved in Bodley MS. Rawlinson, B. 158, pp. 178-80, in an eighteenth-century hand, contain a more explicit statement :—' Ben: Johns: In his old age, grew very poore and haueing borrowed £40 of a Certain woman (mistriss to the E. of Dorset.) She Inveigled him to come and sejourn at her house, he did so, and brought with him all his books, the onely houshould stuff he had, which she haveing In possession, attached the old man, sent to all his friends, but could not amongst them borrow the Money to redeeme them which broke his heart and so he died.'

III

## ARCHDEACON PLUME'S NOTES ON BEN JONSON

MS. 25 A, p. 77.

Here lies Ben Johnſon—who was once one—
yˢ he made of himſ—ſhakſpʳ. tk. yᵉ pen fr̄ him & made yˢ
Here lies Benjamin—wᵗʰ short hair up. his Chin—
Who wl he lived was a ſlow thing—& now he's b̄d is no thing.

5 Ibid., p. 95. Ben Johnſon borr. 50l & pᵈ it ag aft. wˡᵈ h. borr. 100 yᵉ gentl. told him—He h. decᵈ him once & nev shᵈ agⁿ—

Ibid., p. 123. Yᵘ Thing like a Thing, like a Man—sᵈ Ben Johnſon to Sʳ Inigo Jones—who dairs not call him Jackanapes.

Ibid., p. 161. Ben Johnſon at yᵉ Xning of Shakeſp. his child to

w<sup>ch</sup> he w. jnvit g<sup>d</sup> Fr. s<sup>d</sup> to him—now y<sup>u</sup> c̄x̄p. a gt matter—But
I w. giue it a Latin fpoon & y<sup>u</sup> sh. tranſl<sup>t</sup> it.

MS. 25 B, p. 51.
Here lies Ben Johnſon Who once was one—h. own Epit.
Here lies Benjamin—w<sup>th</sup> little hair up. his chin
Who w<sup>l</sup> he liued w. a slow th—& now he is b̄d is Noth}
Shakespr.
If y<sup>u</sup> fall a galloping once s<sup>d</sup> one—to An. yt w. thrown in a gallop
B Johſ<sup>n</sup> s<sup>d</sup> h sh. rath. h. an Acr of witt yn of land—w<sup>r</sup>up.
One called him—Wife Acre—

Ibid., p. 71. One told Ben Johns<sup>n</sup>—ſhakeſp nev. studied for any th. he wrott. B. J. s<sup>d</sup>—y<sup>e</sup> mōe to blame He—[? he] s<sup>d</sup>—Cesar never puniſhes any but for a juſt Cauſe & ar. time mk athyns in Bohemia—So Tom Goff brings in Etiocles & Polynices diſc<sup>ng</sup> of K. Rich. 2<sup>d</sup>.

Ibid., p. 78. B. Johns<sup>n</sup> uſed to w<sup>lk</sup> w<sup>th</sup> a Trunchion Cane & mt. an old Comrague in y<sup>e</sup> ſtreets a long time abſent fell a Baſtinad. him—& chiding him—y<sup>t</sup> he w<sup>ld</sup> putt him to it, now he w. gr. old to diſcipl<sup>n</sup> him—w<sup>n</sup> not ſo abl as w<sup>n</sup> he w. yong—

Ibid., p. 82. B. Johnſon was w<sup>th</sup> yong Wat Rawleigh in France & w<sup>ld</sup> y<sup>r</sup> be drunk—See you my gov<sup>r</sup> s<sup>d</sup> hee—

MS. 30, fol. 6 verſo. Searjant Noy was p̄ſented w<sup>th</sup> theſe verſes frō Ben. Johnſon while he was himſ at his Com̄encem<sup>t</sup> dinner for his degree of Searjant at law, y<sup>t</sup> ſo he might take notice Ben ſtood w<sup>th</sup>out expecting but a call to come to dinner,

 When y<sup>e</sup> w<sup>ld</sup> was drowned, No venizon was found,
  bec: there was no park.
 Here Wee ſit & get never a bitt,
  bec: Noy has all in his Arke.

Ibid., fol. 21 verſo. Ben Johnſon brings in his Gypſies dancing, who robd y<sup>e</sup> ſpectato<sup>rs</sup>—amongſt y<sup>e</sup> reſt there was one Xian, & he had loſt (he ſaid) his practiſe of piety. Y<sup>e</sup> gypſies cleer themſ—Yo<sup>r</sup> book (or ballad) w<sup>r</sup> you call it Is not here—o<sup>r</sup> Society—dos not practiſe piety Y<sup>e</sup> Autho<sup>r</sup> y<sup>t</sup> firſt undertook it Long agoe himſ forſook it.

  19 he] *This word is doubtful.*

## NOTES ON ARCHDEACON PLUME.

Thomas Plume (1630-1704), who died Archdeacon of Rochester, and founded the Plumean professorship of astronomy at Cambridge, was a native of Maldon, to which he bequeathed a library, mainly historical. The manuscripts include several notebooks of contemporary gossip collected by Plume. From these the extracts here printed are taken. In one manuscript (no. 22) he had made a few slight extracts from the opening scene of *Every Man in his Humour*.

Mr. Andrew Clark, in an article on 'Dr. Plume's Pocket-Book' contributed to *The Essex Review* (xiv, pp. 9-20), quoted the chief literary anecdotes, including the Jonson extracts.

1-4. Repeated in lines 13-16. Cf. Bodleian Ashmole MS. 38, p. 181, 'M$^r$ Ben: Johnson and Mr. W$^m$: Shake-speare Being Merrye att a Tauern, M$^r$ Jonson haueing begune this for his Epitaph

> Here lies Ben Johnson that was once one
> he gives ytt to M$^r$ shakspear to make vpp who presently wrightes
> Who while hee liu'de was a sloe things (*sic*)
> and now being dead is Nothinge.'

'A slow thing' refers to Jonson's laboured writing, which was a stock charge against him; cf. Jasper Mayne's lines 'To the Memory of Ben Johnson' in *Jonsonus Virbius*, 1638, p. 30.

> Scorne then their censures, who gav't out, *thy Witt*
> As long upon a *Comœdie* did sit
> As *Elephants* bring forth; and that *thy blotts*
> And *mendings* tooke more time then *Fortune plotts*.

Halliwell-Phillipps in his *Life of Shakespeare*, 1848, p. 146, quoted from 'an Early MS. common-place book' a variant text:

> B. Johnson in seipsum,—
> Here lies Johnson,
> Who was ones sonne;
> Hee had a little hayre on his chin,
> His name was Benjamin!

See also *Drummond Conv.* xvii. 596-7.

2. *tk.* = took.   3. *up.* = upon.   4. bd = buried.

9-11. Plume's abbreviations are very irritating, but his version of this story is interesting. He says 'Ben Johnson, at the christening of Shakespeare his child, to which he was invited, " Good friend ", said to him, " now you expect a great matter, but I will give it a latin spoon, and you shall translate it ".' This anecdote was first printed, from a transcript of Mr. Andrew Clark, in Furnivall and Monro's revision of *The Shakspere Allusion-Book*, 1909. But the better known version of Sir Nicholas L'Estrange in his *Merry Passages and Jeasts*, 1650-5 (British Museum Harley MS. 6395, fol. 2), first printed in Capell's *Notes on Shakespeare* (vol. i, Part ii, pp. 93-4), runs thus:

'*Shake=speare* was Godfather to one of *Ben: Johnsons* children, and after the christning being in a deepe study, Johnson came to cheere him vp, and askt him why he was so Melancholy? no faith *Ben*: (sayes he) not I, but I haue beene considering a great while what should be the fittest gift for me to bestow vpon my God-child, and I haue resolu'd at last; I pry'the what, sayes he? I faith *Ben*: I'le e'en giue him a douzen good Lattin Spoones, and thou shalt translate them.'

16. 'Ben Jonson said he should rather have an acre of wit than of land.' Is this the origin of Thomas Jordan's feeble poem in *Jewels of Ingenuity?*—

> *On Ben Jonson and a Countryman.*
>
> Ben Jonson in a tavern once began
> Rudely to talk to a plain countryman,
> And thus it was: 'Thou dull laborious Moile,
> That, I believe, wert made for nought but toil,
> For every acre of thy land I have
> Twenty of wit.'—'Such acres, Sir, are brave,'
> Replied the countryman: 'what great mistakers
> Have we been of thy wealth, Mr. *Wise-acres*.'

19-21. A confused echo of the passage in the *Discoveries* 'De Shakespeare nostrati' (Folio, 1640, pp. 97-8). Even worse is the accusation of 'making Athens in Bohemia', which must be a development of the comment to Drummond quoted in *Conv.* xii. 208-10.

24. *Comrague.* This form, as distinct from 'comrogue', is used in the sense of 'comrade' in Heywood and Webster's *Appius and Virginia*, 1654, p. 47 (IV. ii), and Heywood and Brome's *Lancashire Witches*, 1634, sig. K.

27-8. See *Drummond Conv.* xiii. 295-306.

29-32. A better text is in Rawlinson MS. Poet. 147, of the Bodleian, p. 88:

> *Ben. Johnson to Noy yͤ Lawyer.*
>
> When the world was drown'd
>     No venifon was found
>         For yⁿ yᵉʳᵉ was neuer a Parke
> And now here wee sitt
>     And haue neuer a bitt
>         For Noy hath all in his Arke.

The text of Rawlinson MS. Poet. 210, fol. 68, subscribed 'Beniamine Iohnson' agrees with this. It has for motto 'Omnia iam fuerant pontus, dama nulla reperta est', with the false quantity 'dăma'. But Plume's anecdote gives the setting, without which the lines are hardly intelligible. Noy was Sir William Noye, appointed attorney-general in 1631, and famous for the uncompromising support he gave Charles I in extending the royal prerogative and encroaching on popular rights.

The quibble on Noy's name and Noah's (helped by the Vulgate 'Noe') is made seriously by R. Hayman in *Quodlibets, lately come over from New Britaniola, Old Newfound-land*, 1628, p. 15, in a poem '*To the right worſhipfull* William Noy, *Eſquire, one of the Benchers of Lincolnes Inne*'.

> *Noah* the ſecond father of all ſoules,
> Had in his *Arke* all beaſts, and feathered fowles.
> You in your *Arke*, as in a plenteous hoord,
> Haue ſtor'd what *Wit*, or *Learning* can afford:
> For all *Lawes, Common, Ciuill*, or *Diuine*,
> For *Hiſtories* of old, or of our time,
> For *Morall Learning*, or *Philoſophy*,
> You are an exact, liuing *Library*......

188  *Notes on Archdeacon Plume*

37-42. A hazy recollection of a passage in *The Masque of Gipsies* (Folio, 1640, pp. 68-9). In l. 39 'he said' should be 'she said'; Christian was a woman. There is a reference to Bishop Bayly's manual, *The Practise of Pietie*, published early in the seventeenth century and frequently reprinted.

## IV

## MEMORANDUMS OF THE IMMORTAL BEN

⟨Me⟩m. I laid yᵉ Plot of my Volpone, & wrote most of it, after a prefent of 10 dozen of ⟨palm⟩ Sack, from my very good Lᵈ T—r; yᵗ Play I am positive will last to Posterity, & ⟨be act⟩ed when I & envy are friends, with applaufe.

5   ⟨Me⟩m. The first Speech in my Cataline, spoken by Scylla's Ghost, was writ after I parted from ⟨my⟩ Boys at the Devil-Tavern; I had drunk well yᵗ night, & had brave notions. Theres one ⟨scen⟩e in yᵗ Play wᶜʰ I think is flat; I refolve to mix no more water with my wine.

10   ⟨M⟩em. Upon yᵉ 20ᵗʰ of May, yᵉ King, Heaven reward him fent me 100l. I went often to yᵉ ⟨Devi⟩l about that time, & wrote my Alchymist bef. I had fpent 50l. of it.

⟨M⟩em. At Christmas my Lᵈ B— took me with him into yᵉ Country; there was great plenty of ex⟨cellen⟩t Claret-Wine, a new
15 Character offered itᵉ. to me here, upon wᶜʰ I wrote my Silent Woman. ⟨My Lᵈ⟩ fmild & made me a noble prefent upon reading yᵉ first act to him, ordering at the fame time a good quantity of yᵉ Wine to be fent to London with me when I went, & it lasted me till my work was finished.

*Text from MS. notes in an eighteenth-century hand in a 1674 Quarto of Catiline, first printed by W. Bang in* The Modern Language Review, *January 1906. David Hughson [i.e. Edward Pugh] had previously printed a copy of the notes from 'an antient manuscript preserved at Dulwich college' in his* London, *vol. iv. p. 40 (issued in 1807); his variants are here collated.*
2 Palm Hughson.   *The last stroke of the* m *is just visible in the MS.*
3 be acted *Hughson*   4 are] be   6 from my Boys] with my friends
7 drunk] drank   Theres] There is   8 scene *Hughson*   mix] drink
11-12 I went ... of it] At that time I went oftentimes to the Devil; and before I had spent forty of it, wrote my ALCHYMIST.   13 At Christmas *om. Hughson*   14 excellent Claret-Wine] excellent *Canary*   16 My Lᵈ smild] my lord was highly delighted   16-17 & made ... to him] and upon my reading the first act to him, made me a noble present   17 quantity] portion *supplied by Hughson as a word missing from his MS.*   18 to London with me] with me to London.   when I went, & *om. Hughson*   19 till] until.

# Memorandums of the Immortal Ben

Mem. The Tale of a Tub, yᵉ Devil is an Afs, & fome others 20
of low Comedy, were written by poor Ben Johnfon. I remember,
yᵗ I did not fucceed in any one compofition for a whole winter;
it was yᵗ winter honest Ralf yᵉ Drewer died, & when I & my Boyℯ
drank bad Wine at yᵉ Devil.
Memorandums of yᵉ Immortal BEN. 25

20 The Tale ... Ass] The DIVILL IS AN ASSE, the TALE OF A TUB   20-23 some ... yᵗ winter] some other comedies which did not succeed, by me in the winter   23 yᵉ Drewer *om. Hughson.*   & when] when

## NOTES.

Professor Bang's text has been clipped by a binder, but, judging from the Hughson text, nothing has been lost. The Hughson text appears to have been edited, and the 'antient manuscript' is no longer at Dulwich. Professor Bang's text is preferable.

2. $L^d\ T—r.$ Thomas Sackville, Earl of Dorset and Baron Buckhurst, was Lord Treasurer from May 1599 to his death in April 1608.

5–9. Compare Robert Baron's *Pocula Castalia*, 1650, p. 113.

    With strenuous sinewie words that CAT'LINE swells
    I reckon't not among<sup>th</sup>' Men-miracles.
    How could that Poem heat & vigour lack
    When each line oft cost BEN a glasse of sack.

10. 20<sup>th</sup> *of May*, in the year 1610.   13. *my* $L^d$ *B*— Unidentified.

14–15. *a new Character.* Dryden in his *Essay of Dramatic Poesy* opens his 'Examen' of *The Silent Woman* with a reply to the criticism that the humour of Morose is forced, and adds, ' Besides this, I am assured from divers persons, that Ben Johnson was actually acquainted with such a man, one altogether as ridiculous as he is here represented ' (*Essays*, ed. W. P. Ker, i, p. 84).

23. *honest Ralf.* Commemorated in the extempore grace preserved by Aubrey (see p. 180, above).

# APPENDIX II

## LETTERS OF JONSON

### INCLUDING THE DRUMMOND CORRESPONDENCE

Letters I to VII were written by Jonson during his imprisonment in 1605 for the unauthorized publication of *Eastward Ho*. They are addressed, I, to an unnamed lord, perhaps the Earl of Suffolk, then Lord Chamberlain; II, to the Earl of Salisbury; III, to another unnamed lord; IV, to a noble lady, 'most honor'd of the Graces, Muses, and mee', probably the Countess of Bedford; V, to a third unnamed lord, probably D'Aubigny; VI, to the Earl of Montgomery; VII, to the Earl of Pembroke.

Of these, only Jonson's letter to Lord Salisbury was known before 1901. It was printed by Gifford in the appendix to his Memoir. The others were discovered by Mr. Bertram Dobell, who printed three of them for the first time in the *Athenaeum*.[1] The manuscript is now in the library of Mr. William Augustus White, of New York, to whom we are indebted for the texts of six of the Letters. I, III, and VII are printed for the first time. The manuscript is a quarto commonplace-book of ninety leaves, containing transcripts of letters, of petitions, and miscellaneous documents from 1580 to 1613. The text of the second letter is taken from the holograph among the Cecil Papers at Hatfield; it is interesting to note that the copy in Mr. White's manuscript is a first draft, which Jonson retouched in the copy actually sent to Lord Salisbury. Mr. Dobell conjectured that Chapman was the writer or collector of the transcripts, a number of which relate to him.

In addition to the Jonson letters here printed, Mr. Dobell gave three similar letters of Chapman—a petition to King James on behalf of Jonson and himself, an appeal to the Lord Chamberlain, and a letter of thanks for pardoning them.

The points of the correspondence are:

1. Jonson and Chapman are in prison together, and alone, on the same charge (Letters II, IV).
2. The charge is founded upon a play, and mainly upon 'two clauses' of it (Chapman to the King, and Jonson II).
3. The 'booke' was presented without the Lord Chamberlain's licence (Chapman to the Lord Chamberlain).

---

[1] 'Newly Discovered Documents of the Elizabethan and Jacobean Periods', March 23 and 30, April 6 and 13, 1901.

4. Their arrest they understand to be the direct result of the King's 'anger' (I, III, IV, VI, VII).

5 They complain that they have been committed to prison 'unexamined and unheard' (I, II, IV).

6. They assert their innocence, and hint that some others are guilty, for whose 'licence' they are vexed (VII). The 'two clawses' are 'both of them not our owne' (Chapman to the King), and have, moreover, been 'so mistaken, so misconstrued, so misapplied, as I do wonder whether their Ignorance, or Impudence be most, who are our aduersaries' (IV).

7. Jonson protests that, since his 'first Error', he has kept his style free from offensive personalities, and challenges an examination of all his past works, including the play now in question, 'whether, I haue euer (in any thing I haue written priuate, or publique) giuen offence to a Nation, to any publique, order or state, to any person of honour, or Authority' (II).

The circumstances of this imprisonment, particularly the statements in Letter II, leave it practically certain that the incriminated play was *Eastward Ho*.

With one exception, the reported circumstances of the trouble arising from this play correspond entirely to those disclosed by the correspondence. The anger of the King which the two prisoners understand that they have provoked by 'two clauses' of the play in question was actually provoked by two conspicuous passages of the extant text. One of them ridicules a knight who had 'stolen' his knighthood, and mimics the King's dialect and pronunciation ('I ken the mon weel', IV. i); the other describes Virginia as peopled 'only by a few industrious Scots, perhaps, who indeed are dispersed over the face of the whole earth', and are notable friends to England 'when they are out on't'. The second and more offensive passage was cancelled during the printing of the 1605 edition—so far as is known, it survives only in the Dyce copy—a proof that it was the prospect of publication, not the performance merely, that stirred the King's anger. These passages Jonson and Chapman expressly ascribe to the third writer, and this, according to Drummond's report, was Marston. But where was Marston? Jonson told Drummond that he himself had 'joined Chapman and Marston in prison', where, so far as appears, all three remained until their joint release. And if he 'voluntarily' joined them, as he says, why this indignant complaint at having been committed, unexamined or unheard, to a vile prison? Jonson had, however, been 'delated' to James by Murray;[1] the 'voluntary' self-imprisonment would seem therefore to have been a judicious anticipation of necessity. The *Conversations* report is not in this point entirely consistent, and may be inaccurate in others, e.g. in the presence of Marston. But assuming its

---

[1] See the *Conversations*, xiii. 273.

accuracy in that point, if Chapman and Jonson were both innocently suffering for an offence which their fellow-prisoner Marston had committed, it is at least conceivable that they should have sought to procure their own liberation from an unjust charge with as little prejudice as possible to the real culprit,—ignoring him entirely, and imputing the offence with studied vagueness to 'other men'. Such a course would certainly not be 'chivalrous', and the suspicion cannot be suggested without reluctance. Marston had made his peace with the author of *Poetaster*, and had offered amends the previous year for his part in the quarrel by dedicating his *Malcontent* to that 'most elegant and weighty poet, his sincere and hearty friend, Benjamin Jonson.' He also contributed eulogistic verses to *Sejanus* (S. R. 1604). But it is tolerably clear that the hearty friend's settled opinion of this impulsive colleague, whom he liked to remember that he had 'beaten' and robbed of his pistol, was, notwithstanding these offerings of incense, one of contemptuous disdain. In the interim, moreover, between the dedication to the *Malcontent* in 1604 and the dedication to the *Sophonisba* in 1606, Jonson had almost certainly given his admirer occasion for renewed ill will. For Marston in the latter passage speaks with unmistakable sarcasm of the method of making a Roman play practised by the author of the very play he had so recently eulogized. 'To transcribe Authors, quote authorities, & translate Latin prose orations into English blanckverse, hath in this subiect beene the least aime of my studies' (sig. A 2). And further, in the address 'To my equall Reader', prefixed in the same year to *Parasitaster*, Marston refers, in equally guarded but not less significant language, to certain men 'of my owne addiction' (i.e. dramatic authors) from whom he had suffered injuries which he is magnanimously ready to forgive. 'Of men of my owne addiction, I loue most, pitie some, hate none: For let mee truely say it, I once only loued my selfe, for louing them, and surely, I shall euer rest so constant to my first affection, that let their *vngentle combinings, discourteous whisperings, neuer so treacherously labour to vndermine my vnfenced reputation*, I shall (so long as I haue being) loue the least of their graces, and only pitie the greatest of their vices.' This is exactly the attitude of the admiring follower who feels himself wronged, and cannot refrain from letting the world know it, but conveys the information in the form of a profession of his readiness to forgive.

The only other current theory of the trouble to which these letters relate is put out of court by the fact that Jonson's letter to Salisbury cannot be earlier than May 1605, the date of his elevation to the title by which Jonson addresses him. The view that Jonson and Chapman were in prison because of some offence given by *Sejanus* in 1603 is made plausible solely by the fact that Chapman's was probably the 'second pen' employed by

Jonson in that play. But the Letters imply that a third author at least was concerned in the offending play, and of this there is no hint whatever in *Sejanus*; Jonson's language makes it absolutely clear that there was none.

Finally, the writers ascribe their imprisonment to the anger of the King, and Jonson complains repeatedly of having been imprisoned without examination. But the trouble over *Sejanus*, according to the *Conversations*, was due to the anger of Northampton; and Jonson, whether imprisoned or not, was certainly examined by the Council.

It only remains to add that Jonson's reference, in his letter to Salisbury, to the 'former benefits' he had received from his correspondent is entirely consistent with the view that *Eastward Ho* was the play out of which his need of further bounty had arisen. These were (1) his prompt release from prison in the *Isle of Dogs* business, 1597, (2) in 1603 the leniency of the Council in the matter of *Sejanus*. There is thence no need to postulate another occasion in order to explain Jonson's plural. M. Castelain's suggestion (*op. cit.*, p. 917) of *Sir Giles Goosecap* is therefore entirely needless, and may be dismissed at once. There is no proof that that play either gave offence in high quarters or was in any way connected with Jonson.

I

⟨To an Unnamed Lord,
probably the Earl of Suffolk, 1605.⟩

Most honorable Lord:

Although I cannot but know yo$^r$ Lo: to be busied w$^{th}$ far greater and higher affaires, then to haue leysure to discend sodainlye on an estate so lowe, and remou'd as myne; yet, since the cause is in vs wholie mistaken (at least misconstrued) and y$^t$ eurie noble and iust man, is bound to defend the Innocent, I doubt not but to finde yo$^r$ Lordshipp full of y$^t$ woonted vertue, & fauoure; wherwith you haue euer abounded toward the truth. And though the Imprisonment itselfe can not but grieue mee (in respect of his Maiesties high displeasure, from whence it proceedes) yet the Manner of it afflicts me more, being commytted hether, vnexamyned, nay vnheard (a Rite, not commonlie denyed to the greatest Offenders) and I made a guiltie man, longe before I am one, or euer thought to bee: God, I call to testimonye what my thoughts are, and euer heue bene of his Maiestie; & so may

I thryue when he comes to be my Iudge and my Kinges, as they are most sincere :

And I appeale to posteritie that will hearafter read and Iudge my writings (though now neglected) whether it be possible, I should speake of his Maiestie as I haue done, without the affection of a most zealous and good subiect. It hath euer bene my destenye to be misreported, and condemn'd on the first tale; but I hope there is an Eare left for mee, and by youre honor I hope it, who haue alwaies bene frend to Iustice; a vertue that Crownes youre Nobilitie. So with my most humble prayer of your Pardon, and all aduanced wishes for yo$^r$ honor, I begin to know my dutie, which is to forbeare to trouble yo$^r$ Lo: till my languishinge estate may drawe free breath from youre Comfortable worde.

Ben: Johnson.

We suppose this first letter to have been addressed to Suffolk, the Lord Chamberlain, because Jonson expressly says in Letter II that he has written to that official, who was the authority to license plays, and because this is Jonson's first letter in Mr. White's manuscript.

## II

### To the moſt nobly⹀vertuous and thrice⹀honor'd Earle of Saliſbury.

Moſt truely honorable, / It hath ſtill bene the Tyranny of my Fortune ſo to oppreſſe my endeuors, that before I can ſhew my ſelfe gratefull (in the leaſt) for former benefitts, I am enforc'd to prouoke
5 yo$^r$ Bountyes, for more. May it not ſeeme greiuous to yo$^r$ Lordſhip, that, now, my Innocence calls vpon you (next the Deity) to her defence; God himſelfe is not auerted at iuſt mens Cries; And you, y$^t$ approach that diuine goodneſſe, and ſupply it here on Earth in yo$^r$ place and honors, cannot employ yo$^r$ Aydes more worthely, then
10 to the commune ſuccour of honeſty, and vertue, how humbly ſoeuer it be plac'd. I am here (my moſt honor'd Lord) vn⹀examined,

*From the holograph in the Cecil Papers, vol. cxiv. 58, endorsed* '1605 Ben Ionson to my Lord'. *In l.* 35 *my is interlined; in l.* 44 Chambellayne *originally. A first draft, without any mention of Lord Salisbury, is in the White manuſcript; a collation follows, but differences of spelling and punctuation have not been noted: compared with the holograph, the White manuscript is laxly punctuated.* 1 Moſt truely honorable] My honorable Lord   6 the Deity] a Deitie

or vnheard, committed to a vile prifon, and (w^th mee) a Gentleman, (whofe Name may perhaps haue come to yo^r Lo:) one M^r. *George Chapman*, a learned, and honeſt Man; The Caufe (would I could name fome worthier) though I wiſh we had knowne none worthy o^r Imprifonment) is, a (the word yrkes mee, that o^r Fortune hath neceffitated vs to fo defpifd a Courfe) a Play, my Lord; wherof, we hope, there is no Man can iuſtly complayne, that hath the vertue to thinke but fauorably of himfelfe, if o^r Iudge bring an æquall Eare; mary, if w^th præiudice wee bee made guilty, afore o^r Time, we muſt embrace the Afinine vertue, Patience./ My noble Lord, they deale not charitably, Who are too witty in another mans Workes, and vtter, fome times, they^re owne malicious Meanings, vnder o^r Wordes. I proteſt to yo^r Honor, and call God to Teſtemony (fince my firſt Error, w^ch (yet) is puniſh'd in mee more w^th my ſhame, than it was then w^th my Bondage) I haue fo attempred my ſtile, that I haue giuen no caufe to any good Man of Greife; and, if to any ill, by touching at any generall vice, it hath alwayes bene w^th a reguard, and fparing of perticular perfons: I may be otherwife reported, but if all, that be accufd, ſhould be prefently guilty, there are few Men would ſtand in the ſtate of Innocence./

I befeech yo^r moſt ho: Lordſhip, fuffer not othermens Errors, or Falts paſt, to be made my Crimes; but let Mee be examind, both by all my workes paſt, and this prefent, and not truſt to *Rumor*, but my Bookes (for ſhe is an vniuſt deliuerer both of great, and fmall Actions) whether, I haue euer (in any thing I haue written priuate, or publique) giuen offence to a Nation, to any publique order or ſtate, or any perfon of honor, or Authority, but haue æqually labord to keepe they^re Dignity, as mine owne perfon fafe; If others haue tranfgreffd, let not mee bee entitled to they^re Follyes. But leaſt in being too diligent for my excufe, I may incurre the fufpicion of being guilty: I become a moſt humble futor to yo^r Lo: that w^th the ho: Lord *Chamberlayne* (to

14 a learned, and honeſt] an honest and learned 16 o^r] of our is, a] is 17 neceffitated] enforst so defpifd a] such a despisde 22 who] that 25 to] for 26 than] then 29 any generall] his 30 perticular perfons] his person 33 moſt ho: *om.* 35-7 and not truſt ... Actions) *om.* 37-8 I haue euer ... to a Nation] I haue euer hetherto giuen offence in any thinge I haue written to a Nation 38-9 any publique] a publicke or any] to any 40 æqually *om.* 41-2 If others ... Follyes *om.* 44-6 that w^th the ho: Lord Chamberlayne ... comming to anfwere] that you will be the meanes w^th the ho: Earle of Suffolke, we may come to our aunswere

45 whome I haue in like manner petition'd) you wilbe pleafd to be the gratefull meanes of ouͬ comming to anfwere; or if in yoͬ Wifdomes it fhall be thought vnneceffary, that yoͬ LLo: will be the moft honor'd Caufe of oͬ Liberty, where freing vs from one prifon, you fhall remoue vs to another, wᶜʰ is æternally to bind
50 vs and oͬ Mufes, to the thankfull honoring of you and yoͬˢ to Pofterity; as your owne vertues haue by many defcents of Anceftors ennobled you to time./

Yoͬ Honors moft deuoted
in heart as wordes./

55            Ben. Ionson

47 yoͬ LLo:] you   50 thankfull] gratefull   53-4 Yoͬ ... wordes *om*.

It is interesting to note that Jonson in lines 18, 19, 22-24, drew upon Martial's preface to his *Epigrams*: 'Spero me secutum in libellis meis tale temperamentum ut de illis queri non possit quisquis de se bene senserit. ... Absit a iocorum nostrorum simplicitate malignus interpres nec epigrammata mea scribat: improbe facit qui in alieno libro ingeniosus est.' In 'The Epistle' prefixed to his own *Volpone*, also written in 1605, Jonson repeats the argument of this letter: 'And, howsoeuer I cannot escape, from some, the imputation of sharpnesse, but that they wil say, I haue taken a pride, or lust to be bitter, ... I would aske of these supercilious *Politiques*, what Nation, Society, or generall Order, or State I haue prouokd? what publique Person? whether I haue not (in all these) preseru'd their dignity, as mine owne person, safe? My WORKES are read, allow'd, (I speake of those that are intirely mine) looke into them, what broad reproofes haue I vsd ...' 'The Asinine vertue, Patience' (l. 21), may also be illustrated from the emblem described in *Poetaster*, v. iii, where Jonson writes of the ass:

  by that beast, the old *Ægyptians*
  Were wont to figure in their *hieroglyphicks*,
  Patience, frugalitie, and fortitude.

The 'first Error' of l. 25 is Jonson's imprisonment for his share in *The Isle of Dogs* (see pp. 15, 16, above). The phrase has special point in such an appeal. Lord Salisbury, then Sir Robert Cecil, was one of the Privy Councillors who sat in judgement on that play.

### III

### ⟨To an Unnamed Lord, 1605.⟩

Noble Lord,

  I haue so confirm'd Opinion of yoͬ vertue, And am so fortified in myne owne Innocence, as I dare (without blushinge at any thinge saue your Trouble) put my Fame into youre hands: which I prefer to my lyfe. The cause of my commyttment

I vnderstand is his Maiesties high displeasure conceyued against me; ffor w^ch I am most Inwardlie sorie; but how I should deserue it, I haue yet I thanke God so much integritie as to doubt. If I haue bene misreported to his Maiestie, the punishment I now suffer may I hope merite more of his Princelye fauoure, when he shall know me trulie; Euerie accusation doth not condemne. And there must goe much more to the makinge of a guiltie man, then Rumor. I therfore craue of yo^r Lo: this Noble Benefitt, rightly to informe his Maiestie, y^t I neuer in thought, worde, or Act, had purpose to offend or grieue him, but w^th all my powers haue studied to shew my selfe most loyall and zealous to his whole disseignes y^t in priuate and publique, by speech & writinge, I haue euer profest it, And if there be one man, or deuill to be produc'd y^t can affirm the contrarie, let me suffer vnder all extremitie, y^t Iustice, nay Tyrannye can inflict; I speake not this w^th any spiritt of Contumacie, for I know there is no subiect hath so safe an Innocence, but may reioyce to stand iustified in sight of his Soueraignes mercie. To which we must humblie submytt our selues, our liues and fortunes.

Ben Johnson.

From the White MS. In the last sentence should we read 'most humblie'?

## IV

⟨To an Unnamed Lady,
probably the Countess of Bedford, 1605.⟩

Excellentest of Ladies.

And most honor'd of the Graces, Muses, and mee; if it be not a sinne to prophane yo^r free hand with prison polluted Paper, I wolde intreate some little of your Ayde, to the defence of my Innocence, w^ch is as cleare as this leafe was (before I staind it) of any thinge halfe-worthye this violent infliction; I am commytted and w^th mee, a worthy Friend, one M^r. Chapman, a man, I can not say how knowne to yo^r Ladishipp, but I am sure knowne to mee to honor you; And our offence a Play, so mistaken, so misconstrued, so misapplied, as I do wonder whether their Ignorance, or Impudence be most, who are our aduersaries. It is now not disputable, for we stand on vneuen bases, and our cause so vnequally carried as we are without examyninge, without hearinge, or without any proofe, but malicious *Rumor*, hurried to bondage and fetters; The cause we vnderstand to be the Kinges indignation, for which we are hartelye sorie, and the more, by how much the less we haue deseru'd it. What our sute is, the worthy employde soliciter, and equall Adorer of youre vertues, can best enforme you.

Ben: Jhonson.

 From the White MS. Professor Schelling, in his edition of *Eastward Hoe*, p. 162, conjectures that this lady is the Countess of Rutland, Sidney's daughter, to whom Jonson addressed *Epigram* lxxix, the twelfth poem of *The Forest*, and *Underwoods*, l. But two other noble ladies are equally prominent in Jonson's poetry—Lucy, Countess of Bedford, celebrated in *Epigrams* lxxvi, lxxxiv, and xciv, and Mary, Lady Wroth, celebrated in *Epigrams* ciii, cv, and *Underwoods*, xxviii. To her he also dedicated *The Alchemist* in the Quarto of 1612 as 'the Lady, most æquall with vertue, and her Blood: The Grace, and Glory of women'. She too was a Sidney.

V

⟨To Esme, Lord D'Aubigny?

1605⟩

 The Noble fauoures you haue done vs, Most worthy Lord: can not be so conceald or remou'd: but that they haue broke in vpon vs, euen where we lye double bound to their Comforts; Nor can we doubt, but he who hath so farre, and freelie aduentur'd to the reliefe of our vertue, will goe on to the vtmost release of it; And though I know yo<sup>r</sup> Lo: hath bene far from doinge any thinge herein to youre owne Ambition; yet be pleas'd to take this protestation, that (Next his Maiesties fauoure) I shall not couet that thinge more in the worlde, than to expresse the lastinge Gratitude, I haue conceiu'd in soule towards yo<sup>r</sup> Lordshipp.

Ben: Johnson.

 From the White MS. Chapman, three of whose letters on the subject of the imprisonment are included in the collection, comments in a letter to the Lord Chamberlain, that 'we heare from the Lord Dawbney, that his highness hath remitted one of us wholie to your Lo: favoure'. This is almost certainly Jonson, who was living with D'Aubigny at this date.

## VI

### ⟨To the Earl of⟩ Mongomerie.

Most worthely honor'd,
     For mee not to solicite or call you to succoure in a tyme of such neede, were no lesse a sinne of dispaire, than a neglect of youre honor; Yo$^r$ Power, youre Place, and readinesse to do good inuite mee; and myne owne cause (which shall neuer discreditt the least of yo$^r$ fauours) is a mayne encouragement; If I lay here on my desert, I should be the more backward to importune you; But as it is (Most worthy Earle) our offence beinge our misfortune, not our malice; I challenge yo$^r$ ayde, as to the common defence of Vertue; But more peculiarlye to mee, who haue always in hart so perticularly honor'd you. I know it is now no Tyme to boast affections, least while I sue for fauours I should be thought to buy them; But if the future seruices of a man so remou'd to you, and low in Meritt, may aspire any place in yo$^r$ Thoughts, let it lye vpon the forfayture of my humanitie, if I omitt the least occasion to expresse them. And so not doubtinge of your Noble endeuors, to reflect his Maiesties most repented on oure partes & sorrow'd for displeasure. I commytt my fortune, Reputation, and Innocence into youre most happie handes, and reiterated protestation of being euer most gratefull.

Ben: Johnson.

From the White MS. Philip Herbert was created Earl of Montgomery on May 4, 1605. He was a patron of Massinger, but his chief claim to literary remembrance is the dedication of the Shakespeare First Folio to him and to his brother William.

## VII

### ⟨To the Earl of⟩ Pembrooke.

Most Noble
          Earle:
     Neither am I or my cause so much vnknowne to youre Lordshipp, as it should driue mee to seeke a second meanes, or dispaire of this to youre fauoure. You haue euer been free and Noble to mee, and I doubt not the same proportion of youre Bounties, if I can but answere it with preseruation of my vertue,

and Innocence; when I faile of those, let me not onlye be abandon'd of you, but of Men. The Anger of the Kinge is death (saith the wise man) and in truth it is little lesse with mee and my frend, for it hath buried vs quick. And though we know it onelie the propertie of men guiltie, and worthy of punishment to inuoke *Mercye*; yet now it might relieue vs, who haue onlie our Fortunes made our fault: and are indeede vexed for other mens licence. Most honor'd Earle, be hastie to our succoure. And, it shall be our care and studye, not to haue you repent the tymely benefit you do vs; which we will euer gratefullye receiue and Multiplye in our acknowledgment.

Ben: Johnson.

From the White MS. 'You haue euer been free and Noble to mee' is illustrated by Jonson's statement to Drummond (*Conv.* xiii. 312-13) that every New Year's Day Pembroke sent him twenty pounds to buy books. Jonson's dedication to Pembroke of *Catiline* and his book of *Epigrams* in the Folio of 1616 both have significant passages. Of his tragedy he says, 'It is the first (of this race) that euer I dedicated to any person, and had I not thought it the best, it should haue beene taught a lesse ambition'; and he dedicates the *Epigrams* as the 'ripest of my studies'. Either dedication is headed, 'To the Great Example of Honor, and Vertue, the most noble William, Earle of Pembroke'.

## VIII

To my worthy & honord frend: M$^r$. Leech.

M$^r$. Leech

I do not offend vsually this way: and therefore one Importunacye may be the better suffred. I pray you to be careful of this Gent$^s$: necessitie, and succoure it willingly, and in tyme, you shall make me euer beholden to you; he y$^t$ helpes in a busines of so great charitie as this, doth not more succor the needers want, than he increaseth his own good name: I pray you S$^r$. to write very effectually, and so I leaue to troble you: least I should do Iniurie to your nature in solliciting you to that, to which of your self, you are so prompt and willing.

Your true louer & frend<br>Ben: Johnson.

From the White MS. Evidently an appeal on behalf of a friend, similar to that in Letter ix. 'M$^r$. Leech' may be the John Leech who was secretary to the Earl of Pembroke. He published in 1620 *J. Leochlæi Scoti Musæ priores*, which included 'Eroticon libri sex', dedicated to Pembroke.

## IX

To my honord & vertuous frend M<sup>r.</sup> Tho: Bond Secretary to my ho: Lord the Lord Chauncellor of England.

S<sup>r</sup>.

I am bold, out of my trust in your frendship, to request your help to the furdering this Gentleman's suite, the bearers, with my lords fauor : who (of my knowledge) is a most honest man, & worthie of a much better fortune, than that he sues for : what it is, he himselfe will best acquaint you with, and the circumstances that should perswade to it, To which I pray you giue credit in all, for I know his Modestie will not vtter any thing subiect to suspition. You binde me to you to be euer thankfull : And they are not the least curtesies, that make more than one beholden. Let him finde I pray you that I haue credit with you by your vndertaking what you can for him chearfully: And I will take care you shall not repent you: If it be any thing to hold

Your poore vnprofitable louer

Ben: Jonson.

From the White MS. 14 louer] *Originally* friend, *which has been erased.*

Letter ix at any rate may relate to 'the poore Man' for whom Jonson interceded to Lord Ellesmere 'the last Terme he sate Chancellor' —Hilary Term, 1617—in *Underwoods*, xxxi and xxxii. Lord Ellesmere appears to have been ready to hear the man without counsel, when a lawyer came forward to defend him without a fee (ibid. xxxiii). 'Mr. Bond, secretary to my Lord Chancellor', has a passing mention in Wotton's *Letters* (ed. Pearsall Smith, ii. 86) as obtaining a Six Clerks' place in 1614. *Thomas Coriate Traueller for the English Wits*, in his letter from the Court of the Great Mogul, 1616, p. 43, sends 'the recommendations of my dutifull respect' to various 'louers of vertue, and literature' including Jonson and 'Maist. Iohn Bond my countreyman, chiefe Secretarie vnto my Lorde Chancellour'. Should 'Tho: Bond' in the address be 'Jho: Bond'?

## X

### To the moſt honorable and honour'd Earle of Saliſbury.

My moſt honorable Lord./

May it pleaſe yo<sup>r</sup> Lo: to vnderſtand, there hath bene no Want in mee, eyther of labor or ſincerity in the diſcharge of this buſines, to the ſatiſfaction of yo<sup>r</sup> Lo: and the ſtate. And wheras, yeſterday, vpon the firſt Mention of it, I tooke the moſt ready courſe (to my preſent thought) by the *Venetian* Ambaſſadors Chaplin, who not only apprehended it well, but was of mind w<sup>th</sup> mee, that no Man of Conſcience, or any indifferent Loue to his Countrey would deny to doe it; and w<sup>th</sup>all engaged himſelfe to find out one, abſolute in all Numbers, for the purpoſe; w<sup>ch</sup> he will'd me (before a Gent: of good Credit, who is my Teſtemony) to ſignifie to yo<sup>r</sup> Lo: in his Name: It falls out ſince, that that Party will not be found, (for ſoe he returnes anſwere.) Vpon w<sup>ch</sup> I haue made attempt in other Places, but can ſpeake w<sup>th</sup> no one in Perſon (all being eyther remoou'd, or ſo conceal'd, vpon this preſent Miſcheife) but by ſecond Meanes, I haue receau'd anſwere of doubts, and difficulties, that they will make it a Queſtion to the Archprieſt, w<sup>th</sup> other ſuch like ſuſpenſions: So that to tell yo<sup>r</sup> Lo: playnly my heart, I thinke they are All ſo enweau'd in it, as it will make 500 Gent: leſſe of the Religion w<sup>th</sup>in this weeke, if they carry they<sup>r</sup> vnderſtanding about them. For my ſelfe, if I had bene a Preiſt, I would haue put on wings to ſuch an Occaſion, and haue thought it no aduenture, where I might haue done (beſides his *Maieſty*, and my Country) all Chriſtianity ſo good ſeruice. And ſo much I haue ſent to ſome of them./

If it ſhall pleaſe yo<sup>r</sup> Lordſh: I ſhall yet make farder triall, and that you cannot in the meane time be prouided: I do not only w<sup>th</sup> all readyneſſe offer my ſeruice, but will pforme it w<sup>th</sup> as much integrity, as yo<sup>r</sup> particular Fauor, or his Maieſties Right in any Subiect he hath, can exact./

Yo<sup>r</sup> Ho: moſt perfect
ſeruant and Louer

Ben: Ionſon

From the holograph in the *Domestic State Papers, James I*, xvi. 30, November, 1605. In line 17 'will' is added in interline. It has been docketed incorrectly '8 Novembr. Beniamin Iohnson to my Lord. 1600'. The letter was first printed in the *Athenaeum* of August 15, 1857, in a review of the *Calendar of State Papers, Domestic Series, 1603–1670*. In *Notes and Queries*, 2nd Series, x, p. 367, Mr. Raymond Delacourt quotes the docket of a warrant dated '7 November, 1605'—'A warr$^t$ unto Beniamen Johnson to let a certaine priest knowe that offered to do good service to the State, that he should securely come and goe to and from the LL's, w$^{ch}$ they promised in the said warrant upon their honors.' The *Athenaeum* reviewer asserted that the warrant was still to be found 'in the Register of the Privy Council'; but there is a break in the Register from January 1, 1602, to February 28, 1613.

The Venetian ambassador in 1605 was Nicolò Molin, whose dispatches on the Plot are in the archives of Venice. The 'Archpriest' referred to in l. 18 was George Blackwell, formerly of Trinity College, Oxford, who held this office from 1598 to 1608, when he was deprived of it for taking the oath of allegiance to King James. The Archpriest had control of the secular clergy, as there was no Catholic bishop in England.


XI

*A Letter from* Ben. Johnson *to Doctor* Donne, *in clearing himself upon a former accusation.*

SIR,

YOu cannot but believe, how dear and reverend your friendship is to me, (though all testimony on my part, hath been too short to express me) and therefore would I meet it with all obedience. My mind is not yet so deafned by injuiries, but it hath an ear for counsell. Yet, in this point, that you presently disswade, I wonder how I am misunderstood; or that you should call that an imaginarie right, which is the proper justice, that every clear man owes to his innocency. Exasperations I intend none, for Truth cannot be sharp but to ill natures, or such weak ones, whom the ill spirit's suspition or credulity still possesse. My Lady may believe whisperinsg, receive tales, suspect and condemn my honestie; and I may not answer, on the pain of losing her; as if she, who had this prejudice of me, were not already lost. O no, she will do me no hurt, she will think and speak well of any faculties. She cannot there judge me; or if she could, I would exchange all glory, (if I had all mens abilities) which could come that way for honest simplicitie. But, there is a greater penaltie threatned, the losse of you my true friend; for others I reckon not, who were never had, you have so subscribed your self. Alas, how easie is a man accused, that is forsaken of defence! Well, my modesty shall sit down, and (let the world call it guilt, or what it will) I will yet thank you, that counsell me to a silence in these oppressures, when confidence in my right, and friends may abandon me. And, lest your self may undergo some hazard, for my questioned reputation, and draw jealousies or hatred upon you, I desire to be left to mine own innocence which shall acquit me, or Heaven shall be guilty.

*Your ever true Lover.*

From *A Collection of Letters, made by S<sup>r</sup> Tobie Mathews K<sup>t</sup>. With a Character of the most Excellent Lady, Lucy, Countesse of Carleile : By the same Author. To which are Added many Letters of his own, to seuerall Persons of Honour, Who were Contemporary with him*, 1660, p. 328. The text is taken from the Bodleian copy, formerly Horace Walpole's (Bliss B. 350). The Letter gives a pleasant glimpse of Jonson's relations with Donne. 'My Lady' (ll. 11–12) is probably Lucy, Countess of Bedford, but Jonson scrupulously confines himself to a general statement of his position. John Donne the younger, who 'edited' the Tobie Matthew collection, may have deleted an explicit reference. In l. 16 should 'any' be 'my'?

A letter of Donne's[1] to an untraced correspondent, dated from Mitcham July 17, 1613, again shows Donne intervening as peace-maker on behalf of his old friend; 'Mr. Holland' is probably Hugh Holland of the Mermaid Club, to whose *Pancharis* Jonson prefixed verses in 1603, and who in his turn prefixed verses to *Sejanus*. ' I did your commandment with Mr. Johnson ; both our interests in him needed not to have been employed in it. There was nothing obnoxious but the very name, and he hath changed that. If upon having read it before to divers, it should be spoken that that person was concerned in it, he sees not how Mr. Holland will be excused in it, for he protests that no hearer but Mr. Holland apprehended it so.'

[1] First printed by Mr. Gosse in *The Life and Letters of John Donne*, ii, p. 16, from the collection of Mr. J. H. Anderdon.

## XII

### WILLIAM DRUMMOND TO JONSON

*To his worthy Friend, Mr.* Benjamin Johnson.

SIR,

Here you have that Epigram which you desired, with another of the like Argument. If there be any other Thing in this Country, (unto which my Power can reach) command it ; there is nothing I wish more, than to be in the Calendar of them who love you. I have heard from Court, that the late Mask was not so approved of the King, as in former Times, and that your Absence was regreted: Such Applause hath true Worth, even of those who otherwise are not for it. Thus, to the next Occasion, taking my Leave, I remain

*Your loving Friend.*

*January* 17. 1619.

From Drummond's *Works*, folio, 1711, p. 234. Gifford supposed that the 'Epigrams' were the two poems afterwards printed in *Underwoods*, viii, ix, 'The Houre-glasse' and 'My Picture left in Scotland'. But Jonson sent these to Drummond later, dating them 'January 19, 1619'. The second of these lyrics is not 'of the like Argument' with the first. Drummond must have sent either two epigrams of his own—he attempted this form of verse, and wrote it very badly—or two by some writer whom he had quoted to Jonson. Jonson no doubt sent a farewell letter on the 19th, but it has not been preserved.

## XIII

### WILLIAM DRUMMOND TO JONSON

i. A first draft of the Letter sent on April 30, 1619.

Sir,

Mr. Fenton shew mee a letter of yours, in which yee remember your freinds heere, but I am particularly beholden to you for your particular remembrance of mee. Other letters of yours I haue not seene. The vncertaintye where to find you, hath made mee so negligent in writing. When I haue vnderstood of your being at London, I will not be so lazie. I haue sent you here the Oth of our Knights, as I had it from Drysdale, haralt, if there be anay other such pieces wherein I can serue you, yee haue but to aduertise mee. Many in this countrye of your friends haue trauelled with you in their thoughts, and all in their good wishes place you well at home. What a losse were it to vs if ought should haue befallen you but good. Because I doubte if these come unto you, I shall commit you to the tuition of God, and remaine

*Your assured and loving freind.*

ii. The same, revised.

*To my good frieind* BEN JONSON.

S<sup>r</sup>.—after euen a longing to heare of your happy iourney, Mr Fenton shew mee a letter from you, remembring all your freinds heere, and particularlie (such is your kyndnesse) mee. if euer prayers could haue made a voyage easie, your must haue beene, for your acquaintance heere in their thoughts did trauelle a long with you. The vncertaintye where to directe letters hath made mee this tyme past not to write, when I vnderstand of your being at London, I shall neuer (among my worthiest freinds) be forgetful of you. I haue sent you the oth of our knights, as it was giuen mee by Harald Drysdale, if I can serue you in any other matter, yee shall find mee most willing. [What a lose were it to vs if ought should haue befallen you but good.] Thus wishing that the successe of your fortunes may [answer our desires,] be equall [to the deserts of your many good parts,] to your deserts, I commite you to the tuition of God.

      Edenbrough
      30 of aprile. 619.

From the autographs in the Hawthornden MSS., vol. ix, in the Library of the Society of Antiquaries of Scotland. 18 happy iourney *substituted for* good estate, *and the whole of this opening phrase an afterthought.* 19 letter from you, remembring all your] Originally 1st letter of yours, in which you remember your. 26 *After* knights *a parenthesis* (if you haue it not before) *is struck out.* In 28–31 words in brackets are the first draft.

The various friends whom Jonson made during the visit are enumerated at the close of Letter xiv, and include 'the beloved Fentons'. They have been identified by David Masson in his account of Jonson's visit prefixed to *The Register of the Privy Council of Scotland*, vol. xi. 1616–1619, pp. clxii–clxix. 'Maister Johnne Fentoun' is mentioned in the *Register* (x, p. 311) in-March, 1615, as 'Keeper of the Register of the Comptrollery', and was elected in June, 1619 (xi, pp. 605–7), Commissioner to the Orkneys and Shetland to demand the dues from foreign fishers. 'A worthy Gentleman, named Master *Iohn Fenton*', brought John Taylor six miles on his way to Dunfermlin (*Pennyles Pilgrimage*, 1618, sig. E).

## XIV

*To my Worthy, Honoured and Beloved Friend Mr.
William Drummond, Edinburgh.*

*Most Loving and Beloved Sir,*

Against which Titles I should most knowingly offend, if I made you not at length some Account of my self, to come even with your Friendship. I am arrived safely, with a most Catholick Welcome, and my Reports not unacceptable to His Majesty: He professed (I thank God) some Joy to see me, and is pleased to hear of the Purpose of my Book: To which I most earnestly sollicit you for your Promise of the Inscriptions at *Pinky*, some Things concerning the Loch of *Lomound*, touching the Government of *Edinburgh*, to urge Mr. *James Scot*; and what else you can procure for me with all speed: Especially I make it my Request, that you will enquire for me, whether the Students Method at St. *Andrew*'s be the same with that at *Edinburgh*, and so to assure me, or wherein they differ. Though these Requests be full of Trouble, I hope they shall neither burden nor weary such a Friendship, whose Commands to me I will ever interpret a Pleasure. News we have none here, but what is making against the Queen's Funeral, whereof I have somewhat in hand, which shall look upon you with the next. Salute the beloved *Fentons*, the *Nisbets*, the *Scots*, the *Levingstons*, and all the Honest and Honoured Names with you; especially Mr. *James Writh*, his Wife, your Sister, &c. And if you forget your self, you believe not in
*Your most true Friend and Lover,*

Ben. Johnson.

*London,* 10th *of May* 1619.

From Drummond's *Works* in folio, 1711, pp. 154–5, where it is followed by the madrigal 'On a Lover's Dust'. See the *Conversations*, xvi. 403, xviii. 645, for the reference to Loch Lomond (l. 9).

Of the Nisbets, Masson notes that Sir William Nisbet of the Dean, a wealthy merchant, was Lord Provost of Edinburgh in 1618, and that James Nisbet was a town councillor that year, and afterwards a Bailie of the town; 'these two were directly concerned with the vote of the Magistrates and Town Council to make Ben Jonson an honorary burgess' (p. clxvii). The Scots included Sir John Scot of Scotstarvet, Director of Chancery, and afterwards Privy Councillor and Senator of the College of Justice. Of the Livingstons there is no special record;

but 'Mr. James Writh' was Mr. James Raith, 'servitor to Alexander Earl of Dumfermling' (*Register*, xi, p. 95), an Edinburgh advocate of high standing. He married Eliza Fowler, and Drummond's mother was a Fowler, so the 'Wife' to whom Ben sent his remembrances 'was a cousin or other relative of Drummond's. In that case, the "your sister" remembered along with Mrs. Raith may have been a sister of Drummond's yet unmarried' (ibid. p. clxvi).

## XV

### WILLIAM DRUMMOND TO JONSON

*To his Worthy Friend Master* Benjamin Johnson.

SIR,
　　　　　The uncertainty of your abode was a cause of my silence this time past, I have adventured this packet upon hopes that a man so famous cannot be in any place either of the City or Court where he shall not be found out. In my last I sent you a description of *Lough Lomond* with a map of *Inch-merinoch*, which may by your Book be made most famous⟨,⟩ with the form of the Government of *Edenburgh*, and the Method of the Colleges of *Scotland*; for all inscriptions I have been curious to find out for you, the *Impressaes* and Emblemes on a Bed of State wrought and embroidered all with gold and silk by the late Queen *Mary* mother to our sacred Soveraign, which will embellish greatly some pages of your Book, and is worthy your remembrance; the first is the Loadstone turning towards the pole, the word her Majesties name turned in an Anagram, *Maria Stuart, sa vertu m'attire*, which is not much inferiour to *Veritas armata*. This hath reference to a Crucifix, before which with all her Royall Ornaments she is humbled on her knees most lively, with the word *undique*; an *Impressa* of *Mary* of *Lorrain* her Mother, a *Phœnix* in flames, the word *en ma fin git mon commencement*. The *Impressa* of an Apple Tree growing in a Thorn, the word *Per vincula crescit*. The *Impressa* of *Henry* the second the *French King*, a *Cressant*, the word, *Donec totum impleat orbem*. The *Impressa* of King *Francis* the first, a *Salamander* crowned in the midst of Flames, the word, *Nutrisco et extingo*. The *Impressa* of *Godfroy of Bullogne*, an ⟨Ar⟩row passing throw three Birds, the word, *Dederitne viam Casusve Deusve*. That of *Mercurius* charming *Argos* with his hundred eyes, expressed by his *Caduceus*,

two *Flutes*, and a *Peacock*, the word, *Eloquium tot lumina clausit.* Two Women upon the Wheels of Fortune, the one holding a Lance, the other a *Cornucopia*; which *Impressa* seemeth to glaunce at Queen *Elizabeth* and her self, the word *Fortunæ Comites.* The *Impressa* of the Cardinal of *Lorrain* her Uncle, a *Pyramide* overgrown with *Ivy*, the vulgar word, *Te stante virebo*; a Ship with her Mast broken and fallen in the Sea, the word, *Nunquam nisi rectum.* This is for her self and her Son, a Big *Lyon* and a young Whelp beside her, the word, *unum quidem, sed Leonem.* An embleme of a *Lyon* taken in a Net, and Hares wantonly passing over him, the word, *Et lepores devicto insultant Leone.* Cammomel in a garden, the word, *Fructus calcata dat amplos.* A Palm Tree, the word, *Ponderibus virtus innata resistit.* A Bird in a *Cage*, and a *Hawk* flying above, with the word *il mal me preme et me spaventa Peggio.* A Triangle with a Sun in the middle of a Circle, the word *Trino non convenit orbis.* A Porcupine amongst Sea Rocks, the word, *ne volutetur.* The *Impressa* of King *Henry* the eight(,) a *Portculles*, the word, *altera securitas.* The *Impressa* of the Duke of *Savoy*, the annunciation of the *Virgin Mary*, the word *Fortitudo ejus* Rhodum *tenuit.* He had kept the Isle of *Rhodes.* Flourishes of Arms, as Helms, Launces, Corslets, Pikes, Muskets, Canons and the word, *Dabit Deus his quoque finem.* A Tree planted in a Church-yard environed with dead mens bones, the word, *Pietas revocabit ab orco.* Ecclipses of the Sun and the Moon, the word, *Ipsa sibi lumen quod invidet aufert*; glauncing, as may appear, at Queen *Elizabeth.* *Brennos* Ballances(,) a sword cast in to weigh Gold, the word, *Quid nisi Victis dolor?* A Vine tree watred with Wine, which instead to make it spring and grow, maketh it fade, the word, *Mea sic mihi prosunt.* A wheel rolled from a Mountain in the Sea, (the word) *Piena di dolor voda de Speranza.* Which appeareth to be her own, and it should be *Precipitio senza speranza.* A heap of Wings and Feathers dispersed, the word, *Magnatum Vicinitas.* A Trophie upon a Tree, with Mytres, Crowns, Hats, Masks, Swords, Books, and a Woman with a Vail about her eyes or muffled, pointing to some about her, with this word, *Vt casus dederit.* Three Crowns, two opposite, and another above in the Sky, the word, *Aliamque moratur.* The Sun in an Ecclipse, the word, *Medio occidet Die.*

I omit the Arms of *Scotland*, *England*, and *France* severally by themselves, and all quartered in many places of this Bed. The workmanship is curiously done, and above all value, and truely it may be of this Piece said *Materiam superabat opus.*

I have sent you (as you desired) the Oath which the old valiant Knights of *Scotland* gave, when they received the Order of Knighthood, which was done with greater solemnity and magnificence.

W. Drummond.

*July* 1. 1619.

From *The History of Scotland, From the year 1423. until the year 1542* ... By William Drummond of Hawthornden, 1655, pp. 263–5. Reprinted 1680. Included in the Folio of 1711 among the 'Familiar Epistles', No. 5, p. 137. In the text of 1655, the Knights' Oath is misplaced, appearing at p. 259; the Folio restores it to its place at the end of this letter. A copy of the letter up to 'Nutrisco et extingo' (l. 25) is in the Hawthornden MSS., vol. ix. The 1655 misspells 'embbellish' in l. 12, and the MS. misspells '*get*' in l. 20. In l. 39 the Folio reads 'leoni', which is a preferable construction. In l. 50 all the texts leave a space after ' and ', as if Drummond had forgotten some further detail. In l. 56 the Folio reads 'instead of making'. In ll. 64–5 1655 and 1680 read 'above in the Sea'; 'Sky' is a correction of the Folio.

### XVI

### To the Right Hon:ble the Earle of Newcastle :~

My Noblest Lord./

and my Patron, by excellence./

I haue here obeyed your coṁaunds, and sent you a packet of mine owne praiſes, wᶜʰ I should not haue done, if I had any stock of modeſtie in store. But obedience is better then Sacrifice; And you coṁanded it. I am now like an old bankerupt in witt, that am driuen to pay debts, on my freinds creditts. and for want of satisfieing letters, to subscribe bills of Exchange./

4ᵗᵒ. Febr: 1631        Your Lo: Deuoted.

Ben: Ionſon./

From Harley MS. 4955, fol 182. The 'packet of mine owne praiſes' consists of three verse-tributes by Lord Falkland, Nicholas Oldisworth, and R. Goodwin.

Letters xvii–xx were first printed by S. A.—i. e. Samuel Ayscough—in *The Gentleman's Magazine*, lxvi, part i, pp. 91–2, February, 1796.

## XVII

### A Letter to the Earle of New Castle./

My Lord

The faith of a fast friend, with the duties of an humble seruant, and the hearty prayers of a Religious Beadsman, all kindled vpon this Altar, to your Hon^r:, my Hono^ble: La:, the hopefull issue, and your right Noble Brother, bee euer my sacrifice./

It is the Lewd Printers fault, that I can send yo^r Lo^p, no more of my Booke done. I sent you one peice before, the fayre, by M^r Withrington, and now I send you this other morcell, the fine Gentleman that walkes in Towne; the Fiend, but before hee will perfect the rest, I feare, hee will come himselfe to be a part, vnder the title of the absolute knaue, w^ch he hath play'd w^th mee; My Printer, and I, shall afford subiect enough for a Tragi-Comœdy. for w^th his delayes and vexation, I am almost become blind, and if Heaven be so iust in the Metamorphosis, to turne him into that Creature hee most afsimilates, a Dog w^th a Bell to lead mee betweene Whitehall and my lodging, I may bid the world good Night.

And so I doo

Ben: Ionson.

From Harley MS. 4955, fol. 202 verso. In line 4 'my Hono^ble: La:' was the Earl's first wife Elizabeth Barret, who died in 1643. The 'Lewd Printer' (l. 6) was John Beale, who printed *Bartholomew Fair* and *The Divell is an Asse* for Robert Allot in 1631.

## XVIII

### An other Lett.
### ⟨to the Earl of Newcastle⟩.

My Noblest Lo:
    and best Patron.

I send no borrowing Epistle to prouoke yo^r Lo^p, for I haue neither Fortune to repay; or securitie to engage, that wilbe taken:

but I make a most humble petition to your Lo:ps bounty, to succour my present necefsities this good time of Easter, and it shall conclude all begging requests hereafter, on the behalfe

Of Yo:r truest beadsman<br>
&<br>
most thankefull seruant<br>
B: I:

From Harley MS. 4955, fol. 203.

### XIX

### An other Letter
⟨to the Earl of Newcastle⟩.

My Noblest Lo: and
            my best Patron.      I haue done your busines, as your Lo:p trusted mee w:th, and the morneing after I receiued by my beloued friend M:r Payne your Lo:ps timely gratuity. I stile it such; for it fell like the dewe of heauen on my necefsities, it came so oportunely and in season. I pray to God, my worke haue deseru'd it, I meant it should in the workeing it. and I haue hope the performance will conclude it. In the meane time I tell your Lo:p what I seriously thinke, God sends You those chargeable and magnificent honors of makeing feasts, to mixe w:th your charitable succors, dropt vpon mee, your seruant: Who haue nothing to claime by of meritt, but a cheerefull vndertakeing whatsoeuer your Lo:ps iudgm:t thinkes mee able to performe. I am in the number of your humblest seru:ts: my Lo: and the most willing; and doe ioy in the good friendship and fellowship of my right learned friend M:r Payne, then whom your Lo:p: could not haue imployed a more diligent & iudicious Man, or that hath treated mee w:th more humanitie, w:ch makes mee cheerfully to infert my selfe into yo:r lo:ps comands, and so sure a Clientele

Wholly & onely<br>
Yo:r Lo:ps<br>
B: Ionson.

From Harley MS. 4955, fol. 203. The 'feasts' referred to in l. 10 are *The King's Entertainment at Welbeck* in May 1633, and *Love's Welcome at Bolsover* on July 30, 1634. The plural 'those chargeable... honors' (ll. 9, 10) perhaps suggests the second entertainment. The two together cost the Earl £20,000.

Mr. Robert Payne is described as 'a divine, and my chaplain, who hath a very witty searching brain of his own' in the preface which the Earl contributed to the *Philosophical and Physical Opinions* of his wife, published in 1655. He was a friend of Hobbes, who refers to him in a letter to the Earl printed in the *Historical MSS. Commission Reports, Portland Papers*, ii, p. 125.

## XX

### An other Lr̃e
### ⟨to the Earl of Newcastle⟩.

My Noble and most honor'd Lord.

I my selfe beeing no substance, am faine to trouble You with shaddowes; or (what is lefs) an Apologue, or Fable in a dreame. I being strucken with the Palsey in the Yeare 1628. had by Sr Thomas Badger some few monthes synce, a Foxe sent mee for a present; wch Creature, by handling, I endeauored to make tame, aswell for the abateing of my disease, as the delight I tooke in speculation of his Nature. It happen'd this present year 1631, and this verie weeke, being the weeke Vshering Christmas, and this Tuesday morneing in a dreame, (and morneing dreames are truest) to haue one of my seruants come vp to my Bed-side, and tell mee, Master, Master the Foxe speakes. Whereat, (mee thought) I started, and troubled, went downe into the Yard, to witnes the wonder; There I found my Reynard, in his Tenement the Tubb, I had hyr'd for him, cynically exprefsing his owne lott, to be condemn'd to the house of a Poett, where nothing was to bee seene but the bare walls, and not any thing heard but the noise of a Sawe, diuiding billatts all the weeke long, more to keepe the family in exercise, then to comfort any person there with fire, saue the Paralytick master; and went on in this way as the Foxe seem'd the better Fabler, of the two. I, his Master, began to giue him good words, and stroake him: but Reynard barking, told mee; those would not doe, I must giue him meate; I angry, call'd him stinking Vermine. Hee reply'd, looke into

5 *Sir Thomas Badger* was appointed Master of the King's Harriers on January 30, 1605 (*Domestic State Papers, James I*, xii. 43). He acted in Campion's masque at Lord Hay's wedding, 1607, and in *Prince Henry's Barriers*, 1610.

25 your Cellar, w^ch is your Larder too, You'le find a worse vermin there. When presently calling for a light, mee thought, I went downe, & found all the floore turn'd vp, as if a Colony of Moles had beene there, or an army of Salt-Peter men; Wherevpon I sent presently into Tuttle-street, for the Kings most Excellent
30 Mole-chatcher to releiue mee, & hunt them: But hee when hee came and veiw'd the Place; and had well marked the Earth turn'd vp, tooke a handfull, smelt to it, And said, Master it is not in my power to distroy this vermine; the K: or some good Man of a Noble Nature must helpe you. This kind of Mole is
35 call'd a *Want*, w^ch will distroy you, and your family, if you preuent not the working of it in tyme, And therefore god keepe you and send you health.

The interpretation both of the Fable, and Dreame is, that I wakeing doe find Want the worst, and most workeing Vermine
40 in a house. and therefore my Noble lord, and next the King, my best Patron: I am necessitated to tell it you. I am not so impudent to borrow any summe of your Lo^p, for I haue no faculty to pay: but my needs are such, and so vrging, as I doe beg, what your bounty can giue mee, in the name of good Letters, and the
45 bond of an euer-gratefull and acknowledging seruant

To your honour

Westminst^r. 20^mo: Dec^bris
    1631                  B. Ionson

Yesterday the barbarous Court of Aldermen
50 haue withdrawne their Chander-ly Pension, for Veriuice, & Mustard. 33^li–6^s–8^d.——

From Harley MS. 4955, fol. 203 verso.

35 *Want*: a quibble on 'want' = 'mole'. Cf. Lyly, *Midas*, I. ii. 53-6 (ed. Bond), '*Licio.* She hath the eares of a Want. *Pet.* Doth she want eares? *Licio.* I say the eares of a Want, a Mole, thou dost want wit to vnderstand me.'. The use survives in dialect (e. g. in Somersetshire).

For the reference to the loss of the pension in the postscript, see Appendix III, xii.

## XXI

⟨To Sir Robert Cotton.⟩

S$^r$, as feriously, as a man but fayntly returning to his defpayr'd health, can; I falute you. And by thefe few lines requeſt you, that you would by this bearer, lend me fome booke, that would determinately fati⟨s⟩fy mee, of the true fite, & diſtance betwixt *Bauli* or *portus Baiarū*, and *Villa Augusta* into w$^c$h (if I erre not) runnes *Lacus lucrinus*. They are neare by my historical ayme to *Cumæ Chalcidenſium Miſenū*, *Auernus*, in *Campania*./
Good S$^r$ addè this to many othér Courtefies you haue done mee that though I chance to furuiue now, I may hereafter dye more in yo$^r$ Debt.
The Booke ſhall be returned this night
w$^t$hout excufe.                You$^r$ infirme

                                  Ben. now./

From the holograph in British Museum Cotton MS., Julius C. iii. fol. 222. Now first printed. 4, &] *Originally* of. 5, or] *Originally* and. No finer testimony to Jonson's scholarship has survived than this letter, written in his latest years after the attack of the palsy. Nothing in his extant writings throws any light on the inquiry, but doubtless he had a literary object in making it. ' The Booke shall be returned this night': was this a precaution taken after Jonson's fire, in which apparently some MSS. of Cotton's perished? See *Underwoods*, xliii. 100, and note.

## XXII

⟨Letter written in a Corner of Thomas Farnaby's Edition of Martial, 1615.⟩

AMICO SVMMO

D.

RICH. BRIGGESIO.

S.

Eccum tibi librum, mi Briggesi, quem heri, penè cum conuitio, a me efflagitasti, mitto. Voluit ad te afferri, etiam hodie; ne diutius moratus, me læsi officii reum apud te faceret. Est Farnabii

mei Martialis. Non ille Jesuitarū castratus, euiratus, et prorsus sine Martiali Martialis. Iste illum integrum tibi, virumq' præbet; nec
10 minùs castum, sed magis virilem. Annotationes etiā suas apposuit tales autem, ut videri possit, sine commentario, commentator. Tu fac, ut illum perlegas protegas; et faueas homini, in tanto sale epulisque Martialitiis, nec insulso, nec jejuno. Dignus enim est, qui vigiliis suis mereatur, ut foret

15        Toto notus in orbe Martialis,

quod de se ingeniosissimus poeta prædicare ausus sit, et vere; suffragante etiam

JONSONIO TVO.

Qui x° Augusti cɔɔ cxxiii
20     amicitiæ, et studii ergô,
hoc levidense
D. D.

First printed in *The Gentleman's Magazine*, 1786, vol. lvi, part i, p. 378. In l. 13 we read 'Martialitiis' for 'Martialiticis', in l. 14 'vigiliis' for 'Virgiliis'. Richard Briggs was probably the brother of Henry Briggs, the mathematician; he was sub-master, and from 1602 to 1630 head master, of Norfolk School.

The affectionate reference to Farnaby as 'Farnabius meus' (ll. 7-8) may be illustrated from his editions of *Juvenal and Persius*, 1612, and Seneca's *Tragedies*, 1613, to which Jonson prefixed commendatory verses (printed in *Ungathered Verse*, xiii-xv). Farnaby in the preface to the *Juvenal* paid a high tribute to Jonson's scholarship. The gibe at the castrated Martial of the Jesuits will be appreciated by any who have seen Jonson's own copy, preserved in the British Museum, of *Chorus Poetarum Classicorum Duplex*, published at Lyons in 1615; it is severely expurgated, but Jonson has supplied all the omitted lines and passages in the margin.

# APPENDIX III

# LEGAL AND OFFICIAL DOCUMENTS

## I

## OFFICIAL PAPERS RELATING TO JONSON'S IMPRISONMENT FOR HIS SHARE IN 'THE ISLE OF DOGS', 1597.

From the Privy Council Register for the Reign of Elizabeth, xxii, p. 346.

Monday in y<sup>e</sup> afternoone.   At the Court at Greenew<sup>ch</sup> the 15<sup>th</sup> of Aug: 1597
preſent

L: Trer̃  Mr Secretarie
L: Chamblẽn  Mr Chauncellor
L: North   of the Excheqr
Mr Comptrollr

. . . . . .

A Lr̃ẽ to Richard Topclyfe, Thomas ffowler, and Ric̀ Skivington eſq<sup>rs</sup>, docto<sup>r</sup> ffletcher and m<sup>r</sup> Wilbraham. Vppon Informac̃on given vs of a lewd plaie that was plaied in one of the plaie howſes on the Bancke ſide contanynge very ſeditious & ſclandrous matter, wee cauſed ſome of the Players to be apprehended & comytted to pryſon, whereof one of them was not only an Actor, but a maker of pte of the ſaid Plaie; ffor as moche as yt ys thought meete that the reſt of the Players or Actors in that matter ſhalbe apprehended to receave ſoche puniſhment as theire Leude and mutynous behavior doth deſerve; Theſe ſhalbe therefore to Req<sup>r</sup> yo<sup>u</sup> to examĩe thoſe of the plaiers that are comytted whoſe names are knowne to yo<sup>u</sup> m<sup>r</sup> Topclyfe, what ys becom̃ of the reſt of theire ffellowes that eith<sup>r</sup> had theire ptes in the devyſinge of that ſedytious matter, or that were Actors or plaiers in the ſame, what Copies they haue given forth of the ſaid playe, and to whome, and ſo⟨c⟩h oth<sup>r</sup> pointes as yo<sup>u</sup> ſhall thincke meete to be demaunded of them, wherein yo<sup>u</sup> ſhall req<sup>r</sup> them to deale trulie

218   *Legal and Official Documents*

as they will looke to receave anie favor. Wee praie yoͧ alſo to pvſe ſoch papers as were founde in Naſh his Lodgingȩ, wᶜʰ fferrys a meſſenger of the Chambʳ ſhall delyver vnto yoͧ, And to Certyfie vs thexamynacõns yoͧ take So &c.

From Register xxiii, p. 13.

At the Courte at Richmonde the 2 of October, 1597.

Present

L. Keeper               L. Northe,
L. Admirall            L. Buckhurst
L. Chamberlaine,      Mʳ Comptroler
Mʳ Secretary, &<br>Sʳ John Forteſcue₀/

. . . . . . . . . . .

Both warrantȩ ſigned by L. Keeper 3 8ᵇᵉʳ, 97. Mʳ Comptroler Mʳ Secretary Sʳ John Forteſcue.

A warrant to the Keeper of the Marshalsea, to releaſe *Gabriell Spencer* and *Robort Shaa* Stage players out of priſon, who were of lat comitted to his cuſtodie. The like warrant for the releaſing of *Beniamin Johnson*.

These documents are preserved in the Public Record Office; they were first printed in Dasent's *Acts of the Privy Council*, vol. xxvii, p. 338, vol. xxviii, p. 33; ll. 7–28 are the fifth, and ll. 36–41 the third entry, of the business transacted at each meeting of the Council. Of the officials then present the Treasurer was Lord Burghley, the Lord Chamberlain George, second Lord Hunsdon, the Lord Keeper Sir Thomas Egerton, the Lord Admiral the Earl of Nottingham, the Controller of the Household Sir William Knollys, the Secretary Sir Robert Cecil, and the Chancellor of the Exchequer Sir Walter Mildmay.

Of the commissioners appointed to investigate and report on the play, Richard Topcliffe (1532–1601) was notorious as a hunter out and torturer of recusants and was an adept at that kind of detective work. Dr. Fletcher was Giles Fletcher, D.C.L., father of the poets Giles and Phineas, and uncle of the dramatist John Fletcher. He too was appointed by the Privy Council to examine recusants in October, 1591. He had been presented to the treasurership of St. Paul's in May, 1597. Roger Wilbraham was active in examining people inculpated in the Essex rising of 1601.

## II

### INDICTMENT AGAINST BEN JONSON FOR THE MANSLAUGHTER OF GABRIEL SPENCER ON SEPTEMBER 22nd. 1598, AT SHORDICHE

From the Jail Delivery Roll, October, 40 Elizabeth, for the County of Middlesex, preserved in the Office of the Clerk of the Peace, the Guildhall, Westminster.

Cogn̄ Indictament̄ petit librum legit vt Clicus signū Cum lr̄a T Et del iuxta formam statut̄ etc.

Iuratores pro dn̄a Regina pn̄tant q^d Beniaminus Johnſon nup Middſß de london yoman Viceſimo Secundo die Septembris Anno regni dn̄e nr̄e Elizabethe dei grā Anglie ffranc' et hib̄nie Regine fidei 5 defenſor' etc Quadragiſimo Vi et armis etc In et ſup quendm̄ Gabrielem Spencer in pace dei et dc̄e dn̄e Regine apud Shordiche in Com̄ Midd pred in Campis ib̄m exiſten̄ inſultū fecit Et eundm̄ Gabrielem cum quodm̄ gladio de ferro et calibe vocat' a Rapiour precij iij^s quem in manu ſua dextera adtunc et ib̄m hāit et tenuit 10 extract' ffelonice ac voluntar' percuſſit et pupugit dans eidm̄ Gabrieli Spencer adtunc et ib̄m cū gladio pred in et ſup dexterū latus ipius Gabrielis vnam plagam mortlem pfunditat' ſex pollic' et latitud vnius pollicis de qua quidem plaga mortali idm̄ Gabriel Spencer apud Shordiche pred in predco Com̄ Midd in Campis 15 predcīs adtunc et ib̄m inſtant' obijt Et ſic Iur' predcī dicunt ſup Sacrm̄ ſuū q^d prefat' Beniaminus ⟨John⟩ſon predcum Gabrielem Spencer apud Shordiche pred in predco Com̄ Midd et in Campis predcīs ⟨die et anno⟩ predcis felonice ac voluntar' interfecit et occidit Contra pacem Dce' dn̄e Regine etc 20

This document was first printed by Mr. John Cordy Jeaffreson in *The Athenaeum* for March 6, 1886. He included it in his *Middlesex County Records*, vol. i, published for the Middlesex County Records Society in that year, pp. xxviii, foll., with valuable comments, some of which we reproduce. The roll has lost its dated wrapper, the writs of 'Venire' and 'Capias' and the Coroner's Inquisitions post mortem. When first it came into Mr. Jeaffreson's hands, it was quite wet. The ink

2 lr̄a T.] Jonson was marked with 'M' on the brawn of the left thumb, but the letter was popularly known as the Tyburn T.   'iuxta formam statut̄', 18 Elizabeth, c. 7.   11 percuſſit *written over an erasure: the scribe at first went on to* eidm̄ (*sic*)   12-13 in et ſup ... Gabrielis *added in interline*.   17 predcum] *The* um *has four minims*.   19 die et anno  *J. C. Jeaffreson*.

is faded, and the roll torn at two points (ll. 17, 19); but the writing is legible. It is endorsed 'Billa Vera'. The Grand Jury, which found it a true bill, probably sat, Mr. Jeaffreson thinks, at 'The Castle' in St. John's Street, Clerkenwell. Jonson would then be arraigned at the next jail delivery. On two points we venture to question Mr. Jeaffreson's conclusions: 'That he was styled "yeoman" in the indictment, whereas the draughtsman, to guard against a dilatory plea, would have styled him "gentleman" had he thought him entitled to bear arms as one of the Johnstones of Annandale.' But did the draughtsman know more about Jonson than that he was an actor? He would not expect an actor to be a gentleman. Further, Mr. Jeaffreson points out that the indictment charges Jonson with being the aggressor—'insultum fecit' 'voluntarie occidit'—whereas Jonson later (i.e. in the account he gave to Drummond) asserted that the conflict was forced upon him. But the law did not recognize duelling: does the legal phraseology really mean more than that Jonson had to take the consequences of killing his man? Finally, Mr. Jeaffreson notes that Jonson forfeited all his goods; otherwise 'ca null' (i.e. 'catalla nulla') would have appeared in the memorandum over his name at the top of the indictment.

A facsimile of the document was given in the fourth volume of the *Records* (1892), at page 350.

## III

## CITATIONS OF JONSON AND HIS WIFE FOR RECUSANCY, 1606.

From *A Book of Corrections or Presentments of the Consistory Court of London*, Book 1605-6, fol. 23 verso. Entry for the Parish of St. Anne's, Blackfriars, under date Friday, 10 January, 1605-6.

Beniaminū Iohnson et  Presented, that they refuse not to
vx̄ dicte poe            Come to divyne servis but have ab-
    xij$^d$            sented them selves from the Coīon beinge
    xij$^d$            oftentymes admonished w$^{ch}$ hathe Con-
Pasch 4 & xviij$^d$      tinued as farr as we Can learne ever
    4 & xviij$^d$       since the kinge Came in he is a poett
    [2$^a$ seffione]     and is by fame a seducer of youthe to y$^e$
    [Tē Pasch]         popishe Religion
    [Cl. Gard in Pasch./

26 Aprilis 1606 Comp$^9$ dictus Beniamyn Iohnson et tā nom̄ suo qu$^a$ vxoris sue humlr̄ petijt absoluc̄ a stā excom̄ ads eos lata cui dn̄s obcit detectiones respondentē that [he hath refused] bothe he and his wife doe ordinaryly to Churche and to his owne pshe Churche

1-8 (& marginal heading) *engrossed in the hand of a clerk.* 9 foll. *Additional notes in a minute hand by some official of the Court. At line* 23 vnder *the note is continued to the foot of the page, being interrupted by the next entry. After l.* 41 Towching *the note is carried over to the foot of fol.* 24. *opposite.* 6, 7 *Bracketed words are struck out.*
11 he hath refused *struck out.*

& fo hath don this halfe yeare but for their receyving he fayethe he hathe refufed to recyve the Coi͞on vntill he fhall be refolved either by the minifter of the p͡fhe or fom̄ other in the fcruple he maketh therin but his wife he fayethe for a⟨n⟩y thing he knowthe hathe gon to Churche & vfed always to receyve the Coi͞on and is appoynted to receyve the Coi͞on to morow   Towching the laſt p$^t$ of the p͡fentm$^t$ for his feduceing of youthe he vtterly denyethe bothe the fact & fame therof or eu͞ going about to feduce or pfwade any to the popifhe religion.  Vnd' d͞ns facta p om' fid t͝a de parendo iuri et ſtando mandatis Eccl͞ie Anglicane d͞ns eos abfolvit   And for his & his wives going to Churche that he bring Certificat vnder the miſtr Mr handfer & the Churchwardens hande of their diligent & ordinarie going to Churche to divine fervis & fermons hereafter, the firſt Court day of the next terme & of their fo continu⟨in⟩ge / Towching his owne not receyving for that he alleagethe fom̄ fcruple of confcienc' whearein he defyrethe to be fatiſſied having as he Confeſſeth heretofore byn of fom̄ othr opinion in Religion w$^{ch}$ nowe vppō better advifement [is] he is determined to alter he defyreth fuch learned men to be [ad] affigned vnto him to confer w$^{th}$ all he pmifing to Conforme him felfe according as they fhall advife him & pfwade him ⟨    ⟩ the [Judg] [Vnde] d͞ns doeth name vnto him m$^r$ Deane of Pawles D: Monford one of the Refidentiaries the D: Lovell & m$^r$ Paffield my L: of Cant. his Chaplens w$^{th}$ whom he fayethe he hathe fom̄ acquaintanc' D: Spenc$^r$ Vicar of St Sepulchers & D: Di͞x pſtor of S Andrewes Vnderfhaft & he is ordered to attend fom̄ one of thes at his own Choys twice a week & Certify of his fo doing & how he is fatisfied [in his confcience] & refolved the laſt Court day of the next terme / Towching the last p̱t of the p͡fentm$^t$ forasmuche as he bothe hathe denyed that eu͞ he went about to feduce any p̱te to popery & for he hath vtterly denyed the fame therof he neu͞ g⟨i⟩ving Caufe therof and being thervppō defyrous the Churchwar- dens or any body fhould iuſtify how they can chardg him herin the

15 Afce Ex *added in the margin.*
24-5 & ordinarie *and* to divine . . . . . . fermons *added in interline.*
26 continuinge] *The minims of* nu *are faint, but apparently the word is incomplete.*    30, 31 *is* and *ad struck out.*
33 *Two words illegible. Perhaps* w$^t$ argm, *i.e.* with arguments. *The writer first wrote* Vnde d͞ns *& then over the line* The Judg: *he then struck out by error* Vnde *and* Judg    34 Monford] *this name is blotted.*    39-40 in his confcience *struck out: over it is written* when he (?), *and this is also struck out.*   40 *After* resolved *one word is illegible.*

## 222 *Legal and Official Documents*

Judg doeth decree the Churchwardens & fwornmen that p̄fented him to be Called into the Court the first Court Day of this next Terme to fpecefy what pticulers they have to Chardge him towching the fame p̄fentmᵗ And he the fame Johnſon is moniſhed to be
50 then therᵉ to [be] ſee farthʳ pſeeding in this Cauſe

*Entry for Wednesday, May 7, 1606 (Ibid., fol. 321 verso).*

To certify of their diligent going to Churche / And he Prefented that he is by fame a feducer of youthe to popiſhe religion / he was moniſhd to appeare to fee farther pſeeding herein he having denyd bothe the fact & the fame & the Churw: weare decreed to be here to fpecifie what pticulers they haue to Chardg him with.

Beniaminꝰ Johnſon et
eius vx̄ ſte Anne black-
friers
55 23. b 1

*Entry for Wednesday, May 14, 1606 (Ibid., fol. 329).*

Beniaminꝰ Johnſon Ste
60 Anne in blackfriers
321. b 1

Prefented that he is by fame a feducer of youthe to popiſhe religion / he was moniſhed to appeare to fee farther pceding herin he having denyed bothe the fact & the fame and the Church Wardens weare decreed to be here to fpecifie what
65                     pticulers they have to Charrdg him wᵗʰ
    px            continuat in hunc diem /

*Entry for Wednesday, June 2, 1606 (Ibid., fol. 334 verso).*

Beniaminꝰ Johnſon et
eius vx̄ p̄o ſte Anne in le
blackfriers
329. a 1
70 23. b 1

Prefented that he is by fame a feducer of youth to popiſhe Religion continuat in hunc diem / he was moniſhed to appeare to fee farther profeding herein he having denyed both the fact & the fame. / They are both to Certify of their diligent & ordinarie going to Churche / he is to Certify how he is ſatiſfied in the ſcruple he made of his receyving the Coiōn by them he was referred vnto to conferr wᵗʰ.

75

Cʳ Gard et Johnſō
Dᵈ px ſtayᵈ at ſeale

50 be *ſtruck out.*

The above documents were brought to light by Mr. Francis W. X. Fincham, Superintendent of the Department for Literary Enquiry in the Principal Probate Registry, in a paper read before the Royal Historical Society on April 14, 1921. The paper was printed in the fourth series of the Society's *Transactions*, vol. iv, pp. 103–39. Mr. Fincham summarized the case and printed the first of the documents.

1. *Beniaminū* ... = Beniaminus Johnson et vxor dictae parochiae. The entries of money payments in the margin are the fines paid for failure to attend. One shilling was the normal fine (Ferdinando Pultan, *A Collection of sundrie Statutes, frequent in vse*, 1618, pp. 611, 920). Apparently 5s. 6d. was the extra toll levied for not taking the sacrament at Easter : as Jonson had failed to do so ever since the king came in, the double payment would cover the two Easters of 1604 and 1605, or payment for his wife. The case was tried before Edward Stanhope, the Bishop of London's vicar-general and official in spirituals.

9. *Compº* ... = Comparuit dictus Beniamyn Iohnson et tam nomine suo quam vxoris suae humiliter petiit absolutionem a sententia excommunicationis adversus eos lata cui dominus obiecit detectionis respondentem. The last word should be 'respondenti'.

16. *for any thing he knowthe*. At this date (January 1606) Jonson was living apart from his wife, from whom he was absent five years when he ' remayned with my Lord Aulbanie ' (*Conv. Dr.* xiii—).

21. *per omnia* = on reviewing all the evidence.

24. *Mr kandſer*. The name is not clear. In Hennessy's *Novum Repertorium* he appears as John Handclir, A.M., appointed on February 19, 1605.

34. *mʳ Deane of Pawles*. John Overall, dean from 1602 to 1614.

*D: Monford*. This appears to be the reading. Thomas Mountforde, D.D., was appointed prebendary of Harleston in St. Paul's Cathedral in April 1597 ; he died in 1632.

35 *mʳ Paffield*. Zacharias Pasfield was Prebendary of Newington in St Paul's, 1604 ; he died in 1616.

37. *Diẋ*. John Dixe was rector of St. Andrew Undershaft from 1597 to 1613. The name ends with a flourish, not a contraction mark.

51. *And he*. The sentence is incomplete.

66. *px* = ' proxime', i. e. postponed to the next court.

76–7. The marginal notes mean, (1) ' The Churchwardens & Jonson are cited' or ' are to be cited '—' Citantur ' or 'Citentur '.

(2) ' Stayed at seal ' = no final decision was taken.

## IV

## JONSON'S DEPOSITION IN THE CHANCERY SUIT WILLIAM ROE VERSUS WALTER GARLAND, 1610.[1]

The document here printed for the first time throws new light on Jonson's relations with the Roe (or Rowe) family, of whom

[1] This is probably the deposition which Dr. C. W. Wallace recorded in *Englische Studien*, xliii, p. 369 (foot-note), that he had found. He quoted the opening words to show Ben Jonson's age. We are not aware, at the time of going to press, that he has made any further use of it. We owe our knowledge of it to the expert advice of Mr. Hilary Jenkinson.

Sir Thomas Roe is the most famous representative. Jonson in his book of *Epigrams* has no less than seven poems addressed to members of this family: to Sir Thomas, epigrams xcviii, xcix; to Sir John, xxvii, xxxii, xxxiii; and to William, lxx, cxxviii. The last of these was plaintiff in an action in the High Court of Chancery in 1610, and Jonson appeared as a witness in his behalf. Jonson's evidence is preserved among the *Chancery Town Depositions* of James I's reign, Bundle 357, in the Public Record Office.

In 1566 Thomas Roe, citizen and merchant tailor of London, acquired from Thomas Heron the manor of Higham Bensted, Walthamstow. He was Lord Mayor of London in 1568, knighted in 1569, and died in 1570. His third son, William Roe, succeeded to the estate. He was born in 1545, educated at Merton College, Oxford, travelled in France and Germany, and was a friend of Immanuel Tremellius and Theodore Beza. He married Anne, daughter of John Cheyney of Chesham Bois. These facts are recorded in his epitaph in St. Mary's Walthamstow, which also says of him, 'Quum pecunia ad vsus publicos exegeretur, ne maior, quam pro rata portione, vicinis suis imperaretur, diligenter curavit, et imperatae, ne tenuiores exhauriri se quererentur, bonā partem ipse dissolvit'. He died on June 29, 1596.

The estate passed to his eldest son, Jonson's intimate friend, Sir John Roe.[1] He was born on May 5, 1581, and was a minor at the time of his father's death. The father's will, proved in 1596, appeals to his widow and his executors to 'be suiters for his wardeshipp, that his vtter spoyle (as much as in them is) maie be preuented'. As Professor Grierson suggests, the father was anxious that a courtier should not 'beg' the wardship of the youth. In the Michaelmas term of 1597 'Row Iohn; Essex, arm. f., 16' is entered on the books of Queen's College, Oxford.[2] He served in Ireland, and perhaps it was there that he was knighted, for there is no official record of his being dubbed. In 1605 Mountjoy, Earl of Devonshire, recommended him to Sir Ralph Winwood, ambassador to the United Provinces, as anxious to serve the States and follow the wars.[3] That he served in the Low Countries and travelled in Russia, we know from Jonson's thirty-second epigram. His foreign service is noticed also in a letter of Sir J. Throckmorton in the *Sidney Papers* (ii, p. 325). Writing from Flushing to Robert, Viscount Lisle, on October 5, 1605, Throckmorton describes an English reverse in the Low Countries and mentions among the wounded 'Sir *John Rooe* sore hurt in the Heade, but he cam of, and recovereth'. He died in Jonson's

---

[1] See the notices in the *Drummond Conversations*, xi. 155–9, xii. 184–7, in Appendix I. The chief facts about Sir John Roe were set forth in Professor Grierson's *Poems of John Donne*, ii, pp. cxxix–cxxxv.

[2] Clark, *Register of the University of Oxford*, ii, Part II, p. 223).

[3] *Hist. MSS. Commission, Buccleugh MSS.* (Montague House), i, pp. 56, 58.

arms of the plague, probably in that very year, or at latest in 1606, before his brother William, after running into debt, sold property on the estate to a creditor.[1]

William Roe, the plaintiff in this suit,[2] was born on September 5, 1585. He was educated at Eton, and went up to King's College, Cambridge, as a scholar in 1604.

He may have succeeded to an encumbered estate; at any rate, his brother the 'infinite spender', as Jonson called him, had sold the manor to his father-in-law, Sir Reginald Argall. During the minority of William, one Walter Garland paid court to him, visiting him both at school and college, and advanced him a total sum of £60, and bought from him for £200—which was a cheap bargain—a property in Clay Street,[3] Walthamstow. The attempt of the family to invalidate this sale caused the lawsuit. William Roe's twenty-first birthday fell on September 5, 1606. It would appear, both from Jonson's evidence and from Lady Argall's, that Garland secured his bargain as soon as the young man came of age.

Four witnesses were summoned on behalf of the plaintiff— Ben Jonson on May 5, 1610, Lady Argall on May 8, Cheney Roe on October 2, and Paul Bowcher (or Burcheer) on November 19. Seventeen interrogations were drafted for the examination of these witnesses.

'Paule Bowcher of Walthamstowe', gentleman, aged sixty, appears as the present owner of the property: he has known Garland three years or more, and he now dwells in the house 'as having bought the fame and the orchard garden doue houfe barne & ftable w$^{th}$ other thapurtenanc℮ and a Clofe of xij acres ... for the fume of two hundred and fiftye pound℮' from the defendant, and he had lately bought 'another field of the def$^t$ called Long Downes pcell of the land℮ in queftion for the fume of fifty pound℮'. He thought the price dear at the time, but he believes he could recover it again because he has improved the property.

'Cheney Rowe of Trinitie Colledge in Cambridge', gentleman, aged twenty-two, and younger brother of William, states the main facts. He has known Walter Garland about six years; Garland was tenant for the house in Clay Street and for other property 'vnto one S$^r$ Reiginald Argall kn$^t$, father in Lawe of this depon$^t$', during the plaintiff's minority. He paid for rent about £30 a year; the property which Garland bought from William Roe was 'worthe

---

[1] In the *Calendar of Irish State Papers*, 1606-8, p. 539, in a list of 'Captains discharged since 1603' he is spoken of as dead.

[2] The authorities whom we have found most helpful in tracing the history of the family are Philip Morant, *History of Essex*, 1768; Mr. G. F. Bosworth, *The Manor of Higham Bensted, Walthamstow*, 1919 (the sixth official publication of the Walthamstow Antiquarian Society); and the Vicar of Walthamstow, the Rev. H. D. Lampen, who allowed access to the parish registers.

[3] Now part of Forest Road.

to be letten by the yeare, about Sixteen pounds'. The fee simple, before the woods growing on the property were cut down, he estimates at about £600; but in spite of depreciation he himself has offered, and is still prepared to give, £300. He testifies from personal knowledge about Garland's visits to Eton, in order to get the estate 'far vnder the value therof, As in the end he did'; and he 'hath bin credibly informed, That the deft made the like Journeys vnto the compt, whilſt he was a fcholler in Cambridge, and vnder age'. The two Roes were at Eton together, but when Cheney went up to Trinity in 1608,[1] his brother had evidently gone down. He speaks of seeing Garland at Eton, but not at Cambridge. He testifies to the money-lending and adds that Garland gave him five shillings at Eton to speak in his behalf. The tip was modest, but the difference in the bribe offered to Ben Jonson shows that Garland had a shrewd eye for value, and he put considerable pressure on Cheney afterwards. Cheney corroborates Ben Jonson's testimony about Garland's insisting that a gentleman paid his debts of honour and Garland's offers of hospitality to William.

The other family witness was Anne, Lady Argall, wife of Sir Reginald, the then owner of the manor, whose age is given as forty-eight. She had known William Roe for twenty years, and Garland for seven. She confirms the statements about the visits to Eton and Cambridge, and the loans. She actually 'intreated the deft diūſe tymes' to desist from both. She called at his house, and, finding him out, appealed to his wife. She was not present at the sealing of the deed of conveyance, but she believes it took place two or three days after William came of age.

William Roe afterwards followed in the steps of his father and brother, and travelled abroad. Jonson's praise of him as the 'good *Æneas* ... imbarqu'd for hell', who 'came backe untouch'd', is hardly borne out by the evidence of one other financial transaction of Roe's later years, communicated to us by Professor J. B. Bury. Thomas Roe, a younger brother of William, who became a Fellow and afterwards Vice-Provost of King's College, Cambridge, died in 1633 or 1634, and bequeathed £200 to the College 'to be employed towards Fires in the Hall'. But William, who was his executor, 'never had the conscience to pay the sum

---

[1] Cheney Roe's career can be fully traced. He matriculated at Trinity College, Cambridge, as a pensioner in 1608; that year he is also entered as a scholar; B.A. in 1610–11; Fellow of Trinity, 1612; M.A. 1614; B.D. 1622; D.D. 1635; Senior Bursar 1619-20; Senior Dean 1635–6; Vice-Master 1638-44 (Rouse Ball and Venn, *Admissions to Trinity College, Cambridge*, 1546–1700, p. 240). He incorporated at Oxford on January 15, 1616; and Foster (*Alumni Oxonienses*, iii, p. 1284) notes his livings—Rampton, 1631, Houghton Conquest, 1636, and Overell, 1637. The Earl of Manchester sequestered him for non-residence in 1647. He died in 1664, and was buried at St. Mary's, Walthamstow, on May 30.

to the College'.[1] He repurchased the manor from John Argall,
son of Sir Reginald; and he died there on December 27, 1667.
He had been knighted at Whitehall on January 22, 1629. He
left legacies to benefit orphans and widows of Walthamstow and
to repair the highway from Higham Hill to Hale End.[2]

The first of the Chancery documents is a parchment sheet
headed,

Interrogatories to be miniſtred to witneſſes to be examined on
the pte and behaulfe of Willm̅ Rowe gentleman Complt againſt Walter
Garland deft.

The names of the witnesses are given in the margin:

 Beniamine Iohnſon Iur̅ 5º Maij 1610
 Dn͠a An͠a Argall iur̅ 8 Maij 1610 Mat. Carew
 Cheigny Rowe iur̅ 2º Octobr̅ 1610
 Paul B(ur)cheer iur̅ 19 Mat. Carew
  Nove͡b 1610 Mat. Carew

Jonson was examined on Interrogatories 1, 12, 13, 14, 15, & 16.
These may be quoted:

1. *Imprimis* doe yow knowe the pties plt and defendt and howe longe
have yow knowne them or either of them.

   \*   \*   \*   \*   \*   \*   \*

12. *Item* what word℈ or meanes have yow hard or knowne the ſaid deft
vſe to entice or pſwade the complt to make ſale of the ſaid
meſſuage and p9miſſes and did not the ſaid Garland amongſt the
reſt of his alluremt℈ or pſwations ſpeake theiſe or the like word℈
vzt that he had knowne divers Noblemen and gentlemen That
had att their full age pformed all ſuch promiſſes as theie had made
during their nonage vnto their Tenn̂t℈ and ſervant℈ and paid all
ſuch debt℈ and ſom̅es of monney as theie had borrowed beinge
vnder age and that that was a great honour vnto them. And
that he hoped the Complt was of no baſe minde but was of as
noble a diſpoſition as anie of the ſaid lord℈.

13. *Item* what ſome or ſom̅es of monney or other Conſideraco̅n did the
ſaid Garland offer vnto yow to pcure a bargaine and ſale to him
from the Complt of the ſaid meſſuage and twentie acres of
ffreehould Land and did he not earneſtlie deſire to effect his

---

[1] From a manuscript in the College Library, *Skeleton Collegii Regalis
Cantab: a Catalogue of all the Provosts Fellows and Scholars of the King's
College of the blessed Virgin Mary and Saint Nicholas in the University of
Cambridge since the foundation thereof anno 1441 usque ad extremam anni
1750. By Anthony Allen Esqre.* Vol. iii, p. 1183.

[2] Gifford, in a note on *Epigram* cxxviii, gave a reference to a 'William Roe'
noticed in Howell's *Letters*, in Letter lxiv, volume ii, of the *Epistolæ Ho-Elianæ*,
1650 (dated August 3, 1644): '*Willi. Ro:* is return'd from the Wars, but he
is grown lame in one of his Arms, so he hath no mind to bear *Arms* any more,
he confesseth to be an egregious fool to leave his Mercership, and go to be a
Musqueteer.' The spelling '*Ro:*' marks an abbreviation, and Gifford, who
used a later edition, did not know of this. It is '*Ro*' in the third edition of
1655. It is therefore unlikely that Howell is referring to any one named 'Roe'
or 'Rowe': you cannot contract a monosyllable.

purpofe therein. And to that end envited yo{w} and the Comp{lt} to his howfe in Walthamftowe where he ftill Continewed to follicite the Comp{lt} to make fale of the fame Howfe and the faid Land therevnto belonginge, and yo{w} to be a meanes to pfwade him thervnto, and of what age was the Comp{lt} when the defend{t} vfed thofe pfwations, and of what age was the Comp{lt} when the writings Conteyning the Conveyance weare fealed by him

14. *Item* did the faid Garland in yor heareing before the faid b9gaine Concluded betweene the Comp{lt} and def{t} alledge that fome pte of the Land would be fownd to be Coppiehould Land And did he not therevpo(n) defire that he might have it for that price wch he then offered faying further that yf he had it he muft be forced to defend the title thereof at his owne charge, and would be Contented foe to doe

15. *Item* was there not fome queftion or doubt made by the Comp{lt} before the faid bargaine was Concluded whether he had twentie acres of ffreehould Land in Walthamftowe yea or noe And did not the faid def{t} therevpon anfwere that he would at his pill finde out twentie acres of ffreehould Landꝰ or to that effect declare the truth herein as yo{w} hard or now remember.

16. *Item* weare Yo{w} prefent at the makeing vpp and concludinge of the bargaine and agrem{t} betwixt the Comp{lt} and def{t} for the faid Meffuage Landꝰ and p9miffes vpon what Confideracōns was the fame Concluded did the def{t} at that time or at anie other time in yor hearinge promife vnto the Comp{lt} two lodging Chambers in the faid meffuage for him and his man and graffe haie and provender for two geldingꝰ naggꝰ or horfes every Yeare for and during the naturall Life of the Comp{lt} yea or noe And was not that pte of the Confideracōn wherevpon the faid bargaine was Concluded and a motive to the Comp{lt} to make fale thereof

The deposition of Ben Jonson was as follows:

p Rowe quer̃.

8 die Maij. 1610.

Año 8, Ia: Regis./

Beniamin Johnson of the Precinct of the blackffreers London gent. aged 37. yeers or theraboutꝰ fworne &c. by direction vpon the 1. 12. 13. 14. 15. & 16th Interr̃./

1. That he doth know the pl: & def{t} in this Suyte, and hath knowne Wm Row gent. named for the compl: about 5. yeares, and Walter Garland named for the def{t}, about 4. yeares./

12. That he hath knowne the def{t} vfe many wordꝰ & meanes to entice, & pfwade ye Compl: to make Sale of the meffuage & Landꝰ in this Int. intended./ And this dept further faith, That amongeft other the Alurementꝰ of the def{t}, hee hath heard him tell the Compl: That he the f{d} def{t}, had knowne diũfe Noble men & Gentlemen, wch had at their full age pformed all fuch pmifses, As they had made in their Nonage, vnto their Tenñtꝰ

& Servuntȩ and paid all such debtȩ & Sumes of money, as they
had borrowed in their Minority, And that It was great honour
vnto them so to doe, And that he hoped the Compl̃ was not of
any base mynde, but of as Noble a disposacēn as any Lord, or
gent: of them all, Or words to that Effect. / And moreover this
dep$^t$ saith That the def$^t$, the rather to make good his f$^d$ Speeches
did at one tyme, in the hearing of this dep$^t$ instance in particular
S$^r$ Roƀt Tirrell of the ffleet (whom he called M$^r$) whose Bounty
(as the def$^t$ alledged) towardȩ him, was exceeding much in that
kynde, The w$^{ch}$ the def$^t$, as this dep$^t$ is verely p̃swaded, did so
highly extoll, to th'ende to move the pl̃: by such sermised Example,
to be bountifull vnto him. /

13. That the def$^t$, did at one tyme offer to giue this dep$^t$ Money
And at another tyme at his owne howse in Waltham Stowe in
Essex he ⟨offer⟩d to bestow a Nag of x$^{li}$ price on this dep$^t$ to
p̃cure t⟨he⟩ Compl̃: to sell vnto him the messuage & Landȩ in
question: Howbeit this dep$^t$ saith That he did absolutely refuse
the def$^t$ȩ f$^d$ Offers, As also to be any Instrument in the Busines,
Otherwise then to p̃swade the Compl̃: to be good vnto the def$^t$,
Not onely in respect of the debt w$^{ch}$ the def$^t$ p̃tested the pl̃: owed
him, But also in regard of many kyndnesses, w$^{ch}$ the def$^t$ p̃tended
he had done vnto the pl̃: And yf it were so that the def$^t$ would
bona fide giue as much for the f$^d$ howse & Landȩ as another
would, then to lett him haue them, before another. / And this
dep$^t$ also saith That the def$^t$ was exceeding earnest w$^{th}$ him to
p̃swade the pl̃: vnto the f$^d$ Bargaine, and to that purpose did many
tymes move this dep$^t$ thervnto, And the sooner to effect his desire
in that behalf did invite the Compl̃: & this dep$^t$, home to his
howse at Waltham Stow aforef$^d$, The compl: then being as this
dep$^t$ thinketh neare vpon his full age. /

14. Hee well remēbreth That the def$^t$ did once, or twice, in
private tell this dep$^t$, he dowbted That some parte of the Landȩ
in question, would fall out to be coppihold Lande, and therfore
said That the price w$^{ch}$ he offred for the p̃misses was Enowgh, By
reason that he might (p̃adventure) bee trowbled to defend the title
therof, Or to that effect, And more to this Int. he canott depose.

15. He doth remēber That at one tyme, before y$^e$ Bargaine was
concluded on, as he taketh yt, there was some question made by
the Compl̃: Whether he had 20. acres of freehold Land in

Waltham Stow or Not: Whervnto the def&#116; made Anſwere to this, or like effect, vizt, Lett me alone to fynde yo&#119; xx&#116;&#121; Acres. /

55   16. Hee was not pñte at the making vp of the Bargaine & Agreem&#116; aforeſ&#100;: ffor he ſaith he was ever againſt yt, vtterly refuſing to be any Witnes thervnto, being a matter w&#99;&#104; he never deſired ſhould come to paſſe, And therfore he ſaith he often pſwaded the Compl: Not to doe any thing w&#116;&#104;out good Advice: 60 ffor that this dep&#116; as he told the pl: did pceiue the def&#116; to be a craftie fellow, & indirect in his practizes: But he ſaith he hath heard the def&#116; ſay That the pl: ſhould be welcome to him, ſo longe as he had any thing to do in y&#101; howſe, both for horſemeat & Mansmeat. But whether that was any parte, or any con- 65 ſidacon of the Bargaine this dep&#116; faith he doth not know Nor more &c.

/ Capt. coram Nicħo Robertē   
in abſenc̃ Mr̃D Nicholſon.     Ben: Ionſon.

<small>In l. 24 'ſermiſed' is written with the abbreviation mark of 'ſer' and followed by the 'r'. In l. 26 'tyme', and in l. 27 'howſe', are interlined. In l. 28, 'offerd', the paper is torn. In l. 28 'of x&#108;&#105; price', and in ll. 50–51 the words 'That at one tyme . . . taketh it', are interlined.</small>

To this practical championship of his young friend Jonson's verse tributes may be fitly appended. They were first printed in the 1616 Folio among the *Epigrams*. Both have a certain note of admonition—the first appropriate in addressing a younger friend. The second opens with a warm expression of affection, 'my ioy to name', much as the poet had greeted Sir John as 'glad-mention'd Roe' in *Epigram* xxxiii. Taken in all its bearings, the lawsuit is an interesting side-light on Jonson's genius for friendship.

Epigram lxx.

To WILLIAM ROE.

When *Nature* bids vs leaue to liue, 'tis late
  Then to begin, my ROE: He makes a state
In life, that can employ it; and takes hold
  On the true causes, ere they grow too old.
Delay is bad, doubt worse, depending worst;
  Each best day of our life escapes vs, first.
Then, since we (more then many) these truths know:
  Though life be short, let vs not make it so.

Epigram cxxviii.

## To William Roe.

Roe (and my ioy to name) th' art now, to goe
  Countries, and climes, manners, and men to know,
T'extract, and choose the best of all these knowne,
  And those to turne to bloud, and make thine owne:
May windes as soft as breath of kissing friends,
  Attend thee hence; and there, may all thy ends,
As the beginnings here, proue purely sweet,
  And perfect in a circle alwayes meet.
So, when we, blest with thy returne, shall see
  Thy selfe, with thy first thoughts, brought home by thee,
We each to other may this voyce enspire;
  This is that good Æneas, past through fire,
Through seas, stormes, tempests: and imbarqu'd for hell,
  Came backe vntouch'd. This man hath trauail'd well.

Of Walter Garland we have discovered nothing further. The Walthamstow parish registers before 1642 are not preserved. But his 'many kindnesses' to impecunious young gentlemen are a sufficient testimonial to him. Robert Terrell, the only other client of his cited in the evidence, was knighted in Royston early in 1607, perhaps in March.

## V

## THE PATENT FOR JONSON'S PENSION OF 1616

Patent Roll, 13 James I, 29 (Roll 2084, No. 12).

D' conc̄ ad vit'  
Beniamino Iohnſon

Iames by the grace of god &c To all men to whome theis p̄ſentȩ shall come Greeting. knowe yee that we for divers good conſideracions vs att this p̄ſent eſpecially moving and in conſideracion of the good and aceptable service done and to be done vnto vs by our welbeloved Servaunt Beniamyn Iohnſon of our eſpeciall grace certaine knowledge and mere mocion have given and graunted and by theis p̄ſentȩ for vs our heires and succeſſors doe give and graunt vnto the said Beniamyn Iohnson a certaine añuytie or penc̄on of one hundred markes of lawfull money of England by the yeare. To have hould and yerelie to receive the said Annuity or pencion of one hundred markes by the yeare to the said Beniamyn Iohnson and his Affignes from the ffeaft of the birth of our lord God lafte paft before the date hereof for and during the naturall life of him the said Beniamyn Iohnson out of the Treafure of vs our heires and succeffors in the Receipt of the Exchequer of vs our heires and succeffors by the handȩ of the Trēr and Chamblaines of vs our heires and succeffors there for the tyme being att the ffoure vfuall termes of the yere that is to fay att the ffeaft of Thannunciacion of the bleffed virgin mary the Nativitie of S$^t$ Iohn Baptift S$^t$ michaell Th'archangell and the Birth of our lord god quartely by even porcions to be paid Although expreffe mencion &c In witnes whereof &c. Wittnes our selfe at Weftminster the firft day of ffebruary.

        p b̄re de priuato Sigillo &c.

This patent is printed by Professor E. K. Broadus in *The Laureateship*, p. *222*.

## VI

## NOTICES FROM THE EXCHEQUER OF RECEIPT MISCELLANEA (Bundle 62)

Anno decimo quinto Iacobi Regis
Mensis Decembris *1617.*/

*Thomas Knyuett* ordinary Groome of the Prince his Highnes Chamber being fent by the Comaundem$^t$ of *S$^r$ Robert Cary* knighte Chamberlaine to the Prince his Highnes from Newmarkett to Chelfey parke to *S$^r$ Iohn Cotton* to feeke *M$^r$ Eliott* to warne him to attend the Prince w$^{th}$ his Hawke after dinner. Alfo another time fent by *M$^r$ Gray* from White hall to Blackfriers to *M$^r$. Iohnson* the Poet to come to the Prince ffor w$^{ch}$ feverall feruices hee prayeth to haue allowance for his paines and charges of his horfe and his botehire too and fro, and to bee rated by the Hono.$^{ble}$ *S$^r$ Robert Cary* Knight Chamberlayne to his Highnes; And paied by the Wor$^{ll}$. *M$^r$ Adam Newton* Receiuo$^r$ generall of his Highnes Treafure.——————   } iiij$^s$

                                            Ro Cary
4$^s$                                    W Alexander:

Menſis Decemb Aō Regni Regē Iacobi quinto decimo

*Thomas Henn* one of the ordinarie groomes of the Prynces Chamber beinge ſent in his highnes ſeruice by the Comaundmᵗ of Mʳ Alexander gent: vſher dailie waiter to his highnes, from the court at Newmarket to Tripford neare Royſtone with a meſſuage to Sʳ Charles Howard, and allſoe one other meſſuage from whithalle to Black fryers with a meſſuage to Benn Iohnſon which ſeruiſes beinge done he returned with anſweares to the places aforſaid, Wherfore he praieth to haue allowance for his horſe and himſelfe his paines and Charges to and fro to be rated by the honnoᵇˡᵉ: Sʳ Robert Carye Knight Chamberlaine to his highnes and paid by the right worſhip: *Mʳ Addam Newton* receuer generall of his highnes Treſſure./——————— } viijˢ

                                        Ro: Cary

8ˢ                                    W Alexander:

## VII

## NOTICES OF BEN JONSON IN THE CITY ARCHIVES OF EDINBURGH, 1618

From the Council Register, vol. xiii, fol. 39.

Vigesimo quinto Septembris Jᵐ vjᶜ Decimo Octauo.

| | |
|---|---|
| Precept Gild Jonsoun burges and gildbrother | Ordanis the Deyne of gild to mak Benjamyn Jonsoun inglisman burges and gildbrother in communi forma. |

Ibid., fol. 42.

Decimo sexto Octobris Jᵐ vjᶜ Decimo Octauo.

| | |
|---|---|
| Precept Ainslie Thesaurer | Ordanis the thesaurer to pay to James ainslie Laite baillie twa hundreth twentie ane pund sex schillingis four pennyis debursit be him vpone the denner maid to Benjamin Jonstoun conforme to the Act maid yranent and compt givin in of the same. |

## 234  Legal and Official Documents

### From the Accounts of the City Treasurer.

*Item* y<sup>r</sup> aucht to be allowed to ye compter payit be him to James ainslie baillie for expenfsis Debursit vpone ane bancquett maid to Benjamin Johnstoune conforme to ane act of Counsell of ye dait ye ⟨   ⟩ day of September 1618         ij<sup>c</sup> xxj lib. vj<sup>s</sup> viij<sup>d</sup>.

### From the Accounts of the Dean of Guild.

*Item,* ye twentie day of Januar Jm vj<sup>c</sup> and nynteene yeirs gewin at directioune of ye counsell to Alex<sup>r</sup> patersone for wrytting and gilting of Benjamine Johnestounes burges ticket being choyes written                                                                                    xiij lib. vj<sup>s</sup> viij<sup>d</sup>.

The above entries were first printed, not very accurately, by David Laing in the *Proceedings of the Society of Antiquaries of Scotland*, 1857, vol. iii, part ii. For example Jonson's burgess-ticket, instead of being 'choyes' written, was 'thryes' written. The Lord Provost was Sir William Nisbet of the Dean, the Treasurer William Rae, and the Dean of Guild David Aikinhead.

## VIII
## JONSON'S HONORARY DEGREE AT OXFORD, 1619

From the *Registrum Vniuersitatis Oxon: de actis in Domo Conuocationis a festo Michaelis Anno D<sup>ni</sup>: 1615. Ad festum Michaelis 1628* (Register N. 23, fol. 76 verso).

Convocatio habita 17° die menfis Julij Anno Dn̄i 1619 Cuius cā erat vt łræ a Cancełłio n̄ro honoratiſſimo ad hanc venełem Domū miſſæ legantur:

Lectæ erant Łræ in favorem Beniamini Johnſon in humanioribus
5 łris egregie docti, vt ad gradū māgri in Artibus pmoveatur.
Supplicat ven̄eli Convocationi Doctorū Māgroȝ Regen̄ et
Ben: John- nō Regen̄ egregius vir Beniaminus Johnſon vt nō obſtantibus
fon    ſtatutis et exercitijs prius p<sup>1</sup>ſtandis et tempore complendo et gratiis in ven̄eli hac domo nō proponendis bona veſtra cū venia
10 ad gradū M<sup>ri</sup> in Artibus in hac Academia admittatur et āctual<sup>r</sup> in Domo Congregationis creetur: cā eſt quod ōni humana literatura
Julij 17° fœliciter inſtructus et eo nōīe a Sereniſß Rege annua penſione eacȝ ſatis honorifica honeſtatus necnō ab illuſtriſß Cancēłłio n̄ro Comite Pembrochiæ com̄endatus et proprio Chirographo
15 dignatus (cā deniȝ ipſa a Delegatis prius approbata) vt poſſit

hodie fpeciali v̄ro favore et gratia fretus titulo hoc Academico et honore infigniri conceditur fimplr

2. *litterae a Cancellario nostro*, Jonson's patron, the Earl of Pembroke. Four letters of the Chancellor were read: one from Sir Henry Savile, one from Dr. Whyte, prebendary of Christ Church, offering £100 yearly to found a chair of moral philosophy, the Chancellor's own letter about Ben Jonson, and also a letter to continue the Vice-Chancellor in office for the following year. The Vice-Chancellor was Dr. Goodwin, Dean of Christ Church; the Proctors were Christopher Wren, of St. John's College, and Bryan Duppa, of All Souls, the future editor of *Jonsonus Virbius*.

Pembroke's commendatory letter unfortunately is not entered on the Register; this seems to have been done only in the case of resident members of the University.

## IX

## THOMAS COOKE HIS BILL, 1620

Mensis Januar. Anno Regis Iacobi Decimo Septimo, 1619.

Thomas Cooke, one of the Gromes of the Prince his chamber, being sent in his Highnes service by ye command of Mr. Walter Alexander, Gentellman Usher, Daily Waiter to the Prince his Highnes, of two Message two severall tymes from the Court at Whitehall into London by Cripellgatt, to warn Mr Ben Johnson the Poet, and the Players at the Blackfriers to atend Hys Highnes that night following at Court, wch severall services being done, he returned each tyme with answer, also being sent another tyme by the lyke comand to the honorabl. the lorde Hubarde with letters wch service being done he returned answer to the Court aforesaid, for wch services he praieth to have alowance for his boot hier and charges to & fro for thre jornies to be 4s. rated by the honrabl Sir Robert Cary Knyght Chamberlin to ye Prince Hys Highnes and to be paid by the worshipfull Mr. Addams Newton, Recever Generall of Hys Highnes Tresurer.

First printed by T. C. Noble in *Memorials of Old Temple Bar*, 1869, p. 99 note, and reprinted by him in *Notes and Queries*, Series IV, vii, p. 183, as in the possession of Mr. John Carter of 17 Fleet Street, endorsed 'Thomas Cooke his bill 1619'. The two copies exhibit some differences of spelling, and are clearly untrustworthy in such forms as 'Jenevar', 'Welter', 'Whitehaell', and 'honarbl' which have been corrected. In l. 12 'octed' has been corrected to 'rated'.

## X

### DEED OF ASSIGNMENT TO JOHN HULL, 1621

From the Auditors' Patent Books, 1620–1624 (E. 403/ 2455/ folio 51 verso) preserved in the Public Record Office.

Beniamin Johnson his assignement to John Hull for his half yeares annuity at Michas. next, 33$^{li}$ and 3$^{li}$ more.

Memorandum that whereas by obligacōn of the date hereof I Beniamin Johnſon am indebted to John Hull Cittizen & founder of london in Thirty and ſix poundℭ payable at Midſomer and Michas next by even porcōns, Now I the ſayd Beniamin haue Aſſigned John Hull to receiue and be payed his ſayd debt out of my Anuall Pencōn payable to me out of M$^r$ Henſhawes office in the kings ma$^{te}$ Excheq$^r$ at Westm$^r$ (that is to ſay) to receiue the xxxiij$^{li}$ to be due to me at Michas next for my halfe yeares Pencōn & thother iij$^{li}$ of the ſayd debt out of the reſidue of my ſayd Pencōn when the ſame ſhaibe due, And to that end I doe deſire and appointe my frend M$^r$ John Burgis to ſee the ſayd John Hull ſatiſfyed his ſayd debt out of & w$^{th}$ my ſayd Pencōn to whom I haue placed ordered and appointed the ſame for the purpoſe afforeſayd

j$^o$ Junij 1621

and to none other pſon nor otherwiſe./ In teſtimony hereof I haue hereto Subſcribed my name the firſt day of June, Anno dn͠i 1621./

Teste          Signed
John Ewen      Ben: Johnſon
Peter Bland    ffrend the last three poundℭ by iuſt debt muſt be 4$^{li}$
                 Signed
                 Ben: Johnſon

3. *John Hull* is mentioned in the Records of the Founders' Company. On February 4, 1604, it was ordered that for 'divers and sundry' violations of his oath he should be 'carried to warde', upon an order from the Lord Mayor, and fined; from 1606 he is mentioned as attending Court meetings, and he became Warden in 1611, and Master in 1617

# Deed of Assignment to John Hull

and 1627 (information kindly supplied by Mr. C. F. Corbould Ellis, Clerk of the Company of Founders).

9. *Mr Henshawes office.* Samuel Henshawe was appointed deputy to Sir Thomas Watson, teller of the Exchequer, on July 19, 1620 (Auditors' Patent Books, 1620-4, E. 403/ 2455/ foll. 20, 21).

16. *John Burgis. Underwoods,* lvii, petitioning for payment of arrears of Jonson's pension, is addressed to him:

*To Master* Iohn Burges.

Father *John Burges,*
Necessitie urges
My wofull crie,
To Sir *Robert Pie*:
And that he will venter
To send my *Debentur.*

## XI

## WARRANT FOR THE REVERSION OF THE OFFICE OF MASTER OF THE REVELS OCTOBER 5, 1621

Patent Roll, 19 James I, 7 (Roll 2251, No. 15).

D' Con̄ Offic̄
Beniamino
Ionſon gen̄

Rex Om̄ibȝ ad quos &c̄ saltm. Cum nos p̄ l̄ras n̄ras patentes magno sigillo n̄ro Anglie sigillat̄ geren̄ dat̄ apud Weſtm̄ vicesimo t̄cio die Iunij, anno regni n̄ri Anglie ffrancie & hibnie primo & Scocie tricesimo sexto, dederim⁹ & conceſſerim⁹ dilco ȝuien̄ n̄ro Georgio Buck militi, p̄ noēn Georgij Buck Armiḡi, Officiū magr̄i 5 Iocoꝛ revelloꝛ & maſcaꝛ omniū & singuloꝛ n̄r̄ Hered₇ & succeſſoꝛ n̄roꝛ coit̄ vocat̄ Revells and maſkes, Ac ipm Georgiū Buck magr̄m iocoꝛ revelloꝛ & maſcaꝛ p̄dict̄ feθim⁹ ordinaw̄im⁹ & constituīm⁹ p̄ p̄dc̄as l̄ras n̄ras patentes, habend₇ gaudend₇ occupand₇ & ex̄cend₇ Offic̄ ill eidem Georgio, p̄ se vel p̄ sufficien̄ deputat̄ suū, siue 10 deputatos suos sufficientes, a tempore mortis Edī Tylney Armiḡi, vel qᵃmcito Offic̄ p̄dict̄ p̄ refignac̄ foriſſcur̄ siue surſumreddicōem vel al̄ quouis legali modo vacaret p̄ t̄mino vite naturalis ip̄ius Georg⟨ij⟩ Buck cum om̄ibȝ domibȝ manſionibȝ regard₇ pfic̄ iur̄ libtat̄ꝑ & aduantaḡ eidem Offic̄ quouismodo p̄tinen̄ siue spectan̄ vel tali Offic̄ 15 p̄tinere vel spectare deben̄. Et insup dederim⁹ & conceſsim⁹ p̄ p̄faŧ l̄ras n̄ras patentes eidem Georgio Buck p̄ ex̄cicio & occupac̄

Offic͠ p̄dicꝯ vadꝯ & feodꝯ decem libraꝝ legalis monete Anglie p ann̄
habendꝯ & p̄cipiendꝯ dicꝯ vadꝯ sibi vel affign̄ ſuis, a tempore mortis
20 dicꝯ Edī Tylney, vel a tempore quo idem Offic͠ p̄ fforiſſcuꝓ ſurſumreddicōem vel aliquo alio modo p̄x̄ vacaret p ꝓmino vite ip̄ius
Georgij Buck de theſauro nr̄o heredum vel ſucceſſoꝝ nr̄oꝝ ad recepꝯ
Sccij nr̄i Weſtm̄ heredum & ſucceſſoꝝ nr̄oꝝ p manus Theſ & 
Cam̄aꝓ nr̄ heredum & ſucceſſoꝝ nr̄oꝝ ibm p tempore exiſten̄,
25 ad feſta ſc̄i Iohis Bap̄te et Natalꝯ dn̄i p equales porcōes ſoluendꝯ,
put p eaſdem ⅼras nr̄as patentes plenius liquet & apparet. Cumcꝫ
etiam nos p alias ⅼras nr̄as patentes geren̄ daꝯ apud Weſtm̄ ꝓcio
die Aprilis anno regni nr̄i Anglie ffrancie & hib̄nie' decimo p
confideraciōn in eiſdem expreſſ[3] & contenꝯ, dedīmi[9] & concefferim[9]
30 dilco & fideli ſuien̄ nr̄o Iohi Aſhley militi vni Gen̄oſ Cam̄e n̄re
priuate Offic͠ magr̄i iocoꝝ revelloꝝ & maſcaꝝ omnī & ſinguloꝝ nrꝯ
heredꝯ & ſucceſſoꝝ nr̄oꝝ cōiꝯ vocaꝯ Revells and maſkes, Ac ip̄m
Iohem Aſhley magr̄m iocoꝝ revelloꝝ & maſcaꝝ p̄dꝯ fecim[9] ordinaūim[9]
& conſtitūim[9] p p̄dicꝯ ⅼras nr̄as patentes hendꝯ gaudendꝯ occupandꝯ
35 & ex̄cendꝯ Offic͠ p̄dicꝯ p̄ſaꝯ Iohi Aſhley militi p se vel p sufficien̄
deputatum ſuū ſiue deputatos ſuos ſufficienꝯ a tempore mortis
p̄nōiaꝯ Georgij Buck, vel qᵃmcito Offic͠ p̄dicꝯ p refignacōem ſurſumreddicōem vel alꝯ quouis legali modo vacaret p ꝓmino vite naturalis
ip̄ius Iohis Aſhley cum om̄ibꝫ domibꝫ manſionibꝫ regardꝯ ꝓfic͠ iuꝓ
40 lib̄taꝯ & aduantagz eidem Offic͠ quouiſmodo ꝑtinen̄ ſiue ſpectan̄ vel
tali Officio ꝑtinere ſiue ſpectare deben̄, Et inſup p eaſdem ⅼras
nr̄as patentes dederim[9] & conceſſerim[9] eidem Iohi Aſhley militi p
ex̄citꝯ & occupacōe Offic͠ p̄dicꝯ, vadꝯ & feodꝯ decem libraꝝ legalis
monete Anglie p Annū habendꝯ & p̄cipiendꝯ dicꝯ vadꝯ & feodꝯ ſibi
45 vel Affign̄ ſuis a tempore mortis dc̄i Georgij Buck militis, vel a
tempore quo idem Offic͠ p foriſſcuꝓ ſurſumreddicōem vel aliquo alio
modo p̄x̄ vacaret p ꝓmino vite naturalis ip̄ius Iohis Aſhley militis de
theſauro nr̄o heredum & ſuccꝯ nr̄oꝝ, ad recepꝯ Sccij nr̄i heredum &
ſucceſſoꝝ nr̄oꝝ p manus Theſ & Cam̄aꝓ nr̄i heredꝯ & ſucceſſoꝝ nr̄oꝝ
50 ibm p tempore exiſten̄ ad ffeſta Natiuitatiſsc̄i Iohis Bap̄te et Na-
talis dn̄i p equales porcōes ſoluendꝯ, put p eaſdem ⅼras nr̄as patentes
plenius liquet & apparet. Quiquidem Georgius Buck & Iohes
Aſhley adhuc ſupꝯſtites ſunt, et p̄nōiaꝯ Georgius Buck rōne mortis
p̄ſaꝯ Edī Tylney Offic͠ p̄dicꝯ & ceꝉa p̄miſſa modo het & ex̄cet, vt ꝺtam
55 inde hem[9] notc̄i. Sciatis qd̄ nos p diūſis bonis cauſis & confide-
racōibꝫ nos ad p̄ſens ſp̄ialiꝯ mouentibꝫ, de gr̄a nr̄a ſp̄iali, ac ex ꝺta

sciencia & mero motu nr̄is, dedim⁹ & conceſſim⁹ ac p p̄ſentes p nob
heredibȝ & succeſſoribȝ nr̄is dam⁹ & concedim⁹ dilco ȝuieñ nr̄o
Beniamino Ionſon geñoſo, dicť Offic̄ magr̄i iocoȣ revelloȣ & maſcaȣ
omiū & singulaȣ nr̄ hered₇ & succ̄ nr̄oȣ cōiť vocať Revells and 60
maſkes. Ip̄mcȝ Beniaminū Ionſon magr̄m iocoȣ Revelloȣ & maſcaȣ
p̄dicť facim⁹ ordinam⁹ & conſtituim⁹ p p̄ſentes. Habend₇ gaudend₇
occupand₇ & excend₇ Offic̄ p̄dicť p̄fať Beniamino Ionſon p se vel p
sufficientem deputatum suū, siue deputatos suos sufficientes, a tempore
mortis p̄noīať Georgij Buck & Iohis Aſhley mit₇, vel qᵃmcito Offic̄ 65
p̄dicť p reſignacōem surſumreddicōem vel alio quouis legať₇ modo
vacauer̄ p ťmino vite naturalis ip̄ius Beniamini Ionſon cum om̄ibȝ
domibȝ manſionibȝ regard₇ pſic̄ iur̄ libtatibȝ & aduantag̃ eidem Offic̄
quouismodo ptineñ siue spectañ vel tali Officio ptinere siue
spectare debeñ.   Et infup de vbiori gr̄a nr̄a dedim⁹ & conceſſim⁹ 70
ac p p̄ſentes p nob heredibȝ & succ̄ nr̄is dam⁹ & concedim⁹ eidem
Beniamino Ionſon p excicio & occupacōe Officij p̄dicť, vad₇ & feod₇
decem libraȣ legalis moneť Anglie p ann̄, habend₇ & pcipiend₇ dicť
vad₇ & feod₇ sibi vel aſſign̄ ſuis a tempore mortis p̄noīať Georgij
Buck & Iohis Aſhley miliť vel a tempore quo idem Offic̄ p foriſſcūr̄ 75
surſumreddicioñ vel aliquo alio modo px̄ vacauer̄ p ťmino vite
naturalis ip̄ius Beniamini Ionſon de thesauro nr̄o heredum &
succeſſoȣ nr̄oȣ, ad recepť Sc̊cij nr̄i Weſtm̄ heredum & succeſſoȣ
nr̄oȣ p manus Theſaurar̄ & Cam̄ar̄ nr̄ heredum & successoȣ nr̄oȣ
ibidem p tempore exiſteñ ad ffeſta Natiuitatis sc̄i Iohis Bap̄te & 80
Natať₇ dn̄i p equales porcōes soluend₇.   Prima solucōe inde
incipiend₇ ad illȣ ffeſť ffeſtoȣ p̄dicť, quod prim̄ & px̄ euener̄
poſtqᵃm p̄fať Beniaminus Ionſon Offic̄ p̄dicť & ceter̄ p̄miſſis gauis̄
fuer̄ Eo qd̄ expreſſa mencio &c.   In cuius rei &c T.R. apud Weſtm̄
quinto die Octobris.                      p br̄e de priuato Sigillo &c. 85

Jonson derived no benefit from this grant in reversion, because Sir John
Astley survived him.  Malone noted (*Variorum Shakespeare*, 1821, vol. i,
p. 418 note) that some attempt must have been made to obtain this
grant for Jonson in the reign of Elizabeth.  Dekker in *Satiro-mastix*
(1602, sig. G 4 verso) makes Sir Vaughan say to Horace, the character
who impersonates Jonson, 'Master Horace, let your wittes inhabite in
your right places; if I fall handsomely vpon the Widdow, I haue some
cossens Garman at Court, shall beget you the reuersion of the Master of
the Kings Reuels, or else be his Lord of Mis-rule nowe at Christmas'.

## XII

## DOCUMENTS RELATING TO JONSON'S APPOINTMENT AS CHRONOLOGER TO THE CITY OF LONDON, 1628, 1631, & 1634

From the *Repertory of the Court of Aldermen, 42, Hamersley Mayor*, fol. 271. This is the sixth entry.

    **Martis** fecundo die Septembris
    1628 Anoc͡ɜ RRͤ Caroli Anglie
    &c. Quarto ; /

**Hamerfley Maior,** Recorder Middleton Gore, Deane Cambell, Ducie Mowlfon Heyling, Parkhurft, Poole, ffen Acton et Abbot et Garraway Vic;

    . . . .

Johnson admit-   **Item** this daie Beniamyn Johnfon Gent is
ted Chronologer   by this Court admitted to be the Citties Chronologer in place of mͬ. Thomas Middleton deceafed ; To haue hold exercife, and enioye the fame place, and to haue and receive for that
Cam͡:      his fervice out of the Chamber of London, the fome of one hundred nobles p Anu͡, to contynue duringe the pleafure of this Court, And yͤ ffirft quarters payment to begin att Michaelmas next ;

From *Repertory 46, Whitmore Mayor*, fol. 8. The twelfth entry.

**Jovis** decimo die Novembris 1631 Annoc͡ɜ
Regni Regis Caroli Angͭ etc. Septimo
**Whitmore Maior,** Barkham,
Lumley, Hamerfley, Deane, Cambell,
Ducie, Raynton, ffreeman, Mowlfon,
Parkhurft, Poole, Clitherowe, ∼ ‖ ∼
Bromfeild, ffen, Abbott, Garraway,
Backhoufe, Acton, et Abdy,

    . . . . . . .

    **Item** it is ordered by this Court that mͬ Chamb̄len
Beniamine   fhall forbeare to pay any more fee or wages vnto
Johnson    Beniamine Johnfon the Citties Cronologer ∼ vntill he fhall have prefented vnto this Court some fruits of his labours in that his place

# Jonson's Appointment as Chronologer

From *Repertory 48, Mowlson Mayor*, fol. 433. The ninth entry.

**Jovis** xviij⁰ die Septembris 1634 Annoq̃  
RRẽ Caroli Angl̃ etc. Decimo /  
**Mowlſon Maior** Recorder ⌒ ‖ - ‖  
Hamerſley Cambell Whitmore Parkhurſt  
Bromfeild ffen Abbott Backhouſse Acton  
Smith Wright Cambell Perry Pratt  
et Harriſon et Gurney Vic /

. . . . . . .

**Item** this day mr Recorder and Sr Hamerſley knight and Aldrañ declared vnto this Court his Matẽ pleaſure ſignified vnto them by the right honoble the Earle of Dorſett for and in the behalfe of Beniamine Johnſon the Cittys Cronologer Where⁄vpon it is ordered by this Court, that his yearely penconñ of one hundred nobles out of the Chamber of London ſhalbe continued and that m̃ Chamb̃len ſhall ſatiſſie and pay vnto him all arrerages thereof /

Ben: Johnson Cittys Cronologor C' m̃kes a yeare

5

10

8 nobles] *Originally* markes *in the entry, with a marginal correction* mistaken 100 nobles p anñ. *The correction was made, and the marginal note crossed out.*

The duties of the office of City Chronologer are specified in the entry recording the appointment of Thomas Middleton on September 6, 1620. He was 'to collect and set down all memorable acts of this City and occurences thereof', and to be ready 'for such other employments as this Court shall have occasion to use him in'; but he is not to print anything so written 'without the allowance & approbation of this Court'. There is a significant entry relating to Middleton in September, 1623: 'Twenty marks given him for his services at the shooting on Bunhill, and at the Conduit Head before the lord Mayor and Aldermen.' Jonson's views on such performances might be guessed, even if he had not written the 'Speach according to Horace' (*Underwoods*, xliv), in which he writes with scathing irony of the City and 'the Battells of thy Aldermanitie'.

In the stead of bold
*Beauchamps*, and *Nevills*, *Cliffords*, *Audley's* old;
Insert thy *Hodges*, and those newer men,
As *Stiles*, *Dike*, *Ditchfield*, *Millar*, *Crips*, and *Fen*.

Jonson's contemptuous reference to the withdrawal of the pension has been given in the letter to the Earl of Newcastle (p. 214 above).

## XIII

### EXAMINATION OF JONSON BY THE ATTORNEY-GENERAL ON OCTOBER 26, 1629

From the State Papers, Domestic, Charles I, cxix. 33.

The examinatiō of Beniamyn Iohnſon of weſtminſter gent, taken this 26th day of october 1628: by me Sr Robert heath his Matyͤ Atturny generall

The ſaid examinant, beinge aſked wheather euer he had ſeen certeyn verſes, begin⟨i⟩ng thus Enioye thy bondage: & ending thus, Englandͤ raunſome here doth lye: & intitled thus To his confined frend &c / & the paper of thos verſes being
5 ſhewed vnto him / He awnſereth, that he hath ſeen the like verſes to thes / And beeing aſked wher he ſawe them; he ſaith at Sr Robert Cottons houſe at weſtminſter: Being further asked vppō what occaſion he ſawe them at that time; he ſaith that coming in to Sr Robert Cottons houſe as he often doth, the paper of thes
10 verſes liing ther vppon the table after dinner, this examinant was aſked concerning thos verſes, as if himſelf had been the auther thereof; thervppō this examinant redd them, & condemned them & wth deep pteſtations affirmed that they were not made by him, nor did he knowe who made them, or had euer ſeen or herd them
15 before, & the like pteſtations he nowe maketh vppō his chriſtianity & hope of ſalvation / he ſaith he took noe coppy of them, nor eu͠ had coppy of them; he ſaith he hath herd of them ſince, but eu͠ wth deteſtation / he being further aſked wheatħ he doth knowe who made or hath herd who made thē, he awnſwereth he doth
20 not knowe, but he hath herd by commō fame that one mr Townleye ſhould make them, but he pfeſſeth truly that he cann not name any one ſinguler pſon who hath ſoe reported it / Being aſked of what quality that mr Townly is, he ſaith his name is zouch Townlye, he is a ſcholler and a diuine by pfeſſion & a
25 preacher / but wher he liveth or abideth he knoweth not, but he is a ſtudient of Chriſtͤ church in oxford / Being further aſked wheatħ he gaue a dagger to the ſaid Mr Townlye ſ & vppō what occaſion ſ & when / he awnſwereth, that on a Sunday after this examinant had herd the ſaid mr Townly preach at St Margaretͤ
30 church in weſtminſter, mr Townly taking a liking to a dagger wth

a white haft which this examinant ordinaryly wore at his girdle & was given to this examinant this examinant gaue it to him two nights aft℮, being invited by m^r Townly to fupp but w^thout any circumſtaunce & w^thout any Relation to thos or any other verſes, for this examinant is well aſſured this was foe done before he fawe 35 thes verſes, or had herd of them / And this examinant doth not remember that ſince he hath ſeen m^r Townlye /

Ben: Jonſon /

14 he *added in interline.*  21 Townleye] *The first* e *is added above the line.*  30 dagger] *The scribe began by writing* ſw[ord], *but struck it out.*  31 white] *The scribe began by writing* wy, *and carelessly altered the* y *to* h.  32 two ... ſupper *added in interline.*  33 aft℮] *The scribe has written* ℮ *for* ᵉ).  37 ſince] *The scribe added a second* that *and struck it out.*

Zouch Townley was a personal friend of Jonson's, and twice wrote verses in his honour. He replied to Alexander Gill's verse attack on *The Magnetic Lady* with a poem beginning,

It cannot moue thy friend firm Ben that he
Whom the Star-chamber censured, rayles at thee.

He also prefixed a tribute to the 1640 edition in octavo of the *Ars Poetica* & some of the minor poems. It is interesting that Cotton's circle mistook the eulogy on Felton for a poem of Jonson's. Townley escaped the consequences of writing a more spirited poem than was usual with him by flying to Holland. The following text of the poem is taken from Sloane MS. 826, foll. 192-193 verso:

### To his confined ffriend M^r ffelton.

Enioy thy Bondage; make thy Prison know
Thou haſt a Libertie thou canſt not owe
To those base Punishments; keep't entire, ſince
Noething but guilt shackles the Conscience.
I dare not tempt thy valient blood to whay,                     5
Enfeebling it with pittie, nor dare pray
Thy Act may mercy finde, leaſt thy great Storie
Looſe somewhat of its Miracle and Glorie.
I wish thy Meritt, labour'd Crueltie;
Stout Vengeance beſt befittes thy Memorie:                    10
ffor I would haue Posteritie to heare,
Hee that can brauely doe, can brauely beare.
Tortures may ſeeme great in a Cowards Eye.
'Tis noe great thing to ſuffer, leſſe to die.
Should all the Cloudes fall out, and in that ſtrife            15
Light'ning and thunder send to take my life;
I would applaude the wiſedome of my ffate,
Which knew to valew mee at such a rate,
As at my ffall to trouble all the skie,
Emptying upon mee Ioues full armorie.                          20
Serue in your sharpeſt Miſcheifes: Vſe yo^r Rack;
Enlarge each Ioynt, and make each sinew crack:

# 244 *Legal and Official Documents*

Thy soule before was streightned, Thanke thy doome,
To shew her vertue shee hath larger roome.
25 Yet, sure, if every arterie were broke,
Thou wouldst finde strength for such another stroke.
And now I leaue thee unto Death and ffame,
Which liues, to shake Ambition with thy Name:
And if it were not sinne, the Court by it
30 Should hourely sweare before the ffavourite.
Farewell: ffor thy braue sake wee shall not send
Henceforth Commaunders Enemies to defend:
Nor will it euer our iust Monarch please
To keep an Admirall to loose our Seas.
35 ffarewell: Vndaunted stand, and ioy to bee
Of publique sorrow the Epitomie.
Let the Dukes Name solace and crowne thy thrall:
All wee by him did suffer, Thou for all.
And I dare boldlie write, as thou dar'st dye,
40 Stout ffelton, Englands Ransome, heere doth lye.

In l. 6 the MS. reads 'to pittie': 'with pittie' is the reading of the printed text in *Wit Restor'd*, and of five British Museum MSS.

The record of this examination was first printed in *The Athenæum* of December 3, 1859, in an article entitled 'New Facts about Ben Jonson'. The 'Facts' were set off with a display of reckless conjecture. It was suggested that Jonson 'may' have been part author of Townley's poem: 'it will be doing no violence to Jonson's habits of association and composition to imagine that, where he confesses to have given the dagger, he may also have lent weight and point to the line.' But, 'finding his sack and pension in peril', he drew back & implicated Townley. Buckingham, of course, was one of Jonson's patrons.

## XIV

### GRANT FROM THE DEAN & CHAPTER OF WESTMINSTER TO JONSON IN HIS SICKNESS, 1629

From Westminster Abbey Muniment 34163, fol. 44.

Jan. 19. 1628 Given by D<sup>r</sup> Price to M<sup>r</sup> Beniamin Ihonfon in his ficknes & want; w<sup>th</sup> Confent of
this I fent to D<sup>r</sup> D<sup>r</sup> Price D<sup>r</sup> Sutton D<sup>r</sup> Grant D<sup>r</sup> Holt D<sup>r</sup>
Price Februarij. 24. Darell, & my Lord of Lincolns good ⎫
by Tho. Bufh— likinge fignified by M<sup>r</sup> Ofbalfton ——— ⎬ 5<sup>li</sup>.
⎭

The above is from a paper manuscript of memoranda of the Treasurer's payments. The entry was first printed by Dr. H. C. Beeching in the *Times Literary Supplement* of January 6, 1905, with explanatory comment: 'My Lord of Lincoln' was Bishop Williams, who was also Dean of Westminster. Dr. Price was Williams's sub-dean. Dr. Sutton was author of a devotional book, *Disce Mori*, reprinted by Newman. Lambert Osbalston was Master of Westminster School; he was made a prebendary later in the year after Sutton's death. He was cited before the Star-chamber for calling Laud, in a letter to Williams, 'the little meddling hocus-pocus', and was the only prebendary of the abbey who took the Solemn League and Covenant. Thomas Bush was a bell-ringer. Dr. Beeching noted: 'The resolution seems to have been adopted in this irregular manner because only five prebendaries were at hand, and six were required to make a Chapter. One would like to know why Dr. Newell, the Treasurer, does not record his own consent.'

Jonson had written in 1626 a tribute to Williams on his being deprived of the office of Lord Keeper (*Und.* lxi). He wrote in 1629 an epigram 'To K. Charles for a 100. pounds he sent me in my sicknesse' (*Und.* lxii).

## XV

### JONSON'S PATENT OF 1630 FOR AN INCREASED PENSION

From the original Warrant, signed by the King, in Rawlinson MS. A 289, fol. 12, of the Bodleian Library.

### Charles R.

Charles by the grace of God Kinge of England Scotland ffraunce & Ireland defendor of the fayth etc To the Threr Chauncellor vnderthrēr Chamblens & Barons of the Exchequer of vs or heires & succrs now beinge & that hereafter ſhalbe & to all other the officers & miniſters of the ſaid Court & of the Receipt 5 there now beinge & that hereafter ſhalbe & to all others to whom these pᵍſentᵉ ſhall come or to whom it ſhall or may appteyne Greetinge. Whereas or late moſt deare father King Iames of happy memorie by his Lreꝫ patentᵉ vnder the Great ſeale of England bearinge date at Weſtmr the firſt day of ffebruary in the 10 thirteenth yeare of his raigne of England (for the confideraconꝫ therein expreſſed) did give & graunt vnto or welbeloved fervaunt Beniamin Iohnſon one añuitie or yearly pencoñ of one hundred markᵉ of lawfull money of England during his life to be paid out of the ſaid Excheqr at the feaſtᵉ of th'añūtiacoñ of the 15 bleſſed virgin Mary, the Nativitie of St Iohn Baptiſt, St Michaell th'archangell & the birth of or Lord God quarterly As by the ſd Lreꝫ patentᵉ more at large may appeare. Which aūuitye or pencoñ together with the ſaid Lreꝫ patentᵉ the ſaid Beniamin Iohnſon hath lately furrendred vnto vs. Knowe yee now 20 that wee for di͠us good confideracõns vs at this p⁹fent efpecially movinge & in confideracoñ of the good & acceptable fervice done vnto vs & oʳ faid fathʳ by the faid Beniamin Iohnfon & efpecially to encourage him to ꝓcede in thofe fervices of his witt & penn which wee haue enioyned vnto him & wᶜʰ wee expect from him are gratioufly pleafed to augment & increafe the faid annuitie or pencoñ of one hundred markę vnto an annuitie of one hundred poundę of lawfull money of England for his life. And for the better effecting thereof of oʳ efpeciall grace certen knowledge & meere mocoñ wee haue given & graunted & by thefe p⁹fentę for vs oʳ heires & fucceffors vpon the furrender of the annuitie aforefaid do give & graunt vnto the faid Beniamin Iohnfon one Annuitie or yearly pencoñ of one hundred poundę of lawfull money of England by the yeare. To haue hold & yearly to receive the faid annuitie or yearly pencoñ of one hundred poundę of lawfull money of England by the yeare vnto the faid Beniamin Iohnfon and his affignes from the feaft of the Birth of oʳ Lord God laft paft before the date hereof for & duringe the naturall life of him the faid Beniamin Iohnfon at the receipte of th' excheqʳ of vs oʳ heires and fucceffoʳˢ out of the Treafure of vs oʳ heires & fucceffoʳˢ from time to time there remayninge by the handę of the Thrēr & Chamꞗlens of vs oʳ heires & fucceffoʳˢ there for the time beinge at the forefaid foure vfuall Termes of the yeare (that is to fay) at the feaftę of Th'an͠utiacoñ of the bleffed virgin Mary the Nativitie of Sᵗ Iohn Baptift, Sᵗ Michaell th'archangell & the birth of oʳ Lord God by even & equall porc͠ons quarterly to be paid. The firft payment thereof to beginn at the feaft of Th'an͠utiacoñ of the bleffed virgin Mary next before the date of thefe p⁹fentę. Wherefore oʳ will & pleafure is. And wee do by thefe p⁹fentę for vs oʳ heires & fucceffors require cōmaund & authorife the fd̄ Thrēr̄ Chauncelloʳ Vnderthrēr̄ Chamꞗlens & Barons & other officers & minifters of the faid Exchequer now & for the time beinge not only to paie or caufe to be paide vnto the faid Beniamin Iohnfon or his afsignes the faid an͠uitie or yearly pencoñ of one hundred poundę of lawfull money of England accordinge to oʳ pleafure before expreffed but alfo from time to time to giue full allowaunce of the fame accordinge to the true meaninge of theis p⁹fentę. And theis pn̄tę or th'inrollment thereof fhalbe vnto all men whom it

# Patent for an Increased Pension

shall concerne a sufficient warrant & discharge for the payinge and allowinge of the same accordingly without any further or other warrant to be in that behalf pcured or obteyned. And further knowe yee that wee of o$^r$ more especiall grace certen knowledge & meere mocoñ have given & graunted & by these p9sentᶜ for vs o$^r$ heires & successors do giue and graunt vnto the said Beniamin Iohnson & his assignes one Terse of Canary Spanish wyne yearly  To haue hold pceive receive & take the said Terse of Canary spanish wyne vnto the sd Beniamin Iohnson & his assignes duringe the terme of his ñrall life out of o$^r$ store of wynes yearly & from tyme to tyme remayninge at or in o$^r$ Cellers within or belonginge to o$^r$ Pallace of Whitehall. And for the better effectinge of o$^r$ will & pleasure herein wee do hereby require & cōmaund all & singuler o$^r$ officers & ministers whom it shall or may concerne or who shall haue the care or charge of o$^r$ said wynes that they or some of them doe deliver or cause to be deliūed the said Terse of wyne yearly & once in every yeare vnto the sd Beniamin Iohnson or his assignes duringe the terme of his ñrall life at such time & times as he or they shall demaund or desire the same.  And theis pñtᶜ or th'inrollment thereof shalbe vnto all men whom it shall concerne a sufficient warrant & discharge in that behalf.  Although exp$^r$sse mencoñ &c.  In witnes etc witnes etc/    Ex per Ro Heath.

Maie it please yo$^r$ most ex$^t$ Ma:$^{tie}$./

This conteyneth yo$^r$ Ma$^{tp}$ graunt vnto Beniamin Iohnson yo$^r$ Ma$^{tp}$ servaunt duringe his life of a pencoñ of 100$^{li}$ p anñ and of a Terse of Spanish wyne yearlie out of yo$^r$ Ma$^{tp}$ store remay(n)ing at Whitehall.

And is done vpon surrender of a former Lres patentᶜ graunted vnto him by yo$^r$ late royall father of a pencoñ of 100 markᶜ p anñ

Signified to be yo$^r$ Ma$^{tp}$ pleasure by the Lord Threr /

Ro Heath

This warrant was first printed by Whalley.

In Patent Roll, 6 Charles I, part 11 (Roll 2543, No. 37), is the 'inrollment' of this warrant. This is printed in Professor E. K. Broadus's *The Laureateship*, pp. 223–5. It is headed in the margin 'D pencoñ Beniamino Iohnson geñoso.' Two trivial variants, due to carelessness, are found in this text: viz.:—34. hold *om.*   67. ꝑceive receive] receive ꝑceive.

In the warrant at ll. 48-9 the engrossing clerk wrote originally 'the feaste ... next enſuing the date of theſe p9ſentꝭ'. Sir Robert Heath has corrected this to 'next before the date'. The correction is copied in the enrolment. The word 'Canary' is added in interline, ll. 66, 68.

The final note, ll. 83-92, is not in the enrolment; it is a summary for the king's own use, to save him the trouble of reading through the warrant. In place of this the enrolment, after the words 'In witnes &c.', adds: 'Witnes our selfe att Westm̃ the three and twentith day of Aprill. ꝑ b̃re de priuato sigillo &c.'

The warrant is endorsed: 'March: 1630 [a correction of 1629] Expl apud Westm<sup>r</sup> vicesĩo sexto [originally 'quinto', & next 'secundo'] die Martij Anno Rꝭ Caroli quinto ꝑ Windebank.'

The warrant is doubtless the King's answer to a poem printed in *Underwoods*, lxxvi:—

> *The humble Petition of poore* Ben.
> *To th' best of Monarchs, Masters, Men,*
>    King CHARLES.
> —Doth most humbly show it
> To your Majestie your Poët:
>    That whereas your royall *Father*
>    JAMES *the blessed*, pleas'd the rather,
>    Of his speciall grace to *Letters*,
>    To make all the MUSES debters
>    To his bountie; by extension
>    Of a free Poëtique Pension,
>    A large hundred Markes annuitie,
>    To be given me in gratuitie
>    For done service, and to come : . . . . .
>    Please your Majestie to make
>    Of your grace, for goodnesse sake,
>    Those your *Fathers Markes*, your *Pounds*.

The grant of 'one Terse of Canary Spanish wyne yearly' from the royal cellars was an additional mark of favour. Professor Broadus is probably right in referring its origin to a similar grant to Chaucer: in Speght's edition of 1602, of which Jonson possessed a copy, the list of Chaucer's rewards includes *unum dolium vini* a year for life (sig. b vi verso). There was a delay in carrying out this grant, & another poem of the *Underwoods* (lxviii), dated in the Folio 1630, is 'An Epigram, To the House-hold', beginning

> What can the cause be, when the K⟨ing⟩ hath given
>    His *Poët* Sack, the *House-hold* will not pay?

with an intimation that, if licensed by the King, he could write a poem that would turn the green cloth blue.

## XVI.
## WARRANT FOR THE ADMINISTRATION OF JONSON'S GOODS, 1637

From the Act Book of the Dean and Chapter of Westminster, No. 4, 1632–44. The second entry under the date 'Vicesimo fecundo die mensis Augusti Año dni 1637', fol. 53.

Beniamini Iohnſon Adčo:
Die et Año predco per venłem virum Iohannem Exton legū dtorēm Surrū &c conceſſa fuit Adcō omnī et ſinguloȓ bonoȓ Beniamini Iohnſon nuper Citē weſtmɼij abinteſtaȓ (vt dicitur defuncȓ, wittimo Scandret vni Credīt dēi defuncȓ, de bene &c in debita iuris forma prius iuraȓ ſaluo iure Cuiuſcumq3.

Inuiū extum viij$^l$. viij$^s$. x$^d$. 5

The existence of this document was first announced in *A Calendar of Grants of Probate and Administration and of other Testamentary Records of the Commissary Court of Westminster*, 1864, p. xviii, by G. H. Rodman, who noted that the Calendar contains the names of Skelton, Camden, Jonson, and Titus Oates.

In l. 3 Surrū = Surrogatum. In l. 6 the bracket is omitted after 'dicitur': 'alleged to be intestate'.

The note in the right-hand margin means 'Inuentorium exhibitum'. According to Mr. Gordon Goodwin, writing on the subject in *Notes and Queries*, Series x, iii, p. 125, the inventory is still in existence.

# APPENDIX IV

## BOOKS IN JONSON'S LIBRARY

These volumes are mainly concerned with Jonson as dramatist, poet, and critic: we may here turn aside for a moment to consider him as a book-collector. There is ample proof that the twenty pounds Lord Pembroke gave him every New Year's Day to buy books were carefully spent. Jonson's library was an arsenal of learning. It impressed contemporaries, some of whom show us pleasant glimpses of it. Selden is a witness of weight, and he has twice recorded his appreciation. In the preface to the first edition of his *Titles of Honor*, 1614, he comments on some popular misconceptions which he has corrected:

> *As in diuers like that of* Crowns *and* Diadems, *which all haue hitherto taught to haue been mongst* Royall Notes *most anciently in* Europe. *I presume I haue sufficiently manifested the contrarie, and answerd their vrged Autorities, producing also one out of* Euripides *his* Orestes, *seeming stranger* [read *stronger*] *against my part then anie other: which, when I was to vse, and hauing not at hand the Scholiast* (*out of whom I hoped some aid*) *I went, for this purpose, to see it in the well-furnisht Librarie of my beloued friend that singular Poet M.* Ben: Ionson, *whose speciall Worth in Literature, accurat Iudgment, and Performance, known only to that* Few *which are truly able to know him, hath had from me, euer since I began to learn, an increasing admiration. Hauing examin'd it with him, I resolud vpon my first Opinion,...*

Again, in a letter 'To my honoured and truly worthy Friend Mr. Ben. Johnson' dealing with another misconception—the Puritan citation of Deuteronomy xxii. 5 as God's veto upon an actor wearing female dress—Selden reinterprets the verse, with a mass of Rabbinical and other lore to support him, and ends the letter thus:

> In the connexion of these no vulgar observations, if they had been to the common learned reader, there had been often room for divers pieces of *European* theology, dispers'd in *Latin* and *Greek* authors of the *Gentiles* and fathers of the church too, and often for parts of mythology; but your own most choice and able store, cannot but furnish you incidently with whatever is fit that way to be thought of in the reading (*Opera Omnia*, ed. Wilkins, 1726, vol. ii, tom. ii, 1696).

# Books in Jonson's Library 251

'Barten Holyday, D. D. and late Arch-Deacon of Oxon.,' whose translation of Juvenal and Persius was published in 1673 after his death, was another learned borrower. He acknowledges the help Selden had given him in procuring a manuscript and Camden in lending a commentary. 'My dear friend, the Patriarch of our Poets, *Ben. Johnson* sent-in also an ancient Manuscript partly written in the *Saxon* Character.' '*Corpus-Christi* & *Ben. Jonson's Manuscripts*' are cited on pages 274 and 277. Probably this is the fifteenth-century manuscript of Juvenal's *Satires* and Horace's *Ars Poetica* now in the Library of St. John's College, Oxford, 'Saxon' being a generic term for any form of older handwriting.[1]

We print a list of Jonson's books which we have succeeded in tracing;[2] each work is authenticated, usually from a library or from a sale catalogue. A supplementary list will appear in the final volume should there be occasion for one. The present list could be swelled by a resort to conjecture. It would be easy to trace in Jonson's text his borrowings from older writers. The author of the *Discoveries* had, in his own phrase to Drummond, not only read but digested Quintilian; for the well-known lyric 'Drink to me only with thine eyes' he culled scattered flowers from Philostratus and wove them into a garland in the style and spirit of the Greek Anthology; the horse-dealer of *Bartholomew Fair* speaks a language largely derived from Gervase Markham's works on farriery; and the hunting technicalities of *The Sad Shepherd* are taken, not always intelligently, from Turbervile. But it will be a sufficient illustration of the width and thoroughness of Jonson's reading if we present the evidence which he volunteered in his own marginal notes to *Sejanus* and *The Masque of Queens*. He annotated both of these compositions relentlessly.

The notes on *Sejanus* are found only in the Quarto of 1605. In a prefatory address 'To the Readers' (¶ 2 verso) he referred to his main authorities thus:

---

[1] The readings noted are those of the manuscript: in *Satire* xv. 27 'Consule Junio (where 'Junio' is supplied in a later hand), and 174 'et ventris indulsit non esse legumen', which Holyday translates 'Nor could his belly some course Pulse obtain'.

[2] We acknowledge our indebtedness to two previous lists: W. C. Hazlitt's list of Jonson's books in *Contributions towards a Dictionary of Book Collectors*, part xiii, pp. 3, 4, and Mr. Robert W. Ramsey's paper on 'Books from the Library of Ben Jonson' contributed to the *Transactions of the Royal Society of Literature*, vol. xxvii, 1897, pp. 139–53, with a supplementary note, pp. 155–7.

I haue quoted the Page, to name what Editions I follow'd. *Tacit. Lips.* in 4º. *Antuerp. edit.* 600. *Dio. Folio. Hen. Step.* 92. For the rest, as Sueton. Seneca. &c. the Chapter doth sufficiently direct, or the edition is not varied.

For his archaeology he depended on the following authorities:

Guillaume Budé, *De asse et partibus eius*, 1522.
Barnabé Brisson, *De formulis et sollemnibus populi Romani verbis*, 1592.
Rhodiginus Caelius, *Lectiones antiquae*, 1517.
Pompeius Festus, *De verborum significatione.*
Lilius Gregorius Gyraldus, *Historiae deorum gentilium syntagma* in vol. i of his collected Works, 1580.
Onuphrius Panvinius, *Reipublicae Romanae Commentarii*, 1588.
Angelus Politianus, *Miscellanea*, 1489.
Johannes Rosinus, *Romanae antiquitates*, 1583.
Johannes Gulielmus Stuckius, *Sacrorum, sacrificiorumque gentilium descriptio*, 1598.
Adrianus Turnebus, *Adversaria*, 1581.

The Turnebus is recorded below; it is the only one of these books that we have traced.

Similarly the elaborate notes to *The Masque of Queens* show his close study of the literature of witchcraft. 'It hath prou'd a worke of some difficulty to me', he writes in the dedication of the Quarto to Prince Henry, 'to retriue the particular *Authorities*', but he did so because the Prince had commanded him to track them out. First he drew upon the classics—the Canidia epode of Horace, the Medea incantation in Ovid, Erichtho in Lucan; with incidental references to Seneca, Apuleius, Philostratus, Josephus, and Eusebius. Then he consulted the later experts, and especially the authorities of the Roman Church, of which he was then a member. A great stand-by was the *Malleorum Quorundam Maleficarum, tam veterum quàm recentiorum authorum, tomi duo*, published at Frankfort in 1582 and 1588. He must have possessed a copy. He used the two tracts of the first volume—*Malleus maleficarum Fr. Iacobi Sprenger, and Fr. Henrici Institoris Inquisitorum, et Fr. Ioannis Nider Theologiæ Professoris Liber vnus Formicarij, qui tractat de Maleficis & eorum deceptionibus.* In the second volume he made use of the seventh author *R. P. F. Bartholomæi de Spina, Ord. Præd. Sacri Palatij Apostolici Magistri quæstio de Strigibus seu Maleficis,* and also his *Apologia quadruplex de Lamijs : contra Io. Franciscum Ponzinibium, V. I. D.* Another book of which Jonson made much use is **Martinus Delrio's** *Disquisitiones Magicæ*, published in two volumes at Louvain in 1599 and 1600. A list is added of other works, with the date of the earliest edition or the earliest Latin translation contained in Bodley :

Cornelius Agrippa, *De occulta Philosophia*, 1531.
Jean Bodin, *De Magorum dæmonomania*, 1581.
Philippus Ludwigus Elich, *Dæmonomagia*, 1607.
Johannes Georgius Godelmannus, *De Magis, Veneficis, et Lamiis*, 1594.
Paracelsus, *De occulta Philosophia*.
Porphyrius of Tyre, *De Sacrificiis et Diis atque Dæmonibus*, 1552.
Johannes Baptista Porta, *Magia Naturalis*, 1562.
Michael Psellus, *De Dæmonibus*, 1577.
Nicholas Remy, *Dæmonolatria*, 1595.

And, of course, we must add King James the First's *Dæmonologia*. Jonson quotes it only once, but a reference to it was tactful.

Sometimes Jonson annotated his books. In view of his censure of Daniel as 'no poet', it would be diverting to examine his copy of *The Ciuile Warres*, 1602, with the text scored and annotated in Greek and Latin. His copy of Scriverius' *Martial*, 1619, shows what we might expect. Jonson was a keen lover of Martial. On page 9 he falls foul of Lilius Gregorius Gyraldus, who is quoted as saying of this poet: 'ex toto eius libro quædam, nec plurima seligerem, bonorum digna lectione, quibus libellum non hercule maximum conficerem : reliqua, quod & ipse ait, scombris & siluris involucra relinquerem.' Jonson comments: 'ô asininè dictū !' On page 10 he annotates a comparative estimate by Muretus of Catullus and Martial. 'Inter Martialis autem & Catulli scripta tantum interesse arbitrer, quantum inter dicta scurræ alicuius de trivio, & inter liberales ingenui hominis iocos, multo urbanitatis aspersos sale': Catullus, he concludes, writes purer Latin. Jonson reproaches him: 'durè, durè, mi Murete, et false.' But the keenest of these side-shafts are levelled at contemporaries. Martial's epigram to the Emperor (iv. 27)—

> Saepe meos laudare soles, Auguste, libellos,
>    Invidus ecce negat : num minus ergo soles ?
> Quid quod honorato non sola voce dedisti
>    Non alius poterat quae dare dona mihi ?
> Ecce iterum nigros corrodit lividus ungues.
>    Da, Caesar, tanto tu magis ut doleat—

is underlined throughout; an index finger points to it in the margin; and against the second line is written the name 'Inigo'. Nowhere perhaps has Jonson indicated so characteristically his attitude to his collaborator.

The epigram 'Ad Cinnam' (i. 89) has another of these personal allusions, though it is veiled in the obscurity of a foreign language:

> Garris *in aurem* semper omnibus, Cinna,
> Garris et illud teste quod licet turba.
> Rides *in aurem*, quereris, arguis, ploras,
> Cantas *in aurem*, iudicas, taces, clamas,
> Adeoque penitus sedit hic tibi morbus,
> Ut saepe *in aurem*, Cinna, Caesarem laudes.

The repeated phrase 'in aurem' is underlined, with a side-note 'S$^r$ T. M$\nu\sigma$.' This was probably Sir Thomas Monson, master of the armoury at the Tower, who was involved in the Overbury murder, and imprisoned for three years till he was allowed to clear himself in 1617. His troubles may have made him cautious. Was he, one wonders, one of the 'Ripe statesmen' derided in Jonson's ninety-second epigram, who

> talke reseru'd, lock'd vp, and full of feare,
> Nay, aske you, how the day goes, in your eare.
> Keepe a *starre*-chamber sentence close, twelue dayes:
> And whisper what a Proclamation sayes?

Often a mere underlining is suggestive. It indicates sometimes a passage which Jonson has transferred to his note-books as literary quarry, or a sentiment which keenly appealed to him. In his copy of Bernardino Partenio's *Horace* in Cambridge University Library he has underlined a sentence of the introduction: 'Poeta non scribit multitudini, excellentissimis tantum ingenijs placere vult.' Even more striking is the folio Sallust in the library of Clare College, Cambridge, with the historical data both in the text and in the commentaries, upon which he drew for his *Catiline*, carefully marked in the margin. The pages of the *Jugurthine War*, on the other hand, are quite unmarked.

Sometimes the notes give clear indication of Jonson's study in a new field. His copy of Arcerius' *Aelian* (Leyden, 1613), now in the Cambridge University Library, is heavily annotated with English equivalents of the Greek military terms and with corrections of the Latin rendering of them: $\dot{\alpha}\pi\grave{o}\ \tau\hat{\omega}\nu\ \dot{\alpha}\rho\mu\acute{\alpha}\tau\omega\nu$, at the foot of page 14, is translated 'in cornubus'. Jonson is shocked and annotates '*Currubus*: vid. errorem D.V. in traductione'. On page 50 he corrects 'systema' and 'stichus' as renderings of σύστρεμμα and στῖφος. On page 11, where Aelian quotes Homer's praise of Menestheus as a tactician—

> τῷ δ' οὔτις μὲν ὅμοιος ἐπιχθόνιος γένετ' ἀνὴρ
> κοσμῆσαι ἵππους τε, καὶ ἀνέρας ἀσπιδιώτας·—[1]

Jonson quotes a very interesting rendering:

> In ordring troopes of horse, & foot
> none could with him contend:
> Nor range them into better formẽs,
> to hurt, or to defend.
>
> Sr E. V.

Chapman's rendering in the *Seauen bookes* of the Iliad (1598, p. 36) is

For Horsemen and for Targatiers, none could with him compare:
Nor put them into better place, to hurt or to defend.

Is 'Sr E. V.' Sir Edward Vere? and is he retouching Chapman's version?

The most curious of these annotated texts is Mr. Sydney Cockerell's copy of the Amsterdam *Lucretius* of 1620. Jonson read this poet with great care, marking the text and giving a few references to Lactantius. Probably Jonson was late in reading him, for we have not traced in the plays or poems any direct borrowings from Lucretius, and by 1620, of course, Jonson had written most of his plays. On the fly-leaf opposite the title-page Jonson copies out Ovid's two references to Lucretius (*Amores*, i. 15. 23-4, *Tristia*, ii. 425-6); the first of these he had translated in the opening scene of *Poetaster*. On page 4 he translates in a vigorous couplet two lines describing the gods of Epicurus:

> Far above grief & dangers, those blest powers,
> Rich in their active goods, need none of ours.[2]

On page 156 he quotes Sir George Sandys's rendering of the lines about Avernus.[3] But the most interesting insertion is

---

[1] *Iliad* ii. 553-4.
[2] *De Rerum Nat.* ii. 649-50:
> Nam privata dolore omni, privata periclis,
> ipsa suis pollens opibus, nil indiga nostri.
[3] Ibid. vi. 740 foll.

on the leaf pasted down on the back cover and unfortunately mutilated. It is a satire in Latin riming verse on the Puritans.

> Surge Muſa
> nō confuſa
> nō est labor ſanus
> dic percitè
> & politè
> Quid fit Puritan⁹
>
> Vafer van⁹
> nunqū plan⁹
> gaudet in obſcuris
> nil in ſcholis
> ſed in ſolis
> Garrulat scripturis
>
> Semet præbet
> qd̄ non debet
> tollit magistratū
> cae⟨nam⟩ vorans
> unquā plorans
> precib⁹ ingratū
>
> albu⟨m⟩ nolens
> & non ⟨vo⟩lens [1]
> philtrā angularē
> sed . . . . . llū
> form . . . . . .
> jungit . . . . . .

How came this cheery doggerel to be written as an epilogue to a text of Lucretius? Is it Jonson's?

The sentiment is Jonsonian, especially in the third stanza. *Semet præbet*, 'he offers *himself*', 'he puts *himself forward*—the emphasis falls on *Semet*—usurping the place of the magistrate, *quod non debet*—a wrong and indecent proceeding. *Tollit magistratum*, like Deacon Ananias in *The Alchemist*, who exclaims when a proposal to coin money is made to him and a timid colleague questions the legality of coining—'Lawfull? We know no Magistrate.'[2] And in the Latin comment on the Puritan which is embedded in the *Discoveries*, Jonson himself states, 'Puritanus Hypocrita est Hæreticus... phreneticè pugnat contra Magistratus, sic ratus obedientiam præstare Deo'.

---

[1] Or possibly 'colens'.   [2] *Alchemist*, III. ii. 149-50.

>       Caenam vorans,
>       unquam plorans
>       precibus ingratum—

*unquam* for *semper*—' ever whining unthankfully in his prayers '—is a solecism which Jonson should have avoided himself or repressed in his most censorious manner if committed by another. But the Puritan type here depicted—'ravenous while the meal lasts, but saying no grace *after* it'—had been elaborated in *Bartholomew Fair*, and the gibe is Jonsonian. When Zeal-of-the-land Busy, after gorging on roast pig, is moved in spirit to testify against the enormities and idolatries of the fair, a bystander comments, 'An excellent right Hypocrite! now his belly is full, he falls a railing and kicking, the Iade ... two and a halfe ⟨pigs⟩ he eate to his share. And he has drunke a pailefull'.[1]

In the last stanza the first word must be 'album': a slight curve at the end of 'albu' may be meant for a contraction mark, but it is extremely doubtful. 'Rejecting the surplice and equally rejecting the square cap' appears to be the interpretation; but *philtram* (feminine) is another solecism. Ducange has the neuter *philtrum* as a by-form of *feltrum* ('felt'), and Jonson has 'a felt of rugg' for a cap in *The Alchemist*, I. i. 36. The last three lines are beyond cure, but a neat suggestion which has been made to us for the concluding rhyme is *circularem* in reference to the 'round' head of the Puritan.

How came the grave scholar-poet to put such a piece as this in a copy of the *De Rerum Natura*? Clearly it was not a composition of the study. But it may well have been an improvisation at the Mermaid or the Devil either by Jonson himself or, more probably, by a joint effort of the 'Covey of Wits' over their wine.[2]

---

[1] *Bartholomew Fair*, III. vi.
[2] Compare the Latin macaronic verses entitled *Conuiuium Philosophicum*, describing a supper of wits at the Mitre on September 2nd, 1611, and preserved among the *Domestic State Papers*, James I, lxvi. 2. It begins:

>       Quilibet si sit contentus
>       vt statutus, stet conventus
>           Sicut nos promisimus:
>       Signum mitræ erit locus,
>       erit cibus, erit iocus
>           optimotatissimus.

The guests are enumerated in comic rhymes: Christopher Brooke, for example, and John Donne appear as

>       Christopherus vocatus Torrens
>       et Johannes Factus.

       Surge Musa
       non confusa—

the Muse is pointedly asked to steady herself for a rapid effort—
'dic percitè'; the piece so composed had associations which
made Jonson anxious to preserve it; and he had recourse to the
blank leaves of—we may suppose—the only book he was carrying
in his pocket at the moment. Some corrosive ink has been
spilled over the title-page, and Mr. Cockerell suggests that this
also was an accident at the tavern.

 The history of one of Jonson's books can be traced even before
it reached his shelves, and from that time onward to its present
resting-place. It is John Davis's Welsh Grammar, which was
a present from James Howell. A whole letter of the *Epistolæ
Ho-Elianæ*, 1645 (section 5, xxvii, pp. 31-2), is devoted to it.

     *To Mr.* Ben. Iohnson.

F ATHER BEN, you desired me lately to procure you Dr.
 *Davies* Welsh Grammer to add to those many you have, I
have lighted upon one at last, and I am glad I have it in so
seasonable a time that it may serve for a New-years gift, in which
quality, I send it you; and because 'twas not you, but your *Muse*
that desir'd it of me, for your letter runs on feet, I thought it a
good correspondence with you to accompagne it with what followes.

'What followes' is a poem of thirty-four lines, but Howell's own
copy of this to Jonson, which he inscribed in the gift-copy, is
a better text to quote. The book has the imposing title:

  *Cambrobrytannicæ Cymraecaeque Linguae Institutiones et
Rudimenta accuratè, & (quantùm fieri potuit) succinctè & compen-
diosè conscripta à Joanne Dauide Rhæso Monensi Lanuaethlæo
Cambrobrytanno, Medico Senensi: Ad Illust. virum Edouardum
Stradlingum Equestris ordinis Cambrobrytannum: Ad intelligend.
Biblia Sacra nuper in Cambrobrytannicum Sermonem & castè
& eleganter versa, non minùs necessaria quam vtilia: Cum
exacta carmina Cymraeca condendi Ratione, & Cambrobrytanni-
corum Poematum generibus, alijsquè rebus nonnullis eòdem
spectantibus, ijsdemque pariter non minùs necessarijs quàm vtilibus.*
[Device] *Londini Excudebat Thomas Orwinus. 1592.*

Coryat is to be the common butt:
    Nam facete super illum
    sicut malleus in anuillum
     vnusquisque ludet.
    Coriati, cum potabit
    Lingua regnum pererrabit
     Nec illum quicquam pudet.

# Books in Jonson's Library

On the title-page Jonson has written his motto and a record of the gift:—'*Sū Ben: Jonsonij* ex Dono *Amicisſimi D. Jacobi Howell.* / Kal. Jan cıɔ ıɔc xxxiv.' Camden prefixes a set of commendatory verses; this may have been a link with Jonson. On the fly-leaf before the title Howell has written :

Howellus Johnsonio ευηρεμειν[1]
Tempestiuè equidem (mî Johnsonî) in manus cecidit Dauisius, vt strenæ locum suppleat. Accipias eum, illo quo datur, anim⟨o⟩[2] felicissimum tibi annum exoptantem. Vale κεφαλὴ μοὶ προσφιλες ά7η & saluti consule, vt pergat amare
                                Tuum
Cal; Jan;                          Ja Howell.

## To THE poett
### Mr Beniamin Johnson
vpon dr Dauis Welsh Gramar.

T'was a tough task, beleeue it, thus to tame
a wild and wealthy language, & to frame
Gramatique toyles to curb her, so, that she
must speake by rule, & sing by prosodie.
such is the power of Art, *Rough things to shap⟨e⟩*[2]    5
*And rich inclosures, of rude Comons make*
Doubtles much oyle & labour went, to couch
into methodique rules, the rugged Dutch.
The Rabbies passe my reach, but iudg j can
ſomething of *Clenārd* and *Quintilian*    10
And for those moderne dames, I find they three
are only lopps cutt from the Latian tree
And easie twas to hewe them into parts,
The tree it self so blossoming with arts.
I haue bin shewed of *Irish*, & *Basquence*    15
Impfect rules coucht in an Accidence,
But j find none of these hath t'ane the start
of *Dauies*, or that shewes himself more man of Art,
Or that in smoother method, & short way,
the Jdiomes of a language did display.    20
This is the toung, the *Bards* sung in of old,
& Druyds their dark knowledg did vnfold,
*Merlin* in this his prophecies did vent,
wch through the world of fame beare such extent

---

[1] Evidently meaning 'good luck'; it is Howell's attempt to reproduce εὐημερεῖν.
[2] One letter is cut off in the margin.

S 2

This spoak that soñe of Mars, that Britain bold,  25
Who first mongst Christian Worthies is enrolld,
This *Brennus* when He to desire & glutt
the mistresse of the world did prostitut
This *Aruiragus*, & braue *Catarac*
sole free, when all the earth was on Romes rack  30
This *Lucius* who on Angells wings did soare
to *Rome*, & wold weare diademe no more.
And many *Heros* more, w<sup>ch</sup> shold j tell
This new yeare scarce wold serue me, so *Farewell*.

The printed version is revised with care; thus, in the reference to the Romance languages, instead of 'easie twas to hewe them into parts', Howell writes '*square* them into parts' (l. 13), and he curtailed the alexandrine in line 18 by writing 'or that proue more men of art'. In the edition of 1650 the letter is stupidly misdated 'Cal. Ap. 1629'; the year was, as Jonson's inscription shows, 1634, and the book was not a present for All Fools' Day.

Howell had had to hunt for his copy; he wrote to Jonson earlier in 1633, 'I cannot yet light upon Doctor *Davies* his Welsh Grammer, before Christmas I am promisd one' (*Epistolæ*, xvii, p. 23). After Jonson's death the book passed to Gilbert Bennett, who has written his name on the title-page. Finally Pepys acquired it, and it is now preserved in the Pepys Library at Magdalene College, Cambridge.

Many other friends and admirers must have offered similar tributes. We record gifts from Sir Kenelm Digby, William Drummond, Clement Edmondes, Edmund Gunter, Lord Herbert of Cherbury, Hadrianus Marius, Sir John Radcliffe, Selden, and Henry de Vere, Earl of Oxford; of these, Edmondes, Gunter, and Selden present copies of their own works. But we have nothing from Camden, 'the glory and light of our kingdom', to the inspiration of whose scholarship Jonson paid unstinted acknowledgement.[1] To twenty-three published works of his friends and literary acquaintances Jonson prefixed commendatory verse: he must have had copies of all these books, but we have traced only Edmondes's *Obseruations vpon Cæsar's Commentaries*, Mabbe's *Celestina*, and Selden's *Titles of Honor*. We have not found, for example, his copy of *The Faithful Shepherdess*, of Chapman's *Hesiod*, of Browne's *Pastorals*, of Drayton's *Battaile*

[1] In the opening of the King's Coronation *Entertainment* and in *Epigram* xiv.

*of Agincourt*, or of the First Folio of Shakespeare. How priceless a First Folio would be with marginal indications of the thousand lines that Shakespeare should have blotted, and an authoritative statement clearing away all doubts whether he did blot

      Cæsar did never wrong, but with just cause.

Jonson's collection had its vicissitudes. The most memorable was the fire commemorated with spirit and humour in 'An Execration upon Vulcan' (*Und.* xliii). This happened probably in or about the month of October, 1623. Ten years later Jonson narrowly escaped having another fire. Howell, in the very letter in which he expresses a hope that he will procure 'before Christmas' a copy of Davis's Welsh Grammar, concludes: 'So desiring you to look better hereafter to your charcole fyre and chymney, which I am glad to be one that preservd from burning, this being the second time that *Vulcan* hath threatned you, it may be because you have spoken ill of his wife and bin too busy with his hornes . . .'[1] It is pleasant to contemplate 'Father Ben' and 'Yo<sup>r</sup> Son, and contiguous neighbour, J. H.' plying buckets manfully and averting the catastrophe. On this occasion at any rate 'being sealed of the tribe of Ben' proved something more than a spiritual tie.

Another danger which the library ran was revealed in the frank confession to Drummond: 'Sundry tymes he hath devoured his bookes .j.[2] sold y<sup>m</sup> all for Necessity.'[3] Jonson must at such moments have waited impatiently for the dawn of New Year's Day and the renewal of Lord Pembroke's bounty.

It was Jonson's habit to inscribe his books with his motto and his name. The motto was 'Tanquam Explorator', in reference to his habits of reading. He took it from Seneca's *Epistles* (ii. 5), 'Soleo enim et in aliena castra transire, non tanquam transfuga, sed tanquam explorator'. This he wrote at the top of the title-page. Below, at a clear space in the margin—usually just above the imprint—he wrote 'Sū Ben: Jonsonij', or, if the book was large and the margin correspondingly ampler, 'Sū Ben: Jonsonij liber'. In the list printed here the books have the motto and the

---

[1] A reference to the 'Execration', ll. 6–10, 216. The letter is in *Epistolæ Ho-Elianæ*, 1645, section 5, xvii, pp. 22–3. The date is 1633.
[2] 'j' in modern usage is 'i.e.'
[3] *Conversations*, xiii. 328–9.

inscription of ownership, unless the omission is noted. Other forms of signature are possible, but only early in Jonson's life, except in a small book, such as the duodecimo *Ignoramus* in Bodley. The inscription in his copy of Puttenham's *Arte of English Poesie*, which we reproduce, is exceptional. But the signature 'Ben Johnson' in the Bodleian copy of Augustine Vincent's *A Discoverie of Errours In the first Edition of the Catalogue of Nobility, Published By Raphe Brooke, Yorke Herald*, in 1622, is not genuine. Jonson doubtless possessed a copy of the book. In *The New Inn* (II. vi. 28) he has a punning reference to a character who 'studies *Vincent* against *Yorke*', and who will 'conquer If she read *Vincent*': moreover, Vincent championed Camden against Brooke's attacks. Similarly the entry of Jonson's name on the title-page of the British Museum copy of the *Hypnerotomachia Poliphili* is a forgery. Other books excluded from the list are J. J. Scaliger's *Epistolae*, Leyden, 1627, in the Dyce Library at South Kensington, and Stephen Ritter's *Poetica Prosometria*, Frankfort, 1619, in the library of Trinity College, Cambridge. It is not possible to guarantee all the books in the following list, but as many as are accessible have been examined.

The books are classified under the seven headings of Manuscripts, The Scriptures, English Works, Greek and Roman Writers, Renaissance and Later Writers, Antiquities and Scholarship, Language and Grammar.

## MANUSCRIPTS.

Statius. *Thebais.* Now Royal MS. 15 A xxi in the British Museum, of the early thirteenth century, on vellum. It belonged to John Russell, Bishop of Lincoln (1480-94), whose autograph is on folio 1. An earlier owner's name is erased. Jonson's motto and autograph—'Sum Ben. Ionsonii liber e dono Thomæ (Strange?)'—are erased on folio 2. At the foot of folio 3 is Sir Robert Cotton's autograph. For Thomas Strange see Jonson's *Bible* in the next section.

Salomon, King of Israel. *Opus de arte magica, ab Honorio ordinatum.* A fourteenth-century manuscript, Sloane 313, in the British Museum. Jonson's motto and autograph are on folio 9. Analogous to Solomon's work on alchemy which Sir Epicure Mammon possessed (*Alch.* II. i. 82).

*Speculum Christiani.* Now MS. Hh. 1. 13 in the Cambridge University Library, of the fifteenth century, on vellum. Ascribed to John Watton in MS. civ of Corpus Christi College, Oxford. Printed by William de Machlinia, *c.* 1483.

Juvenal, *Satires*, and Horace, *Ars Poetica.* Now MS. 192 in the Library of St. John's College, Oxford, of the fifteenth century, on vellum. Inscribed 'Sum Ben: Ionsonij ex dono D. Io. Radcliffe equ: Aurati'. Favourite passages are marked. For Sir John Radcliffe see *Epigr.* xciii.

Terence. Now MS. 87 in the library of St. John's College, Oxford, of the fifteenth century, on vellum. A few corrections and glosses: e.g. *ne* is glossed 'certe', *faxo* 'faciam'.

## THE SCRIPTURES.

Bible. *Biblia Sacra Vulgatae Editionis Sixti V. P. M. jussu recognita.* Antwerp, 1599. On the back of the title-page in Jonson's autograph 'Ex dono D. Thomæ Strange, 1605, Beniamin Ionsonius. Benedicā Dominum in omni tempore, semper laus eius in ore meo—Ps. xxxiii'. (Sotheby's, 31 March, 1906.)

Psalms. *The whole Psalter translated into English Metre.* Archbishop Parker's version printed by John Day in or about 1567. Owned by Samuel Woodford, author of *A Paraphrase upon the Psalms* (1668), who wrote on the fly-leaf, 'There was written in this book, but the leaf was by accident torn out: "This is Ben Jonson's Booke. Price worth Gould".' (Hazlitt.)

## ENGLISH WORKS,

*Including Translations and Chronicles.*

Chapman, George. *Seauen Bookes of the Iliades of Homere, Prince of Poets, . . . ¶ Translated . . . by George Chapman, Gent.* London, 1598. No motto. (British Museum.)

Chaucer, Geoffrey. *The Workes of our antient and learned English poet G. Chaucer, newly printed.* T. Speght's edition, 1602. (Hazlitt.)

Cooper, Thomas (Bishop of Winchester). *An Admonition to the People of England.* London, 1589. The title-page with Jonson's autograph is in Rawlinson MS. 3 D (p. 46) of the Bodleian.

Chronicles, English. *Rerum Anglicarum Scriptores post Bedam Præcipui, ex Vetustissimus Codicibus Manuscriptis nunc primum in lucem editi.* London, 1596. William of Malmesbury, Henry Archdeacon of Huntingdon, Roger Hovenden, the Chronicle of Ethelward, Ingulf of Croydon, edited by Sir Henry Saville. Pages 1-20 annotated by Jonson, but there is neither autograph nor motto on the title-page. (The Library of the English School, Oxford University.)

Daniel, Samuel. [*The Ciuile Warres betweene the Houses of Lancaster and Yorke, in six bookes*, 1602.] No title; the text scored, and marginal notes. (Christie's, 5 December, 1906.) This must be the copy which Hazlitt noted as the *Works* of 1602, 'with many passages underscored and MSS. notes in Latin and Greek'.

Edmondes, Clement. *Obseruations vpon Cæsars Commentaries.* Collected edition, 1609. Inscribed 'Clement Edmondes commendeth himselfe to Ben: Johnson and dedicateth this booake to his Vertues and his Love to Clement Edmondes'. Jonson gave the copy away, with this inscription: 'Optimū Belli Magistrū, etiā Authorem cum doctissimis commentarijs Amici eruditiff. quem ipfe mihi, & Mufæo meo dono concefferit, & dignatus fit, In æternum pignus amoris, amicissimo, fiue potiūs amicitiæ ipfi D. Hen. Theobaldo Ben. Ionfonius æternum amicus, vouet.' See *Epigr.* cx, cxi. (British Museum.)

Greville, Fulke, Lord Brooke. *Certaine Learned and Elegant Workes.* London, 1633. (Huth Library.)

Guicciardini, Francesco. *The Historie ... conteining the Warres of Italie ... reduced into English by Geffray Fenton.* London, 1599. This copy passed to Thomas Cotton, who erased Jonson's signature. See *The Antiquary*, March, 1901, p. 89. (Sotheby's, 8 November, 1897.)

Gunter, Edmund. *The Description and Vse of his Maiesties Dials in White-hall Garden.* London, 1624. Inscribed 'Sū Ben: Ionsonj ex dono Authoris'. The dedication to the King speaks of '*these poor fruits of my younger Studies when I was Your Maiesties Scholler in* Westminster *and* Christchurch'. No motto. (British Museum.)

James VI, of Scotland. *His Maiesties Poetical Excercises at vacant Hours.* Edinburgh, 1591. (Hazlitt.)

Mabbe, James. *The Spanish Bawd represented in Celestina: or, The Tragicke-Comedy of Calisto and Melibea.* London, 1631. Autographs of Jonson and of a friend of his, Francis Cornwall. (Quaritch, 1909.)

Marston, John. *Tragedies and Comedies collected into one volume.* London, 1633. Not Jonson's actual copy, but the title-page inscribed by him has been inserted. (Dyce Library, South Kensington.)

Montaigne. *The Essayes ... of Lo: Michaell de Montaigne ... now done into English* [by John Florio]. London, 1603. Jonson's autograph has been deleted, and also his note on the price he paid for the book: 'Liber Manassis et Henrici Northondel Iunctim, emptus prætio septem solidorum Anno Domini 1604.' Some of the errata have been corrected in the text. (British Museum.)

Montemayor, Jorge de. *Diana, ... Translated out of Spanish into English by Bartholomew Yong.* London, 1598. Title-page in the possession of J. P. Collier, according to David Laing, *Notes on Ben Jonson's Conversations with William Drummond*, p. 35.

Norris, Sir John, and Sir Francis Drake. *Ephemeris Expeditionis Norreysii and Drakis in Lusitaniam.* London, 1589. (Sotheby's, 23 July, 1906).

Puttenham, George. *The Arte of English Poesie.* London, 1589. This copy contains, after p. 84, four cancelled leaves omitted in the pagination. See facsimile. (British Museum.)[1]

Selden, John. *Titles of Honor.* London, 1614. (Hazlitt.)

Spenser, Edmund. *The Faerie Queen: The Shepheards Calendar: Together with the other Works of England's Arch-Poët, Edm. Spenser: ¶ Collected into one Volume, and carefully corrected.* London, 1617. With numerous MS. notes. (Crossley's Sale, July, 1884.)

---

[1] The quotation from Heraclitus is found in Aristotle, *de Partibus Animalium*, i. 5. ἐκέλευε γὰρ αὐτοὺς εἰσιέναι θαρροῦντας· εἶναι γὰρ καὶ ἐνταῦθα θεούς. But Jonson quotes it from the epilogue to Aulus Gellius' *Noctes Atticae*, § 12, where the earliest editions substituted it for the correct reading πολυμαθίη νόον οὐ διδάσκει.

# THE ARTE
## OF ENGLISH
### POESIE.

Contriued into three Bookes: The first of Poets
and Poesie, the second of Proportion,
the third of Ornament.

AT LONDON
Printed by Richard Field, dwelling in the
black-Friers, neere Ludgate.
1589.

# IO. BAPTISTAE
## PIGNAE CARMINVM
### LIB. QVATVOR,

AD ALPHONSVM FERRARIAE
PRINCIPEM.

His adiunximus

CAELII CALCAGNINI CARM. LIB. III.
LVDOVICI AREOSTI CARM. LIB. II.

CVM PRIVILEGIO.

VENETIIS,
EX OFFICINA ERASMIANA,
VINCENTII VALGRISII.

M. D. LIII.

## GREEK AND ROMAN WRITERS.

Aelianus, Claudius. *Tactica,* . . . *Editio Nova. Operâ ac studio Sixti Arcerii.* Leyden, 1613. Carefully annotated, with glosses and corrections. See pp. 254–5. (Cambridge University Library.)

Aristaenetus. ΑΡΙΣΤΑΙΝΕΤΟΥ ΕΠΙΣΤΟΛΑΙ. *Aristaeneti Epistolae Graecae. Cum Latina interpretatione & Notis.* 3rd ed., Paris, 1610. (Emmanuel College, Cambridge.)

Aristophanes. *Comoediae Vndecim cum Scholiis Antiquis.* Edited by Odoardus Bisetus. Geneva, 1607. (Fitzwilliam Museum, Cambridge.)

Aristotle. *Opera Omnia quæ extant, Græcè & Latine. Authore Guillelmo Du Val.* Paris, 2 vols., 1619. (St. John's College, Cambridge.)

Arrianus, Porphyrius, Heliodorus, Oppianus, &c. *De Vita et Natura Animalium.* Lyons, 1533. (Hazlitt.)

Athenaeus. *Deipnosophistarum libri quindecim,* ed. J. Dalechamp, with Casaubon's notes. Lyons, 1612. Inscription erased probably by the owner who signs himself 'Henrici Jacobij 1640'. (Bodleian.)

Catullus, Tibullus, and Propertius. *Opera omnia quæ exstant. Cum variorum . . . commentariis.* Paris, 1608. 'This copy is injured by damp, and may have been a salvage from the fire.' (Hazlitt.)

*Chorus Poetarum Classicorum Duplex; Sacrorum et Profanorum Lustratus Illustratus.* Lyons, 1616, 2 vols. An expurgated text; Jonson has supplied the lacunae in the margin, which has been badly cropped by the binder. (British Museum.)

Cicero. *Opera Omnia quæ exstant. A Dionysio Lambino Monstroliensi ex codicibus manuscriptis emendata . . . Fuluii Vrsini . . . notæ.* Geneva, 1584. (Cambridge University Library.)

Diodorus Siculus. *Bibliothecae Historicae Libri XV, de XL . . . Studio & labore Laurentii Rhodomani Cherusci.* 2 vols., Hanau, 1604. (Kepier School, Houghton-le-Spring.)

Euclid. *Elements of Geometrie,* with preface by John Dee. London, 1576. (Sotheby's, 2 April, 1857.)

Eustathius. *De Ismeniæ et Ismenes Amoribus.* Paris, 1617. (Hazlitt: a copy sold at Sotheby's, March, 1895, with an extra title inserted, containing Jonson's autograph.)

Greek Dramatists and Lyrists. ΕΛΛΗΝΕΣ ΠΟΙΗΤΑΙ ΠΑΛΑΙΟΙ. ΤΡΑΓΙΚΟΙ ΛΥΡΙΚΟΙ ΚΩΜΙΚΟΙ ΕΠΙΓΡΑΜΜΑΤΟΠΟΙΟΙ. *Poetae Graeci Veteres, Tragici, Lyrici, Comici, Epigrammatarii.* Geneva, 1614. (Cambridge University Library.)

Greek Heroic Poets. ΟΙ ΤΗΣ ΗΡΩΙΚΗΣ ΠΟΙΗΣΕΩΣ ΠΑΛΑΙΟΙ ΠΟΙΗΤΑΙ ΠΑΝΤΕΣ. *Poetae Graeci Veteres Carminis Heroici Scriptores, qui extant, omnes.* Geneva, 1606. Texts of Homer, Hesiod, Orpheus, Callimachus, Aratus, Nicander, Theocritus, Moschus, Bion, Dionysius, Coluthus, Tryphiodorus, Musaeus, Theognis, Phocylides, Pythagoras, Apollonius Rhodius, Oppianus, Quintus Smyrnaeus, Nonnius. Latin version 'Cura ac recensione Iac. Lectii'. (Cambridge University Library.)

Hermes Trismegistus. *Opuscula, cum fragmentis . . . Item Asclepii Discipuli adiecta.* London, 1611. Inscription erased: 'Ex dono Honorandi Amici D. Ioannis Radcliffe Equitis Aurati.' The book passed to Selden, who has written at the top his motto περὶ παντὸς τὴν ἐλευθερίαν. For Radcliffe see above, in the Manuscript section. (Bodleian.)

Herodotus. *Historiarum Libri IX ... Cum Vallæ Interpretatione Latina ... ab Henrico Stephano recognita, & Spicilegio Friderici Sylburgii. ... Excerpta è Ctesiæ libris.* Geneva, 1618. (Cambridge University Library.)

Horace. *Bernardini Parthenii Spilimbergii in Horatii Flacci Carmina atq. Epodos Commentarii Quibus Poetae artificium, & via ad imitationem, atq. ad Poetice scribendum aperitur.* Bound up with this, *Q. Horatii Flacci Sermonum Libri quatuor, seu, Satyrarum Libri duo. Epistolarum Libri duo.* Venice, 1584. A full text of Horace with the commentary of Bernardino Partenio; much of the second part is underlined. (Cambridge University Library.)

Horace. *Blasii Bernardi, Foroliviensis, Medici, De Laudibus Vitæ Rusticæ Commentarius in secundam Oratii Odem, e libro epodon.* Florence, 1613. The text of the Epode 'Beatus ille', with Bernardus' commentary. (A. C. Swinburne's copy, sold at Sotheby's, 19 June, 1916.)

Juvenal and Persius. *D. Junii Juvenalis Satyrorum Libri V. preterea A. Flacii Persii Satyrorum Liber unus cum Commentariis Eilhardi Lubini.* Hanau, 1603. (Sir Edward Brabrook.)

Longus. *Daphnis et Chloe.* Florence, 1598. (W. A. White, Esq.)

Lucian. *Luciani Samosatensis Dialogi Octo, Marini Dialogi XV, Charon siue Contemplantes,* &c. The motto appears to have been cut off by the binder. Paris, 1530. (Hodgson's, 20 March, 1907.)

Lucretius. *De Rerum Natura.* Amsterdam, 1620. Fully described above, pp. 255-8. (S. C. Cockerell, Esq.)

Martial. *M. Val. Martialis Nova editio. Ex Museo Petri Scriverii.* Leyden, 1619. Many notes: see pp. 253-4, above.

Gruterus, Janus. *Notæ in Martialis Epigrammata.* Apparently issued as a supplementary volume to Scriverius' *Martial*; volume ii, consisting of *P. Scriverii Animadverisones* (sic) *in Martialem*, 1618; volume iii, a collection of notes by Lipsius, J. J. Scaliger, Pontanus, and Gruterus, 1619. (James Crossley: *Times Literary Supplement*, 14 August, 1919.)

Minucius Felix, Marcus. *Octavius.* Oxford, 1627. The misprints are corrected in Jonson's hand from the list of errata. (Francis Edwards, 14 November, 1908.)

Plato. ΠΛΑΤΩΝΟΣ ΑΠΑΝΤΑ ΤΑ ΣΩΖΟΜΕΝΑ. *Platonis opera quæ extant omnia. Ex noua Ioannis Serrani interpretatione, perpetuis eiusdē notis illustrata ... Excudebat Henr. Stephanus.* 3 vols., Paris, 1578. Each volume has an autograph inscription :
Vol. i. 'Ad promouenda ftudia fua. Sum Ben: Ionsonij ex dono amplissimi illustriſsq' Herois: Henrici Com: de Oxenford.'
Vol. ii. 'Ad promouenda ftudia. Donū amplissim. Herois Illustriff. Do. Henrici comitis oxoniensis exto et Ben Ionsonij liber.' At top of the page, ' 3 volumes pet. 04$^1$-00$^s$-00$^d$' This volume is dedicated to King James I.
Vol. iii. 'Ad promouēda ftudia fua. Donum ampiffimi (sic) Herois Illuftriffimiq. D. Dom. Hen. de Vere. Com. Oxonienf. Exto. Et

Ben: Ionsonij Liber.' The price is repeated at the top of the page. (Chetham Library, Machester.)

Pythagoras. *Τὰ τ͂ Πυθαγόρᾱ, σωζόμψα. Pythagorae Fragmenta, quae ad nostram aetatem pervenerunt.* Ed. Joachim Zehner. Leipzig, 1603. (Emmanuel College, Cambridge.)

Sallust. *C. Crispi Salustii Latinorum Historicorum Præstantissimi, Opera, quæ quidem extant, omnia.* With commentaries of Valla and eight others, and *Constantii Felici Durantini Historia Coniurationis Catilinariæ.* Basel, 1564. (Clare College, Cambridge.)

Stobæus, Joannes. *Dicta Poetarum, quæ apud Io. Stobæum, exstant: emendata et Latino carmine reddita ab Hugone Grotio. Accesserunt Plutarchi & Basilii Magni de usu Græcorum Poetarum libelli.* Paris, 1623. (Puttick's, 7 February, 1895.)

Suetonius. *C. Suetonii Tranquilli XII Caesares, Et in eos Laeuini Torrentii Commentarius auctior et emendatior.* Antwerp, 1578. (Cambridge University Library.)

Valerius Maximus. *Dictorum Factorumque Memorabilium Libri IX.* Antwerp, 1574. (Hazlitt.)

Virgil. *Symbolarum Libri XVII quibus P. Virgilii Maronis Bucolica, Georgica, Aeneis, ex probatissimis auctoribus declarantur, comparantur, illustrantur. Per Iacobum Pontanum de Societate Iesu.* Augsburg, 1599. The text of Virgil, interpreted by Pontanus' commentary. (Cambridge University Library.)

## RENAISSANCE AND LATER WRITERS.

Arithmaeus, Valentinus (Lignitio-Silesius). *Pericula Poetica, siue Somnia metrica tentata et repræsentata.* Frankfort, 1613. (Britwell.)

Bacon, Francis. *Francisci de Verulamio . . . Instauratio magna.* 1620. *Pars Secunda Operis quæ dicitur Novum Organum.* (Balliol College, Oxford).

Barnesius, Joannes (Benedictinus). *Dissertatio contra Æquiuocationes.* Paris, 1625. (Cambridge University Library.)

Barth, Caspar von. *Fabularum Æsopicarum Libri V. Phœnix. Psalmi XVII. Erotopægnion. Satira in Bavium. Alcæus Latinus. Elegiarum Lib. IV. Jamborum Lib. II. Lyricorum Lib. II.* Frankfort, 1623. (British Museum.)

Bolsec, Jérôme Hermès. *De Ioannis Calvini, magni quondam Genevensium ministri, vita, moribus, rebus gestis, studijs, ac denique morte Historia.* Cologne, 1580. A Latin version of a French original. Bound up with it is Columbanus Vrancx, *Malleus Calvinistarum,* Antwerp, 1590. (Cambridge University Library.)

Buchanan, George. *Rerum Scoticarum Historia.* Edinburgh, 1586. Presented by Drummond to Jonson, with autograph signatures of both: 'Ex eius Dono, Sum Ben Ionsonii.' (Sotheby's, 2 April, 1857.)

Christianovic, Stanislaus. *Examen Catholicum Edicti Anglicani, quod contra Catholicos est latum, Auctoritate Parlamenti Angliae . . . Anno Domini M.D.C.VI.* Paris, 1607. The copy has been badly cropped by the binder, who has cut off half the signature and all the motto. (Lincoln Cathedral Library.)

Erasmus, Desiderius. *Familiarium Colloquiorum opus, nunc postrema cura ab Authore recognitum.* Paris, 1527. (Sotheby's, 26 October, 1916.)

Gratius, Ortwinus. *Duo Volumina Epistolarum Obscurorum Virorum, ad D. M. Ortuinum Gratiū, Attico lepóre referta, denuò excusa & a mendis repurgata.* Frankfort?, 1557. (British Museum.)

Gruterus, Janus. *Pericula, id est; Elegiarum Libri IV. Manium Gulielmianorum Lib. I. Epigrammatum libellus. Harmosynes siue Ocellorum liber primus.* Heidelberg, 1587. (W. A. White, Esq.)

*Harangues et Actions publiques des plus Rares Esprits de nostre temps. Faictes tant aux ouuertures des Cours souueraines de ce Royaume qu'en plusieurs autres signalées occasions.* Paris, 1609. (Bodleian.)

Hornmoldus, Sabastianus. *In Crapulam pro Sobrietate; seu votum de vitanda et fugienda ebrietate ex diversis authoribus decem epigrammatum centuriis celebratum.* Basel, 1619. (British Museum.)

*Hymnorum Ecclesiasticorum, Ab Andrea Ellingero, V. Cl. emendatorum, Libri III. Accessêre Ioseph Lib. II. Autore Hieronymo Fracastorio. Et Marc. Ant. Flaminii, Hercul. Strozæ, Basilij Zanchij, & aliorum quorundam huc pertinentes Hymni.* Frankfort, 1588. (Trinity College, Cambridge.)

La Faye, Antoine de. *Emblemata et Epigrammata Miscellanea selecta ex stromatis Peripateticis A. Fayi.* Geneva, 1510. (Eton College.)

*Melanthe Fabula Pastoralis acta coram Jacobo Mag. Brit. Franc. & Hibern. Regi Cantabrigiae. Egerunt Alumni Coll. Sac. & Indiv. Trinitatis Cant.* Cambridge, 1615. (Sotheby's, 23 July, 1906.)

Mirandula, Octavian (editor). *Illustrium Poëtarum Flores, Per Octauianum Mirandulam collecti* . . . Lyons, 1579. (Purdom's Catalogue, 1923.)

Mirandula, Scipione. *Cynthia Coronata seu Serenissima Maria Austriaca Inclitissimo Principe Carolo Sole suo auricomo cincta: Augustissimo Gemino vtriusque Genio sacra.* London? 1623? No motto. (British Museum.)

Montaigne. *Essais de Messire . . . Montaigne.* 2 vols., Bordeaux, 1580. (Sabin, 1907.)

Ocland, Christopher. *Anglorum Praelia.* London, 1582. (Sotheby's, March, 1891.)

Petrarcha, Francesco. *Opera quæ extant,* ed. J. Herald. Basel, 1581. (Hodgson, 18 March, 1915.)

Pigna, Giovanni Baptista. *Carminum Libri Quatuor* together with *Caelii Calcagnini Carm. lib. iii,* and *Ludovici Areosti Carm. lib. ii.* Venice, 1553. (British Museum.)

*Poetæ tres elegantissimi emendati & aucti, Mich. Marullus, Hieron. Angerianus, Joannes Secundus.* Paris, 1582. (Dobell.)

Quercu, Leodegarius à. *Flores Epigrammatum, ex optimis quibusque authoribus.* Paris, 1560. The title-page with Jonson's autograph is in Rawlinson MS. 1387, fol. 47, of the Bodleian.

Ruggle, George. *Ignoramus. Comœdia Coram Regia Maiestate Iacobi Regis Angliæ.* London, 1630. Signature at the top of the page; no motto. (Bodleian.)

Savonarola, Girolamo. *Triumphus Crucis, sive De veritate Fidei. Libri IV. Recens in lucem editus.* Leyden, 1633. Inscribed 'Sum Ben: Ionsonij

# Books in Jonson's Library

ex dono perillustr. Equitis D. Ken. Digbæij.' (Shakespeare Birthplace, Stratford-on-Avon.)

Thomas, Paulus (Engolismensis). *Poemata.* 2nd ed., Paris, 1627. (Trinity College, Cambridge.)

Torrentius, Laevinus. *Poemata.* Antwerp, 1579. (Trinity College, Dublin.)

Vanninius, Guido. *Carminum Libri Quattuor.* Lyons, 1611. (Trinity College, Cambridge.)

Vives, Juan Luis. *Opera, in duos distincta tomos.* Basel, 1555. (St. John's College, Cambridge.)

## ANTIQUITIES AND SCHOLARSHIP

Aleander, Hieronymus (Junior). *Antiquae Tabulae Marmoreae, Solis effigie symbolisque exculptae Accurata explicatio.* Paris, 1617. (J. H. Rogers collection, Philadelphia, sold in May, 1895.)

Bellenden, William. *De Tribus Luminibus Romanorum. Libri sex-decim.* Paris, 1634. Dedicated to Charles I of England. (Cambridge University Library.)

Camerarius, Philipp. *Operæ Horarum Subsiciuarum siue Meditationes Historicæ. Centuria et Editio correctior, atque auctior, Altera.* Frankfort, 1606 (misprinted 1506). (Mitchell Library, Glasgow.)

Castalio, Josephus. *Variæ Lectiones et Opuscula quorum nomina post epistolam.* Rome, 1594. Bound with this are two other works of Castalio, *De Antiquis Puerorum Prænominibus* and *De Vergili Nominis Scribendi Recta Ratione*, with the same imprint ; and also two works not necessarily part of the original volume—*Io. Antonii Viperani De Obtenta Portugalia a Rege Catholico Philippo Historia*, Naples, 1588 (pencil-marked), and *Io. Thomae Minadoi Pro Sua de Bello Persico Historia aduersus ea Quae illi à Ioanne Leunclauio obijciuntur Disputatio*, Venice, 1595. (Cambridge University Library.)

Caussino, Nicolò. *De Symbolica Ægyptiorum Sapientia.* Cologne, 1623. (Dobell, January 1917.)

Donatus, Marcellus (Ponzani Comes). *Scholia siue Dilucidationes Eruditissimæ in Latinos plerosque Historiæ Romanæ Scriptores.* Venice, 1504. (Cambridge University Library.)

Dornavius, Caspar. *Amphitheatrum Socraticæ Joco-Seriæ, hoc est, Encomia et Commentaria Autorum, qua Veterum, qua Recentiorum, prope omnium: quibus res, aut pro vilibus vulgo aut damnosis habitæ, styli patrocinio vindicantur, exornantur.* Hanover, 1619. (Cambridge University Library.)

Gesner, Conrad. *Historia Animalium.* 4 vols., Zurich, 1555. (Hazlitt.)

Gesner, Conrad. *Mithridates. De Differentiis Linguarum tum veterum tum quæ hodie apud diuersas nationes in toto orbe terrarū in usu sunt.* Zurich, 1555. (British Museum.)

Gruterus, Janus. *Lampas siue Fax Artium Liberalium.* 5 vols., Frankfort, 1602–5. Signature preserved in vols. ii, iii, and iv, which all have marginal notes and underlinings in pencil. (W. Ashburner; and formerly M. Stapylton, James Crossley. See *Times Literary Supplement*, 10 July, 1919.)

Heinsius, Daniel. *Aristarchus Sacer, siue ad Nonni in Iohannem Metaphrasin exercitationes.* Leyden, 1627. (American Art Association, 26 January, 1922.)

Manutius, Aldus. *De Quaesitis per Epistolam Libri III. Aldi Manutii. Paulli F. Aldi N.* Venice, 1576. (Cambridge University Library.)

Marolois, Samuel. *Opera Mathematica, Geometrie, Perspective.* 3 vols., La Haye, 1614–16. The signature torn out of the first volume, fragmentary in the second, intact in the third. (Royal College of Physicians.)

Melissus, Paulus (i. e. Paul Schede). *Meletematum Libri VII, Paraeneticorum Libri II, Parodiarum Libri II, Psalmi aliquot Anno Christi MDVC recens editi.* Frankfort, 1595. (Hazlitt.)

Panciroli, Guido. *Notitia utraque Dignitatum, cum Orientis, tum Occidentis.* Lyons, 1608. With motto, autograph, and the words 'Guidus Pancirolus de notitia utraque' in Jonson's handwriting. (Star Library: Puttick's, 12 June, 1917.)

Roa, Martin de. *Singularium Locorum ac Rerum Libri V. In quibus cum ex sacris tum ex humanis litteris multa ex Gentium Hebræorumque moribus explicantur.* Cordova, 1600. Inscribed 'Ex dono Ed. Herberti Equitis Amiciss. Doctiss.' Passed to Thomas Morton, Bishop of Durham, who presented it to St. John's College. Bound up with the copy, and no doubt issued with it, is de Roa's *De Die Natali, Sacro, et profano, Liber vnus. Singularium item Locorum, liber VI.* Cordova, 1600. (St. John's College, Cambridge.)

Scaliger, Joseph Juste. *Epistola de vetustate et splendore Gentis Scaligeræ.* Leyden, 1594. (Manchester University Library.)

Scaliger, Joseph Juste. *Jos. Justi Scaligeri Julii Caesaris a Burden Filii Opuscula, varia aute hac non Edita, nunc vero multis partibus aucta.* Frankfort, 1612. Carefully marked, and a few notes: e.g. p. 282 where 'Gulielmus Gilbertus *Glocestrensis*' is corrected '*Colcestr.*' (Dyce Library.)

Selden, John. *De Diis Syris Syntagmata.* Leyden, 1629. (Puttick's, 16 February, 1898.) According to F. Cunningham in a note on the Drummond *Conversations*, ix, a copy of the 1617 edition 'with autograph and MS. notes by Ben Jonson' was in the Bright Sale.

Selden, John. *Jani Anglorum Facies Altera.* London, 1610. Inscribed 'Sū Ben: Ionsonij Liber ex dono Authoris mihi chariss'. (Sotheby's, 23 July, 1906.)

Sweertius, Franciscus. *Selectæ Christiani Orbis Deliciæ ex Vrbibus, Templis, Bibliothecis, et aliunde.* Cologne, 1625. (Quaritch, May, 1908.)

Turnebus, Adrianus. *Adversariorum Tomi III.* Basil, 1581. (J. E. Cornish, Manchester, c. 1880.)

Vossius, Gerardus Joannes. *De Historicis Græcis Libri Quatuor.* Leyden, 1624. Chapters i–v marked and slightly annotated. The copy passed to Gerard Langbaine, who also annotated it, and then to Ralph Bathurst, who gave it in 1659 to Trinity College, Oxford.

Wower, Joan à. *De Polymathia Tractatio.* Presentation copy to Jonson, 'Eruditissimo viro B. Jonsonio D. D. Hadrianus Marius'. Basel, 1603. No motto. (British Museum.)

## LANGUAGE AND GRAMMAR.

Amerotius, Hadrianus. *Compendium Graecæ Grammaticæ.* Louvain, 1520. (Corpus Christi College, Cambridge.)

Beumlerus, Marcus. *Nova Latinae Linguae Grammatica.* Zurich, 1595. Title-page recorded as surviving in *Notes and Queries*, 1865, 3rd series, viii, p. 403.

Davis, John. *Cambrobrytannicæ Cymraecaeque Linguae Institutiones et Rudimenta.* London, 1592. Fully described above, pp. 258–60. (Magdalene College, Cambridge.)

Friderus, Petrus. *De Lingua Latina Opus Absolutum: Quo nova planè, diùque desideratâ methodo, vera Latinitatis ratio atque usus, praeceptis paucissimis & explicatissimis perfectissimé docetur. Opus Grammaticum, ut exiguum, ita omnibus Scholis utilissimum.* Basel, 1592. (Old Town Library, Leicester.)

Geneva Greek Grammar. *Graecae Grammatices in usum Genevensis Scholae perscriptae pars prima.* Geneva, 1568, 'Apud Ioannem Durantium'. The title-page was sold as a part of a collection of autographs at Messrs. Hodgson's, 7 February, 1923.

Lily, William, and Erasmus, Desiderius. *De octo orationis partium constructione libellus, a Guil. Lillo, emendatus ab Erasmo.* London, 1540. (Cottrell-Dormer Library, sold at Sotheby's, October, 1924.)

Linacre, Thomas. *Thomae Linacri Britanni de emendata structura Latini sermonis libri VI. . . . recogniti a Ioachimo Camerario Pabepergensi . . . Accessit libellus eiusdem Camerarij de arte Grammatica & figuris dictionum.* Leipzig, 1556. On the title-page, after Jonson's signature, there follows a pedigree of owners. The second owner records himself: 'Sum Leonardi Darei. An: 1632,' and he has also appended the date 1620 to Jonson's own signature. There is no record of this transfer being a gift: did Jonson sell the book? (T. Loveday, Esq.)

סֵפֶר הַשָּׁרָשִׁים עִם הַנִּגְזָרִים. *Dictionarium Hebraicum, ultimo ab autore Sebastiano Munstero recognitum, et ex Rabinis, praesertim ex Radicibus Dauid Kimhi, auctum et locupletatum.* Basel, 1564. (Messrs. J. and J. Leighton, 1921.)

# INTRODUCTION TO
# 'A TALE OF A TUB'

# A TALE OF A TUB

*A Tale of a Tub* has come down to us only in the second Folio (1631–40), where it occupies the last place among the completed plays. It was licensed for Queen Henrietta's Men on May 7, 1633, and probably performed by them at The Cockpit in the course of that year; but the only performance actually recorded took place on January 14th of the following year, before the Court. Sir H. Herbert, whose office-book contained this entry, adds that the play was 'not likte' by the courtly audience. With this slight and solitary indication of contemporary opinion, the *Tale of a Tub* passed into a period of neglect which few have attempted to disturb. The circumstances of this only known performance were unpromising, had the play been intrinsically more attractive than it is. Jonson had at last been definitively worsted in his long intermittent struggle with Inigo Jones for the predominant position in the purveyance of the Court masques. Jones had complained, somewhat unreasonably, that *Love's Triumph through Callipolis*, performed on Twelfth Night, 1630-1, was published with the poet's name preceding the artist's on the title-page; and his anger had led to Jonson's being 'discarded' on the following and subsequent occasions. Jonson had bitterly resented this humiliation, had retorted in the 'Expostulation' and elsewhere, and his wrath was still unexhausted when he prepared the *Tale of a Tub* for performance in 1633. Once more the author of the *Poetaster* resorted to his old weapon of dramatic caricature. But the vigour of his arm was sadly diminished since his crushing assault upon Marston and Dekker. Jonson is no longer the young Titan, indulging a grimly boisterous laughter as he pounds and riddles his assailants. He is an ageing and bedridden man of letters, whose resentment of his wrongs was embittered by the sense of its ineffectiveness. It is striking evidence of the prestige which Jonson, slighted as he was, still retained, that Inigo in alarm procured the suppression of the passages reflecting upon himself.

### I

It is now recognized that the attack upon Inigo is confined to certain scenes, easily detachable from the context, and that the bulk of the play, whatever its date, was written without any reference to him or to their feud. No play of Jonson's in fact offered less obvious occasion for satire upon the Court-architect than this comedy of Middlesex clowns. But precisely its grotesque irrelevance fitted it for Jonson's malicious purpose. It was doubtless sweet to exhibit the prosperous favourite of Whitehall hobnobbing, as their fellow, with the tinkers and farriers of Islington and Hampstead, and designing a wedding-masque for the village-constable's daughter. Medlay the cooper offered a hold for this design, for no better reason than that his name, or nickname, of In-and-In gave an opening (like 'inlay' and 'ingine' in v. ii. 60, 61) for a pun upon Inigo, not too sorry for the Jonson of 1633 to seize.[1] Medlay, as represented in the first three acts, appears not a whit elevated above his companion wiseacres of the Finsbury council. It is he, for instance, who confounds 'warrants' with rabbit-warrens ('Cunni-borroughes' in III. i. 35). Such a man could not suddenly be converted into an impersonation, however grossly caricatured, of the immensely versatile and brilliantly accomplished artist without some evident 'straining o' the stuff'; and in the 'interloping' scene of the fourth act this humble dullard abruptly puts on a new character. All the four clowns of this

---

[1] Medlay as Inigo was possibly not Jonson's first thought. Cf. v. ii. 72, where after In-and-In has undertaken the masque, Tub asks:

    Ha' you nere a Cooper
  At *London* call'd *Vitruvius*? send for him.

'Vitruvius' can hardly be other than Inigo; but then Inigo would have to be distinct from In-and-In Medlay of Islington.

scene, in fact, display a sudden interest in their ancestry, but apparently only in order to lend plausibility to the account which Medlay, in his new role, volunteers of his own 'godsire' In-and-In Shittle, the weaver, who had given him the same name, as serving

> A Joyners craft, bycause that wee doe lay
> Things in and in, in our worke.

But his real quality was that of '*Architectonicus professor*, rather'. Inigo was actually the son of a weaver, and had begun life as a joiner. The original Medlay was a cooper, and the wish to point the allusion to Inigo has at least introduced some ambiguity into the description of his trade.[1] Even this scene, however, hardly prepares us for the denouement of v. ii, where Medlay is pointed out as the one man in Middlesex who can make a masque, and who, besides 'devising' it, insists on writing it too:

> Hee'll do't alone Sir, He will joyne with no man :
> Though he be a Joyner, in designe he cals it,
> He must be sole Inventer.

His clownish dialect, too, abruptly becomes educated English ; he even begins to display pedantic affectations, and the inkhorn words ('feasible' and 'conduce') of the travelled Inigo, hitherto wholly unknown to him, fall with every sentence from his rustic lips.[2] He has even Latin enough to

---

[1] He is called a 'Cooper' in the List of Persons. In I.iv. 40-1, however, he rejoins to Clench's 'I'll ha' *Tom Tiler* For our *Iohn Clay*'s sake' with 'And I the jolly Joyner, for mine owne sake'; and in III. vi. 8 f., where Turfe says to him, of the legend of Guy of Warwick :

> You shall worke it
> Into a storie for me, neighbour *Medlay*,
> Over my Chimney ;

which is more plausible of a 'Joyner' than of a 'Cooper'. Both these passages, as is noted below, belong stylistically to the later manner.

[2] Contrast e. g. the following :

(1) *Cle.* I veare, they ha' made 'hun away. *Med.* No zure ;
　　The Justice
　　　　Dare not conzent to that . . . .
　　　　　　　You are right, *D'oge*!
　　Zet downe to a minute, now tis a'most vowre. (v. ii. 2 f.)

misquote a technical phrase, though he 'stands not' on his Latinity.[1] Naturally, Medlay's masque is meant to throw ridicule on Inigo. And from the standpoint of Jonson's own masque-making art, this production is dull and pointless enough. None the less it must be pronounced to fail completely as satire no less than as poetry or drama. It is not absurd enough. Had Jonson genuinely wished to ridicule the masque-making efforts of Middlesex clowns, he might have given the original Medlay a piece on the lines of *Pyramus and Thisbe*. But he wanted something at once palpably far below his own work, yet such as Inigo might credibly have produced. 'Inigo claims to be the only maker of masques: see what sort of masque he will produce if you give him a free hand!' This was doubtless Jonson's underlying thought. But in making him produce merely this saltless rhymed repetition of the not very succulent story just enacted, Jonson only threw into relief the defects of his own play, and ran a grave risk of drawing on to his own head the resentment he intended for Inigo. The audience which 'disliked' the rest of the play would have shouted down the masque.

It may then be taken as beyond doubt that the scenes in question (the 'interloping scene' in Act IV, v. ii. 28–75, v. vii to the end) were a later addition to an original play composed with a different intention and without direct satire upon Jones.[2] It remains to consider the date and circumstances of the composition of this original play.

Dryden included the *Tale* among Jonson's 'dotages', and the view that it was a work of his old age, if not his very last play, appears to have been universally held until the

and (2) *Med.* If I might see the place, and had survey'd it,
    I could say more: For all Invention, Sir,
    Comes by degrees, and on the view of nature;
    A world of things, concurre to the designe,
    Which make it feazible, if Art conduce.   (v. ii. 54 f.)

[1] v. vii. 11.
[2] The possibility is of course not excluded that these 'new scenes' had some kind of counterpart, probably more drastic in style, in the original play which they now replaced.

time of Collier. That scholar pointed out the obvious fact that there are numerous allusions to 'the Queen' (e. g. I. iv. 53: 'Do's any wight parzent hir Majesties person?'); and Mr. Fleay, besides accepting this as certain, assigned the play categorically to the year 1601 on the ground of supposed allusions to books and events of that year. The view that it is Elizabethan in origin is now held by almost all who have closely examined the play.[1]

That Jonson in 1633 was bringing upon the stage not a play which he had just composed, but one written long before, of which he was rather ashamed, and which he only used under dire stress of need, is the hypothesis which most readily explains the unwonted tone of the Prologue and the motto. They are apologetic, and it was not Jonson's wont to apologize. He scoffs openly at his 'ridiculous' play. Not merely because it is full of dull-witted rustics; it might be that and still be as arresting as Tolstoy's *Power of Darkness* or Balzac's *Les Paysans*. But the play itself, he confesses, or rather proclaims, is yet duller than the dull rustics themselves,—'inficeto inficetior rure'; as if he hoped to persuade the audience not to damn his play by agreeing with them in advance that it deserved to be damned.[2] The Prologue is, in effect, the work of a man whose old spirit was subdued,—the spirit which had once browbeat his audience with the assurance that his play, by God, was good and they might like it if they chose. Yet this disdain can hardly have expressed his mind about the play when it was written. Though very far from a masterpiece, the *Tale of a Tub* is the work of a man full of humorous observation and comic zest. These witless rustics are drawn with

---

[1] Especially by Small (*Stage Quarrel*, p. 14), Scherer (Bang, *Materialien*, Bd. 39), Baskervill, *English Elements in Jonson's Early Comedy*, p. 76 f. Miss F. Snell, on the other hand, in her Yale thesis edition (1915) holds the entire play to belong to Jonson's old age. But Miss Snell's result is based upon misleading statistics.

[2] Even if, as we cannot doubt from the context of Catullus's verse, Jonson thought of Inigo in quoting it, he could not expect the reader to apply a motto placed on the forefront of a play to a person caricatured by an unimportant character in it.

abundance of wit, with unmistakable gusto and a flowing invention.

Jonson cannot indeed make the dullness of his rustics as delightful as that of Shakespeare's Athenian artisans, or his own later gulls; and poetic charm, such as invests Shakespeare's rustics or those of his own *Sad Shepherd*, was here evidently beside his purpose, if not beyond his power. But his peculiar virtuosity in painting fatuous pretentiousness is already unmistakable, and it was exercised with no less unmistakable zest. That did not prevent his giving the play a title of half-ironical disparagement,—according to the current fashion which Shakespeare followed in his *As You Like It* and *What You Will*.[1]

The view that Jonson, in 1633, revived a play substantially written many years before was first suggested by the occurrence already noticed of numerous allusions to 'the Queen';[2] and many critics have sought no further evidence. But might not Jonson, it has been asked, writing under Charles I, deliberately place the scene in Elizabeth's reign?[3] The possibility is not to be denied,—he practised this 'historic' writing in the Folio text of *Every Man in his Humour* and perhaps elsewhere. But if the allusions are appropriate to a date on other grounds probable, the burden of proof decidedly lies upon those who support that hypothesis. Now a date in the middle of the nineties, which answers that condition, is not inconsistent with the other time-indications of the same kind. Thus Metaphor, the justice's clerk, has seen 'King *Edward*, our late Leige, and soveraigne Lord', ride forth in state (I. v. 32 f.). Hugh, as Captain Thumbs, professes to have fought at St.

---

[1] Cf. I. iv. 25:
    *A Tale of a Tub*, Sir; a meere tale of a Tub.
    Lend it no eare I pray you.

[2] 'I charge you in the Queenes name, keepe the peace' (II. ii. 30), and often.

[3] Dr. E. K. Chambers (*Eliz. Stage*, iii. 373–4) has even suggested Queen Mary's. This would suit the allusion to the late king Edward, bnt would be grossly out of keeping with the mention of Faustus.

Quentin's in 1557 (III. ix. 15), and Rasi' Clench the farrier claims '*Rasis*... King *Harry's* doctor' as his 'God-phere' (interloping scene). But none of them need be more than elderly men on this account.[1]

## II

It remains to consider the substance and form of the play itself, apart from the easily detached Inigo-scenes grafted upon it. It is in the technique of style and metre of composition and character-drawing that the difference between a young and an old man's work must, if anywhere, betray itself. But a preliminary word may be said, first, on the general character of a piece on which posterity has been too content to accept the contemptuous estimate with which its author ushered it into the world.

In its subject-matter, cast of society, and atmosphere, the *Tale of a Tub* undoubtedly stands, at a first glance, in sharp contrast with the rest of the Jonsonian drama. His province, in the work of his prime, was the Town, with its decadent corruptions and affectations. The country-side did not, on the whole, interest him. For the eccentricities of the rustic in town, whether a sturdy Downright or a simple Sogliardo or Stephen, he had the keenest relish; and he occasionally carried his audience on a brief excursion to witness the serio-comic exploits of a Sordido in the country; but rustic humours, as such, were to all appearance of no account for his art. A play, then, like the *Tale of a Tub*, in which the scenery and the whole personnel are, in respect of Jonson's London, unequivocally rustic, where the whole plot is concerned with the rivalries, tricks, and solemn futilities of rural Middlesex, and the contrast of country simplicity or downrightness with urban cunning or craft nowhere arises, would stand out as a striking anomaly in Jonson's dramatic career had it been written at any time between 1598 and

[1] That chronological consistency is in any case not to be pressed too severely appears from the fact that 'old *Iohn Haywood*', who died in 1580, is to be called in if necessary for the masque (v. ii. 74), while there are allusions to Faustus and Friar Bacon of the later eighties.

1616. Again, its plot turns entirely upon a series of rivalries in love; a theme to which, in the dramas of his maturity, Jonson habitually assigned the insignificance to be expected from one whose moments of romantic insight were so fitful and so rare; for even the comedy of love calls for quicker sympathies with this side of life than he ever unmistakably displays.

The nature of the subject-matter, then, so far as it goes, tends to rule out the play from the great central period. We may go farther and say that, as between apprenticeship and 'dotage'—the really crucial question—this consideration affords the only plausible ground for holding that the *Tale of a Tub* may have originated in the poet's old age. For there is no doubt that in his later years, if his normal distaste for country humours did not abate, he at least compelled this reluctant matter not infrequently to take the impress of his art. His fame as a masque-writer took him repeatedly to great country-houses in remote parts of England, and the readiest way of furnishing forth the antimasque was to call in the 'local talent' of shepherds and village clowns. His four-hundred mile walk through the length of rural England, too, was hardly undertaken only to save his purse. Three years after that adventure, he produced in *The Gypsies Metamorphosed* (1622) a veritable riot of rustic humorous types, including a clown called 'Puppy' like one in the present play. Twelve years later still, in *Love's Triumph at Bolsover* (1634), he gratified his malice against Inigo by exhibiting the great Court-architect as he exhibits him here, consorting familiarly with a herd of village craftsmen. The beautiful Theocritean poetry of *The Sad Shepherd*, again, which seems to warn off any attempt to put the rude clownage of the *Tale of a Tub* near it in date, departs even more completely from Jonson's characteristic domain of Town society. And not long probably before 1619, he had brought in 'clowns making mirth and foolish sport' 'contrary to all other pastorals' in the lost *May Lord* (*Conversations*, xvi).

But, clearly, parallels of this kind are not decisive. And they leave quite untouched the hypothesis that Jonson may have dallied with this *prima facie* un-Jonsonian kind of matter in the obscure experimental years before the well-defined new departure of 1598. Our information concerning this first phase of Jonson's dramatic career consists, as we have seen, of the following facts:

(1) In September 1598, shortly before the production of *Every Man in his Humour*, Meres included him in a list of the chief English dramatists, as one of the 'best in tragedy'.

(2) This is supported by entries in Henslowe's *Diary* which show that in December 1597 he received payment for the plot of a play which he was to finish by the ensuing Christmas. This may have been the plot which he handed over to Chapman, who by October 1598 had written two acts of a tragedy on it.

(3) In the summer of 1597 he took part in completing Nashe's *Isle of Dogs*.

(4) Meres' eulogy makes it certain that he had written by 1598 at least one or two plays of which we have no record, and his assertion to Drummond in 1619 that 'the half of his plays were not in print' goes to confirm this. What is more important, we may infer from Jonson's not having published any play earlier than 1598 in the Folio edition of his *Works* that all that he had written earlier was unsatisfactory to his mature taste.

(5) While the composition of *Every Man in his Humour* marked a new departure in various points of comic technique, the verse and style of its earliest text are still very imperfectly moulded to the writer's ideals; so that when he revised the play, he left hardly a sentence as it stood, while scenes and persons remained practically unaltered. It may thence be inferred that the stylistic and metrical divergences of the Quarto from the Folio represent characteristics of the young Jonson, still imperfectly overcome in 1598; and that his dramatic speech of 1595-7 will have had these character-

istics in a yet more pronounced degree. In any case the style and verse of the last plays stand unmistakably apart from both.

### III

Between the first definitely datable verse of Jonson's—that of the first Quarto of *Every Man in his Humour*—and that of his last decade, the divergence is, in fact, as pronounced as that between Shakespeare's verse in the early plays and in *Coriolanus* or *The Winter's Tale*, and in a large degree the divergence is of the same kind. Both poets, notwithstanding their enormous psychological disparity, began with a nice conformity to metrical and stylistic norms, and ended in the lordliest licence. But Shakespeare is a poet alike in his decorum and in his audacities; and his expression, exquisitely and spontaneously poetic at the outset, gathers imaginative range and volume as it grows more sombre and more complex. Jonson's diction, in the plays, is rarely poetic; and apart from the isolated *Sad Shepherd* it shows a progressive elimination of poetical phrase. His verse in the Quarto of *Every Man in his Humour* is severe and somewhat stiff, far as yet from the colloquial ease attained in the final version of the play. Like the young Shakespeare he still uses occasional passages of rhyme. But hardly a line has less than ten syllables, or more than eleven, and while the sense is no longer moulded with anything like Marlowan regularity in the single line, 'light' or 'weak' endings are rare, and the normal movement and structure of the metre are scrupulously emphasized. In the later plays, on the contrary, while the five-foot norm is on the whole strictly observed, it is as if for the purpose of playing fast and loose with all the other norms—number of syllables, verse music, recognition of metrical breaks in the sense pauses; while all colloquial abbreviations and elisions are freely admitted.[1]

[1] Miss Snell, in her edition of this play (Introd. p. xxvi f.), gives a table of the proportion of 'extra syllables' in the successive plays, which shows that the number steadily and pretty uniformly increases from

The fundamental fact in the problem of the present play is that it presents, in different portions, both these Jonsonian manners, and each in a somewhat extreme and accentuated form. Of the abundant presence of the late manner there is no question, and in the 'interloping' and other 'Inigo' scenes of 1633 we have a definite criterion for the rest. Without doubt a large part of the play was written, in its present form, about that time. The opening scenes are full of examples of a style of verse closely resembling that of the Inigo-scenes. Thus Canon Hugh's speech (I. i. 12 f.):

> What! Squire, I say? *Tub*, I should call him too:
> Sir *Peter Tub* was his father, a Salt-peeter-man;
> Who left his Mother, Lady *Tub* of *Totten-*
> *Court*, here, to revell, and keepe open house in;
> With the young Squire her sonne, and 's Governour
> Basket-
> *Hilts*, both by sword, and dagger: *Domine,*
> *Armiger Tub,* Squire *Tripoly, Expergiscere.*

But there are equally unmistakable, though much rarer examples of a totally different manner. They are not distributed evenly through the play, nor yet concentrated in any one scene or act; but occur most often in Act III. Take this speech of Squire Tub to his intended father-in-law Turfe (III. iii. 3 f.):

> *Turfe,* I am privie to thy deepe unrest:
> The ground of which, springs from an idle plot,
> Cast by a Suitor, to your daughter *Awdrey*—
> And thus much, *Turfe,* let me advertise you:
> Your daughter *Awdrey*, met I on the way,
> With Justice *Bramble* in her company:
> Who meanes to marry her at *Pancridge* Church.
> And there is Chanon *Hugh,* to meet them ready:
> Which to prevent, you must not trust delay;
> But winged speed must cross their slie intent:
> Then hie thee, *Turfe,* haste to forbid the Banes.

*Every Man in his Humour* (5 per hundred lines) to *The Magnetic Lady* (24·8). She finds that the proportion for the Inigo-scenes almost exactly coincides with that for the rest of the play, and hence concludes that the whole play originated at the same (late) period. Statistics, like fire, are a good servant but a very bad master.

This is not only quite unlike the later Jonson, it is not, in any respect, characteristically Jonsonian at all. Eight lines out of the eleven present some kind of departure from colloquial idiom; the formal phrasing, the quasi-poetical inversions, the timid balance of sentence and line, are in sharp contrast to the mature Jonson's habitual massive and, with all its severe conformity to 'art', personal and idiomatic speech. It is quite unlike the dramatic speech of his culminating period, and it differs from it in the fashion, not of an old man whose mastery is slipping from him, but of a novice still feeling his way.

There is no question of an accommodation of style or rhythm to the character. Tub can talk quite otherwise in the Inigo-scenes, as in v. vii. 19 f. :

> No, Mr. *In-and-In*, my *Tale of a Tub*,
> By your leave, I am *Tub*, the Tale's of me,
> And my adventures! I am Squire *Tub*,
> *Subjectum Fabulæ. Med.* But I the Author.
> *Tub.* The Worke-man Sir! the Artificer! I grant you.
> So *Skelton*-Lawreat, was of *Elinor Rumming*:
> But she the subject of the Rout, and Tunning.[1]

Such contrasts would suffice to dismiss the suggestion that the numerous unmistakable affinities of the play with the drama of Elizabeth's last decade are due to deliberate archaism on Jonson's part. For he must then, in style and verse, either have archaized in a most uncharacteristically fitful and capricious way, leaving the bulk of the writing untouched by archaism, or, if we can suppose the homely rough speech of these village folks to be intentionally archaic as well as rustic, he must have adopted, in the same play, two radically different conceptions of 'archaism'.

The style occurs in considerable tracts throughout the play, chiefly in the parts of Tub, but also at times in those of Turfe and Awdrey. Compare, for instance, Turfe's reply

---

[1] In Tub's part there are other occasional inconsistencies which point to an original text, unequally revised. Thus for the most part he does not use dialect. But in III. iii. 32, 34, he says 'vetch' and 'velonie' like Turfe.

to the above speech of Tub, and Awdrey's reflections on her situation in III. vi. 27, with the intervening speech of Turfe:

> Was ever silly Maid thus posted off?
> That should have had three husbands in one day;
> Yet (by bad fortune) am possesst of none?
> I went to Church to have beene wed to *Clay*;
> Then Squire *Tub* he seized me on the way,
> And thought to ha' had me: but he miste his aime;
> And Justice *Bramble* (nearest of the three)
> Was well-nigh married to me; when by chance,
> In rush'd my Father, and broke off that dance.
> . . . . . . . .
> Husbands, they say, grow thick; but thin are sowne.
> I care not who it be, so I have one.

Such passages do not, however, form the staple of the play. On the contrary, there are everywhere examples of a style which in homely and colloquial vigour, in rustic raciness and uncouthness, Jonson never surpassed. The talk of the wiseacres in Turfe's house at Kentish Town, e. g. (II. i), undergoes the minimum of either stylistic or metrical restriction in becoming verse-dialogue; and Turfe himself falls into it without reserve; as in this speech of II. i. 9 f.:

> Well said, *To-Pan*: you ha' still the hap to hit
> The naile o' the head at a close: I thinke there never
> Marriage was manag'd with a more avisement,
> Then was this marriage, though I say't, that should not;
> Especially 'gain' mine owne flesh, and blood;
> My wedded Wife. Indeed my Wife would ha' had
> All the young Batchelers and Maids, forsooth,
> O' the zixe Parishes hereabout: But I
> Cry'd none, sweet *Sybil*; none of that geare, I:
> It would lick zalt, I told her, by her leave.

or the speech beginning

> I do defy 'hun, so shall shee doe too,

and ending

> I thought, I had had 'un as zure as in a zaw-pit,
> Or i' mine Oven. Nay, i' the Towne-pound:
> I was so zure o' hun: I'ld ha' gi'n my life for 'un,
> Till he did start. But now, I zee 'un guilty,
> As var as I can looke at 'un. Would you ha' more?
> (IV. i. 30 f.)

Apart from the marks of dialect, the affinities of this verse and style are rather with the talk of the lower characters in *The Staple of News*, *The New Inn*, and *The Magnetic Lady* than with anything in the early plays. In these he still used prose largely for the homelier characters and situations.

It remains to conclude that the *Tale of a Tub*, as we have it, represents an original, the date of which is approximately defined by the style and verse of the 'early' passages; i.e. in the neighbourhood of the first version of *Every Man in his Humour*, and decidedly before rather than after it. It will be seen below that its dramaturgic character also strongly supports this view. It shows no trace of 'Humours', and must have preceded the decisive new step deliberately taken by Jonson in September, 1598, with *Every Man in his Humour*, whether his lofty opinion of that piece as the one model for comedy was publicly proclaimed (or even as yet privately entertained) on this first occasion or not. The date 1596-7 fairly satisfies these conditions.

But was it entirely written in verse? The facts allow no peremptory decision. Jonson's choice of prose or verse for different plays fluctuates (in *Volpone* all verse, in *Epicoene* all prose, in *The Alchemist* all verse), while the choice between them for different scenes or situations in the same play is far less logical or consistent than in Shakespeare. But the abundant use of prose in all the early plays down to *Sejanus*, and the predominant use of it in *Every Man in his Humour* and *The Case is Altered* (the two nearest in date, on our hypothesis, to this play) for homely characters and scenes, make it difficult to believe that in 1596-7 Jonson would have made his Middlesex clowns speak in verse. His thoroughgoing use of verse for all purposes and characters begins, as far as we know, with *The Alchemist*, where the drastic brutalities and professional hocus-pocus of the three knaves, and the sordid calculations of their dupes, are all reflected with perfect art in a metrical form capable also, as in the Mammon speeches, of lurid Baudelaire-like splendours of poetry. In *Bartholomew Fair* he returned to prose; but this uniform yet loose and all-accommodating vesture of verse was Jonson's final choice. He would be likely, then, in adapting an old play, of mixed verse and prose, for performance in 1633, to recast it in a uniformly metrical garb.

The verse and the prose would not, however, fare equally in the revision. The prose would as such necessarily disappear, and the verse that replaced it would resemble the original verse which Jonson was then composing. The verse, on the other hand, satisfying the formal conditions as it stood, would not be radically refashioned. Much would be tolerated, or but slightly altered, by the aged and bedridden poet, which would have come out differently had he written it anew. On the whole, the early verse would partially survive and the early prose would be wholly replaced by late verse. Such a hypothesis appears to explain better than any other the striking stylistic and metrical inequalities of the text. It is supported by the fact that the passages most palpably 'early' chiefly occur in situations of romantic or sentimental tone (or what passes for such in the Jonsonian world), such as the wooing of Squire Tub.[1]

### IV

The presence of style and verse only explainable as the work of Jonson's prentice years offers the surest criterion for the date of the original *Tale of a Tub*. But a number of other features provide concurrent, if often less cogent, testimony.

Plot-structure is confessedly a treacherous test. But it affords ground, in the present case at least, for some plausible surmise. Though far from the consummate mastery of *Volpone* or *The Alchemist* in this respect, the plot of the *Tale* is by no means unskilful. Jonson came to dramatic writing steeped in Latin comedy, and we may confidently

[1] See especially II. iv. 47–59.

assume that his very earliest play detached itself sharply from the loose incoherence still frequent in the Elizabethan stage in the early nineties. But it is no transcript from Latin comedy in terms of English life, like *Ralph Royster Doyster* or *The Comedy of Errors*; it is rather an original bit of English life seen and modelled in a mind instinct with classic ideals. Jonson, never a servile classicist, shows himself here decisively of the school of *Gammer Gurton's Needle*, not of *Ralph Royster Doyster*, still less of *The Comedy of Errors*. The usual motive—the struggle for the possession of a girl—provides an intrigue which is worked out with unfailing clearness and cogency. As a picture of life and human nature—even rustic human nature—it is no doubt elementary. But if it lacks the power of Jonson's ripe invention, so it is without the perverse prodigality of his elaborating intellect, which even so early as *Every Man out of his Humour* so seriously clogged the action, and in all the plays of his last period impaired the value of the whole design by monstrous extravagances, such as the mutually unknown husband and wife of *The New Inn*, or the garden and well episode in *The Magnetic Lady*. There is no trace as yet even of the allegorizing pedantry which was responsible for so much learned symbolism in plays of all periods after the first;—the Fountain of Self Love in *Cynthia's Revels*, the eructation-scene of *Poetaster*, the 'Lady Pecunia' of *The Staple of News*, the 'reconciling of Humours' in *The Magnetic Lady*. In this, as in many other points, it is nearest to the unpretentious and good-humoured lucidity of *Every Man in his Humour*, where the Humour-theory, with all its hazards for a man of Jonson's temper, was still a servant, discreetly employed for the proper ends of drama, not a despotic master overriding them. The struggle for a girl reappears there, but only as an almost devitalized rudiment; Edward Kno'well and Bridget—most perfunctory of lovers—are in fact the victims of Jonson's persistent attachment to Plautine precedent. In the *Tale of a Tub*, the love-business, though without a breath of romance, is genuinely at the root of the whole action. The rivalry of several suitors was of course no novel theme in England. Its obvious dramatic opportunities were exploited in several plays (to go no farther back) of the seventies, eighties, and nineties, as *Common Conditions* (1576), *Mucedorus* (printed 1598), *Wily Beguiled* (c. 1595), *The Merry Wives* (1599). In others, as *Englishmen for my Money* (1598), *The Taming of a Shrew* (c. 1594), two or more daughters are the subject of similar intrigues.[1] Some of these were doubtless later than the original *Tale of a Tub*; others, in particular *Mucedorus*, he evidently knew;[2] that love intrigue was so little Jonson's natural way in drama confirms the suspicion that he was here against his later wont complying with a vogue. Yet it is clear that his critical instinct is already awake; his classical discipline asserts itself unmistakably; in no English play up to this date had the Unities been so approximately observed as in this comedy of country-folks and clowns, and very few could offer a plot so well traced, coherent, and so free from the idleness which Hamlet was justly to rebuke in the bulk of the plays of his time. Thus the unity of time is already carried out in the *Tale of a Tub* as completely as in any of its successors: the whole complicated action is carried through in a day. In regard to the so-called 'unity of place', Jonson did not at once impose on himself the severity he finally exercised; but from the first he innovated sharply upon the chartered freedom in this respect for which the popular stage had been gaily abused, in words still freshly remembered, by Sidney. Whether we look to the number of changes of scene apparently intended, or to the geographical area of their variation, the *Tale of a Tub* is somewhat freer than the Humour plays of 1598–1601, as these are freer than the bulk of their successors. In *Every Man in his Humour* there are (approximately) twenty shiftings of scene, in *Every Man out of his Humour* seven-

---

[1] Baskervill, *English Elements in Jonson's Early Comedy*, 83 f.
[2] Cf. below, pp. 296–7.

teen; in the former we pass to and fro between various localities all in or near the present City; in the latter, between the City and the country. *Volpone* has some eighteen changes, *Epicoene* and *The Alchemist* ten; and in all three the plot is focused in a single spot—the house of Volpone or Morose, the laboratory of Subtle and Face, with brief occasional shiftings to the street, or a neighbouring building. Of the plays of the last period, *The Staple of News* has only eight changes, and the localities are all in the City. In *The New Inn* (with nine changes) practically everything happens in different rooms of the inn; in *The Magnetic Lady* (with fourteen changes) in different rooms of Lady Loadstone's house.

In the present play there appear to be twenty changes of scene; and we pass perpetually from one to another of five or six suburban hamlets or their neighbourhoods; Lady Tub's house at Totten Court, Turfe's at Kentish Town, Preamble's at Maribone, the fields near Pancras, the country near Maribone, the country near Kentish Town. This degree of variation, roughly within the present Northwest district, clearly distinguishes the play from contemporary Romantic drama in one direction, and in the other no less clearly from the practice of Jonson's later years; while it corresponds closely with his practice in the Humour plays of 1598–1601, thus going to confirm the contention that the play belongs in origin to the earlier date.

If the *Tale of a Tub* still falls short of Jonson's later rigour in regard to shiftings of place, it realizes the unity of action, as Jonson understood it, with a completeness which he was very rarely again to equal. For the Humour theory, which was soon to transform both for better and worse his dramatic practice, had not yet, to all appearance, occurred to him, and the demon of learned allegory was still held at arm's length. His natural and scholarly bent towards a unified and organic type of drama was thus free from the two most formidable disintegrating influences which threatened it, which were soon to run riot in *Every Man out of his Humour* and *Cynthia's Revels.* Even *Every Man in his Humour* is rather an ingenious entanglement of several disconnected actions than a single action. But in the *Tale of a Tub* all the persons high and low have a single preoccupation—the disposal of the hand of Awdrey Turfe; even Lady Tub, who is resolved that anyhow her son shall not win her; even Awdrey herself, who cares not who wins her, provided only she be won. While the plot thus shows considerable artistic skill, it is fresh and natural; none of Jonson's plays smells less of the lamp. Between its simple tricks and elementary disguises and the perversely manufactured confusions of *The New Inn* and *The Magnetic Lady* there is the difference which separates the spontaneous vigour of youth from the factitious violence of flagging genius.

Yet it must be allowed that the action is not quite so perfect in what may be called longitudinal as in lateral unity. The entire personnel is caught in the meshes of a single interest; their several enterprises do not, however, form a single action, but a series of at least two, so markedly detached that the play pauses between them. The first three acts are occupied by parallel attempts on the part of the three rival groups. Towards the close of the third act (III. vii) Tub and Preamble have both been foiled, and the ground appears clear for a return to the original situation and the marriage of Awdrey to Clay. Then Hugh concerts a new device, and the action starts as it were *da capo*, but soon developing fresh and lively variations. Even in his ripest days, longitudinal integration was not always complete; in *Volpone* itself the action reaches a natural conclusion with the triumph of Volpone and Mosca at end of Act IV, and starts afresh with their new plot in Act V.

A few traces, further, of pre-Jonsonian methods of plot-management have survived even in the revised version. Thus Canon Hugh, disguised as Captain Thumbs (III. ix), comes forward and explains the situation to the audience with the naïveté of the early stage:

> Thus as a begger in a Kings disguise, . . .
> Comes Chanon *Hugh*, accoutred as you see,
> Disguis'd *Soldado*-like: marke his devise:
> The Chanon, is that Captaine *Thum's*, was rob'd:
> These bloody scars upon my face are wounds.

In II. iv. 49 f. Tub similarly describes his operations as if he were an onlooker:

> Now th'adventurous Squire hath time, and leisure,
> To aske his *Awdrey* how she do's, and heare
> A gratefull answer from her.

Both these occur in speeches conspicuously early in manner. So, Metaphor addresses himself:

> Make no delay, *Miles*, but away.  (IV. i. 109),

or refers to himself by name (IV. ii. 80).

## V

If the plot foreshadows in constructive quality Jonson's maturest comedy, and is relatively free from his failings, the characters represent rather an early experiment in a manner which he subsequently and finally abandoned. They are all slightly, though not unskilfully, drawn; the staple of character' is thin and unsubstantial; not one shows a trace of that conscious and aggressive virtuosity in the painting of social types which emerged in his work with the comedy of Humour, but of which the Humour comedy was only the first and most doctrinaire expression. In this 'rustic' comedy there is at most a hint and vague promise of the power which, applied to the town-populace, lays bare in *Bartholomew Fair* the significant cleavages in human nature and in the national life, and makes that drama, with its profusion of sordid and shabby personages, so massive and so great a play. That the persons are all, contrary to Jonson's wont, rustics, justifies no inference as to its date. What is of importance is that there is nowhere an approach here to the elaboration of character for its own sake—often at the cost of the business of the play—which the later Jonson could rarely resist. In the *Tale of a Tub*, as originally conceived and composed, Jonson's main concern is unmistakably the plot. For its sake promising openings for character elaboration are neglected, lively sketches left incomplete. Of the long passages, even whole scenes, of mere character exposition which abound elsewhere throughout the Jonsonian drama, there is here nothing; and if the play has gained in rapidity and directness, it has no less lost in brilliance and power. Jonson's natural method is first to make his personages clear and then to set them in motion; its extreme consequence is the monstrous exposition—some four acts long—of *Every Man out of his Humour*, following a voluminous Theophrastean analysis of all the persons. In his greatest plays he corrected this extravagance; but such masterly opening scenes as those of *The Alchemist* owe much of their quality to the power which makes every stroke of the scurrilous dialogue that hurries us into the midst of things at the same time add something to the sinister clearness of the portraits of the three rogues. The opening scene of the *Tale of a Tub* sets the action going with no less directness; the incident of Canon Hugh wakening Tub at dawn with his baleful news, and Tub descending in his dressing-gown to concoct countermeasures, is admirably contrived. But neither here nor later is either Tub or Hugh much more than a clever sketch. And it is precisely types such as these, with a well-defined professional status, that most uniformly called forth Jonson's elaborating bent. Compare Hugh with the Puritans of *The Alchemist* or *Bartholomew Fair*, or with Brainworm, his counterpart in function,—both descending from the serviceable slave of Roman comedy; Justice Preamble with Clement or Overdo, or Tub with Cokes of Harrow; and we realize how far Jonson still was from the discovery of his full power. Above all, compare this parson and lawyer, drawn with a pen that scarcely throws off in passing, and never stays to emphasize, a single professional trait not needed for the working of the plot, with the wonderful Chaucerian full-length portraits of Parson Palate and Master

Practice (ostentatiously paraded with the author's signature), which prolong the leisurely exposition of *The Magnetic Lady*. It is difficult to believe that Jonson could, within a year or two, write under the influence of conceptions so radically different of dramatic art. The *Tale of a Tub* is in fact sharply marked off in almost every point of inner technique from the other 'dotages'. Of the abstract symbolism of *The Staple of News* and *The Magnetic Lady* it has as little as of the ultra-romantic extravagance of *The New Inn*. It is far from being great drama; but the ascription of its clownish matter and atmosphere to the decaying powers of the poet seems to be an example of the same kind of confusion as that which so long obscured the classical excellence (for its time) of *Gammer Gurton's Needle*.

It remains to consider Jonson's treatment of the suburban rustics who compose the staple of the personnel. Here there is little material for comparison in his own work. But many slight traits connect these scenes and characters with the dramatic fashions of the nineties. The blundering artisans of *A Midsummer Night's Dream* and the blundering country-folks of *Love's Labour's Lost* were assuredly known to Jonson; the clowns of *Mucedorus* and Munday's *John a Kent and John a Cumber* have left scarcely mistakable traces in his play.[1] The common rusticity is differentiated with much liveliness of invention. Thus the servants of the gentlefolks make a distinct group. Pol-marten, Metaphor, Hilts, have each their specific trait variously proportioned between the jester and the gull. Hilts is sketched at the outset with charm—

> A testie Clowne: but a tender Clowne, as wooll:
> And melting as the Weather in a Thaw:
> Hee'll weepe you, like all *Aprill*: But he 'ull roare you
> Like middle *March* afore.   (I. i. 77 f.)

The stupid, pretentious high constable, with his subordinates, the headborough, petty constable, and third-

---

[1] This is made probable by Baskervill, *English Elements*, p. 83.

borough, can hardly be separated from the vogue of satire upon constables which is exemplified in Lyly's *Endimion*, in the old *Leir*, and in the Dull of *Love's Labour's Lost*, and culminates in *Much Ado* and Middleton's *Blurt Master Constable*. All four express themselves freely by means of proverbs, like the Nicholas of *The Two Angry Women*, a nearly contemporary piece. Jonson's mature comedy rejected or severely curtailed the role of the professional jester; replacing him partly by the natural humourist of other callings, such as Cob the water-bearer, or Juniper the cobbler, partly by his great speciality, the 'gull'. His comic figures of both kinds detach themselves increasingly from the old and vigorous tradition of Elizabethan clowns and jesters, which Shakespeare, though endlessly refining and poetizing it, never abandoned. In the present play this detachment is only incipient. We are still in close touch with that tradition. These rural constables and tradesfolk blunder unconsciously, but their blunders are often of the lineage of those perpetrated, with countless variations of ignorance and mischief, in the less determinate 'clowns' of the earlier drama. Thus Clay, who in cowardice as well as fatuity comes nearest to the later gull, is made to echo a confusion of speech which had previously befallen Mouse in *Mucedorus* and Bullithrumble in *Selimus*:

> I have kept my hands, here hence, fro' evill speaking, Lying, and slandering; and my tongue from stealing.
> (III. i. 61-2.)[1]

Turfe himself, airing his fatuous self-importance among his subordinates, excites ironic amusement like that provoked by bully Bottom as the uncontested leader of the clowns of Athens, and Dogberry, compassionating the feeble wits of Verges; 'Hee's i' the right', declares Puppy,

> He is high Constable
> And who should reade above 'hun, or avore 'hun?
> (I. iv. 46-7.)

---

[1] Eckhardt, *Die lustige Person* (*Münchener Beiträge*), p. 325.

but his assurance, unlike Dogberry's, deserts him in the presence of superiors.

One character, however, offers more than these incidental connexions. In Hannibal Puppy the clown-jester unmistakably survives, the only unequivocal specimen of the species in the Jonsonian drama. Mr. Baskervill has pointed out his close affinity to Mouse of *Mucedorus*. Though a serving-man, his part is chiefly made up of the quips, puns, wilful 'misunderstandings', and humorous freedoms of various kinds, which formed the professional jester's repertory. Thus his colloquy with Lady Tub (III. iv. 10 f.) brings him into the fellowship of Lyly's Licio and Petulus in *Midas*,[1] of Speed and Launce and of the Clown in *Twelfth Night*. Affected misunderstandings are a part of his method, as of theirs, though the Shakesperean figures, at least, hardly touch the depths of banality in which Puppy is at home:

> *Lad.* Sirrah, whose man are you?
> *Pup.* Madam, my Master's.
> *Lad.* And who's thy Master?
> *Pup.* What you tread on, Madam.
> *Lad.* I tread on an old Turfe.
> *Pup.* That *Turfe*'s my Master. (III. iv. 18.)

Compare in Act III, Scene v, the play upon the 'tale' (tail) and 'sun' (son). The whole episode is a crude variation of the motive so pleasantly touched in the chartered bantering of Olivia and Rosalind by their respective jesters. Puppy has also the whimsical fancy which was a no less stock resource of the professional jester; and he indulges it not ineffectively in the description of his hunger, and of the preparations for the 'Bride-ale' (III. ix. 54 f.):

---

[1] Cf. in the *Midas*, I. ii:
> *Licio.* She hath the eares of a Want.
> *Pet.* Doth she want eares?
> *Licio.* I say the eares of a Want, a Mole.

and Speed's retort to Launce after a similar feat:
> Well, your old vice still, mistake the word.

>                   The night before to day
> (Which is within mans memory, I take it)
> At the report of it, an Oxe did speake;
> Who dy'd soone after: A Cow lost her Calfe:
> The Belwether was flead for 't: . . .
>                   the very Pig, the Pig
> This very mornin, as hee was a rosting,
> Cry'd out his eyes.

This is passable Elizabethan fooling, in the vein of Launce and of Launcelot Gobbo, even of Touchstone; but it bears little resemblance to anything else in Jonson's extant and undoubted work. His gulls are more irredeemably fatuous, his cunning serving-men more pointed and practical. The merry Onion in *The Case is Altered* is somewhat of a kindred spirit, but cannot with certainty be assigned to Jonson.

Puppy too, like so many clowns of the non-Jonsonian stage, has his fits of doggerel; as in III. iv. 28 f., when he calls for help against his importunate 'Valentines':

> In stead of Bils, with Colstaves come; in stead of
>     Speares, with Spits;
> Your slices serve for slicing swords, to save me, and
>     my wits;

and later in the dialogue with Lady Tub. So Onion, in his relief at Jaques's departure (*The Case is Altered*, IV. viii *ad fin.*), vents a doggerel couplet.

A different kind of significance attaches, finally, to the girl who is the centre of the plot. Awdrey is the principal link between these rural clowns and the persons of higher condition. Few comedies which turn solely upon the winning of a wife are so successfully denuded of the romance of love; and few men were better qualified for the denuding process than Jonson. Yet there is an unmistakable disparity here between his matter and his genius. He is not at home in this world where squires and judges throw every other concern to the winds for the sake of marrying a constable's foolish daughter. The plot in its ultimate purport belongs to romance, and no handling can change its nature. Its essential features remain, like shrivelled rudiments, in the midst of the more vital comic stuff. The plays of the eighties and nineties offer many examples of the attempt to accommodate romantic themes to comedy. In plays actually derived from Romances the heroines, like Amadine in *Mucedorus*, often retain their sentimental, semi-poetical speech. Greene originated the pleasant compromise which we know as 'romantic comedy', where a love-story, treated with freshness and charm and of serious but not tragic interest, is interwoven with frankly comic episodes; and from these mixtures of grave and gay Shakespeare advanced to such miracles of mingled wit and passion as Rosalind. But another school of dramatists, trying to get rid of romantic sentiment altogether, translated its persons and themes with varying degrees of success into terms of homely, often sordid, realism. The euphuistic or Arcadian periphrases in which the heroines of Greene and Lodge had signified their love-passion were replaced by a frank and enterprising sexuality, and their ideal constancy to an ideal lover by a ready acceptance of the best match to be had. Some heroines of this type are still rather constructed than observed; and the fatuous as well as sensual Silena of *Mother Bombie* is more unpleasing than the robustly animal Mall in *The Two Angry Women of Abingdon*. Jonson's Awdrey is probably the extremest example of this anti-romantic type to be found in the Elizabethan drama. Her crude desire for a husband neither breaks out in volcanic impetuosity, as with Mall, nor even translates itself into the arch coquetries of a more innocent type of country-girl; she is a vulgar and phlegmatic hoyden, with a keen eye to the main chance, but little concerned to choose among her three suitors provided she is assured of one, and finally accepting completely unperturbed a suddenly improvised fourth. Yet Awdrey is drawn with wit and skill; she is in perfect keeping with the atmosphere and the temper of the play; and her half-illiterate speeches are rich in traits imagined with cynical insight into the mind of her type, such as her reflection when she hears of the arrest for robbery of the unlucky Clay (II. iii. 17 f.) : '

> I thought he was a dissembler; he would prove
> A slippery Merchant i' the frost. Hee might
> Have married one first, and have beene hang'd after,
> If hee had a mind to't. But you men,
> Fie on you.

# INTRODUCTION TO
# 'THE CASE IS ALTERED'

# THE CASE IS ALTERED

*The Case is Altered* was first published in 1609, being entered in the Stationers' Register on January 26th of that year. The title-page appears in two forms; the earlier: 'Ben: Ionson, His Case is Altered', the later: 'A Pleasant Comedy, called: the Case is Altered written by Ben Ionson'. Neither can have been authorized by him. He did not include it in the edition of his Works (1616); nor was it printed (notwithstanding many modern assurances to the contrary), either in the posthumous second volume of that edition (1630-41) or in the Folio of 1692. The external evidence of its authenticity is, then, prima facie by no means strong. But it is to be remembered that Jonson gave to the world, in 1616, as his 'Works', only those pieces by which he wished to be judged; and that he told Drummond three years later that 'the half of his comedies were not in print'.[1] We know too that several of the plays which he excluded (e. g. the tragedies referred to by Meres) were admired; they presumably conformed, therefore, to prevailing standards of method rather than to the straiter Jonsonian orthodoxy announced in *Every Man in his Humour*. This description certainly applies to *The Case is Altered*. The supposition that the play was substantially Jonson's, but that in 1609 he disapproved of it, and would have preferred not to be known as its author, is supported by the fact (discussed in the critical introduction) that in one copy the words 'written by Ben Ionson' in the second title-page are deleted.

The play had, according to the title-page of the Quarto, been played 'sundry times' by the Children of Blackfriars, i.e. of the Chapel. It was then certainly at least ten or eleven years old. Some prima facie difficulty is caused by the opening scene. Unmistakable satirical allusions there

---

[1] *Convers.*, xvi. 393.

to Antony Munday, as Balladino, and to a recent eulogy of him as the 'best plotter', show that this scene followed the appearance of Meres's *Palladis Tamia*, where this singular judgement is in fact pronounced. A no less unequivocal allusion by Thomas Nashe, in *Lenten Stuffe*—'Is it not right of the merry coblers cutte in that witty play of *the Case is Altered*?'—shows that our play was then already well known. Now *Palladis Tamia* was entered on the Stationers' Register in September 7, 1598: *Lenten Stuffe* in January 11, 1599. These dates would almost suffice to show that the scene in question must be later than the play at large. And the text contains proof that it was in fact an afterthought. In IV. v a bit of dialogue has been retained which shows that in the original version Valentine was engaged to write the 'prety *Paradox* or *Aligory*' which Juniper in the present text requests of Balladino (I. i). The scene was hardly added before 1600, for at that date there is reason to think that Munday had no grievance against Jonson.[1] That it can be little later is shown by Balladino's sarcasms upon Humour plays, then at the height of their vogue, but still a comparative novelty. The play itself, in view of Nashe's allusion, and of the vogue of the 'merry cobbler' which it implies, can be probably dated 1597-8. When Jonson rewrote this scene, *The Case is Altered* thus belonged to a past phase of his technique. The day of such work was for him, as a serious occupation of his art, gone by. He had deliberately turned from the comedy of romantic adventure to the comedy of 'humorous' character-types. He was addressing himself with growing exclusiveness to the more refined class of his audience who could relish the finer method. Hence he can openly deride, in this scene, 'the common sort' who 'cared not for't', or 'knew not what to make on't', who 'look'd for good

---

[1] Mr. Crawford has pointed out (10 *N. and Q.* vol. xi, p. 41 f.) that four passages from *The Case is Altered* are quoted in Bodenham's *Belvedere* (1600), edited by 'A. M.', initials plausibly identified with those of Munday. Munday would not, he urges, have included quotations from a play in which he was himself satirized.

matter, they, and were not edified with such toys'; who in short liked above all a rousing story. And Munday ('in print for the best plotter') was the very man to supply this plebeian interest: 'Tut giue me the penny', he is made to say, 'giue me the peny, I care not for the Gentlemen I, let me haue a good ground, no matter for the pen, the plot shall carry it.' But precisely this language might have been used, a couple of years earlier, by the author of *The Case is Altered* himself. No doubt the subordination of plot interest, in the Humour plays, was a passing phase of Jonson's art. The great comedies of his second period were to be masterpieces of plot-structure. But the plot of *The Case is Altered* is in every structural quality pre-Jonsonian. Jonson was never simple, in the sense of Molière or Racine; he loved to exhibit a fundamental motive multiplied in a crowd of parallel circumstances; but while he multiplied the circumstances he did not, in his mature plays, multiply the motive. A motley procession of dupes visit and revisit the laboratory of Subtle, and each has his distinct adventure and catastrophe; but the laboratory and its operations never cease to be the centre of interest. In *The Case is Altered* the interest is divided, and, it would seem, deliberately divided. The interweaving of two stories in the same plot was not, like the mingling of grave and gay, a long-established usage of the Elizabethan stage; but during the nineties, furthered by such brilliant examples as the *Midsummer Night's Dream* and *The Merchant of Venice*, it had made rapid progress both in vogue and status. Of this vogue, up to 1600, *The Case is Altered* is, outside Shakespeare, perhaps the most considerable example.

## II

Jonson has taken his two stories from separate plays of Plautus, the *Captives* and the *Aulularia*. The *Captives* represents an incident in a war between Elis and Aetolia. Hegio, an Aetolian, is the father of two sons. One of these had been stolen, many years before the date of the action, by the slave Stalagmus, as a child of four years. The other, Philopolemus, has been recently captured in battle, and is retained a prisoner in Elis. In order to ransom him, Hegio purchased two Elian prisoners, Philocrates and his slave Tyndarus. These two have arranged between themselves to exchange names and conditions. When Hegio therefore proposes to send the slave to Elis to negotiate the exchange, it is Tyndarus under the name of Philocrates who remains in his hands. Unluckily for the stratagem, Aristophontes, another Elian captive, who knows Philocrates well, has been allowed to visit the supposed Philocrates in Hegio's house. Confronted with the peril of immediate exposure, Tyndarus plays a desperate and audacious game, and almost succeeds in persuading Hegio that Aristophontes is a madman (III. iv), but is finally unmasked. Vainly he pleads that he has only acted the part of a loyal servant to his master. 'Then ask him for your reward!' retorts the furious Hegio, and dispatches him in double fetters to the mines to do an extra heavy tale of work. Finally Philocrates returns, with Philopolemus and the slave Stalagmus, and Tyndarus, who had been purchased as a child by the father of Philocrates as a present for his son, is discovered to be Philopolemus's long-lost brother. In a transport of joy and compunction Hegio orders his instant release and sends Stalagmus, loaded with his fetters, to suffer in his place. The efforts of a parasite, Ergasilus, to procure a dinner from Hegio interrupt without very sensibly relieving the action.

The plot of the *Aulularia* is still simpler. The miserly Euclio, who wishes to pass as a poor man, has found a vessel (*aula*) full of treasure. In all haste he buries it again, and the fear of its discovery becomes thenceforth his ruling preoccupation. A well-to-do neighbour, Megadorus, seeks the hand of his daughter, Phaedra, who has, unknown to either, been seduced by Megadorus's nephew, Lyconides. Euclio, greatly alarmed by a proposal which he can only account for by supposing his treasure to be discovered, declares that he can give no dowry; but when Megadorus still persists, and further offers to provide the wedding feast, reluctantly consents. The cooks put into his house by Megadorus, however, renew his alarm, and he secretly transfers the treasure to the temple of Fides. Strobilus, a slave of Lyconides, who has been sent to watch operations in his master's interest, observes him, and finally discovers and abstracts the treasure. Phaedra gives birth to a child, and Megadorus breaks off the match. Euclio, still ignorant of this event, finds his treasure gone. Lyconides, overhearing his frantic outburst, and knowing nothing as yet of the treasure, confesses his crime. The last act is incomplete, but it is evident that Euclio, overwhelmed by the threefold blow—the loss of the treasure, his daughter's seduction, and her repudiation—willingly accepts Lyconides' offer to marry Phaedra and keep the treasure as her dowry.

The two plays belong to widely contrasted types of Plautine comedy. The one, in the main, a serious romance, touching not without power the springs of generous emotion and tragic pathos; the other a satirical exposure of a ridiculous vice. Both move essentially in the sphere of private life; but the domestic crisis of the *Captives* depends upon distant military events. Both have to do with the drama of men's demeanour under loss; but Hegio grieving for his sons is pathetic; Euclio, who repeatedly suffers the pang of losing his treasure before it is actually lost, is purely ludicrous. Both combine serious and comic interest, though in different proportions. The sentiment and pathos of the *Captives* are interrupted and relieved at intervals by the parasite Ergasilus; the comic exploitation of Euclio has a serious incident in the seduction of his daughter. The two plays, in short, in spite of, and to some extent in virtue of, their marked unlikeness, were not ill adapted for manipulation as joint sources of an Elizabethan Romantic comedy. And the *Captives* offered further, like many other Roman comedies, some special features of incident familiar to medieval and later romance—the loss and recovery of children, confusion of identity, chivalrous loyalty to a friend. The situation, in particular, of Tyndarus taking the place of Philocrates, and incurring the penalty by his devotion, is parallel to that of Antonio paying Bassanio's debt and barely avoiding death in consequence. Love, however, the most indispensable of Romantic motives, is wholly lacking—an exemption indeed which Plautus, in the Epilogue, expressly claimed as its peculiar merit. And the *Aulularia*, which did offer love interest in a rudimentary form, was in temper and theme utterly unromantic. Further, if both plays, even separately, lent themselves to the Romantic taste for mingling serious and comic effect, they did not, even combined, lend any support to the equally pronounced Romantic taste for a plot full of incident and crowded with persons, and acknowledging very elastic limits of space and time.

Plautus had in fact managed his romantic story with the economy both of time and place traditional in the classical drama of all periods. If his play fell short of the ideal rather suggested than laid down by Aristotle, it was quite secure from Sidney's amusing strictures upon the Romantic dramas of his day. Philocrates crosses the gulf to Elis and returns; the duration of this short journey (a few days apparently) measures that of the supposed action; while the scene remains from first to last in the neighbourhood of Hegio's house. The action of the *Aulularia* seems to be limited to one day, and the scene observes similar narrow limits.

### III

The conversion of these materials into a thoroughgoing Romantic comedy would, then, have been no very exacting task. But *The Case is Altered* is not a thoroughgoing Romantic comedy. Its author was not bent on repudiating every suggestion of specifically 'classical' technique or character. As we might suppose from his evident familiarity with Latin comedy, he shows a decided respect for its ways in its own sphere, and where he qualifies them it is with a temperate and sparing hand. Moreover, when he innovates most boldly, and launches out into developments for which the challenging examples lay altogether in the modern drama close at hand, this quasi-romantic work sometimes, like the Gothic of Sir Christopher Wren, betrays a greater natural affinity of spirit to the technique it supersedes than to that which it simulates. When he crowds the canvas with figures, when he multiplies motives, when he marshals almost all the men of the piece as rival lovers of Rachel de Prie, he seems an ultra-Elizabethan. When he tries to paint Rachel herself, and love, he is an English Plautus trying to write in the Elizabethan style. When he takes obvious pains to multiply the links which connect his several stories, and compels the motley throng of persons concerned in them to do their business, so far as it comes on the stage, within reasonably narrow limits of place and time, he is an Elizabethan who recognizes the substantial validity, in these points, of ancient technique.

It is true, of course, that he was not the first Elizabethan to pay some tacit, perhaps unconscious, homage to the 'Unities' even in Romantic plays. Sidney's sarcasms in the *Apology* would have found far less application to the Romantic comedies of the nineties than to those of the beginning of the eighties. Shakespeare, in particular, was working out a new technique which went far to reconcile the virtue of Romantic drama with the truth of classical criticism. Even *The Two Gentlemen of Verona*, the loosest in composition of the comedies written by him before *The Case is Altered*, was far from approaching in extravagance the pieces held up to ridicule by Sidney. The action of *The Merchant of Venice* moved only to and fro between Venice and Belmont, and occupied only a few months: that of *The Comedy of Errors* went on in a single city and occupied a single day. When, later on, he admitted exceptionally wide limits of space or of time, as in *King Henry V* and *The Winter's Tale*, an explaining chorus or apologetic prologue testified eloquently to the growing force of the rule. Yet the Prologue to *Every Man in his Humour* shows how vigorously those extravagances still throve at the date of that play.[1] *The Case is Altered*, then a recent, perhaps the latest sensation of the stage, bears the strongest witness to its author's resolve to attenuate, if he could not wholly evade them. No child new swaddled in the first act becomes a greybeard in the fifth; no chorus wafts us over the seas; there are far-off rumours of battle, but no mimic warfare is brought upon the stage. The action begins with the departure of Paulo for the campaign in which he is taken prisoner, and ends with his release and return; if not a matter of days, as in Plautus, it need not occupy more than a few weeks. Everything, again, happens in the same city—Milan, or in the country near. In respect to the 'unity of place', *The Case is Altered* occupies precisely the position of *Every Man in* and *Every Man out of his Humour*; in respect of the 'unity of time' it is less 'romantic' than *Sejanus* or *Catiline*. The play thus acquired, in spite of its multiplicity of interest, a certain concentration and rapidity. That the writer had achieved a real unity of action is less evident, though he clearly exerted much resource in the effort. Some absurd incidents, such as Onion's wooing of Rachel, seem to spring in part from his desire to bind his wandering sprays of story together.

When we look, however, to the working out of the stories themselves, it becomes apparent that he is, in intention at least, an Elizabethan, aiming at modern and Romantic effects, developing every germ of cognate interest in Plautus, but ready, on occasion, to throw Plautine precedent completely aside, and give free scope to the dramatic discoveries of another society and another time. Even when he is closest to Plautus in situation, he is new and fresh in detail,

---

[1] Although written, in our view, several years later, the Prologue was adapted to the circumstances of 1598, and refers only to plays of that or an earlier date.

his extraordinary gift of inventing characteristic traits being in fact already mature, while in plot-construction and characterization he was still an apprentice.

## IV

Take, first, the handling of the Plautine motive of separation and recovery of children. The Roman treatment of this theme was in general, to the northern instinct, wanting in tenderness. Shakespeare had preluded the prodigal hilarities of *The Comedy of Errors* with the father's pathetic story of shipwreck and separation. He had also reinforced the pathos as well as the gaiety by adding a second pair of twins. The author of *The Case is Altered* was clearly of the same mind when he provided a second abduction and a second restoration, and doubled the good and evil hap of Hegio's son, Camillo, with the similar situation of Euclio's daughter, Rachel de Prie. Rachel, like Camillo, had been abducted as a child, and her recovery and restoration to her brother, Chamont, contributes to the symmetrical neatness of the denouement. The character of Count Ferneze, the father of Camillo and Paulo, is drawn with some power. The rude and primitive vehemence of Hegio is recalled in his bursts of tempestuous anger, but his nature is more romantically varied and modulated; he is less headstrong, and, in his son's phrase, more 'wayward' (I. vi 85). His anger and cruelty are rooted in grief, and the pathos which is merely implicit in Hegio is invoked and even emphasized by a series of telling and sometimes delicate strokes. He tells Maximilian, in a passage eloquent with passion, of ' that blacke, and fearfull, night '—still remembered as if it were yesterday—when he lost Camillo (I. ix). When Camillo actually appears, a prisoner and supposed to be Chamont (IV. ii), the father involuntarily recalls his lost son, and hastily thrusts the remembrance away:

Faith had *Camillo* liu'd,
He had beene much about his yeares, my Lord.
—He had indeed, well, speake no more of him.

When, by a daring dramatic stroke, he is about to commit Camillo to the gallows, it is again the image of the child he thinks lost which rises before his eyes and compels him to 'foolish pity':

> Stay, what forme is this,
> Stands betwixt him, and me, and holds my hand?
> (V. ix. 21, 22.)

But Ferneze's gusts of sorrow or anger are crossed by gayer moods. Like Justice Clement he is easily placated by wit. He can bandy chaff with Onion, and insist upon the rogue's pardon at the hands of an offended guest (I. viii); he can rally Juan-Angelo upon his fourteen mistresses (II. v), approve Christophero's suit to the beggar's daughter, and then make love to her himself (II. vi). The recovery and recognition scene, on the other hand (V. xii), is surprisingly ineffective. 'O my dear *Paulo* welcome!' is the only greeting to the son whose capture he has passionately resented. And even the discovery of his long-lost child, in the prisoner whom he has just tortured, plucks from him words of no more penetrating pathos than the commonplace

> O happy reuelation! ô blest hower!
> O my *Camillo*!

Ferneze is, however, not the only finder or loser. The whole action appears to be preoccupied with the pursuit or loss or recovery of three precious things: Ferneze's sons, Rachel, and Jaques's treasure. In the fifth act these three lines of development are brought to a simultaneous climax with a machinelike precision of symmetry which effectually banishes pathos and approaches burlesque. The scene (V. xi) where the Count, Christophero, and Jaques by turns declaim their despair in a sort of catch, is more like the gay finale of *As You Like It* than anything else in the Elizabethan drama that professes to be serious:

> *Count.* O my sonne, my sonne.
> *Chris.* My deerest *Rachel*.
> *Iaq.* My most hony gold.

*Count.* Heare me *Christophoro.*
*Chris.* Nay heare me *Iaques.*
*Iaq.* Heare me most honor'd Lord.

This is but one of the points in this extremely resourceful play in which we have to contrast the writer's lavish provision of dramatic apparatus with his imperfect command of its powers.

But the *Captives* possesses a second, perhaps even stronger attraction for Elizabethan Romantic drama, in its central situation, where the sentimental interest of fidelity involving a tragic penalty is made more piquant by mistaken identity. The Tyndarus-Philocrates story is taken over with all its essential incidents in the fortunes of Chamont and Camillo. Camillo, like Antonio in *The Merchant of Venice*, barely escapes the penalty of the obligation he has incurred. The sentiment of fidelity to such obligations is continually provoked in the course of the play; but in a temper more akin to satire than to sentiment; as an expectation frustrated. The writer shows a curious disposition to emphasize the disappointments in store for those who anticipate fidelity. The faithful Camillo is an exceptional figure in a society full of people who betray confidence, or whose confidence is betrayed, or who combine both roles in their own person.

Each of Rachel's lovers either receives the confidence of an unsuspecting rival, whom he proceeds to betray, or innocently betrays such confidence himself. Onion entrusts his secret to Christophero, who has a similar secret of his own; Christophero asks permission of the Count to marry, which the Count first cordially gives, and then proceeds to make love himself to the object of Christophero's affections. Paulo commits Rachel to Angelo, a friend for whom he borrows in anticipation Hamlet's glowing words to Horatio, as one
        whome my election hath design'd
As the true proper obiect of my soule. (I. vi. 31, 32.)
And Angelo, like Ferneze, proceeds to make love to her himself. Jaques de Prie is the trusted steward of Chamont.

but he has stolen his treasure and abducted his daughter. And Pacue, the page, after being charged to secrecy, makes known the change of roles between Chamont and Camillo, with disastrous results to the latter. Jaques de Prie has his prototype in the slave Stalagmus who abducted the child Philocrates. But the treachery of Pacue is deliberately substituted, as the means of disclosure, for the much more effective device of Plautus—the excellent scene in which Tyndarus plays his desperate game of self-repudiation with the amazed and all but baffled Hegio being thus lost without any compensation. We must not, however, take the writer of *The Case is Altered* for an indignant moralist or a bitter cynic because he has a turn for exposing the seamy side of friendship. The atmosphere of the play is by no means oppressive with moral consciousness; and even the victims of these betrayals condone them with remarkable facility. In this respect the play falls into line with the convention of easy forgiveness already fairly well established in Romantic comedy. Proteus in *The Two Gentlemen of Verona*, Angelo in *Measure for Measure*, like Iachimo later on, all receive mercy instead of justice from those friends whose trust they have grossly betrayed; and though it is easy to distinguish between the light-hearted indulgence of Valentine for his friend, and the lofty benignity of Posthumus's or Prospero's 'vengeance', yet there was no time in Shakespeare's life at which he rejected this motive in Romantic comedy. Even Shylock was doubtless understood by every one, including the author, as treated with Christian lenity. Angelo's offence against Paulo, in our play, is as grievous as that of Proteus; but a single burst of eloquent anger satisfies his resentment for this wrong, and the traitor is restored to confidence with a 'Come Signior *Angelo*, hereafter proue more true' (V. viii. 78). Jaques de Prie, who has stolen his master's treasure and his infant daughter, is similarly forgiven, with no better pretext; and even presented, as a free gift, with the treasure he has stolen (V. xiii). This is a deliberate departure from the stern retribution meted out at the close of the *Captives* to the slave Stalagmus, who is sent to the horrible tortures from which Tyndarus had just been released. The only persons who receive any punishment at all at the 'happy and vnlookt for ioyes' of the finale are those whose successful robbery of the robber has chiefly contributed to bring his crime to light; and they suffer nothing more grievous than the stocks.

V

If the author of *The Case is Altered* exhibits only a thin and uncertain vein of romance where he was developing the quasi-romantic motives already offered by his Plautine sources, how was it with the motive of which they furnished only the barest hint, but with which Romantic comedy could least of all dispense? A love-interest there had to be, and if we do not spontaneously class *The Case is Altered* with *As You Like It* or *Love's Labour's Lost* as a comedy of romantic love, it is not because it is deficient in love-making. A considerable proportion of the men in the play, from Count Ferneze to the groom in his hall, pay their addresses to Rachel de Prie. All suppose her to be a beggar's daughter; but this makes no difference in their desire to marry her. Virtue and beauty completely carry the day with them all over considerations of interest or of class. Yet in spite of this wide diffusion of romantic magnanimity, the amount of sentiment actually expended on Rachel is extremely small. Paulo alone resembles the ardent lovers of Romantic drama, and neither the brief parting scene nor the briefer scene of his return, which exhausts their visible intercourse, suggests that love was, as such, of much interest to the writer. What he cares for is love at cross-purposes, love producing entanglements and betrayals, and putting wise men off their balance. Rachel herself is, indeed, touched with a charm rare among the women of Jonson. But the charm lies rather in the quiet strength of character with which she supports the embarrassments of her position than in any grace or spirituality of speech. She is delicately but very slightly drawn; comparable neither as a dramatic creation nor for intrinsic importance in the plot with Julia in *The Two Gentlemen of Verona*, far less with **Portia**, among the heroines of recent drama; little more than a 'gracious silence', like Virgilia, innocently provoking the admirations which set men at odds. It is only when we think of the terrible talking Julia of *Poetaster*, or of the wooden Bridget of *Every Man in His Humour*, that we feel the relative quality of drawing shown in her reticent figure, and wonder whether indeed she be the work of the same brain. The suit of the Count for Rachel's hand is a daringly romantic motive, very imperfectly justified by character or circumstance, but Jaques de Prie's avarice had to be alarmed by receiving the proposals of a person of higher status than his own for his daughter's hand. Plautus accounts quite satisfactorily for the situation; his Megadorus is a rich man who, for very intelligible reasons, desires to marry the daughter of a poor man. The whole transaction begins and ends in considerations of cool common sense. The author of *The Case is Altered* naturally wished to retain the miser's comic alarm; the Count, as the person whose suit was most difficult to explain, and therefore most alarming, had precisely for that reason to sue, and not even directly to herself but to the 'beggar' father in person. But he wished to transfer this situation from the matter-of-fact world of Plautus, where it is quite natural, to a romantic soil: his Count is no Megadorus, but a Cophetua, who willy-nilly 'loves a beggar-maid'. Romance would require him to court the beggar-maid; but the comic ulterior purpose requires him to approach her father. The situation remains; the character is altered, and the new wine agrees very ill with the old bottles. It is hardly credible that a great noble, so far gone in love with a beggar's daughter as seriously to seek her hand, should be able coolly to analyse and discount his own emotions, to see at once with, and through, the lover's eye:

I spide her, lately, at her fathers doore,
And if I did not see in her sweet face
Gentry and noblenesse, nere trust me more:
But this perswasion, fancie wrought in me,
That fancie being created with her lookes,
For where loue is, he thinkes his basest obiect
Gentle and noble; I am farre in loue. (II. vi. 37-42.)

No such objection can be taken to the suit of Christophero. But it is characteristic of the technique of the play that by means of his suit the Megadorus-Euclio scene is reproduced in duplicate.

In addition to these three lovers, who represent in some sort Lyconides and Megadorus, Rachel has two others who have no counterpart in Plautus. Angelo is before all things the treacherous lover. The motive of treachery in love recurs with an almost mechanical persistence throughout the play: the Count betrays Christophero, and Christophero, Onion; but Angelo is a dishonest wooer as well as a disloyal friend.

Onion is the burlesque lover of the piece. To parody in a homely amour the highflown romance of dignified lovers had before this been a frequent function of the dramatic clown. Launce enumerating the 'cate-log' of the merits of his milkmaid anticipates Touchstone's wooing of Jane Smile, and of Audrey. Onion too has set his heart on 'a poor man's daughter', and he hopes, as Touchstone will presently follow him in doing, that his mistress is 'none of the honestest', and for a reason that Touchstone only bettered—because other wise she would not have him (II. ii).

The other love affairs belong wholly to the author of *The Case is Altered*. With the two daughters of Ferneze we pass definitely from the domain of Plautus into territory characteristically if not exclusively Elizabethan. Again and again, from the last decade of the sixteenth century onwards, the growing severance of the national life into two opposed camps reflected itself upon the stage in contrasted figures of grave and gay, of the 'melancholy' and the festive. Shakespeare himself in *Twelfth Night* glanced with impartial mockery at the foibles of both. And Jonson, with his peculiarly alert scent for the humours of the time, had been before Shakespeare. At the Court of Cynthia the serious Arete plays a part, not unlike that of Malvolio, among the revellers who have drunk 'the New Fountain waters' which they vainly offer her; to Moria and Philautia and Phantaste she is 'good ladie *Sobrietie*', 'the extraction of a dozen of *Puritans*, for a looke', and with a 'set face ... as shee were still going to a sacrifice' (IV. v). In the 'case of matrons colour'd blacke' (II. iii. 1), Aurelia and Phoenixella, the author of our play drew a similar contrast with even more emphasis. Aurelia and Phoenixella do not merely 'exhibit' their several humours, they announce and expound them, and with much felicity of illustration. The incorrigibly gay Aurelia, who refuses to set her face even for a dead mother because she wears mourning, is nearer of kin to the Jonsonian sisterhood of Sempronias and Saviolinas than to Shakespeare's Beatrice. Her sprightly nature is hard at the bottom as well as on the surface. Phoenixella, on the other hand, has, like Milton's Penseroso and the Lady in *Comus* (whom her language recalls), her hidden and lofty joys—

> I meane that happy pleasure of the soule,
> Deuine and sacred contemplation
> Of that eternall, and most glorious blisse,
> Proposed as the crowne vnto our soules. (II. iv. 35–8.)

On each of these maids the author, with his usual generosity, has lavished two masculine figures—their 'servants' Angelo and Francisco, and the seeming strangers, Chamont and 'Gasper', whose advent throws both sisters into a 'taking', and banishes all other thoughts of love. It is subtly imagined, and with a delicacy of imagination rare among the Elizabethans, Shakespeare apart, that the sister upon whom their mother's death prints more deep 'effects of sorrow' is instinctively drawn to the unknown Camillo by the likeness to her mother which she has been the first to perceive (VI. ii).

## VI

The story of Euclio and his treasure, unlike that of Hegio and his sons, offered little analogy to the subjects of Elizabethan romantic comedy. The passion for money had rarely as yet been brought into English drama. And the moneyed man, when he occurred, had been a terrible rather than a sordid figure. Barabas and Shylock are money-kings, formidable and unscrupulous in getting and spending alike, who amass with passionate greed, but turn their hoards into weapons for the destruction of any man who threatens their profits. It is only incidentally that Shylock is amusing, as in his divided laments over his ducats and his daughter; and Barabas is never amusing. Euclio is wholly without the grandeur or the pathos with which even the lesser and more repellent of these great creations is at moments touched. He is a niggard whose only notion of thriving is not to spend. Poverty has made the parsimonious habit second nature, and when he finds a treasure one day, he becomes a hoarder pure and simple. It has been objected to the consistency of Plautus's representation, that a thoroughgoing miser would not have surrendered the treasure, when found, even in the shape of his daughter's dowry. He would have made the rich son-in-law provide the dowry himself, as he makes him provide the wedding feast. Both Jonson and Molière seem to have felt this difficulty; they have, at any rate, both obviated it, though in quite different ways. Harpagon's only thought to the last is to recover his beloved 'cassette'; Anselme, far from getting a dowry, has to pay the 'commissaire' and pay for the miser's wedding coat, as the price of his consent. Jaques de Prie cannot, naturally, for a moment be compared as a study of character with Harpagon. He has, indeed, isolated traits, due to Jonson's dramatic invention, which are not unworthy of Molière; as in his parting cautions to Rachel (II. i) for the security of his house. Euclio in this situation gives clear matter-of-fact instructions. Jaques's anxiety shows itself more dramatically (like Kitely's) in nervous hesitation between different expedients: Rachel is first to lock herself in:

> Lock thy selfe in, but yet take out the key,
> That whosoeuer peepes in at the key-hole,
> May yet imagine there is none at home . . .
> But harke thee *Rachel*: say a theefe should come,
> And misse the key, he would resolue indeede
> None were at home, and so breake in the rather:
> Ope the doore *Rachel*.[1]

But Jaques is far less consistently wrought out than Harpagon. Harpagon is a Molièresque creation on a Plautine base; Jaques is rather a Euclio transposed and elaborated, a classical nucleus overlaid with trappings of more romantic circumstance and more poetic speech, and provided with a sinister past, not strikingly in keeping with his disposition. This timid miser, who shudders at a courteous word, was once a criminal on a grand scale, who carried off his lord's treasure and his infant daughter—a Stalagmus in short, grafted upon a Euclio. He has worse to fear than demands on his purse; and as the recovery of his lost treasure has been preceded by his confession of the theft, he is glad, miser as he is, to be allowed to resign it to its owner. Molière secured the consistency of his miser's character by dropping the surrender; Jonson—for he it surely was—by altering the circumstances. And Jonson gives his miser, too, some flashes of the lyric exaltation which the passion of avarice assumes only in more highly strung souls than Euclio's. He has moments which recall the outbursts of Barabas, of Volpone, of Mammon, and are not even distantly suggested in the pedestrian anxieties of Euclio. Volpone, singing his morning hymn to his treasure, hails it as 'Thou sonne of Sol, but brighter then thy father'. And Jaques salutes his gold as 'a sweet companion', 'my deere child', and 'King of Kings' (III. v). He even has moments of visionary rapture. 'See see, it was an Angell cald me

[1] This is well commented on by Castelain, *u.s.* p. 202.

forth', he cries on seeing the gold pieces at his feet (V. ii. 5):

> Gold, gold, man-making gold, another starre,
> Drop they from heauen? no, no, my house I hope
> Is haunted with a Fairy,

and then he calls with curious incongruity, as if the voice of Euclio suddenly revived in him, upon his household god, 'my deere *Lar*'. More than this, he has gleams of human tenderness, unexpected and moving as Shylock's cry for his daughter. He steals the treasure, but if he also steals the two-years' child it is

> Because it lou'd me so, that it would leaue
> The nurse her selfe, to come into mine armes,
> And had I left it, it would sure haue dyed. (II. i. 38 f.)

But he is quite without the keen dramatic imagination, as he is without the inexhaustible resource, of the Fox. His ruses are not the acts of one savagely and insolently sporting with human credulity, but the desperate devices of a timid man to avoid discovery. He forestalls Volpone's glowing language; but the low cunning which buries his hoard under a delusive bed of dung is that of farmer Sordido, secreting his harvest of grain in the earth:

> Who will suppose that such a precious nest
> Is crownd with such a dunghill excrement?
> (III. v. 14, 15.)

## VII

While the comic quality of Euclio is thus modified by alien hints of peril and of poetry, the genuine humour of the slave Strobilus, the chief contriver of Euclio's comic harms, is reproduced, with abundant heightening of native Elizabethan fun, in the jesters and serving men of our play. Strobilus is duplicated in Onion and Juniper; and the treasure-stealing scene (IV. ix) gains in piquancy by the combination of two scenes of Plautus: Juniper is caught by Jaques and searched, like Strobilus in *Aulularia*, IV. iv, while the 'ingenious and turbulent' Onion, who has escaped by climbing a tree, watches, from that coign of vantage.

like Strobilus in IV. vi, the miser unwittingly betray his buried treasure. It is an excellent addition that Onion is one of Rachel's lovers, and that he and Juniper are prosecuting his suit (instead of merely, like Strobilus, watching the house in the interest of his master's suit), when caught by Jaques; and their sudden comic conversion from the business of love by the prospect of the gold has no counterpart in the original. In their radical influence upon the action they resemble the clever slave of Plautus and Terence rather than the Elizabethan serving-man, whose function was habitually jest, not stratagem. In this respect Onion and Juniper belong to the category not of Launce and Speed, Launcelot or Touchstone, but of Brainworm or even Buffone. They apply the salutary medicament to Jaques's swollen humour. But this Plautine or Jonsonian function is worked out by characters singularly fresh and unscholastic, full of the vernacular sap and savour of Elizabethan London.

The London shoemaker, sitting at work in his shop, and singing or cracking jests with the passers-by, had already hit the fancy of novelist and playwright; and for some years before 1597 the stage cobbler had been a stock type with well-defined traits, like the braggart soldier, but altogether English and very near to life. He was commonly a sturdy humorous fellow, independent and plain-spoken towards prince and nobles, like the millers and 'pinners' of folk-legend; full of pithy phrases, but also given to learned allusions and big words, which he vented in mangled forms. Comic effect was thus complicated in him with the charm of robust character. And the comic effect itself rested partly upon mere blundering, but partly, as in the jests of the Court fool, upon genuine humour and wit. The cobbler in fact tended to become a variation upon that hackneyed type—a jester who might be employed by the Court, and who could face it when needful with the easy truculence and chartered licence of the Court 'fool', or the country 'pinner', but who was in reality a City craftsman to the core. Ralph in *The Cobbler's Prophesie*, Strumbo in *Locrine* (both of the eighties), were followed by Deloney's famous Simon Eyre in *The Gentle Craft* (1597) and Dekker's adaptation of him in *The Shoemaker's Holiday* (1599). The type was thus in fashion in 1598, the probable date of our play, and Juniper clearly belongs to it, but his speech shows a stressing, characteristic of Jonson, of the quasi-learned traits.[1] He is a hardened picker-up of learning's crumbs; his brain, like Touchstone's, battens on the scraps of erudite phrase that come his way, and delivers them with a sedulous persistence far beyond Touchstone's. Though a much better wit than Master Stephen or Sir Andrew, he snatches at a new and sounding word with an avidity like theirs, and reproduces it, sometimes with not less ineptitude; which Onion then proceeds to carry a step farther. '*Caprichious?*' he cries on hearing Valentine speak of the censors of the 'Utopian' stage as 'a few *Caprichious* gallants'; '*Caprichious?* stay, that word's for me.' 'Coragio!' he presently exclaims to Onion, who has had his head broken; 'be not *caprichious*! what?' '*Caprichious?*' returns Onion; 'not I, I scorn to be *caprichious* for a scratch' (II. vii). His sham erudition has been thought, with little reason, to aim deliberately at the learned pedantry of Gabriel Harvey,[2] and his phrases are in fact at times merely pretentious, not inaccurate. And even his blunders have little of the virtue of the genuine malapropism. They are apt to be abstruse without being funny; they darken his meaning without those unintended felicities of suggestion which mark the genus on the lips of Dogberry, Winifred Jenkins, or Mrs. Malaprop herself.

### VIII

Was *The Case is Altered* written as a whole by Jonson? Neither external nor internal evidence allows of a quite

---

[1] The literary affinities and antecedents of Juniper have been set forth by C. Baskervill, *English Elements*, &c., p. 94 f. On his relations to Eyre cf. Stoll, *Mod. Lang. Notes*, 1906. Juniper's 'learned' vocabulary is studied by H. C. Hart in 9 *N. and Q.* vols. xi and xii.
[2] By Hart, *u. s.*

cogent reply. But we seem to be justified in laying down, first, that he almost certainly wrote considerable sections of it, especially those founded on the *Aulularia*, and exhibiting the 'humours' of the miser; secondly, that there is no part which he might not have written, and that the play as a whole is such as we should expect from a man of his temperament, proclivities, and training, adapting himself, at the outset of his career, to a vogue only partially congenial to him. A young dramatist, still struggling for success, its author aspired to produce a comedy of the type brilliantly exemplified within recent years or months by *The Two Gentlemen of Verona*, the revised *Love's Labour's Lost*, *The Merchant of Venice*. A trained scholar, with a keen, but not fanatical relish for classical technique, he perceived more clearly than most of his fellows how readily the plots and personnel of Latin comedy lent themselves to the purpose of such plays. Naturally, it was in this promising region that he sought the materials for his own. He found in one play a story of serious, sentimental interest, in another one of vigorous satirical humour; and he mingled these ingredients as romantic fashion required, but with unusual and imperfectly successful efforts to weld them into a single coherent action, and restrict them within moderate limits of place and time. All that his Plautine sources offered of either serious or comic motive he transferred resolutely to his modern scenery and setting; developing with evident care the love-story of which they contained barely a hint. But the handling of all this romantic matter, original or derived, betrays, together with a remarkable virtuosity in the invention of effective situations and effective detail, a decided poverty of sentiment. Scenic opportunities for passion are provided in unfailing abundance, but the ample apparatus is imperfectly put to use. There is a prodigious amount of love-making, but little or no convincing love; recoveries of lost children, but little pathos; betrayals and treacheries in profusion, treated with little dramatic and less of ethical *entrain*.

But we easily recognize, also, the marks of the Jonson who was to emerge, and to remain. The ingeniously elaborate plot construction; the multiplicity of parallel variations; the joy in sheer abundance in which he was an Elizabethan through and through;—in these things, as well as in a number of motives and phrases repeated or improved later on,[1] *The Case is Altered* prophesies as surely of the humorous invention of the mature Jonsonian drama as, in its less natural and spontaneous beauties, it catches a faint reflex of the passion and splendour of the early romances of Shakespeare.

[1] The following examples may be specified: Onion's fencing bout (II. vii) is a crude forecast of Bobadill's display. The ceremonious rehearsal of the pages (IV. iii) anticipates the courtiers' rehearsal in *Cynthia's Revels*. Jaques's precautions against thieves (II. i. 54) recur, in fuller detail, in *The Devil is an Ass* (II. i. 168–76). The satirical sketch of audiences at a contemporary theatre (II. vii) reappears in more finished form in the Induction to *Every Man out of his Humour*. The malapropism 'epitaphs' for 'epithets' (II. vii) is repeated in *Cynthia's Revels*, IV. iv; the phrase 'speak legibly' (V. iv) in *Every Man in his Humour*, I. iv; and Maximilian's phrase (of Juniper), 'his tongue has a happy turne when he sleepes' (I. viii), in *Poetaster* (III. i) of the bore in the Sacred Way.

# INTRODUCTION TO
# 'EVERY MAN IN HIS HUMOUR'

# EVERY MAN IN HIS HUMOUR

## I

*Every Man in his Humour* was first printed in Quarto in 1601, having been entered in the Stationers' Register on August 4, 1600. It was not again printed until 1616, when, after an elaborate revision, it was placed first in the Folio edition of Jonson's Works. The Quarto title-page describes the play as having been 'sundry times publickly acted'. The Folio title-page gives the date: 'a Comedy acted in the year 1598.' A letter of Tobie Matthew in the State papers, dated September 20, reports the performance of 'a new play called, Every man's humour'. That the play was then in fact new is confirmed by the silence of Meres, whose *Palladis Tamia* was published in the early autumn of the same year. For Meres, Jonson was merely the author of some not very distinguished tragedies. Yet *Every Man in his Humour* was clearly more successful than anything he had yet done. Aubrey calls it his 'first good' play. Rowe preserved a tradition that Shakespeare intervened to secure its acceptance by his Company. He in any case acted in it, his name heading the list of players added by Jonson to the Folio text.

In the Folio text the play, without material alteration of substance or import, underwent a thoroughgoing modification of form.[1] The character of the changes is set forth in some detail in the Appendix. Here it will suffice to say that they mark a very definite advance in technical and stylistic maturity; the scene, in particular, being transferred from Italy to London, thus assimilating this play to the series of

[1] Mr. Simpson, in his edition of this play, Oxford, 1919 (referred to henceforth as Simpson, *ed.*), p. xiii f., has shown that the Folio text must have been printed from the Quarto text as revised by Jonson, not from a freshly prepared manuscript.

later comedies from *Epicoene* onwards. At what date was this revision carried out?

External evidence is wholly wanting, and in default of it two alternative hypotheses until lately held the field.

(1) F. G. Fleay argued that it took place before 1603, on the ground that the sovereign, in the Folio text, is always referred to as 'the Queen'.[1] But it is plain that Jonson meant his play to stand in no open contradiction with its place in the Folio in the forefront of his comedies, or with the date assigned to it in the title-page. Similarly in the *Tale of a Tub*, when he revived and revised it in 1633, he left intact the allusions to 'her Majesty'. And the advance in maturity referred to strongly favours a much longer interval than three or four years.

(2) Brinsley Nicholson, followed by Professor Castelain,[2] proposed a date about 1606, on the following grounds:

(*a*) Nicholson (in the *Antiquary*, July and September, 1882) pointed out that Bobadill's exploit in the Quarto (E 4), 'Shalbe some ten years ago ... at the beleagring of *Ghibeletto*', is replaced in the Folio (III. i. 103) by one at 'Strigonium', i.e. Gran in Hungary. Gran was actually taken from the Turks in 1596-7. It is perhaps more likely that Bobadill's 'ten years', fictitious in the Quarto, is *not* accurate in the Folio. Cf. his 'twenty score, that's two hundred' (Fol. IV. vii. 82).

(*b*) The oaths freely scattered through the Quarto text are in the Folio toned down or excised. Since the stylistic changes of the Folio are in general, on the contrary, towards a more drastic realism, it is reasonable to conclude that Jonson was conforming to the Act against oaths of 1605-6. But this obviously proves nothing against a later date.

(*c*) Nicholson, *u.s.*, again followed by M. Castelain, argues that a phrase in Wellbred's letter in the Folio version points to the same date: 'I haue such a present for

---

[1] Replacing 'the Duke' (of Florence) in the Quarto. So in Folio, IV. vii. 62, xi. 21-2, v. v. 18 (*ed.* Simpson).
[2] *La Vie et l'Œuvre de Ben Jonson*, pp. 873 ff.

thee (our Turkie company neuer sent the like to the Grand SIGNIOR'). An enormous sum (£5,322) was in fact paid by the Treasury in December, 1605, to the Company of Levant merchants 'for a present to the Grand Seignior' (*Calendar of Domestic State Papers, James I*, xv): the unusual amount of the 'present' being attested by the fact that the merchants had petitioned the Crown to bear the cost.

It will be seen that while (*a*) is of no weight, (*b*) and (*c*) establish 1606 only as the *terminus a quo* for the revision. Its limits of date are thus the ten years 1606–16.[1] But there are reasons, as shown by Mr. Simpson (*ed.* p. xxxi f.), for drawing the limits closer.

(1) The revised play, with its definitely English scene and personnel, groups itself closely with the English comedies from *Epicoene* onwards. And it is more likely to have followed the initial success of this manner in that play than to have been itself the pioneer.

(2) The Folio edition was probably prepared by Jonson during 1612. It contains no work, and no allusions to events, of later date. The alterations in the original texts, considerable in the older plays, cease altogether in *The Alchemist* (1610), *Catiline* (1611), and the *Epigrams* (entered on the Stationers' Register in 1612). The more radical revision of *Every Man in his Humour* is most naturally explained as a part of the process.

Cognate considerations apply to the determination of the date of the Prologue. The Prologue is first found prefixed to the Folio text of 1616. Its absence from the Quarto affords some presumption that it did not then exist, but does not preclude its having been written for and spoken at the original performance in 1598, and afterwards suppressed. Yet this latter hypothesis involves grave difficulties.

[1] Dr. E. K. Chambers (*Elizabethan Stage*, iii, p. 360) points out that the King's men revived the play for a performance before King James on February 2, 1605. The Audit Office Accounts of that year specify, 'On Candelmas night A playe Euery one In his Umor' (ibid. iv, p. 172). 'This revival', Dr. Chambers argues, ' would be a revision, and in fact seems to me on the whole the most likely date.'

Jonson's first original comedy had just been accepted by the leading company of his time, perhaps on Shakespeare's recommendation. Jonson was at no time a respecter of persons; but is it credible that even he would have chosen this occasion for a string of sarcasms upon the repertory of the company, with unmistakable reflections on the work of its famous playwright, himself an actor in the play? Was this an occasion, even, on which a man whose success was still in the balance would loftily invite his audience to 'see One such, to day, as other playes should be'? The temper of the Prologue is not too arrogant for Jonson, but its arrogance suits better a time, subsequent to the theatre-quarrel, in which his status was more assured. Further, it implies a security of conviction in dramatic theory which it is very doubtful whether Jonson had in 1598 or even in 1601 attained. *Every Man in his Humour* in its original form bears clear marks of an artist still feeling his way towards an ideal comic art; it is not consistently wrought out; different methods clash in it, and those that predominate are not in perfect keeping with the dogmas peremptorily announced in the Prologue.

His career during the next few years was still one of bold, even colossal, adventure. *Every Man out of his Humour* and *Cynthia's Revels* are singular sequels to a play just put forth, by the same author, as the ideal comedy. It is rash to dogmatize without more data than we possess; but the contents and tone of the Prologue alike suit best with the years ushered in by *Epicoene* and *The Alchemist*, when Jonson had definitively abandoned the exotic scenery and personnel and the abstract schematism, and begun to devote himself in reality to showing 'an image of the times'. In other words, the Prologue was probably written to introduce the new text of the play, one far more in keeping, as will be seen, than the old with the ideal of comedy it set forth. That the satirical allusions in the Prologue touch no play later than 1598 is to be explained in the same way as the deliberately introduced allusions to 'the Queen' in the Folio text: Jonson is concerned to retain the atmosphere of 1598, when, as he tells us, the play was first performed.

The play, in its final shape, thus belongs to two periods of Jonson's artistic development, ten or more years apart. To the first it owes the entire dramatic substance of plot, character, and dialogue; to the second an infinity of heightening strokes of style and traits of characterization The invention and personnel reflect the man at twenty-six; the style, the man approaching forty. But the ideal of comedy formulated in the Prologue was already, in substance, pursued in the play of 1598, though as yet imperfectly grasped and incompletely executed.

## II

The most definite source of the technique of *Every Man in his Humour* is the art of classical comedy, as formulated by Renascence criticism, particularly by Sidney in the *Apology for Poetry*, published some three years before the performance of the play. It embraced, in particular, the following principles:

(1) The Unities of Time, Place, and Action.
(2) Unity of tone: no admixture of tragic with comic matter.
(3) Truth to life: in the sense, not of modern realism, but of congruity with what is typical, or normal, in custom, action, and character.

These principles, however, in the powerful and original temperament of Jonson, received an individual colour and interpretation. He does not consciously innovate, and he remains the formidable and uncompromising champion of classical technique. But the dramas in which he himself applied it are sharply marked off from any other 'classical' dramas in literature. *Every Man in his Humour* conforms more closely to the above principles than any of its successors. But even here the counterplay of the Jonsonian temperament can be traced.

1. Of the *three Unities*, the unity of Time is not merely observed—the action falling within approximately twelve hours—but its whole course is laid out with meticulous precision, from early morning in Kno'well's house to supper-time at Justice Clement's.[1] The unity of Place is sufficiently complied with—all the scenes falling within the then limits of London.

The unity of Action, on the other hand, Jonson, here and later, applies in a manner distinctively his own. The plot of *Every Man in his Humour* is a complex of several actions, ingeniously tangled together. The more pronounced plot-disintegration of the following play is already foreshadowed, and the same cause is already at work: the satirist's desire to exhibit 'every man' suffering the effect of his 'Humour'. The series of particular actions which thus result do not yet break up the entire complex, but they prevent our ascribing to it the massive and articulated coherence of *Volpone* or *The Alchemist*. And the unity of these great dramas was won not by surrendering the multiplicity of minor actions so congenial to his Elizabethan passion for profusion, but by compelling them to become integral parts of the single all-embracing action. No wonder that Jonson transcribed with high appreciation, in the *Discoveries*, the passage in which Heinsius takes the side of those who understood the unity of a work of art to consist, not in simplicity, but in the oneness of many parts.[2] It may be noted that want of unity is not emphasized, in the Prologue, among the failings of the contemporary drama.

2. *Unity of tone* was certainly aimed at by Jonson, although, in the original version, not completely attained. In this canon also, Jonson was following Sidney. In common with the great body of Renascence critics, Sidney regarded comedy as an instrument of ethical reform—it was

---

[1] The time indications are given in detail by Simpson, *ed.* p. 117, and will be found in the commentary to the play in the present edition.
[2] See the concluding section of the *Discoveries*.

to hold up a glass for the bettering of manners; and this ethical way of approach, though perfectly compatible with pure comedy, was liable to infuse into it an earnestness, even a bitterness, out of keeping with the comic spirit. Sidney, in whose noble humanity the comic spirit had little part, admitted with obvious reluctance that laughter, 'a scornful tickling' due to our perception of some deformity, might sometimes legitimately be produced by comedy. In Jonson, too, the reformatory and punitive temper of the Juvenalian satirist was yet more deeply ingrained than disinterested delight in humour. Its complete dominance was to issue in the ferocious comedy of *Volpone*. Our present play, after undergoing a most stringent revision, was left a piece of pure comedy. But in its first form young Lorenzo's passionate denunciation of the enemies of poetry, and even the savage punishments inflicted on the exposed and baffled Gulls, impaired the unity of comic tone.

3. Jonson aimed, finally, at *Truth to Life*. Renascence criticism interpreted its principle that comedy should be *imitatio veri* by its other doctrine of *decorum* or congruity. Both action and character were limited by the demand, in other words, that they should be in keeping with the normal and the customary. This was grounded upon the condemnation, pronounced by Aristotle and Horace alike, of personages in drama not modelled upon the type of their class,—women who were not timid, old men who did not glorify by-gone days. So Sidney defined comedy as 'an imitation of the common errors of our life', and threw the whole weight of his emphasis on the 'delight' which it produces by representing 'things that have a conveniency to us and our nature', in contrast, as just stated, with the laughter produced by mere oddity. Ethical and prudential motives had their part here also. A 'crafty Davus' or a 'vainglorious Thraso' on the stage were not there merely to amuse; they were to give us an 'experience, what is to be looked for' from crafty or vainglorious persons in general; which they could not do unless they were typical examples themselves.

Jonson, in make of mind, was, up to a certain point, naturally disposed to this typical and normal handling of character. His characters tend to be simple and in one plane, not because he held, like the idealist Sidney, that poetry should ignore the unedifying or inconsistent particulars in the interest of its lofty 'seriousness', but because his mind, strong rather than subtle, saw humanity as a collection of trenchantly defined groups. He seizes character under one aspect, because he sees it so; neglecting, because he does not see them, the cross-play of impulses, the inconsistencies and conflicts, the mingled strength and weakness, of which they are normally composed. His observation was prodigiously active and acute; but its energy was spent in accumulating illustrations of a single dominant trait, not in distinguishing fine shades. The nuances fell together for him, and the vast complexes of detail which his veracious eye collected, and his unsurpassed memory retained, grouped themselves about a few nuclei of ludicrous character.

On the other hand, there were elements in Jonson which conflicted with the broad generic painting of moral types contemplated by Sidney and the other critical advocates of dramatic decorum. Hard and unimaginative as his portrayal of character is, it is based upon the individual life about him, not upon abstract reflection; his personages are real men seen from a particular angle, not moral qualities translated into their human embodiments. Bobadill may be ranged, if we will, with the long line of military braggarts from Plautus's Pyrgopolynices onward; but that description is almost as rudimentary, considered as a summary of Jonson's creation, as it is when applied to Falstaff. Great scholar and doughty theorist as he was, Jonson lived in no secluded academe, but in the welter of Jacobean London, jostling in the crowd with friend and foe, glorying and drinking deep in the tavern with his fellow-poets, as in later days with his 'sons'. If the scholar's memories mingled constantly with his vision of men, he no more saw men merely 'through the spectacles of books' than Milton saw Nature; if theoretic abstraction occasionally, as in *Cynthia's Revels*, gained the upper hand, in all his freshest work, and notably in the present play, his characters are not constructed, but seen.

It remains to ask, What, then, did Jonson precisely mean by giving the comedy in which his partly typical, partly individual, presentation of character was first vigorously displayed its challenging title?

### III

We may, in the first place, distinguish three currents of literary tendency quite independent of the 'humour' fashion in origin, which nevertheless called in this piquant and flexible catchword [1] to their support, modifying its content but also themselves taking its colour.

(1) The stock Elizabethan analysis of character was the simple and summary one of the dominant trait or masterpassion. It achieved its highest reach in the characterization of Marlowe's sublime monomaniacs; it broke down before the profounder psychology of Shakespearean tragedy.

(2) Among dramatists and critics of the academic and courtly schools, the Renascence doctrine of *decorum* in the treatment of character—involving a similar dominance of a single trait—held rank, from the seventies onward, as literary orthodoxy. Before receiving the eloquent sanction of Sidney's *Apology*, it had been laid down by Edwards in the prologue to *Damon and Pithias*, 1571, and by Whetstone in the dedication of *Promos and Cassandra*, 1578.

(3) In the latter half of the reign this way of conceiving character further found support in the literary fashion of the typical character-sketch, consisting of a collection of

---

[1] The history and usage of the term, and of the various literary fashions associated with it, have been elaborately studied, among others by Baskervill, *u. s.*, ch. iii; Harris, *Modern Language Notes*, x, 'The Origin of the Seventeenth-century Idea of Humour'; Penniman, *Poetaster and Satiro-mastix*, p. xliii f.; Simpson, *ed.* Introduction. Cf. also Spingarn, *Critical Essays of the Seventeenth Century*, I. xv.

traits caught from the London life of the day. By Lodge and Nashe, in particular, this kind of sketch was carried out with keen veracity of observation and incisive brilliance of style. The fashion was powerfully promoted early in the nineties by the example of the *Characters* of Theophrastus (ed. Casaubon, 1592), where the whole method was an enumeration of characteristic traits,—of the things which the 'surly' or the 'affected' man would be likely to do or say.

The term 'humour', on the other hand, which came in literary usage to be a frequent synonym for the predominating trait of character, was, as is well known, not of literary origin at all. Properly a term of medieval physiology for one of the four essential fluids which composed the human 'temperament', it had come by the later sixteenth century to denote whatever element of character, through unequal mixture of the fluids, dominated the rest.

But the term rarely preserved the neutral usage of science. As a ready formula for human infirmities, it lent itself aptly to the Elizabethan turn for satire, and acquired a predominantly satiric usage. It rested on an analysis of character which rudely traversed Elizabethan heroics. The ideal which it presupposed was not the single-souled ardour of a superman, 'lift upward and divine', like Tamburlaine, but a perfectly balanced character like that of Shakespeare's Brutus, in whom 'the elements' were

> So mixed . . . that Nature might stand up
> And say to all the world, 'This was a man';

or the Jonsonian Crites—'a creature of a most perfect and diuine temper . . . in whom the humours and elements are peaceably met, without emulation of precedencie'.[1] Unluckily, on this analysis, the mass of men who were not in this sense perfect bore the brand not of mere incompleteness but of deformity. Preponderance connoted not superiority, but excess; and hence 'humour' acquired a suggestion of something odd or overbalanced, which coloured the entire

[1] *Cynthia's Revels*, II. iii.

Elizabethan usage of the term. The psychological platitude that every man has a dominant trait received a more cynical application in the satiric dogma that every man has his characteristic folly—a conclusion promoted by its concurrence with the derisive commonplaces of the Book of Proverbs and *The Ship of Fools*. The medieval love of classifying and cataloguing human infirmities, which culminated in Brandt's memorable shipload, persisted far into the Elizabethan period, and still survived at its close, under the new terminology of 'humours'.

Further, within this field of satirical or derisive usage the connotation of the term fluctuated widely, but in the main in one or other of several fairly well-defined directions. It drifted away from the darker to the lighter faults, from vices to follies; from cruelty or lust to social ambition or jealousy. It drifted away, in another direction, from the close connexion with character to denote mere passing impulse and caprice, or even a mere trick of manner or dress—'a yard of shoe-tie' or 'a three-piled ruff'. It drifted, again, towards a special class of follies—those of infatuated vanity and affectation. Here the nexus with character was retained, but the stress was laid upon the perverse developments of it which consist in pretending to a character not one's own. Among the accentuated social ambitions of later Elizabethan and Jacobean London this third application throve with especial vigour, like the term 'snob' under the not very dissimilar conditions of Thackeray's England. 'These are complements, these are humours,' says Moth after enumerating the tricks of the fashionable lover.[1] Cob, the water-bearer in our play, does not know the word, but Pizo-Cash, the merchant's clerk, is proud to explain to him that 'humour'—for which Cob says 'rheum'—'(as tis generally receiued in these days) it is a monster bred in a man by selfe loue, and affectation, and fed by folly'.[2]

---

[1] *Love's Labour's Lost*, III. i. 23.
[2] Quarto, III. i (sig. F3 verso). In the Folio version humour is treated as

What then was Jonson's theoretic position in regard to these floating currents of aesthetic doctrine, literary fashion, and popular psychology? There is no room for doubt that he was, in the first place, a whole-hearted adherent of the doctrine of *decorum*, as put forward, in particular, by Sidney. It is equally clear, further, from his classical exposition in the Induction to *Every Man out of his Humour*, that he not only accepted but insisted on the doctrine of 'Humours', in that stricter sense of the term which made this doctrine a proximate physiological and psychological counterpart of the aesthetic doctrine of *decorum*; that is, as a term applicable where

some one peculiar quality<br>
Doth so possess a man, that it doth draw<br>
All his affects, his spirits, and his powers,<br>
In their confluctions, all to runne one way;

while he openly derided, as 'more then most ridiculous', the loose popular usage of the word for the mere 'apish, or phantastike straine' which leads a coxcomb to don 'a pyed feather' or a 'three-piled ruff'. At the same time, the Humour psychology by its inveterate accentuation of obliquities fell in with and reinforced Jonson's ingrained bias towards the satirist's outlook upon human character. His Humour scheme became a new weapon in the hands of the satirist, and a new allurement to satire, seducing him later to those extravagances of biting analysis in which the business of the play stands still, and the satirist forgets the comic poet.

And finally, the realist in Jonson, his grip upon concrete fact, his eye for individual and local traits, for the very habit of mind and body in which each man lived, insensibly counteracted the mere rendering of types, infusing into the picture a peculiar Jonsonian richness not to be precisely paralleled elsewhere. Even if, in Mr. Spingarn's words, 'the conception of " humours " and of their function in comedy . . .

a peculiar foible of the fashionable world—'a gentleman-like monster, bred, in the speciall gallantrie of our time' (III. iv). This passage is misleadingly dated 1598 by the *N.E.D.* (*s.v.*).

is in a measure the adaptation of a fashionable phrase of the day to Sidney's theory of comedy, . . . the genius of Jonson has intensified and individualized the portrayal of character beyond the limits of mere Horatian and Renaissance decorum'.[1] The Humour motive, by its greater flexibility, contributed to this freer handling, by releasing the poet from the traditional categories of comic types. It provided a bridge between classical theory and modern life, and helped to render it possible for the master of satiric comedy, the doughty champion of classicism, and the most powerful of Elizabethan realists, to be united in the same man. In addition, by throwing the dramatic emphasis upon character at the cost of incident, it threw into the background, once for all, the comedy of mere intrigue.

### IV

How far was Jonson's conception of a Humour play, of a play based upon a comic exploitation of Humours, original? The answer is clear. In the severer acceptation of the term which Jonson championed, he stood, so far as we know, alone. His comedy of Humours would thus be, to this extent, original had he done nothing more than represent character from this new point of view. His more significant innovation lay in making the exhibition of the Humours the sole function of plot. But something known as a comedy of Humours was already in existence. A year or more before Jonson's play, one actually had appeared called, by Henslowe, the 'comedy of vmers' or 'the vmers', now shown to be identical with Chapman's *An Humorous Day's Mirth*. The piece was repeatedly performed at the Rose during the spring and summer of 1597. 'The sky hangs full of humour,' it is remarked at the outset, and rain may accordingly be expected; but 'the day is nevertheless likely to prove fair'; 'for we shall spend it with so humorous

---

[1] In *Critical Essays of the Seventeenth Century*, I. xv. Mr. Spingarn has thus qualified his earlier simple identification of 'humour' treatment of character and *decorum* (*Literary Criticism of the Renaissance*, p. 88).

acquaintance as rains nothing but humour all their lifetime.'

George Chapman, like Jonson a scholar writing for the popular stage, fluctuated between the deeper and the more current shades of meaning. His 'humorous' people all have some warp of disposition; but with some of them it is quite merged in a ridiculous trick of manner; as in Blanuel, whose humour of 'compliment' impels him to give a punctiliously literal *quid pro quo* for the polite phrases he receives; or in Martia, who has the humour of singularity, eschewing like Armado the idiom of the base vulgar. The humours of Florilla the 'Puritan' and Dowsecer the melancholy philosopher go somewhat deeper, for even in 1597 Puritanism was understood to mean more than the use of an eccentric phraseology. Yet what could be less Jonsonian than this young and beautiful Puritan lady, married to a count—a piquant anomaly, not a type? It is only in Labervele, the jealous husband, and Countess Moren, the jealous wife, that the warp of disposition altogether predominates over tricks of manner or of speech. Moreover, and this is the vital point, Chapman has made very little attempt to bring his plot into organic relation with his Humours. The central interest, such as it is, is provided by the tricks of the mischief-loving courtier Lemot; an interest of intrigue rather than of character, even when his victims, like the 'jealous' Labervele and Countess Moren, have some claim to be examples of genuine 'humour'.[1] The tricks themselves are of a curious and fantastic ingenuity, far removed from the everyday homeliness of Jonson's incidents. Romance and passion, so peremptorily excluded from the Jonsonian Humour plot, quicken the temperature of several scenes. 'This is no humour, this is perfit iudgment, . . . nay, he's more human than we all are,' says the King of Dowseler. And Marcia, 'Oh were all men such, Men were

[1] It is needless to do more than mention 'the humorous Mirth of Dick Coomes and Nicholas Proverbes' in Porter's nearly contemporary *Two Angry Women of Abingdon*. These humours, besides consisting solely of oddities, form merely an episode.

no men but gods; this earth a heaven; ... and who would not die with such a man?' Chapman anticipated Jonson in using the Humour motive in drama, but he did not anticipate the Jonsonian Humour play.

## V

Few Elizabethan plays owe less, in fact, to the stimulus or guidance of previous literature than *Every Man in his Humour*. Its plot, clearly devised by the poet himself for his own purpose, had as a whole no counterpart in Elizabethan or in any other literature; what other known playwright would have lavished his utmost resources of wit and labour upon one so severely denuded of sensational appeal? But certain parallels to particular incidents and personages can be adduced which are hardly accidental.

Some hints of the typical scheme of Plautine comedy—so freely appropriated in *The Case is Altered*—are clearly to be detected. The pair of elderly citizens, deceived and outwitted by a pair of lively young men; the shrewd servingman who plays their game—in the intervals of playing his own; and the bragging soldier,—these stock ingredients of Plautus's plots are traceable in rudiment in Jonson's.

Chapman's *Humorous Day's Mirth* again, however remote from Jonson's work in conception, and however inferior to it, supplied some hints for his salient group of Gulls, the zest and salt of the play.

The gull was, as a literary type, the creation of the nineties, and in particular of the group of writers who, about the middle of the decade, first introduced into English the mingled wit, coarseness, and cruelty of Roman satire. In its earlier use the term denoted merely the credulous simpleton who is made game of by his fellows. But harmless fools of this kind hardly satisfied the needs of the new satire, for which ferocity was *de rigueur*; its instrument was the wheel, and it called for victims more substantial than butterflies. Sir J. Davies's epigrams on the gull put a new construction on his character admirably adapted for this purpose. Fundamentally 'witless' the gull remains; he is no longer, however, a helpless innocent, but poses as a gallant and a wit,—'he which seemes, and is not wise'. He is the would-be fashionable fool, at once pretentious and spiritless, who wears a silver-hilted sword but meekly accepts an insult, parades as a successful wooer but runs away at sight of a velvet gown, and relies for making a figure in company on a stock of picturesque oaths, laboriously got by heart, or a 'melancholy' silence. A year or two later, Davies's portrait was resumed, with even heightened scorn, by Guilpin in the *Skialetheia*.[1] Such a society inevitably created its swarm of foolish pretenders—in other words, the 'gulls' of the more flagrant type delineated by the satirists. Social and literary developments, entirely independent in origin, here concurred. Most of the traits of Davies's gull reappear in Labesha, but his figure, however contemptible, is not yet touched with the acridity of the satirist, which in fact only entered the drama with the Stage Quarrel at the close of the decade. The satirist posed as a moral censor, and used his wit to rend and mutilate; Chapman wrote as a dramatist, whose traditional aim and function were to amuse; and Labesha is meant to be, and for an Elizabethan audience doubtless was, purely laughable.

Stephano and Mattheo both owe something to Labesha, but they are even more 'witless'. Most of the general traits taken by Chapman from Davies are borrowed by Jonson from Chapman for his Stephano, together with the suggestion of one or two dramatic situations due to Chapman himself. Thus, Stephano's evasions when called to make good his swaggering boasts are plainly modelled upon Labesha's; but the execution is more incisive. The childish threat and the transparent subterfuge are stock expedients of both Gulls. Labesha, when threatened by Moren,

[1] Cf. Baskervill, *English Elements in Jonson's Early Comedy*, p. 108 f., and especially Routh, 'London and the Development of Popular Literature', *Cambridge Literary History*, vol. iv, p. 316 f.

declares that he will 'go and tell your lady'; when dared by Lemot to make good a rash insult he retreats hastily into compliment:

> *Le.* Sirra, tell me what you know me for, or else by heaven, I'll make thee better thou hadst never know how to speak.
> *Labesha.* Why, sir, if you will needs know, I know you for an honourable gentleman and the kings minion, &c.

Stephano's *voltefaces* when confronted by Musco and young Lorenzo are clearly of the same brand.

### VI

The preceding sections have attempted to give an account of the influences, inner and outer, which co-operated with Jonson's powerful mentality to produce his first notable comedy. It remains to illustrate, in more detail, the working out of his design in the characterization —a constituent of drama of even more surpassing importance, as we know, in his judgement, at this stage, than was 'action' in Aristotle's.

The two elder men are not yet the insistently ridiculous figures of Jonson's later comedy, or of the Plautine heavy father whom they vaguely recall. Kno'well[1] indeed delivers himself of much genuine wisdom, and has even, without ground, been compared with the flawless metal of the later Asper and Crites, who speak Jonson's mind if they do not reflect his person. That Jonson did not represent himself in this or any other character of the play may be safely inferred from Dekker's taunt that he had 'left Horace' (i.e. himself) 'out of' it.[2] And Kno'well clearly had, in Jonson's view (himself at the standpoint of twenty-five), some characteristic weaknesses of elderly men. Even his gravely elaborate counsel to the unteachable Stephen was an amiable fatuity, and for his son's literary dreams he shows

---

[1] The later names are used for convenience, even when the reference is to the Quarto text.
[2] *Satiro-mastix*, Preface, sig. A 2 verso.

(especially in the early text) something of the philistine contempt of the traditional stage father in such circumstances. His indignant comments on Wellbred's letter mark a like excess of asperity. It is one of the signs of the greater realism of the Folio text (involving here, as often, the softening of a Humour trait) that Wellbred's letter there fairly justifies his resentment.

In Kitely the Humour motive is carried out with no suggestion of ambiguity. He is the best example in the play of its working in Jonson's hands. Neither jealousy nor avarice had yet been painted in English drama so soberly and justly, yet wholly within the limits of comedy. The germs of Shylock and Iago in him make no headway against the inertia of a timorous citizen in 'flatcap and velvet-shoes', whose brooding plots are appropriately cut short by the household bell which summons his wife's 'dear musse', not to any 'terrible feat', but to the parlour for breakfast. Kitely's own image for his state, when he says that his brain is become a mere 'hourglass' for the running sands of barren suspicion, admirably describes the disintegration of will and purpose which makes his inexhaustible suspicions harmless. The excellent scene with Cash (III. iii) may recall its tragic counterpart, King John's hesitating disclosure of a graver secret to Hubert; but even if he owed anything to this suggestion, Jonson's treatment is entirely his own, and he has added at least one happy touch—Kitely's final pretence, after disclosing his mind, that the real secret is still untold, followed by a solemn adjuration to the clerk not to disclose it to his mistress.

Of the young men, on the other hand, Edward Kno'well suffers perceptibly from having been designed for two functions, of neither of which he is allowed the full benefit. As the 'hero', who woos and wins the hardly credible Bridget, he has from the first a merely nominal existence. As representative of the 'humour' of idle poetry, he lingers, in the mature play, only as an ineffectual ghost. The situation of the poetic son in conflict with a worldly-wise father, albeit one who had himself in youth been similarly addicted, clearly had an interest for Jonson's imagination, and probably for his memory; but as Lorenzo's great outburst in the Quarto text shows, it was not easily kept true to the atmosphere of comedy; even his fuller treatment in *Poetaster* is curiously stiff and dry. Edward Kno'well is left, in fact, not so much a Humorist himself as one who contributes to procure the saving ridicule and exposure for the Humorists proper—a young University man of wit and culture about town, whose ironical sarcasm of various shades, from the openly jocose which suffices for cousin Stephen, to the incisively urbane, applied to Matthew and Bobadill, is the principal instrument in the intellectual discomfiture of the gulls.

Edward Kno'well's match with Bridget is a palpably rudimentary survival from the Plautine plot-scheme. It is completely divested of romance without any compensating addition of comic *vis*, Humorous or otherwise. She is capable of accepting the egregious Master Matthew as her 'servant', yet shows on the whole enough good sense to disqualify her as a representative of any other Humour than that of insipidity. The other women, Dame Kitely and Tib, are pleasant enough sketches of the London housewife of the day, without any specifically 'humorous' traits. Both become momentarily 'jealous' of their husbands, without ground, but with ample provocation. Jonson knew something of the Humours of women, as *Every Man out of his Humour* was soon to show. But, on the whole, the anonymous writer who capped our piece in 1609 with an *Every Woman in her Humour* had every excuse for interpreting Jonson's title in the sense of *Vir*, not of *Homo*. *Mulier* remained a blank space in the canvas, worthy to be better filled.

In Brainworm, on the other hand, the chief contriver of the comic harms, Jonson's power of building lifelike character of composite materials is brilliantly displayed. The wily intriguing slave of Plautus, who helps the son to deceive the father, was easily adapted to the further business of provoking exhibitions of humour and providing traps for fools. In Jonsonian comedy the shrewd provoker and exploiter of follies was to become a more and more indispensable role, and Brainworm is only the first of a series of counterparts in this function—Buffone, MaciIente, Mercury in *Cynthia's Revels*, Mosca, Face. But Brainworm, unlike his successors, is still a genial figure. His plots are at bottom a laughable jest, carried out without malignity towards his victims, and his wit wins him forgiveness and the right hand of fellowship from the genial distributor of punishments and rewards.

Such a role, however, did not lend itself readily to the broad typical manner of the Jonsonian Humour. The old soldier begging on the strength of his campaigns, the 'coney-catcher' imposing on simpletons in this disguise, were common figures in the streets, and Brainworm's masquerade is elusive enough to deceive his shrewd master; the man himself, however, was no kinsman of the English rogue, but an original mixture of the devoted servant, the exploiter of humanists and gulls, and the genially mischievous wag. The second trait marks him off from all previous clowns and fools; the first from Chapman's gamesome aristocrat Lemot.[1]

With the group of Gulls we reach the focus of the play as a comedy of Humours. The contrasts of town and country did not enter English drama with Jonson, but no one had delineated so incisively as he the distinctive breeds of foolish pretender proper to the two. The young man of good family and means sent by his friends in the country to be introduced to town society, and the London shopkeeper's son, pushing his way into the company of gallants and scholars, offered tempting points of analogy and divergence even on the low level of the gull type. Native fatuity is compounded in Stephen with the ordinary helplessness of a novice fresh to the town. He has not even the accomplish-

---

[1] Miss W. Smith (*Mod. Phil.* v. 562 f.) has pointed out his resemblance to the Italian zany.

ments to be expected of the country-bred; his first escapade is to buy a hawk, but he is helpless without 'a booke to keepe it by'. With cruel consistency Jonson despoils him of every shred of masking disguise. He has not the wit to give his sham even a moment's semblance of reality; he imposes upon no one save—an incisive touch—his fellow-gull of the town; and the scene in which the two gulls exchange admiring compliments has, save that both are artlessly sincere, something of the quality of Molière's Orgon and Tartuffe kneeling to each other. Both aspire to be thought men of fashion and gallantry, both make pretensions to verse and to success in love; but their relative competence in all these matters is nicely graded. Matthew is the son of a fishmonger, and apparently needy (he has but two shillings in his pocket), but he has a veneer of fashion quite beyond the better-born Stephen's reach. Matthew takes lessons in swordsmanship; Stephen's soldierly ambition extends only to the possession of a Toledo—which proves 'a poor prouant rapier',—and a mastery of military oaths which he forgets at the critical moment. Matthew is a voluble pretender to poetry, knows where to steal, and in his melancholy moods, as he gives out, will 'ouer-flow you half a score, or a dozen of sonnets at a sitting'; the more artless Stephen naïvely discloses his intellectual nakedness in his 'posy', and his notion of the fashionable humour of melancholy is (like Blanuel's) to sit in dogged silence on a stool.[1]

The third Gull, Bobadill, is the most original and subtle creation of the three. He approaches two or three conventional types, but falls within none. On the one side he

---

[1] The theory, championed by Mr. Fleay and Professor Penniman, that Matthew stands for the poet Daniel rests upon wholly insufficient evidence. That Jonson did not think greatly more of Daniel's poetry than of Matthew's, is clear. But Matthew is fundamentally a fraud. Daniel, for Jonson, though 'no poet', was a 'good honest man' (*Conversations*, iii). Matthew steals bodily, and from Marlowe no less than from Daniel; if he alters anything, the result is 'a parodie! with a kind of miraculous gift, to make it absurder then it was' (Folio); where the critical point touches Daniel sharply enough, but distinguishes him no less decisively from his wretched 'parodist'.

derives obviously from the long line of military braggarts, headed by the Plautine Pyrgopolynices and (for the English stage) by Ralph Roister Doister. He has yet more in common with later types like Crackstone in *The Two Italian Gentlemen*, and Basilisco in *Soliman and Perseda*, where the bragging soldier affects a courtly speech instead of the boisterous language of the camp.[1] He is a great swearer still, but his oaths show curiosity and research. This variation of the *Miles* type had already much in common with the gull, and in 1598, when the gull vogue was at its height, it needed no great reach of invention to bring the two fatuities together. Yet Bobadill is not the gull of pure breed any more than he is the bragging soldier of tradition. The gull was a witless pretender to accomplishments and valour. Bobadill, however empty his pretensions to valour, is not without a certain order of accomplishment. His camouflage is beyond the reach of the common gull. Wellbred sees through it at once; but Cob, who entertains no illusions about Master Matthew, thinks his guest, notwithstanding his humble way of life and evident poverty, a very fine gentleman, and wonders at his skill in taking 'this same filthy roguish tobacco'; Matthew and Stephen are lost in admiration of the great man. He has some virtuosity at least in the 'bookish theoric' and phraseology of the military art. There is talent in the design and handling of his camouflage. But these accomplishments, such as they are, form only his second line of defence. His first is a discreet reserve culminating in the 'melancholy' to which the gull of every breed was prone to resort. It is this trait which detaches him most sharply from the military braggart of tradition, his other analogue. The blustering swagger of a Roister Doister was less in keeping with the more artificial manners of 1598 than this dejected hauteur of the unrecognized hero, who deals more in hints and innuendo than in loud assertion, and narrates his impressive feats with affected reluctance, in response to persistent

[1] Baskervill, *u. s.* p. 123 f.; Graf, *Der Miles Gloriosus.*

questioning. It is thus that Bobadill is drawn out by the ironical questions of young Kno'well. Bobadill is by nature like the normal gull, thin-blooded and spiritless; but while the gull put on high-astounding airs and was immediately detected, Bobadill affects a pose better calculated for the game he plays. He is 'not for the general', and cultivates a dignified seclusion as a safeguard against curious scrutiny and dangerous tests: ' I confesse, I loue a cleanely and quiet priuacy, aboue all the tumult, and roare of fortune.' His habitual attitude of lofty connoisseurship and critical disdain allows his valour to be presumed; but we are to understand that it is a valour governed by calculation and science, 'deliberate', not impulsive, and altogether opposed to 'the filthy humour of quarrelling' in such a man as Downright, just as his 'few' but choice words are contrasted with Downright's dearth of good words in his belly—' all old iron, . . . a good commoditie for some smith, to make hob-nailes of '. Scientific mastery of warfare, rather than heroism, is the professed character of Bobadill's soldiership; a trait excellently illustrated in his famous plan for the defeat of forty thousand by twenty; no scheme of prodigious valour coping, Quixote-like, with enormous odds, but a mechanical succession of ordinary single combats, man to man. His collapse immediately after, when Giuliano-Downright rushes in, is equally in the manner of one accustomed to resort to theoric to cover his deficiency of blood: '(Body of me) I had a warrant of the peace, serued on me, euen now, as I came along, by a water-bearer.' The new-style Miles, taken at a disadvantage, covers his retreat, not with noisy swagger, but with the good citizen's plea for submission to law and order.

Bobadill is no doubt the most consummate character in the play, and the whole group of gulls stands in the front rank of Jonsonian portraiture. But *Every Man in his Humour* would have missed much of its enduring vitality if the satirical exposure of morbid excesses and hollow shams were not accompanied by a rich infusion of the pure comedy which arises from the ebullience of robust, hearty, and healthy natures. In spite of its nominal subject the play does not depict a stricken or perverse society; it is not a museum of deformed types, of abnormal specimens; a breezy sanity pervades the atmosphere as it characterizes the art. The genial wit of Brainworm has its part in this effect; but it is due mainly to three delightfully imagined and trenchantly drawn figures, Downright, Cob, and Clement. Downright is a four-square piece of human nature, honest and valiant to the core, a country squire, like Stephen, but wearing with complete unconcern the garb of the *inficetum rus* which Stephen helplessly struggles to lay aside. His rude sincerity, equally incapable of affection and of polish, is admirably pitted against the hollow accomplishment of Bobadill. To be sure, like Hotspur, whose scorn for ballads, expressed in similar terms on the same stage a few months before, Jonson very probably recollected, he preferred 'cheese and a bagpipe' to the sound of a rhyme. Bobadill dismisses him as a 'peremptory clown', but Jonson vindicates the sturdy oak-stump of a man against the melancholy master of martial etiquette, whose own taste in letters was measured by his admiration of the rhodomontade of the old *Spanish Tragedy*.

Cob is a 'character' of the town, as Downright of the country; but his temper is gay, not choleric. Like Juniper in *The Case is Altered*, he is a humorist in the modern sense, and his burlesque account of his ancestry and tirade against the fast-days so fatal to his kinsman the red herring are among the few pieces of sheer fun in the Jonsonian drama. Like most of the Elizabethan jesters he has a shrewd perception of the follies around him. He may pass for a Jonsonian version of the official clown, adapted to the circumstances and atmosphere of his bourgeois stage. But he has neither the chartered independence of the professional jester nor his triumphant wit. He is just a poor citizen, with a house, a wife, and an occupation; he jests over his water-carrying, as Juniper over his cobbling and Hamlet's clowns over their grave-making. His honest simplicity sets him, like Downright, in lively contrast with the affected fools and knaves with whom he has to do. But he is also largely their butt and victim. Bobadill sponges upon and beats him; the merry Justice makes a show of sending him to jail. It is with difficulty that he is allowed, by procuring Bobadill's arrest, to share in bringing about the final discomfiture of the gulls.

Finally, in the old magistrate who composes the issues and reconciles the 'humours', the judicial temper of Jonson is for once happily reconciled with his comic invention. Like the King in Chapman's *Humorous Day's Mirth* he is a genial Minos, who enters with huge gusto into the situation, runs riot in humorous make-believe, and extemporizes rollicking burlesques of the bad poet's verses; but who also distributes rewards and punishments in the end, shrewdly and not (in the final version) too severely. The two sides of his character are signalized before we meet him. He is 'an excellent rare ciuilian and a great scholler', also 'the onely mad merry olde fellow in Europe'.[1] His nearest analogue in the drama is the Sir Thomas More of a probably contemporary play.[2] The mingled whimsicality and shrewdness in his character is admirably imagined and admirably sustained. His uproarious delight in Brainworm's mischievous wit ('my mistris BRAYNE-WORME! to whom all my addresses of courtship shall haue their reference') is only the extravagant side of a hearty joy in poetry (more glowingly expressed in the Quarto) which breaks down, as it did in Jonson himself, all class distinctions. The foolish Justice was a stage convention; Clement is an individual figure, who performs an indispensable function in the Humour play, but stands outside the Humour scheme.

*Every Man in his Humour* is assuredly not Jonson's greatest comedy. Nor is it that which bears the strongest and clearest stamp of his mind. But it is, in an intelligible sense, his best. Among the other plays, all those which

---

[1] Quarto III. ii: 'an excellent good Lawyer, and a great scholler' in the Folio (III. v).
[2] Cf. Baskervill, *u. s.* p. 139.

might compete with it for this distinction, evade, in one way or another, purely comic standards. *The Alchemist*, and still more *Volpone*, are sinister to the verge of tragedy. Even *Epicoene*, the most laughable of Jonson's plays, and in Dryden's judgement the first of all English comedies, is built, with whatever technical mastery, upon a supposition too eccentric to afford a basis for drama of universal significance. In *Every Man in his Humour* Jonson does not as yet give free rein to—he has hardly as yet discovered—the more individual ways of his genius. The language of the Prologue probably gives too definite and dogmatic an edge to the reforming ideas which clearly seethed in the mind of its author when he wrote the play. But he meant reform, not defiant self-assertion; a standard and imitable example of a play 'such as other playes should be', not a sinister-sublime vindication of poetry, like *Volpone*, or a colossal exposure of a colossal abuse, like *The Alchemist*. And he knew that such reform could not be effected by trampling ruthlessly on the tastes of the audience, tastes which in very important respects he shared. Himself a true Elizabethan, he drew together the popular and the academic tradition in comedy, as Kyd and Marlowe a decade before had done in tragedy, and into a not less vital and enduring fusion. He first, and once for all, showed how the rich abundance and variety of incident and character which the Elizabethan, like every other populace, demanded could be secured under the conditions of an art which excluded all aid from legend and romance, from the prodigal use of space and time, from mimicry of grandiose events and marvellous spectacles; which dealt merely with the familiar types, the humdrum incidents, the characteristic foibles, delusions, snobberies, of bourgeois London. Above all he showed how the zest of comedy could be had, without any stirring or sensational plot, by the mere collision of different kinds of warped or opinionated human nature, when these were observed by an eye and through a temperament at once so patiently acute, so drily veracious, as Jonson's, and bodied forth by a pen so incisive and so clear. The impression made upon the contemporary world by the new way in Comedy is not easily measured. For he followed it up the next year by a play in which the Humour theory was worked with immeasurably more stringent and aggressive force as a weapon of social satire. And *Every Man out of his Humour* was the prelude to two years of fierce personal polemics with fellow-playwrights. Jonson became one of the best-hated of his literary contemporaries, and the undoubted interest excited by the first Humour play was forgotten in the resentment roused by its successors. Shakespeare, who seems to have approved of the present play, took part in the 'Stage Quarrel' against Jonson in 1599–1601. Most of the reprobating voices date only from the second Humour play. The Puritan Schilders who in 1599 attacked the 'bad humour' of 'such humorists' may have had the first in mind, but he was an irreconcilable who aimed at the 'overthrow of stage plays' altogether.[1] The pointed and weighty criticism addressed, in 1601, by 'W. I.' to Jonson as 'Monsieur Humorist' together with a 'Satirist' and an 'Epigrammatist', clearly has in view the more accentuated phase of Humour satire. But a few years later the Humour fashion spent itself; the noisy animosities it had provoked subsided; its more ephemeral products were forgotten. Jonson himself had discovered a new vein of invention even more fully consonant to his genius, and stood on a pinnacle of secure fame as the author of *Volpone* and *The Alchemist*. But its freshness and geniality, its wealth of pure comedy, its one or two immortal figures, have enabled *Every Man in his Humour* to survive this and all later changes of mode. The greatest modern master of English humour chose it, two hundred years after Jonson's death, for a memorable performance;[2] and of all Jonson's works it is this by which to the great body of educated readers he is most generally known.

---

[1] For this and the other literature adduced in this paragraph the reader is referred to Mr. Simpson's account (*ed.* p. lix f.).
[2] In 1845, when Dickens played Bobadill.

# APPENDIX V

## THE QUARTO AND THE FOLIO

| Summary | Page |
|---|---|
| I. External changes: | |
| 1. Scene and Persons | 355 |
| 2. Scene division | 356 |
| II. Changes affecting style and language: | |
| 1. Punctuation | 361 |
| 2. Diction | 361 |
| III. Structural changes | 369 |

THE extraordinarily minute and systematic revision which resulted in the Folio text is full of instruction for the student of Jonson's art. Its characteristic features are accordingly set forth in what follows.[1]

### I. *External Changes.* 1. *Scene and Persons.*

The scene was changed from Florence to London, and the persons were provided with English names. Only Clement, Cob, and Tib bore English names in the first version. The original play thus corresponded, in its ostensible scenery and local colour, with its successor, *Every Man out of his Humour*. There is, however, a distinction. The foreign locality in the latter play is merely a transparent disguise for London. The marks of locality can be readily translated into their London equivalents, and a host of actual places are introduced under their actual names: the Inns of Court, Fleetbridge, the Star Chamber, &c. In Act III. i-vi, the fiction is dropped and the scene explicitly laid in 'the middle isle in *Pauls*'; and 'here at London' occurs in the dialogue. In the Quarto version of *Every Man in his Humour* the convention of Italian scenery is much better sustained, and even where London and its localities were clearly in his mind, some show is made of finding at least Italian, if not Florentine equivalents. Thus 'the Friery' stands for 'the Tower', which later replaced it; 'the Realto', for 'the Exchange'. And when young Lorenzo is said to be 'of deare account, in *all our Academies*' (Fol. 'in *both our vniuersities*'), Jonson is plainly adapting his expression to what he knew of the different circumstances of Italy.

---

[1] The most systematic comparison of the two texts is that of Grabau in his edition of the Quarto, *Shakespeare Jahrbuch*, Bd. xxxviii, from which many of the following details are drawn; cf. also Simpson (*ed.* p. ix f.).

There is a corresponding difference in the personal names. The Italian names of *Every Man out of his Humour*—Sordido, Fungoso, Deliro, &c.—are mere satirical epithets conveyed in Italian terms, and carry no local colour whatever. The Lorenzo, Prospero, Stephano, Bianca, of *Every Man in his Humour*, were simply familiar Italian names.

But Jonson knew too little of Italy for effective realism, even had this been his aim. The transfer to London liberated his vast fund of local knowledge. The London of the Folio is crowded with precise localities which have only vague general equivalents in the Florence of the Quarto. It acquires a distinct physiognomy and atmosphere, as Florence never does. We hear of Fleet Street, Coleman Street, Thames Street, Houndsditch, Shoreditch, Whitechapel; of local features, like the Artillery Garden, and Islington ponds; of suburbs, like Hogsden and Finsbury, Similarly, well-known London personages are introduced. The following examples are typical:

Q. Act I, Sc. ii.

Then will I be made an *Eunuch*, and learne to sing Ballads.

I am sent for by a priuate gentleman, my most speciall deare friend, to come to him to *Florence* this morning.

Why cousin you shall command me and 't were twise so farre as *Florence* to do you good.

F. I. iii.

Well, if he read this with patience, Ile be gelt, and troll ballads *for M*ʳ*. IOHN TRUNDLE*.

I am sent for, this morning, by a friend i' the old *Iewrie*, to come to him; It's but crossing ouer the fields *to More-gate*.

You shall command me, twise so farre as *More-gate*.

2. *Scene Division.*

If the change of locality is in keeping with the general tendency towards a vernacular realism which marks the Folio text, the system of scene divisions reflects an equally characteristic approximation to the technique of Roman comedy. The Quarto version follows in general the usual Elizabethan plan of marking a new scene with every change of place. In the Folio Jonson introduces a further division, at the entrance of each fresh person. The Folio is also more consistent in carrying out its scheme; no scene divisions being marked in the Quarto in the fourth and fifth acts, where the place certainly shifts repeatedly: in the fifth, for instance, from the street before Cob's house to the house of Clement. At the same time the matter is now redistributed among the five acts, with the view apparently of better marking its natural divisions. Thus the Thorello-Kitely household is introduced to us at the beginning of the second act, instead of at the close of the first; and the fifth act is wholly devoted to the denouement in the house of Clement, the scene before Cob's house being transferred to the fourth. Modern editors have usually combined the act divisions of the Folio with the normal Elizabethan principle of scene division adopted in the Quarto. The following table, drawn up by Grabau, exhibits the correspondences:

| Q. | F. | Mod. |
|---|---|---|
| I. i | I. i, ii | I. i |
| ii | iii | ii |
| iii | iv, v | iii, iv |
| iv | II. i, ii, iii | II. i |
| II. i | iv | ii |
| ii | v | iii |
| iii | III. i, ii | III. i |
| III. i | iii, iv | ii |
| ii | v | ii |
| iii | vi, vii | iii |
| iv | IV. i, ii, iii | IV. i |
| v | iv | ii |
| vi | v | iii |
| IV. — | vi–ix | iv–vii |
|  | x–xi | viii–ix |
| V. | V. i–v | V. i |

Jonson seems to have regarded the more frequent scene division as dispensing with the usage of marking exits and entrances; even where these occur within the scene, they are uniformly left to be supplied by the intelligence of actor and reader. In this point the Quarto directions are uniformly explicit, and at times render clearer the intention of the Folio, as in Q. III. ii, where Pizo-Cash, in the search for Francisco, has four several exits and returns. The Folio merely directs: *Cash goes in and out, calling.* On the other hand the Folio adds a few descriptive touches, of some value; as in I. ii, *Knowell laughes hauing read the letter.*[1]

[1] Grabau, *u. s.* p. 85.

## The Quarto and the Folio

**II. *Changes affecting style and language.* 1. *Punctuation.***

During the interval between the Quarto and the Folio, Jonson's theory of punctuation, still in his day largely a matter of individual choice, underwent a decided change. The punctuation of the first leaves much to the reader's discretion, that of the second seems designed to deprive him of any excuse for going wrong. The Quarto punctuation helps to more rapid delivery, such as Hamlet a little later desiderated in his players. The Folio punctuation is designed to further a more deliberate and balanced delivery. The comma, for instance, in the Quarto is more sparingly used, and also covers a larger range of values; it is often replaced in the Folio by a semicolon, colon, or even a period. A few lines from the first scene may be compared:

| Q. | F. |
|---|---|
| Nay looke you now, you are angrie vncle, why you know, and a man haue not skill in hawking and hunting now a daies, ile not giue a rush for him; hee is for no gentlemans company, and (by Gods will) I scorne it I, so I doe, to bee a consort for euerie *hum-drum*; hang them *scroiles*, ther's nothing in them in the world, what doe you talke on it? | Nay, looke you now, you are angrie, vncle: why you know, an' a man haue not skill in the hawking, and hunting-languages now a dayes, I'll not giue a rush for him . . . He is for no gallants companie without 'hem. And by gads lid I scorne it, I, so I doe, to be a consort for euery *hum-drum*, hang 'hem scroyles, there's nothing in 'hem, i' the world. What doe you talke on it?[1] |

**2. *Diction.***

The changes in diction are partly, like the redistributions spoken of in I. ii, designed simply to give the same matter in a more supple and expressive form. But most of them show that Jonson's ideal of dramatic expression had itself been modified. He not merely removes obscure and harsh phrases, he shows a definite bent towards colloquial, even homely, idiom, and a decided dislike for the rhetorical, abstract, or bookish phrase into which he had often fallen in the earlier version. The text is corrected, and in parts wholly rewritten, from this point of view. Yet no such

[1] On some further points of punctuation see Simpson, *ed.* xiii.

process was likely to be quite consistently carried out. And the matter is complicated by the fact that even in the revised version Jonson used a certain rhetorical cast of phraseology as a distinguishing trait of the speech of certain characters. But even in these characters this trait is less accentuated; and it may be said generally that, while differences in degree of colloquialism are still preserved in the Folio, there is a general shifting of speech character towards the colloquial extreme; the only exception being in the case of the Gulls, whose affected singularity of speech is still further heightened. Thus e. g. :

>   Q. II. iii. *Prospero* (Wellbred). Lord I beseech thee, may they lie and starue in some miserable spittle, where they may neuer see the face of any true spirit againe, but bee perpetually haunted with some *church-yard Hobgoblin* in *seculo seculorum*.
>
>   Fol. III. ii, sub fin. . . . Would we were eene prest, to make porters of; and serue out the remnant of our daies, in *Thames*-street, or at *Custome*-house key, in a ciuill warre, against the car-men.

The most obvious case is the simple substitution of ordinary for pedantic or inkhorn terms. Thus:

Prospero (Wellbred) calls Bobadilla and Matheo his two *zanies*; in the Folio his *hang-bys*;

Musco-Brainworm has the phrases:

> 'but a servant to *God-Mars*' (Q. sig. F). Folio, '*the drum*'.
> 'three or foure other tricks *sublated*' (ibid). Folio, '*remou'd*'.

The Folio shows a similar preference, as a rule, for the more colloquial forms of grammatical usage. E. g. *'hem* for *them*; *-es* (3 pers. sing.) for the sententious or poetic *-eth*[1] occasionally admitted in the Quarto,

>   as Q. sig. I 4 verso: '*Hesp.* That *toucheth* not me brother.' Folio, '*touches*'.

In comparing the language of individual characters in the two texts we have to distinguish between the introduction of a more colloquial standard of comic speech throughout the play, and the modification of the characters towards more familiar and homely types. It is not easy to draw the line in practice, but on the whole we may say that, while Jonson sought to make his persons

---

[1] On the colloquial character of *-es* cf. Franz, *Shaksp. Grammatik*, § 2.

speak unmistakably in the fashion of their class-types in actual London, he also in several cases modified their class complexion, and in general brought them farther from the academic and bookish world. The test of the latter is, of course, the occurrence of changes which cut deeper than mere modifications of language.

It is probable that Jonson meant both his old men, Kitely and Kno'well, to be more unequivocally 'City men', in breeding and habits of mind, than their prototypes, Lorenzo and Thorello. The rhetoric, without being entirely excised, is curtailed and compressed, so that what remains has the air of a momentary fancy flight instead of their normal cast of expression.

Thus Kitely's soliloquy in III. iii retains still a splash or two of the aureate phrase which decorates the original almost throughout: he levels a taunt at 'fleering oportunitie'; he alludes, as his fellow Kno'well also does, to the golden fruit of the Hesperides and its guardian dragon. But he is not allowed to follow Thorello in the eloquent tribute to beauty's power which follows,—more in the vein of Shakespeare's Biron than of an anxious and rather sordid City merchant. Compare the swift fervour of Thorello's

> Oh beauty is a *Proiect* of some power,
> Chiefely when oportunitie attends her:
> She will infuse true motion in a stone,
> Put glowing fire in an Icie soule,
> Stuffe peasants bosoms with proud *Cæsars* spleene,
> Powre rich deuice into an empty braine.
> (Q. III. i. 22 f.)

with the slow ejection, clause by clause, of Kitely's

> No beautie, no; you are of too good caract,
> To be left so, without a guard, or open!
> Your lustre too'll enflame, at any distance,
> Draw courtship to you, as a iet doth strawes,
> Put motion in a stone, strike fire from ice,
> Nay, make a porter leape you, with his burden!
> (F. III. iii. 22 f.)

also, the common shop-term *caract* (carat) for the bookish *project*.

Similarly compressed and actualized is Kitely's hourglass image already quoted:

> And my imaginations like the sands,
> Runne dribling foorth to fill the mouth of time,
> Still chaung'd with turning in the ventricle.
> (Q. III. i. 42 f.)

—my' imaginations runne, like sands,
Filling vp time; but then are turn'd, and turn'd.
(F. III. iii. 50, 51.)

Still more significantly, his sententious verses against jealousy at the close are now accommodated to the more familiar tone of the revised play; two being transferred to Clement, whose talk readily assimilated these tags of verse, while the rest are introduced as a quotation: 'I ha' learned so much verse out of a iealous mans part, in a play.' And his Latin scraps disappear. 'If he should prooue *Rimarum plenus*', he says of Piso; 'But should he haue a chinke in him', is Kitely's version.

The elder Lorenzo, similarly, without being deprived of his early training as a 'scholar' (I. i), ceases, as old Kno'well, to mingle the rhetoric of schools so freely in his daily speech. . He opens Prospero's letter not merely, like Kno'well, to see whether style and phrase answer his son's praises, but with an epicurean relish, in anticipation, for style and phrase in themselves—

> Both which (I doe presume) are excellent,
> And greatly varied from the vulgar forme,
> If *Prospero's* inuention gave them life.

And when he has read it he comments in a style worthy of Prospero:

> The modest paper eene lookes pale for griefe
> To feele her virgin-cheeke defilde and staind
> With such a blacke and criminall *inscription*.

So again his absurdly pedantic injunction to Stephen—

> Cosen, lay by such superficiall formes,
> And entertaine a perfect reall substance—

is replaced by a pithy proverb:

> I'ld ha' you sober, and containe your selfe;
> Not, that your sayle be bigger then your boat.

His reproof to Brainworm (II. v) shows slighter changes of the same kind. Instead of being 'rapt with admiration' he is 'taken with some wonder'; instead of contrasting Brainworm's mental 'constitution' with his 'exterior' figure, he compares the 'frame and fashion' of his mind with his 'outward' presence.

Here and there this elimination of scholastic abstraction or rhetoric involved a larger change. Lorenzo senior is apt to think as well as to talk in generalities; his actions, probably determined by the grooves of habit and prejudice, are decorated with sounding commonplaces. Old Kno'well has a more concrete mind, and fetches his guiding maxims out of his own experience. The rhymed soliloquy which opens II. ii in the Quarto is wholly rewritten, and the changes are full of interest. With Lorenzo the problem of his son's misdeeds is only a particular case of the unhappy truth that Reason, whom Nature with admirable art appointed to sway our unruly affections, nevertheless in the majority of men reigns but does not govern. Kno'well's reflections (II. v) are a direct and bitter indictment of the manners and morals of the day, so grievously inferior in all points of breeding to those of his own youth. Old age not reverenced, babes suckled in ill customs, youth baited with provoking meats—dressed snails, Venetian courtesans—and primed with the first commandment 'Get money; still, Get money, Boy; No matter, by what meanes.' In these packed and weighty verses we seem to hear the sterner tones of the Jacobean Jonson,—the tones of *Volpone* and *The Alchemist*, and of the additions in Act IV of *Cynthia's Revels*.

The vividly sketched character of the Justice is not sensibly modified in the Folio. But in keeping with the homelier prevailing tone most of his Latin scraps and one highflown piece of rhetoric disappear. The latter is the beginning of the sententious speech in the fifth act, the remainder of which was rewritten on other grounds: 'I *Lorenzo*, but election is now gouernd altogether by the influence of humor, which insteed of those holy flames that should direct and light the soule to eternitie, hurles foorth nothing but smoke and congested vapours, that stifle her vp, and bereaue her of al sight & motion. But she must haue store of *Ellebore*, giuen her to purge these grosse obstructions.'[1] This might be spoken by Asper in the second Humour play. Jonson properly felt that Clement's solemnity must be unmistakable burlesque.

The far more remarkable excision in the part of young Lorenzo-Kno'well does not strictly involve a modification of his character. But it greatly affects our practical conception of it. Young Lorenzo delivers an impassioned defence of poetry. Young

[1] Quarto, sig. M verso.

Kno'well's interest in poetry we have to take upon trust.  He lives, too, it must be remembered in a more pedestrian society than young Lorenzo.  Old Lorenzo and Thorello might have understood his eloquent apology for poetry, but on the City fathers of the new style it would have been thrown away.  Dramatic probability and stylistic consistency thus concurred in counselling the substitution for that lyric outburst on Kno'well's part, of a simple assent to the rough and ready vindication of the 'good poet' offered by the old magistrate in the final scene :

> There goes more to the making of a good *Poet*, then a Sheriffe, M<sup>r</sup>. KITELY.  You looke vpon me !  though, I liue i' the citie here, amongst you, I will doe more reuerence, to him, when I meet him, then I will to the Major, out of his yeere. . . .
> E. *Kn.* Sir, you have sau'd me the labour of a defence.

Jonson clearly does not abandon his idea of Edward Kno'well as a devotee and student of poetry; for his father repeatedly complains that such he is.  But he strips his language of every remnant of poetical quality or literary allusion.  Thus where young Lorenzo talks of Tamburlaine and Agamemnon, Kno'well is put off with the ' sergeant major' or the 'lieutenant-colonel'.[1]

Prospero, again, like his friend, is not permitted, as Wellbred, to exhibit the gifts of style and phrase with which, however, he continued to be credited.  His letter to Lorenzo, in the Quarto I. i, is stuffed with the inkhorn ingenuities of a crude academic wit.  The letter to young Kno'well (Folio I. ii) is at once more unaffected and more coarse ; its lively vernacular contains hardly a learned touch '*viaticum*' and is full of City flavour.  'Old Jewry', ' Hogsden ', ' our Turkey Company ', ' the Guildhall ' ; as a letter it is more characteristic of the well-to-do merchant's son than the other of the undergraduate, and it goes further to explain the anger of its first reader.

If a Kitely and Kno'well suffer some curtailment of their rhetoric, ' natural humorists ' like Cob are provided with a more thorough-paced vernacular.  Kno'well and Kitely still fall at moments into the loftier vein.  Downright and Cob lose such momentary incongruities as they originally possessed.  For the heightening touch take Downright's 'perboyl'd, and bak'd too, euery mothers sonne' (IV. i) in place of the simple 'damned'

---

[1] Quarto III. ii; Folio III. v.

of the Quarto. For the effacement of an incongruity take Cob's effusive gratitude to the Justice for his release (Folio III. vii). In the Quarto a false note is struck by his

> O diuine Doctor, thankes noble Doctor, most dainty Doctor, delicious Doctor. (Q. III. iii.)

In the Folio this drops into a homely English water-carrier's

> O, the Lord maintayne his worship, his worthy worship.
> (F. III. vii.)

Downright's proverbs are mostly new in the Folio. This trait is deliberately introduced, for the Folio makes Bobadill, in his contemptuous description of him, already quoted, expressly allude to it: ' He ha's not so much as a good phrase in his belly, but all old iron and *rustie prouerbes*! a good commoditie for some smith, to make hob-nailes of' (I. v). Did Jonson take this hint from Nic. Proverbs in *The Two Angry Women of Abingdon*?

Bobadill and Matthew have, conversely, a penchant exactly for the highflown or pedantic language which it was Jonson's normal policy to excise. Here then we naturally find his procedure reversed. Thus Bobadill affects to find his opponents 'opposite *in diameter*' to his humour (IV. vii) instead of merely opposite; while Master Matthew's awestruck admiration finds vent in a tribute to his 'vn-in-one-breath-vtter-able skill' (Folio I. v) for 'very rare skill' (Quarto).

The revision of the Gulls' parts in the later text is, indeed, hardly carried out in the same temper as the rest of the play. His insistent demand for closer realism gives way to his yet more ingrained zest for satiric humour. Maturity, which had confirmed the first trait, had only added to the satirist's ruthlessness and power.

The result is that Master Stephen's fatuities are exhibited with an added emphasis which makes him more amusing, but also brings him a degree nearer to farce. It is only in the Folio (I. iii) that Edward Kno'well plays upon his cowardice by pretending to have laughed at him. This is skilfully worked in. In the Quarto Stephen comments on Lorenzo's 'laugh' to himself. 'Oh, now I see who he laught at. . . . By this good light, and he had laught at me, I would haue told mine vncle.' This, as already stated, was perhaps imitated from Chapman.

It may be recalled, without pressing the fact, that in the meantime a better gull had appeared, Master Slender in *The Merry*

*Wives.* Slender's brisk evasion of the threatening quarrel with Pistol and Bardolph (I. i) possibly suggested the similar adventure of Master Stephen with Edward Kno'well in (I. iii).

The underlying motive of all Jonson's changes may be summed up as the more consistent preservation of the tone and atmosphere of comedy,—of comic decorum. This is often effected by quite small changes in the dialogue. Thus Brainworm's quiet chaff of Master Stephen, his master's nephew, is in the Folio disguised in equivocal terms or irony, and no longer breaks out in puns. Compare the dialogue (I. ii), where the pun of Musco is handed over to Stephen:

| Q. | F. |
|---|---|
| *Step.* But I haue no boots, thats the spite on it.<br>*Mus.* Then its no boot to follow him. . . .<br>*Step.* Nay to see, he stood vpon poynts with me too.<br>*Mus.* Like inough so; that was, because he saw you had so fewe at your hose. | STEP. But, I ha' no bootes, that's the spight on't.<br>BRAY. Why, a fine wispe of hay, rould hard, master STEPHEN.<br>STEP. No faith, it's no boote to follow him, now. . . . 'Pray thee, helpe to trusse me, a little. He dos so vexe me.<br>BRAY. You'll be worse vex'd when you are truss'd, master STEPHEN. |

In the same spirit, the bizarre punishments to which Clement between jest and earnest sentences his 'two signior Outsides', Bobadill and Matthew, are reduced to a harmless sport. The confinement all night in the cage, the exposure in bonds at the market-cross, one in a motley coat, the other in sackcloth and the 'ashes' of his burnt poems,—all this belonged to the Aristophanic world of comic fancy whose magnetism never ceased to draw Jonson, but from which he, in the revised version, resolutely turned away. The elaborate public Nemesis accordingly shrinks to a penitent fasting in the court 'while we are at supper'. The comic Triumph and the comic Nemesis now provided for Brainworm and for Stephen are in admirable keeping with the needs of the case, as well as with the tone of the play:

CLEM. O! I had lost a sheepe, an he had not bleated! Why, sir, you shall giue Mr. DOWNE-RIGHT his cloke: and I will intreat him to take it. A trencher, and a napkin, you shall haue, i' the buttrie, and keepe Cob, and his wife companie, here ; whom, I will intreat first to bee reconcil'd : and you, to endeuour with your wit, to keepe 'hem so.

Step. Ile do my best.

In the Quarto Brainworm-Musco is dismissed before the conclusion with only a hearty expression of his approval : 'Body of me a merry knaue, &c.' (Q. v. i). In the Folio Clement pays a far more emphatic tribute to his wit : 'Master bride-groome' (to Kno'well), 'take your bride, and leade : euery one, a fellow. Here is my mistris. Brayne-worme ! to whom all my addresses of courtship shall haue their reference.'

### III. *Structural Changes.*

Here and there a link in the dramatic nexus is strengthened. Thus Prospero's letter (Q. I. i), excellently characteristic as it is, scarcely explains Lorenzo's indignation, nor his anxiety for his son, which is the occasion of his expedition to town and subsequent adventures. Wellbred's letter, besides making the old merchant's disappointment in his expectation of fine phrases much more intelligible, contains allusions which justify his comment—

> From the *Burdello*, it might come as well ;
> The *Spittle* : or *Pict-hatch*,—

and the more personal animus of his jeremiad in Folio II. v.

On the other hand, an undesigned weakening of the nexus of motive has resulted, in the view of Adolph Buff (*Engl. Stud.* i. 181 f.), from the excision of some lines in Act v, where Giuliano suddenly appears before Cob's house, inquiring of his sister Biancha for his lost cloak :

> *Bia.* Not I, I see none.
> *Giu.* God's life I have lost it then, saw you *Hesperida*?
> *Tho. Hesperida*? is she not at home?
> *Giu.* No she is gone abroade, and no body can tell me of it at home. (Quarto, Sig. K 3 verso.)

This reply of Giuliano's, excised in the Folio, with what precedes, certainly explains how Thorello-Kitely comes to be aware of his sister's absence when he replied to the Justice's question : 'Where is Wellbred?' 'Gone with my sister, sir, I know not whither.' But it is perhaps more reasonable to suppose that Kitely is taken to have asked this obvious question when he found his sister absent, without this elementary inquiry being actually put into dialogue.[1]

There are often signs that Jonson was trying to simplify and compress. In Folio IV. viii a superfluous entry has been struck out. Instead of Clement and Thorello entering together fuming at the departure of Pizo and Biancha, Kitely alone bursts in, in one breath exclaiming at the 'plot' laid against him, and inquiring for his sister.

More important is the excision of repetitions of the same motive. Jonson was overfond of emphasizing his points by iteration, and we have seen him adding illustrations of traits of character already sufficiently distinct. None the less, he felt the long-drawn-out reverberations of humours 'wandering on as loth to die' in the last act to be excessive, and curtailed them at two principal points. The Justice's exuberant overflow of extempore verse, and the trophies of Matthew's 'pocket-muse', are each limited to a single specimen. And Thorello-Kitely is relieved of the recrudescence of jealousy which overtakes him in the last hundred lines of the Quarto.

Finally, Musco-Brainworm's explanation to the court of the 'errors' in which he has had so large a hand, entirely superfluous as it is to the spectator, is reduced to the narrowest compass.

There can be no question that the revised play is at every point—disregarding one or two trifling inadvertences—superior in execution to the original. It is equally certain that the essential stuff of invention was there from the first, and that neither characters nor plot are materially enriched. The advance is not in genius but in craftsmanship, in cunning and skilful elaboration of the existing material. Jonson has not carried out with complete consistency the transformation he designed. The familiar tone is not uniformly sustained; some patches of rhetoric perceptibly purple here and there the texture of the close-knit but sober woof. But on the whole the play was brought palpably nearer to the ideal of Comedy which Jonson probably at the same time formulated in the famous Prologue. If *Every Man in His Humour* still remains, what Meredith declared Jonson's comedies at large to be, 'a scholar's excogitation of the Comic', it comes, in its final form, nearer than any of its successors, until *Bartholomew Fair*, to showing an 'image of the times'.

[1] Cf. Simpson, *ed.*, p. xviii–xix.

# INTRODUCTION TO
# 'EVERY MAN OUT OF HIS HUMOUR'

# EVERY MAN OUT OF HIS HUMOUR

## I

*Every Man out of his Humour* was entered on the Stationers' Register on April 8, 1600, and published in the same year. It had been acted by the Lord Chamberlain's men at the Globe, in the course of the preceding winter.[1] Exact data are wanting for the time of composition; but a number of indications point to the conclusion that it had been mainly written during the year 1599, and was in fact its author's principal literary occupation during that year. Since *Every Man in his Humour* must belong to the last months of 1598, Jonson's admitted habit of scarce 'bringing forth a play a year' (''Tis true. I would, they could not say that I did that'[2]) furnishes a presumption that *Every Man out of his Humour* was not finished till towards the end of 1599. The Globe Theatre itself, built as it was of the timbers of The Theatre, can hardly have been ready until far on in the year, for The Theatre was not pulled down before the end of 1598. Several allusions to the play of *Histriomastix*, produced not earlier than August 1599, make this date a definite *terminus a quo*.[3] Some more doubtful indications may be passed by.[4] The play was twice published in quarto, with Jonson's initials on the title-page, in the course of 1600, by W. Holme. A further issue by N. Ling also appeared with the same date. Its enormous length had been curtailed in performance; the

[1] Cf. the close of the Epilogue in the Quarto text, discarded in the Folio:
entreat
The happier spirits in this faire-fild Globe, . . .
That with their bounteous *Hands* they would confirme
This, as their pleasures *Patent*: which so sign'd,
Our leane & spent Endeauours shall renue
Their Beauties with the *Spring* to smile on you.
[2] Apologetical Dialogue to *Poetaster*, ll. 182-3.
[3] Small, *The Stage Quarrel*, p. 21.   [4] Cf. Small, *u. s.* p. 22.

full text 'as it was first composed' was now set before the reader.[1]

With one notable exception, however. At the close of the Quarto text Jonson tells us, with ill-concealed disgust, that the play 'had another *Catastrophe* or Conclusion, at the first Playing', which, as bringing the Queen upon the stage in person, was by 'many' not relished, and therefore ' 'twas since alter'd'. He adds a series of reasons why 'a rightei'd and solide *Reader*' must dissent from this judgement. The effect of the alteration on the character of the second Conclusion is discussed below.

The play is printed with great care, evidently under Jonson's personal supervision: and he even took special pains to ensure for this, his first published play, an impressive entry into the world. The brilliant 'Character of the Persons' which he now prefixed to the text was a daring and somewhat questionable innovation, which might promote the immediate success of the drama, but suggested unfavourable reflections upon the dramatist whose persons needed to be thus explained. But the device was probably effective enough in this case. The reader who picked up the Quarto on a bookstall might well have been repelled by the portentous 'Induction'; but the piquant epigrammatic descriptions, in which Jonson's mastery was far surer than in dialogue, and which equalled anything of the kind yet done in English prose, must have gone far to commend the chalice to his hesitating lips. These brief concise sketches superficially recall the 'Characters' of Theophrastus, soon to be expressly imitated by Hall and his successors. Jonson, like Theophrastus, analyses by an enumeration of traits. But there are very few traces of actual borrowing, and the contrast in style is enormous between the pedestrian, matter-of-fact description of the Greek and Jonson's brilliant and pointed epigrams. Mainly through Jonson's example, here

---

[1] It may be conjectured that the 'cuts' were the obviously detachable parts of Mitis and Cordatus; possibly also the Induction. This would explain why in *Cynthia's Revels* he wove his character studies into the text of the play.

and in the yet more elaborate character analyses of *Cynthia's Revels*, epigram became the ruling preoccupation of the subsequent Character writers, even of those who most closely followed the method, ethical rather than satirical in aim, of the Theophrastian 'Character'. In this feature Jonson's pieces derive rather from the master of epigrammatists, Martial, the chief model of his own verse epigrams, than from the master of the 'Character'. But they make no pretence to the artistry of Martial's composition; they are not 'Epigrams', but a string of epigrammatic traits; and in this respect they contributed to confirm the Theophrastian tradition of structural formlessness in the later English Character.

## II

The title of *Every Man out of his Humour* appears to announce it as a companion piece to its immediate predecessor;—a sister comedy with an inverted motive, somewhat as *Love's Labour's Won* may have been a converse to *Love's Labour's Lost*, or as Fletcher's *The Tamer Tamed* turned the tables upon *The Taming of the Shrew*. It is clear, however, that the relation between the two Humour plays is not of this kind at all. *Every Man out of his Humour* is neither a counterpart nor a contrast, neither a companion piece nor a sequel, to *Every Man in his Humour*. It is a second handling of the same theme, with a more direct satiric purpose and a more uncompromising and defiant originality of method. Jonson had won his spurs; and less than the success of his first great comedy would have sufficed to remove any restraint imposed by regard for the stage tradition upon his unfledged genius. Whether the earlier play was already introduced to its first audience with the haughty declarations of the Prologue is, as has been said, very doubtful. It is certain that, however sharply *Every Man in his Humour* traversed certain romantic proclivities of the stage, it powerfully appealed to the en-

grained realism of the Elizabethan audience. It did not
give them all that they wanted; but it gave them, with
a vigour and brilliance paralleled as yet only in the contemporary glory of Falstaff's Eastcheap, what they wanted
most. It was put forward, explicitly or not, as a model
or a standard play, towards which it was desirable the
Elizabethan practice should gravitate; and Elizabethan
practice did in fact so gravitate. No such claim can ever have
been advanced or entertained in regard to *Every Man out of
his Humour.* Jonson himself, entirely confident as he was of
its merits, well knew that they did not lie in conformity to
any school of drama, new or old. The play was 'strange,
and of a particular kind by it selfe'; to be approved possibly by the humanists of the Inns of Court, but 'how it
will answere the generall expectation, I know not'. If he
claims that it is 'like *Vetus Comoedia*', the likeness lies in its
vigorous independence of tradition, and he puts into the
mouth of Cordatus a sketch of the history of ancient comedy
in which the entire development of the *genre* is exhibited
as a series of innovations in dramatic method. In Aristophanes 'this kind of *Poeme* appeared absolute, and fully
perfected'; nevertheless, his successors, Menander, Plautus,
and the rest, had wholly changed its character.[1] If classical
comedy was thus built upon the defiance of precedent, 'I
see not then, but we should enioy the same licence, or free
power, to illustrate and heighten our inuention as they did;
and not bee tyed to those strict and regular formes, which
the nicenesse of a few (who are nothing but forme) would
thrust vpon vs'. This, far more than the peremptory classicism of the Prologue to *Every Man in his Humour* expresses
the inner mind of Jonson. It is the spirit which years later
speaks ('albeit by adoption') in the sinewy prose of the
*Discoveries* under those notable rubrics '*Natura non effoeta*'
and '*Non nimium credendum antiquitati*'.—'Truth lyes

[1] *Vetus Comoedia* in this passage necessarily means Greek and Roman
Comedy. But there was no inconsistency, as Baskervill, *u. s.* p. 212,
suggests, in his use of the phrase 'Comoedia Vetus in England' to
Drummond (*Conv.* xvii. 410) for the ancient native drama.

open to all; it is no mans *severall*'; 'For to all the observations of the *Ancients*, wee have our owne experience.'[1] This haughty confidence in innovation can never have been altogether strange to Jonson: in the present play we see it for the first time let loose without reserve upon the traditional structure and method of the comic drama.

Close and continuous as was Jonson's connexion with the drama, immense as were his services to it, drama as then or at any previous time practised was not an instrument perfectly fitted to serve his aims in literature. He did not approach the stage 'as wishing to delight', but with the imperious bent of a critical and scornful nature, to inveigh, to instruct, to eradicate, to amend. His natural gift for drama was moreover probably matched by his gift of analytic and epigrammatic description. To reduce these powerful conflicting faculties to the service of the drama is commonly a slow and difficult process. The exuberant poet of *Brand* and *Peer Gynt* had sternly to transform his whole artistic method before he achieved the terrible reticence of *Ghosts*. But Ibsen's dramatic instinct was from the outset surer and stronger than Jonson's; he thought in drama where Jonson thought in epigram and invective; his social satire never crushes or starves his action, hardly ever overlays or retards it. The most directly polemical aim does not relax his grip upon plot, or the grip of his plot upon us. In the masterpieces of his maturity Jonson was to find a dramatic expression no less potent for the Juvenal that chafed within him. But at the present stage that consummation was still remote, and the impatient Juvenal has forged for himself a satire roughly accommodated indeed to the forms of the traditional drama, but fundamentally inspired and controlled by the purpose of 'stripping the ragged follies of the time, naked, as at their birth'. His description of the play as 'a Comical Satire' emphasizes this purpose, and justifies us in regarding the play, with Baskervill, as a deliberate extension to the theatre of the literary fashion

[1] *Discoveries*, Folio, p. 89.

of satire set going by Lodge, Davies, Marston, and Hall in the later nineties. At the same time, Jonson was convinced that he had both provided satire with fresh and potent weapons and in effect struck out a fresh and potent type of play. And the result must always have extraordinary interest as a dramatic experiment. Few dramatists have so boldly refashioned the instrument they found to fit it to say what they wanted. Jonson knew the hazards of the experiment, but had no misgivings as to its merit:

>     Onely vouchsafe me your attentions,
>     And I will giue you musicke worth your eares,
> while,
>                     if we faile,
>     We must impute it to the onely chance,
>     *Arte* hath an enemy cal'd *Ignorance*.[1]

### III

The effect of this satiric aim upon the drama is apparent in every point of dramatic plan. It affects the plot-structure, the choice of characters, the dramatic business, the presentment of the entire piece.

Jonson declared in the Induction that he would

>     to these courteous eyes oppose a mirrour,
>     As large as is the stage, whereon we act:
>     Where they shall see the times deformitie
>     Anatomiz'd in euery nerue, and sinnew.

The figure is that used by Hamlet to express the aim of drama in general; but Jonson's application of it betrays too clearly the havoc wrought upon his plays by his fierce dissection of his material. He, like Shakespeare, holds up 'a mirror' before his audience; but what their 'courteous eyes' see in it is not breathing nature, the very age and body of the time, his form and pressure, but a collection of pathological specimens, labelled and classified. He did not start, as the master of those who know and of those who criticize had laid it down that 'drama' ought to start, with

[1] Introduction, ll. 62-3, 214-16.

action, or the imitation of a piece of life; but with a set of persons singled out for their representative obliquities. The 'Humours' of the personages in *Every Man in his Humour* are mostly the amusing foibles of estimable men; even the gulls are ridiculed in a gayer temper than their counterparts here; harmless women like Bridget give place to foolish pretenders like Saviolina; and the Jonsonian Falstaff, Clement, who distributes reward and punishment at the close, is attenuated into the lean and bitter Macilente. Yet Jonson claimed complacently, through the mouth of Cordatus, to be restoring the comedy founded upon *imitatio vitae*. He thought he was putting a comedy of real life— ' neere, and familiarly allied to the time '—in the place of the comedy of fantastic intrigue, ' cross wooing' with a clown for serving man (III. vi). But what he 'imitated' in life was above all its heterogeneous sequence, its motley kaleidoscopic disarray. Few Elizabethan plays ministered so richly to the Elizabethan appetite for profusion of material as this work of the doughty advocate of classic art. It was assuredly no desire to conciliate that here overpowered the classical instinct for order and unity. It was simply that Jonson gave the rein to the impulses of a temperament censorious and aggressive in unsurpassed degree; a temperament in which the critical severity which discovers misdoers everywhere was combined with the militancy which relishes the battle the more the greater the numbers of the foe, and the rigour which suffers no fault to go without its meed of punishment. That a play so inartistic in composition should be the deliberate production of the most self-conscious artist among the Elizabethans strikingly illustrates the complexity of the forces which actually moulded and shaped his work. The man of letters remained supreme, imposing the form of literature on everything he wrote. It was a bold, and for a writer so deeply imbued with classical ideals of art a noteworthy, experiment; one, however, of which he himself finally recognized the futility, and which even a generous criticism, admitting to the full the power and brilliance of the writing, is forced to class with the literature which we admire but hardly enjoy.

Jonson was, in effect, applying his dramatic instrument in a fashion familiar enough in medieval and sixteenth-century satire, and not unknown to the Greeks.  For nearly a hundred years before him *The Ship of Fools*, in Barclay's version, had supplied a homely picturesque figure for the damnatory formula of a satirist as stern as Jonson: 'stultorum plena sunt omnia.'  Sebastian Brandt, like Jonson had seriously attempted to 'anatomize the time's deformity' in his catalogue of fools, and his ship's crew comprehends in effect representatives of all that he thought noxious in the German society of his time.  That Jonson knew the analogous collection by Theophrastus of the 'fools' of Athens, we have already seen.  Neither Brandt nor Theophrastus, however, appears to have had any influence upon Jonson's choice of representative 'humours'.  His anatomy of society reflects, even more than theirs, the bias of the anatomist's own character, time, and place.  Brandt's fools are, above all, people who offend the prudential instincts of a sober, timid, German scholar of the later fifteenth century. Theophrastus's types are, above all, people who offend an Athenian's nice sense of social tact and good breeding.  To Jonson, a powerful and militant nature, careless of conventions, and holding his own in all societies, like his great namesake, by force of mind and character little aided by nice observance of proprieties, the most offensive kind of 'humour' sprang rather from lack of character than from lack of manners.  His 'humorists' are not, in general, the men of blunt, discourteous self-assertion, but those who, like the Thackerayan 'snob', are lost in some mean or fatuous admiration;—fools of fashion, like Fastidius Brisk, the twin fops Clove and Orange, Puntarvolo, whose foppery, like Jaques's melancholy, is a subtle concoction of his own brain; and in yet more desperate case the rustic Sogliardo, who will have the name of a gentleman, though 'he buys it', and Fungoso, Brisk's luckless ape.  Or they are infatuated lovers, like

Deliro who dotes on Fallace, and Fallace who dotes on Brisk. Saviolina is the dupe of her intellectual vanity, and Sordido of his faith in almanacs. Shabbiest and shadiest of pretenders, but clever enough to play his game for awhile and by no means the worst drawn, is Shift, the professor of 'skeldring and odling', an inferior variant of Bobadill. His name was used again in *Epigram* xii. The mean or fatuous ambitions loomed larger to Jonson's critical eye. Of the failings of the critical temper itself, on the other hand, this most critical of Elizabethan intellects was perhaps but imperfectly aware. But he was acutely alive to, and deeply resented, the infirmities which simulate the severity of criticism,—the uncritical malignity of the ribald and the envious man. The 'scurrilous, and prophane Iester' that 'with absurd *simile's* will transforme any person into deformity' was as abhorrent to Jonson as the unprincipled railer habitually is to the convinced satirist. Macilente, the 'man well parted, a sufficient Scholler, and trauail'd', approaches Jonson on another side, and more nearly. Jonson was too haughtily self-conscious for envy; but the bitter gibes with which Macilente seeks to correct the blind injustice of Fortune have an unmistakable affinity with those levelled by Jonson's masterful but not malignant criticism. Both men, however Jonson might take sides against them, resembled him to the popular eye. And both, though in the play primarily as victims and objects of the satirist's dramatic exposure, gravitate, as if by natural congeniality, to the satirist's side, and become his agents and executants. The fact, however, that Macilente undoubtedly speaks much of Jonson's mind, and that his voice often elusively resembles the familiar accents of his creator, readily leads to the surmise that the victims of the 'comical satire' may be of similarly personal origin or even simply stand for particular persons in Jonson's *milieu*. Mr. Fleay even postulates this as self-evident; but his actual attempts at identification in detail betray obvious embarrassment, and do not seem to have been convincing even to himself.

## IV

Jonson was, it is true, if we may trust his own dates, already the object of literary attacks. For three years, he wrote in the 'Apologetic Dialogue' to the *Poetaster* in 1601,

> They did prouoke me with their petulant stiles
> On euery stage.

And, if again we may trust him, he had forborne to retort until 'at last, vnwilling', he resolved to try what shame could do, and wrote *Poetaster*. It is tolerably certain that his forbearance had not been completely maintained so long; but the statement justifies a presumption against a purely personal interpretation of the intervening plays, only to be overborne by strong evidence. Marston and Dekker, the poets who bore the brunt of *Poetaster*, cannot be shown to have attacked Jonson before the date of *Every Man out of his Humour*; and Marston had even, in *Histriomastix*, introduced a portrait of Jonson with evidently complimentary intention, an intention for which Jonson was probably far from grateful, but which he can hardly have met by pillorying his admirer.[1] And there is no character in the play who can be plausibly 'identified' with either. Critics who take for granted that they must be in the play somewhere discover them, respectively, now in Brisk and Carlo, now in Clove and Orange. The only ground for connecting Marston with Brisk is that Hedon and Crispinus, in the two following plays, where they clearly point to Marston, are generically akin to Brisk, while Clove's affected speech includes various words used by Marston. But Small has shown (*u.s.* pp. 45–6) that the Marston traits of Crispinus are almost entirely those which he does not share with Brisk, and that of Clove's affected words only six out of thirty-nine occur in Marston too. With Dekker-Buffone-Orange, the case is still more hopeless. The whole assumption does imperfect justice to

---

[1] Cf. Fleay, *Biog. Chron.* ii. 71.

the serious and even lofty aims of Jonson in this second Humour play. With whatever success, his aim was to expose the 'time's deformity', the characteristic vices and follies of the day, not to ridicule individuals. Living examples of these humours had assuredly been encountered by Jonson in plenty; Fastidius Brisk was to be met at every fashionable ordinary and on the stage of every theatre; and features caught from particular individuals and noted on particular occasions assuredly mingled with others drawn from his vast reading to furnish forth the prodigious wealth of characteristic traits by which the several 'humorists' with such unflagging pertinacity exhibit themselves. In this sense a particular dandy or simpleton may be said to be glanced at, if we choose; but he is only an insignificant part of the object at which it is levelled. In general the portrayal is much more liable to the charge of being too generic than of being too individual; artificial and unreal invention is a peril much more in question than a too photographic realism; how stiff and 'made-up', for instance, is the figure of Sogliardo set beside his counterpart in the previous play, Master Stephen! In two or three cases it seems possible to connect incidents in the play with real or traditional events of Jonson's time; but we must beware of assuming that because he borrowed the incidents he also identified the persons. Thus Brisk's duel with Luculento so closely resembles that of Emulo with Sir Owen in *Patient Grissel* that both are plausibly regarded as founded upon an actual duel for which Mr. Fleay has confidently provided combatants and a cause of quarrel.[1] Aubrey has, again, preserved the tradition of a calumnious bully, Charles Chester, whom Sir W. Ralegh 'once beat in a tavern and sealed up his mouth, i.e. his upper and nether beard, with hard wax', which doubtless suggested the sealing of Buffone's lips by Puntarvolo (V. vi). So neat a retribution was necessarily rare in actual life, and overtook, by a happy accident, only a single member of the Chester-Buffone

---

[1] His speculations are acutely dissected by Small, *u. s.* p. 188.

tribe. But its symbolical appropriateness to the offence exactly fitted it to serve as comic Nemesis for an offender in whom the whole tribe was embodied.

### V

Whatever personal elements may be interwoven in the intricate texture of the plot and characters, these must then be regarded as predominantly typical in intention. Certainly if we regard them as a complete expression of what Jonson took to be the 'deformity' of the time, we cannot credit him with a very deep or comprehensive scrutiny. They represent chiefly the foibles incident to jealously emphasized class distinctions, and fierce ambition for place and wealth. Some of the gaps in his picture Jonson was himself subsequently to fill in. *Cynthia's Revels*, *The Alchemist*, *Bartholomew Fair*, to go no farther, lay bare 'nerves and sinews' of the time's deformity which are either not at all or but very slightly 'anatomized' here. Inadequate as it is, however, to the complexity of a great and growing civilization, this collection of 'humorists' was yet motley and individual enough for their characteristic activities to resist ready inclusion in any straightforward and coherent plot. The several Humours become so many centres of action among which the interest, such as it is, is scattered. There is no common business in which all the persons or any considerable group of them take part; and the private business on which each is bent is palpably contrived with a view to the one business which absorbs the dramatist,—that of exhibiting and 'curing' Humours. Besides its effect in thus scattering the interest over a number of detached or slightly connected operations, the satiric aim has affected the quality of much of these detached actions themselves. The whole content of each of these miniature plots is of elementary simplicity. The 'humorist' has, normally, but two things to do: to exhibit his humour, and to be tricked, jostled, or persuaded 'out' of it. Both processes lead easily to developments of doubtful dramatic value. When Macilente enters explaining that he is possessed with envy, or Sogliardo announcing that he means to be a gentleman at all costs, we are reminded of the 'program' speeches of the primitive Elizabethan stage. When Sordido hangs himself on the stage we are reminded of its crude violence.[1] The poisoning of Puntarvolo's dog is a trick worthy of a pre-Shakespearean clown. There is little trace as yet of that predilection for symbolic and allusive incident,—the *idolon* of the study,—which was soon to be so unsparingly indulged. The Fountain of Self-Love, and the forced eructations of Crispinus, in the following plays, were foreshadowed at most in the stopping of Carlo's mouth, a piece of 'symbolism' not too recondite, as we saw, to have been actually carried out. Yet this, like Puntarvolo's farcical dialogue with his own gentlewoman, and the Sordido and Saviolina scenes, already mentioned, from Castiglione, still more the original conversion of Macilente referred to below, has little claim to be an example of *imitatio vitae*. The invention, even when brutally realistic, smells indefinably of the lamp, so rarely suggested in the fresh homely atmosphere of the earlier play.

The comic 'catastrophes' are otherwise of varying degrees of dramatic merit. No complex or subtle psychology is involved or applied. The 'cure' is usually of the rough practical kind which teaches fools who cannot be taught otherwise, but teaches them rather caution than wisdom. Sordido's 'conversion' by the curses of the rustics who have unwittingly cut him down is powerfully conceived, but far too summarily handled to be psychologically convincing;

---

[1] Both this incident and Sogliardo's scene with Saviolina (v. ii) were suggested, as Bang has shown (*Eng. Stud.* xxxvi. 340 f.), by Castiglione's *Courtier*. Jonson was conscious of the objection to hanging in a comedy and vainly attempted to rebut it by the example of Plautus's Alcesimarchus in the *Cistellaria*. Alcesimarchus puts his sword to his breast in the presence of his mistress, and is restrained from using it: Sordido actually hangs himself. And even had Alcesimarchus carried out his purpose, the legitimacy of a death by the sword on the stage does not warrant that of a death by the halter.

Sordido, accustomed to trample with brutal cynicism upon the interests of his neighbours, can hardly have been so deeply moved at the discovery that they hate him, or have discovered it now for the first time. Two only of the 'catastrophes' stand out, as examples of high comedy, and one of them is worthy of the stage which within the next two years was to witness the production of *Twelfth Night* and *Much Ado about Nothing*. The catastrophe of which Deliro and his wife are the subjects is ingeniously contrived to cure two humours at the same time; for Fallace's discomfiture is Deliro's disillusion; and if Fallace's cure is but of the external kind, if she is only taught to be more cautious in her entertainment of Fastidius Brisk's successor, Deliro is radically healed of 'doting' for ever. Still better both in design and execution is Saviolina's discomfiture (v. ii), which at the same time explodes the pretensions of Sogliardo. The plot laid by Macilente and the rest for her exposure is admirably adjusted to her dominant foible, as it is to Sogliardo's, and has the air of providing them both with what they most desire. It may seem that Saviolina is too easily taken in; for a clown trying to play a gentleman is not in reality at all like a gentleman trying to play a clown. Sogliardo bungles his French and Italian; the gentleman would have dropped his French and Italian altogether, and bungled his dialect. Saviolina betrays her quality as an observer of men in concluding Sogliardo's social rank from the mere trappings of phrase which may be donned and doffed like any other suit. It is reserved for her tormentors to point to the ci-devant farmer's horny palm—an argument which its owner's naïve explanation, 'Tut, that was with holding the plough', immediately clinches beyond appeal.

## VI

Two of the Humours, Buffone and Macilente, hold a position apart in so far as they are the principal agents in the 'cure' of the rest. Others have incidental parts in the 'surgery'. Saviolina, who snubs Fastidius Brisk, shares to that extent in his ultimate cure, as Brisk himself does in that of Fungoso, and the Hinds in that of Sordido. But in the main it is Buffone and Macilente, types of the reviling tongue and the malignant eye, who, simply in the exercise of these 'humours' of their own, discover and expose the humours of the rest. The contrast between these sharp correctors and gay mischief-makers, like Brainworm or Lemot, measures the distance traversed by Jonson in passing from comedy touched with satire to satire under comic forms. The exceptional position thus assigned to these two is highly characteristic. The satirist is too convinced of the need for sharp chastisement of folly to deal hardly with those who chastise it from questionable motives. He might have exhibited them sapping innocent happiness and blasting just reputation; he chooses to employ them in the salutary business of pricking bubbles and dispelling dreams. Hence they figure virtually in a double capacity, as the objects of the dramatist's satire and as his executants, and Macilente, at least, does not escape the ambiguous air which this double function involves. They stand between the common herd of victims, the *numerus infinitus stultorum*, whom they chastise, and the solitary embodiment of indignant virtue and his friends, being allied in dramatic function to both. Hence, though finally cured themselves also, their cure is reserved till the very end, when their surgery upon others is virtually complete. And their 'cure' when it comes seems to be the most superficial and external imaginable: a temporary pause is induced in the maladies, with every prospect of their breaking out again in undiminished virulence when Buffone releases his lips from the wax, and when fresh fuel has arrived to replenish the fading fires of Macilente, whose

>    humour (like a flame) no longer lasts
> Then it hath stuffe to feed it.

Macilente was played by the same actor as Asper, and speaks the Epilogue significantly in Asper's place. In spite of his hint that 'the shift' (to Asper's dress) would have been somewhat long, Macilente and Asper are distinguished rather to the intellect than to the imagination; Macilente's animosity against those more fortunate than himself assumes, as it goes on, more and more the complexion of Asper's intolerance of folly, until at the close we find that the 'fuel' for lack of which his 'humour' flags is not the prosperity of which his and Carlo's victims have been relieved, but the 'folly' of which they have 'repented'.

In the original text, Jonson had, it is true, provided a kind of explanation for Macilente's abrupt conversion. He comes to the Court bent on maligning whatever he encounters there. But the wonder of the Queen's presence strikes the personification of envy suddenly dumb; then, recovering heart, he addresses her in glowing eulogy, his 'humour' completely changed. Dramatically, this is a dangerous approach to the *deus ex machina*; but it at least avoided the blank unreason of Macilente's conversion in the present text.

## VII

The intellectual scorn towards which Macilente approximates is the unalloyed passion of Asper. In Asper, Jonson for the first, but by no means for the last, time drew his ideal poet. If Asper bears an unmistakable resemblance to Jonson himself, it is because Jonson, like other men of massive personality, on the whole was what he wanted to be, and did, in literature, what he desired should in literature be done. Through Asper's lips Jonson utters, with a passionate eloquence, the lofty and vehement scorn which was one of the driving and shaping forces of his art, and one of the moods in which he most nearly approached poetry. As a character, Asper is a notable creation, more human and sympathetic than any other figure in this drama of eccentrics. In his rugged Jonsonian fashion, he has something both of the grandeur and of the pathos of

Molière's Alceste. No mere prologue sufficed for an exposition of what was in effect Jonson's apologia for his own prospective policy and practice as an artist, and in particular a defence of the present play. He laid hands, accordingly, on a device which may be best described as a compromise between the traditional Induction and the classical chorus or Grex.[1] The preliminary debate of Asper with his friends, and the intervening discussions of the two latter, contain admirable dialogue and not ineffective by-play. But their dramatic vivacity is subordinate to the business of exposition and self-defence. The two friends Cordatus and Mitis serve at first, like Pope's Arbuthnot and Horace's Trebatius, to give the poet occasion, by their prudent or timid warnings, vigorously to indicate his action and expound the object of his campaign. Then, after Asper's withdrawal, Cordatus, 'a man inly acquainted with the scope and drift of the Plot', learnedly expounds the doctrine on which it rests, while the gentle Mitis grows yet more obviously a mouthpiece for the difficulties likely to be occasioned in the conventional hearer by Jonson's 'strange' and 'particular' comic methods. His pertinacity in raising objections is as remarkable as his facile acquiescence in Cordatus's replies. 'You have satisfied me, sir', he rejoins, like Master Stephen, but without the motive and cure of Master Stephen's embarrassing situation. It was not for nothing that Jonson refused to 'afford character' to a person whose whole dramatic existence consists in alternate exercise and surrender of the critical spirit. But Mitis's loss of 'character' is only an extreme instance of the general impoverishment of drama in the interest of rhetoric and satiric quality which marks this play as a whole.

[1] The affinities of Jonson's Inductions to earlier Elizabethan examples in the work of Peele, Greene, and Nashe, are described by Baskervill, *u.s.* p. 146 f.

# INTRODUCTION TO
# 'CYNTHIA'S REVELS'

# CYNTHIA'S REVELS

## I

*Cynthia's Revels, or the Fountaine of Self-Love* was entered on the Stationers' Register on May 23, 1601, and published in quarto in the same year.[1] It had been acted some months before, by the Children of the Queen's Chapel, at Blackfriars. A play so obviously, even ostentatiously, addressed to the Queen may be presumed to have been designed for performance at Court; but there is no evidence that it ever was performed there. The motto prefixed by Jonson to the printed play even points to rebuff in that quarter.

*Quod non dant proceres dabit histrio,—
Haud tamen invideas vati, quem pulpita pascunt*

would have been an oddly chosen legend for a play so full of exalted eulogy of the *proceres*, had not the *proceres* in some rather pointed way failed to respond. It is the utterance of a proud and sensitive man, who had imperilled his dignity and his self-respect by an extravagant bid for the recognition of the Queen, without obtaining it.[2]

The only trustworthy evidence of the date of the first performance is furnished by Jonson's own statement in the Folio that this took place in '1600'. If *Every Man out of his Humour* was produced, as we hold, early in 1600, *Cynthia's Revels*, which bears the marks of yet more prolonged stylistic elaboration, cannot have been finished

---

[1] The above title is Jonson's final version, as given in the Folio. The Quarto has *The Fountaine of Selfe-loue, Or Cynthias Reuels*. The S. R. entry is 'Narcissus, or the fountaine of selfe love'. The identity of this last with the Quarto has been questioned; but it seems to be established by the fact that Walter Burre, to whom the former was entered, was the publisher of the latter.

[2] Jonson's clumsy introduction of the Queen to assist the climax, in the original version of *Every Man out of his Humour*, had been resented, as we know, and the passage cancelled. Was the elaborate and honorific presentment of the Queen in the present play Jonson's attempt to make good this failure?

at Jonson's normal rate of progress—a play a year—before the last months, or weeks, of the year. The performance may therefore be probably dated in December.[1]

If this was approximately the date, it is not difficult to conjecture a ground for the Queen's indifference. In those months of 1600 the brilliant career of one long favoured by her warm friendship was approaching its tragic close. Essex had been in nominal custody since 1599; more serious action was taken against him in June, 1600, when he was removed from his offices; early in the following February the discovery of the desperate plot organized in his name sealed his fate, and he perished on the scaffold on the 25th. At any possible date for the completion of the play, then, the ill-omened adventure of the former favourite loomed large in the public eye. When Jonson in the most pointed fashion alluded to the story of the rash lover Actaeon, punished by Diana-Cynthia for his presumption, an audience much less alive to classical allusions than the Elizabethan must inevitably have made this application.[2] The Queen's treatment of the popular favourite, and the resentment it provoked, are unmistakably glanced at, and Jonson obviously seeks to pose as her loyal defender. 'Black and enuious slanders', we are told, are 'hourely breath'd against her, for her diuine iustice on ACTAEON' (I. i). And, at the close, Cynthia herself is introduced deprecating the censure passed on her by 'some', as 'too seuere, and sowre'; she was stern only to the 'proud' or 'the prophane',—

> For so ACTAEON, by presuming farre,
> Did (to our griefe) incurre a fatall doome.

The question remains, however, how much of Essex's story is implied in these allusions. It has been widely

---

[1] Professor Thorndike (*The Influence of Beaumont and Fletcher on Shakespeare*, p. 17) has shown strong grounds for believing that Jonson dated the year from January to December.
[2] So Ward, *English Dramatic Literature*, ii. 353; Hoffschulte, *Über Jonson's ältere Lustspiele*, 1894; Small, *Stage Quarrel*, 23. Fleay thought Nashe's imprisonment for the *Isle of Dogs* to be referred to, but this seems to have nothing but the 'dogs' to recommend it.

assumed that the references to Actaeon as 'pursued, and torn by Cynthia's wrath' and to his 'fatal doom' refer to Essex's execution, and must therefore have been added after February 25, 1601. This interpretation certainly adds point to the parallel. But the easy hypothesis of subsequent insertion ought not to be lightly resorted to. It is only necessary if the parallel would otherwise not merely be incomplete, but would altogether fall to the ground. Actaeon's fate need not be even approximately reproduced (it was in no case literally reproduced) in that of Essex, provided that at the date of writing enough had happened to make the parallel, so far, piquant and telling. Now by far the most striking resemblance between the two stories had come about as far back as September, 1599, when Essex burst into the Queen's chamber in his riding-habit to find her 'with her hair about her face',—as near an approach as an Elizabethan mortal was likely to make to gazing on ' Cynthia's naked loveliness '. The comparison of this scene with Actaeon's offence was a felicitous piece of satiric wit, and Jonson was not the man to discard it because, at the time he wrote, the tragic sequel was only an impending possibility. It is quite tenable that, Actaeon having only suffered a mild imprisonment, from which he had since been released, with loss of offices, Jonson used the phrases about his 'tragic doom' and his having been 'pursued and torn by Cynthia's wrath' as admissible symbols for the more moderate punishment, or even that he used them solely of the Actaeon of legend. And this is supported by the fact that Cynthia, in defending her severity to him, wholly ignores the graver charges which in the following February led to his execution, and dwells only on the tactless audacities of September, 1599:

> Seemes it no crime, to enter sacred bowers,
> And hallowed places, with impure aspect,
> Most lewdly to pollute? Seemes it no crime,
> To braue a *deitie*?[1]

[1] Act v, scene xi, 19-22.

And if the punishment inflicted on Actaeon seems beyond comparison with anything that Essex suffered before 1601, we must consider that Jonson is translating history into terms of mythology, and that to represent a deity as lightly forgiving a mortal's insult would have been an error in style.

The view, then, that the Actaeon passages as they stand belong to the original text, and were therefore written before the Essex tragedy was complete, is on the whole to be preferred.

But if these were indeed the terms in which Jonson put forth his venture for Court favour, it is not difficult to understand his failure. Elizabeth, with all her robust capacity for digesting praise, was not likely to relish an apology which in denying her faults pointedly emphasized (in the manner of her own 'bitter fool' Pace) the fact that they were 'the talk of the town'—an apology gratuitously and somewhat patronizingly put forward on the public stage. The apologist moreover was a plebeian playwright who had, a few months before, narrowly escaped the gallows and still bore the felon's brand; while his very defence of her was but an incident in what was plausibly understood as a stupendous glorification of himself. And even had it not been so understood, Cynthia is in dramatic importance altogether overshadowed by the homely scholar in black, and Crites is in every sense the Master of her Revels.

II

The immense and undisguised complacency with which Jonson regarded this piece provokes the derision of the modern reader, and is puzzling to the most sympathetic student of Jonson's art. Clearly there is no question of applying classical standards to a play so deliberately denuded of dramatic structure (for everything in Jonson is deliberate) that we with difficulty allow it to be drama at all. Whatever Jonson was here doing, he was not following, however independently, in the steps of the ancient predecessors he was accustomed to proclaim. Far from it, he comes forward announcing his own complete originality.

>In this alone, his MVSE her sweetnesse hath,
>She shunnes the print of any beaten path;
>And proues new wayes to come to learned eares.[1]

There was at all times more of the innovator than of the traditionalist in Jonson, and here the innovating enterprise, in the region of dramatic art, reaches its climax. Yet still we ask, what then was this 'new way', and since classical example was flung to the winds, in what did its appeal to 'learned ears' consist?

A cursory comparison of the play with *Every Man in his Humour* and with *Every Man out of his Humour* makes clear that in these three plays there is a continuous evolution—the satiric, moralizing, and abstract elements of Jonson's mind acquiring a steady domination over the dramatic genius proper—an evolution promoted by his popularity precisely among the aristocratic elements of the audience, to which allegory and satire at the cost of the groundlings appealed. In *Every Man in his Humour* comic genius is still supreme and the abstract Humour philosophy blent with observed humanity to delightful purpose. In *Every Man out of his Humour*, the philosophy, more freely indulged, has half strangled the dramatic life, while dramatic structure is plainly traceable. In the present play, finally, satire, moralizing, and allegory entirely overpower and extinguish dramatic action, while the dramatic elements of character and dialogue survive indeed in great vigour, but owe their vitality mainly to brilliant description and vivacious repartee.

The immense vogue which satire acquired in the later nineties sprang less from any sudden access of the satiric temper than from the almost simultaneous discovery between 1595 and 1600 of a number of new and piquant instruments of satiric expression. Lodge and Hall introduced the

[1] Prologue, ll. 9-11.

'Satire' as a definite species, and emulated the weighty and compact verse, the character-sketches, and the lofty moral tone, of Juvenal and Horace. Harington modelled coarse and biting Epigrams on Martial. Jonson himself, as has been seen, had called in the Theophrastian Character to reinforce the proper satiric weapons available for comedy in the preface of *Every Man out of his Humour*, besides the interludes of Juvenalian invective which punctuate its course. In *Cynthia's Revels* he sought to devise a form in which these satirical elements would be integral parts of the play.

This new type of 'comical satire' was to exhibit the new modes of satirical expression in the heightened context of dramatic dialogue and scenery. Hence the gallery of brilliant 'Characters' which virtually constitutes the second act; hence the great invectives of Crites, hence the all but completely static 'plot'. 'Words, aboue action: matter, aboue words': so Jonson, in the Prologue, ominously defined the special virtue of his poetry; and he could not have expressed more decisively his deliberate departure from a purely dramatic ideal than by thus putting action in the last place, not in the first. In place of action as a coherent whole, we find a number of embryonic or fragmentary actions, very loosely and inorganically connected. Moreover the fragments are drawn not merely from different stories but from heterogeneous story-types. In this it is at once marked off from *Every Man out of his Humour*, where the story-elements, though fragmentary too, are at least drawn from the same quarry of modern actuality. In our play modern actuality has also furnished the preponderating materials and colour. But at least three distinct story-types cross and mingle in this motley web: classic myth, moral allegory, and the intrigues and pastimes of Elizabeth's Court.

The myth-element has already been incidentally noticed. The death of Actaeon serves chiefly as occasion for the final apologia of Cynthia. But the 'Fountain of Self-Love'

## Cynthia's Revels 399

might well have become the *idée mère* of a great satiric comedy which would have been comedy as well as satire. Aristophanes had here magnificently shown the way, and his example has clearly told upon Jonson. It is to the example of *The Birds* and *The Clouds* primarily that we must ascribe both the frank use of mythic or fantastic incident against the canon of Jonsonian realism, and the admission of serious and beautiful lyric poetry (as in Echo's Song) contrary to the rigour of the comic spirit. The fundamental device, the 'Fountain of Self-Love', is in itself a brilliant satiric development of the mythic *Fons* by which Narcissus perished for the love of his own image,[1] and it might have set going a comic action as rich in satire and in drama at once as the adventure of Peisthetairos and his companion.

And, in fact, this device seems designed to play a much more decisive part in the action than it ultimately proves to do. It is announced with obvious complacency in the Induction, and brought forward with striking wealth of mythic apparatus and the emphasis of italics in the first scenes.[2] But after the first act it disappears with the rest of the mythic scenery, and the references to its transforming water, which from time to time recall it, are felt as incongruous and irrelevant interruptions to dramatic business which goes on, such as it is, not merely in another place but on another plane of reality. Some sixteen years later, in *The Devil is an Ass*, and later still, in *The Staple of News*,[3] Jonson could turn such incongruities as these to humorous account; here they only embarrass him. The Fountain of Self-Love is no less superfluous than Pug the 'Stupid Devil' among the 'humours' of Jonsonian London; and for a like reason. Pug found his occupation gone in a city which could give him points in the knowledge of evil. Amorphus and Asotus, Hedon and Anaides, are from the

---

[1] His words *Uror amore mei* (Ovid, *Met.* iii. 463) give the clue to the idea.
[2] As already noticed, the play as entered in the Stationers' Register was actually entitled 'Narcissus'.
[3] Cf. Argurion here with Lady Pecunia.

outset steeped in 'self-love'; the 'new water', whatever its Circean virtues, cannot transform them; it can at most make their habitual intoxication a little headier and more blinding. They belong to the purely human and actual world of the Humour comedy, where all the sport was made by the play and counterplay of different varieties of folly. Jonson, the arch-enemy of dramatic 'monsters', here brought one into this drama of men. But he could not, or could not yet, make it at home there.

The theme of Pug is more directly anticipated in a third mythic motive, the descent of Cupid and Mercury to mix with mortals in human disguise. But this too is turned to no great account. They take service as pages, and are only at rare moments distinguishable from other members of that lively fraternity; as when Cupid in the final masque bethinks himself of his arrows but finds them of no avail against Phantaste and Amorphus, who have drunk of the Fountain of Self-Love, and equally blunt against Crites, who disdains to drink of it.

### III

The masque which this by-play relieves is the principal contribution of Court usage to this composite plot. It has some claim indeed to be regarded as the cardinal incident of the piece. It is the main event of the 'Revels' which we learn in the first scene Cynthia intends to hold, but which actually (in the final version) open only in the second half of the last act. One recalls the *Midsummer Night's Dream*, with its opening announcement of the wedding celebrations which conclude the play and upon which all its lines of action converge. But the brilliant dramatic invention which there makes the interim pass so lightly for us was not in Jonson's plan even if it had been in his power; and he has filled the interval with what is meant to be a scathing picture of the Court futilities which the masque is finally to expose and to punish. These scenes are among the most tedious, as they are among the best written, that he has left us.[1] They have not the virtue of his masterly realism; for he had not yet, as he could boast a few years later, 'come so nigh' to the beauties of Whitehall,

> to know
> Whether their faces were their owne, or no,[2]

and they painfully lack, in consequence, the humour which, in Jonson, was rooted in, and nourished by, observation. Under such conditions, a society game (IV. iii), expositions of the 'noble science of courtship', and rehearsals of it with a friend to take the lady's part (III. v), were dramatically hazardous materials even when Satire was the main end, notwithstanding the brilliant Shakespearian analogies to scenes like these, by which they may possibly have been provoked.[3] No doubt it was impracticable in any case to apply the frank methods of the Humour plays to the inner circle of the Court. Cynthia, too candidly portrayed, might have been taken for a kinswoman of the many-robed Phantaste, rather than for a patron of the sober-stoled 'Puritan', Arete. And long tradition had established as the only admissible representation of the Queen in literature a colourless personification of virtue in which truth of detail was rather avoided than sought. The courtly celebration of Elizabeth was in fact a school of symbolism, which directly incited to indirect, allusive, and allegorical modes of poetic speech, and not seldom induced them in writers to whom they were normally strange. Spenser, to whom they were the breath of poetry, had run riot in splendid symbols for her, and Shakespeare had paused in his fancy Dream (not improbably a Court play) to dally exquisitely with the transparent legend of Cupid's vain assault upon maiden Moon. In taking the Court then as his scene, still more by introducing the Queen in person, Jonson committed himself to some degree of symbolism. Foreign to what was strongest

---

[1] Several of them (in particular v. i–iv), remarkable in both respects, first appear in the Folio.
[2] *Underwoods*, xlii. 35–6.
[3] Compare Amorphus's instruction of Asotus how to woo him as the Lady Lindabrides, with Rosalind and Orlando.

and richest in his art, it appealed with dangerous force to
the scholastic and abstract side of his intellect.  The
consecrated emblem Cynthia acted as a nucleus from which
allegorical influences radiated in all directions through the
substance of the drama.  There thus arose a strange
encounter which is not the least interesting feature of this
undramatic play—between the realist and the symbolist in
Jonson, between the poet who had anatomized the deformity
of the times in the Humour plays and the poet who was
presently to beguile the fancy of the Jacobean Court with
his masques.  The throng of courtly fops and pretenders,
so obviously indigenous in Jonsonian London, mingle in the
palace chambers with antique gods and allegorical personifications, with Mercury and Cupid, Arete and Hesperus, and
the silent shapes of Phronesis, Thauma, and Timê.  The very
scene of the action, though always in or near the palace,
changes its complexion and latitude with the changing
persons.  The opening, where Mercury with his caduceus
meets Cupid with his bow, while Echo chants exquisitely
to the music of the fountain in which Narcissus was
drowned, transports us at once into the artificial myth-world
of the masque ; and we hear without wonder that ' Cynthia's
Revels' are to be held in the wild Boeotian vale of Gargaphie,
where Actaeon perished at her bidding.  But with the
approach of the revellers, the spell of courtly myth and
allegoric fancy is broken, and the true Jonsonian world of
the London streets surges in upon the stage.  Echo flies,
and Mercury and Cupid abruptly retire, at sight of the alien
Amorphus who is 'neither your *Minotaure*, nor your *Centaure*,
nor your *Satyre*, . . . but your mere trauailer'; and the
traveller's talk presently indicates that he and we are no
longer in Gargaphie at all, but north of the Alps,[1] and in
fact nowhere but in ' this our *Metropolis* ', with its parish
churches, its conduits, and its Puritan magistrates, zealous
for the due measuring of coal and cleaning of streets.

[1] 'Since I trode on this side the *Alpes*, I was not so frozen in my
inuention ' (I. iv).

For the most part, as we have seen, the two artistic methods are kept apart in the handling of character. The Humours, however much they have lost in individual sharpness, do not become mere personifications; the personifications hardly simulate realism. But in the group of Court women, Moria, Philautia, Phantaste, Argurion, to whom we may add Gelaia, the page of Anaides, the two manners curiously cross and mingle. In the lively description of Argurion in particular, as Gifford well remarks, 'the literal and metaphorical sense is so blended as to form a very distinct, though an amusing representation'. She is not only 'a *Nymph* of a most wandring and giddy disposition', but a symbol for money. ' Shee spreads as shee goes. . . . Your yong student (for the most part) shee affects not, only salutes him, and away: a *poet*, nor a *philosopher*, shee is hardly brought to take any notice of; no, though he be some part of an *alchemist*. She loues a *player* well, and a *lawyer* infinitely: but your foole aboue all' (II. iii). Even Asotus's wooing of her catches the allegorical infection; and Amorphus would hardly have recommended her to his suit by the singular argument that she had been his father's love before, if this had not been simply a way of saying: ' Make money, as your father did.'

In thus applying classic myth to the dramatic presentment of Elizabeth's Court, Jonson had at least one distinguished precursor. Lyly's Court plays of the eighties had captivated the young Shakespeare in 1590, and, notwithstanding the enormous subsequent strides of the drama, they obviously retained some attraction for the Jonson of 1600, whose critical disdain excepted hardly any other dramas of that decade. Utterly inferior as Lyly was to Jonson in weight of mind, in artistic seriousness, and in poetic power, his aims were not altogether unlike, and he had pursued them with an adroitness which Jonson at this stage had neither sought nor attained. Lyly too had come forward as a reformer at once of literature and of manners, and he had contrived by sheer literary virtuosity to win an enthusiastic vogue for his style, and at least a hearing for his ideas, at Court. Jonson could afford to despise the crude preciosity of Euphuism and the puerile artificiality of Lyly's plots, as well as the tenuity of their intellectual or ethical substance. But he saw in Lyly's device of touching Greek myth to contemporary and courtly issues a fruitful idea which might be taken up into his more masculine technique and used to further his more comprehensive aims.

The most notable feature of the device was of course the use of the Cynthia- or Diana-myths in transparent allusion to the Queen. 'Cynthia' had indeed long been her established title in poetry, but Lyly had done more than any one else to set the fashion, and no one else had woven the allusion into drama with so much elaborate ingenuity as he. In Endimion wakened from slumber by Cynthia's kiss Lyly had symbolized the story of a favoured suitor, as Jonson hinted at the end of a rasher one in the doom of Actaeon. Lyly's Cynthia, like Jonson's, appears as the presiding sovereign power deciding all causes and assigning reward and punishment. But we need not ascribe to Lyly's example traits which belong to the common classical tradition, such as the hostility of Cupid to the chaste goddess and her nymphs. Rather we find Jonson freely developing the Lylyan device of a mythic Court play in a way wholly his own, as in the brilliant (if abortive) application of the Narcissus-myth in the courtly Fountain of Self-Love.

## IV

And both the myth-device and the courtly application contributed to introduce in *Cynthia's Revels* a third type of plot-interest—the conflict between good and evil. The Morality—if we allow the name to plays with both real characters and personifications—had hardly disappeared from the Elizabethan boards when Jonson began to write. He cannot be suspected of any wish to revive this obsolete dramatic kind. But his treatment of characters as the acting out of a single dominant 'humour', though psychologically much better grounded than the simple allegoric schemes of the Morality writers, tended in dramatic practice to become a collection of personified faults corresponding to the evil powers of the Moral play. On the other hand, his passion for vindicating and reforming, his militant idealism and his robust arrogance, all prompted him to introduce representatives of moral excellence, as in *Every Man out of his Humour*, to preside over the discomfiture of the faulty types and loftily point the moral. The purpose of addressing the Queen, and of invoking her immaculate virtue against the serried follies of her Court, involved the introduction of yet other ideal figures, and, what still further added to the Morality effect, set up a sharp moral cleavage in the very structure of the piece. Some vestige of the Humour treatment still clings to the vindictive forces of *Every Man out of his Humour*;—Asper is suspect of harshness, Macilente is lean with envy; but Cynthia is flawless, Arete is embodied Virtue, and Crites, their confederate and confidant, a 'divine' person compounded of all the humours in their right and perfect proportion. The Morality aspect of the play is naturally most pronounced in the masques. Here allegorical abstractions were at home, and if Amorphus, Asotus, and the rest of the masquers have hitherto been no mere abstractions but 'men in their humours', in the masques they figure primarily as examples of the particular vice which each disguises with the attributes of its 'neighbour virtue'. When Amorphus appears as Eucosmus, 'neat and elegant', Anaides as Eutolmos, as 'duly respecting others', Philautia as 'Storge' or 'allowable self-love', the stress is inevitably shifted from the human actors to their ethical import; they become figures in an allegory, not merely persons with expressive names. The adoption by vicious characters of names of Virtues was moreover a familiar motive of the Morality; and even the refinement (pointing to the influence of Aristotelean ethics) by which the Virtue chosen is conceived as the Vice restricted to due measure, as Liberality for Prodigality, is already approached in Skelton's

*Magnificence.*[1] And all pretence of dramatic value is wanting in the mere abstractions 'Phronesis', 'Thauma', 'Timê', 'Phronimus'. Finally, the example both of Lyly and of the later Moralities, such as *The Three Lords and the Three Ladies of London,* is reflected in the elaborate symmetry of the grouping. Here is no question of art concealing art; the grouping is artificial and its artifice is openly paraded. The four foolish courtiers match the four foolish Court ladies; and both pairs are confronted by the four virtuous ladies in the train of Cynthia, three of whom, Phronesis, Thauma, and Timê, serve no other function whatever. The Morality character culminates in the introduction of these three abstractions—*nomina et praeterea nihil.*

### V

Myth and morality have thus had their way with Jonson. Never before had his unsurpassed gift of direct observation of contemporary human life suffered so large an intrusion of fanciful or abstract elements, never had his efforts to combine these discrepant types of motive and material fallen so far short of complete fusion. Yet clearly in details and in single characters the great realist painter of Elizabethan London is unmistakable still, and in brilliance of literary expression he even surpassed all his previous achievements. The shady gallants and seedy men of letters of Elizabeth's last decade were once more, as in *Every Man out of his Humour,* hit off with admirably incisive strokes. None of them can rank as a great comic creation, but several of them stand high in the narrower and lower field of the satiric Character.

Did any of them directly stand for or 'represent' individual enemies of Jonson? Were they acts of reprisal on his part for assaults on theirs? Much space has hitherto been occupied with discussion of questions of this type. In particular Hedon and Anaides have been 'identified' with Marston and Dekker. Doubtless he drew freely from these familiar acquaintances for the traits of the types

---

[1] Baskervill, *u. s.* p. 251.

he portrayed. Beyond question, too, Dekker took the figures of Anaides and Hedon for deliberate caricatures of himself and Marston;[1] and Marston seems to have done the same.[2] But Jonson's language in the Apologetical Dialogue to *Poetaster* justifies us in holding that the decisive step from the type with individual traits to the intentional satiric portrait was taken only in that play; they had indeed attacked Jonson for three years; but he had adhered to his principle of 'sparing persons and dealing only with faults', until

> I, at last, vnwilling,
> But weary, I confesse, of so much trouble,
> Thought, I would try, if shame could winne vpon 'hem,

and therefore emptied the vials of his indignation unmistakably upon the heads of his two assailants in the *Poetaster*.

It is needless, then, to dwell upon the attacks levelled by Marston and Dekker at Jonson since *Every Man out of his Humour*. Marston's insignificant *Jack Drum's Entertainment*,[3] possibly the earliest, is too ambiguous in its possible references to Jonson, to count as a noticeable exercise of the 'petulant style'.[4] The earlier attacks of Dekker, indicated by Jonson in the above-quoted words, as well as the origin of the quarrel with him, elude us. His great counterblast *Satiro-mastix*, though provoked by the supposed attack upon him in *Cynthia's Revels*, was forestalled by the crushing direct castigation of the *Poetaster*. But his evident conviction that in Hedon or Anaides Marston and himself were directly pilloried demands a brief examination of the pair.[5]

Hedon and Anaides are clearly not to be regarded as mere anticipations or first sketches of the later pair,

---

[1] *Satiro-mastix*, I. ii, ed. 1602, sigg. C, C 2 verso.
[2] In *What You Will*, II. i. 169 ff.
[3] After March, 1600; entered in the Stationers' Register in September, 1600.
[4] Small (*Stage Quarrel*, p. 94 f.) identifies Jonson with the elder Brabant; Fleay, with John fo' de King.
[5] The discussion which follows has been greatly facilitated by the tabulation of the traits of Hedon and Anaides, Demetrius and Crispinus, in Small's *Stage Quarrel*, p. 31 f.

Crispinus and Demetrius. Much of the typical generality of the Jonsonian Humour lingers about both; Hedon is in most points recognizably of the type of the fashionable gallant, a near kinsman of Fastidius Brisk. Brisk's resources consist much in his wardrobe, his pomander, and his mirror. Hedon shares his foppery, is thought 'a verie necessarie perfume for the presence', and is even ' for that onely cause welcome thither'. Both profess wit, Hedon contriving for his mistress 'Arcadian' extravagances of comparison, as Brisk breaks into Platonic figure to convey his sense of 'the essentiall felicitie of your court'.[1] Brisk 'sweares tersely, and with variety'; Hedon is a cunning deviser of pretty 'far-fet' oaths (II. ii). Brisk can punctuate a compliment with the viol; Hedon sings a song, and turns a rhyme, and likes to play the patron of musicians and other artists.[2] But these literary and artistic dexterities are very lightly touched; Hedon is a courtier with a turn for preciosity, not yet the sharply individualized poetaster-plagiary Crispinus who entreats the ladies to entreat him to sing. His preciosity, too, is, in spite of his passion for singularity, a common form of debased Elizabethan; not yet the clotted and strenuous 'Gallo-Belgian' dialect of Crispinus-Marston. In outward appearance, again, the figure of Hedon shows a similar warp from the Brisk type. He 'weares clothes well', but they are only 'sometimes' in fashion. The Protean splendour of Brisk appears more than a little damaged in him; but he is not yet the shabby gentleman of the fretted satin sleeve and the stained velvet bases who smarts under the taunts of Horace in the *Poetaster* (III. i). There is nothing in all this that definitely connects Hedon with Marston, and neither Marston nor any one else would probably have suspected a connexion had not Jonson

---

[1] 'You that tell your Mistris, Her beautie is all composde of theft; Her haire stole from APOLLO's goldy-locks', &c. (*Cynthia's Revels*, v. iv); cf. *Every Man out of his Humour*, IV. viii.

[2] Marston appears to have had some interest in music, perhaps derived from his Italian grandfather; his plays abound in musical allusions and imagery.

introduced two other less ambiguous traits. He makes Hedon a bitter assailant of Crites, his own mouthpiece and antitype; and he gives his Anaides a doughty but disreputable ally, such as Marston had already presumably found in Dekker.

Dekker is a much obscurer figure to us, at this time, than Marston. But there is every indication that Anaides is, as a satirical creation, a counterpart of Hedon. He belongs to the tribe of Buffone as Hedon to the tribe of Brisk. But he has certain traits which diminish the resemblance to Buffone and anticipate the more incisive features of the Demetrius of the *Poetaster*. Like Buffone he is a scurrilous and blasphemous railer—'*impudence* it selfe', speaking 'all that comes in his cheekes', and 'lightly occupies the iesters roome at the table' (II. ii). He is not, however, like Buffone, a hungry parasite, a 'good feast-hound, or banquet beagle', who jests for his dinner; indeed he has a certain pretension to social standing, has come into some land 'by chance', declines to know any one beneath him in clothes, and to drink to any one below the salt. He is proficient in all the 'illiberal sciences'—cheating, drinking, swaggering, whoring, as Hedon in the liberal arts of fencing, riding, music. Even his amours are of a grosser type; Hedon courts a mistress with high-flown compliments, Anaides lavishes taffeta gowns and satin kirtles on a 'punquetto', while he plays the niggard to his friends. His intellectual vices too are those of rude nature, not of culture, like Hedon's; he does not understand Latin, but dares to quote it (as Demetrius would trace Jonson's thefts from the classics, 'but that I vnderstand 'hem not full and whole', and he bears a bitter grudge against Crites for having once challenged him to construe his quotation. He is even less than Hedon a literary man; and while Hedon makes a certain approach to the later Crispinus, Anaides detaches himself completely at this point from Demetrius, the 'dresser of plays about the town'. Both pairs, however, agree completely in their hatred of Crites-Horace; and here too Hedon and Anaides, otherwise so distinct, fall completely into line; the 'light voluptuous reueller' and the 'strange arrogating puffe' are for Jonson natural foes of the scholar; and they assail Crites with an animosity which falls nothing short of that displayed by Crispinus and Demetrius against Horace. But they are not yet, like these, satirical *portraits*.

In these characters, then, personal motives qualified the type without destroying its typical quality. In the other characters no personal reference has been made in any degree probable.[1] Amorphus is a new Puntarvolo, Asotus continues the line of Master Stephen and Fungoso, Saviolina reappears in Philautia, Deliro and Fallace in the Citizen and his Wife. In the freshest scenes these old pieces are not so much developed or varied, as combined anew; Asotus, the best of them, exhibits the humour of desperate social ambition as the blundering pupil of the travelled gallant instead of the vain emulator of the fop. The scene (III. v) in which Amorphus instructs him in the art of courtship by personating the lady may perhaps, as already noticed, owe a hint to Rosalind and Orlando, whose wooing had first been enacted a few months before.[2] It is still upon the pretenders and futile aspirants, the snobs of Jacobean London, the people whose footing at Court is precarious or exceptional, that Jonson's dramatic satire fastens with most success. Even in this congenial domain, however, he continually uses, or abuses, his gift of analytic description, never more brilliant than now, to supplement a reserved or suspended dramatic power. Whatever may be thought of them as parts of dramatic scenes, the scathing anatomy (in III. iv) of the types of vulgar courtier, 'the knot of spiders' whose webs will be dissolved when Cynthia arrives, or the yet darker confessions of the Court ladies in Act IV, scene i, are masterpieces of nervous and discriminative

---

[1] F. G. Fleay on unconvincing grounds identifies Amorphus with Harington.
[2] Other reminiscences of Shakespeare may perhaps be found in Moria, Philautia, and Phantaste's discussion of their wooers (IV. i; cf. *Merchant of Venice*, II. i).

phrase. Yet the stir and wealth of life are ill exchanged for these serried rows of satiric portraits, all, in spite of their brilliant variety of costume and accoutrement, painted in the same sombre shades and with the same harsh emphatic touch.

*Cynthia's Revels* is thus, in most points, inferior to even the less excellent of the two earlier Humour plays. Where old matter is retained it is rehandled with less power and freshness; while the new inventions, rich and splendid as they are in detail, do little but embarrass movement and confuse effect. Yet as a document of Jonson's intellectual idealism, of his scorn for the rampant follies of the world, this 'Comical Satire' is impressive. The figure of Crites, not a whit less trenchantly drawn than that of Asper in *Every Man out of his Humour*, has a much more dramatic and significant part in the plot. Asper the Presenter figures only as a passionate chorus to his own play. Crites is its hero, the champion of wisdom and virtue in the war with Vice and Folly, the trusty executant of Cynthia, and her favourite poet. The more languid conduct of affairs here is thus far compensated that the affairs have, under all their triviality, their blended σεμνότης and βαναυσία, a larger issue; they symbolize with whatever idleness of arabesque a conflict of mighty opposites, not merely the comic encounter of fool with fool. As the central figure of the Court, Crites might well have proved a colourless abstraction like the rest. Happily, however, not a little of Jonson's own character has infused itself into this ideal embodiment of his cause. The likeness in certain points is unmistakable; the Jonson of the Preface to *Volpone* or to this very play in the Folio is audibly echoed in his speech and in his tone. But this is not to say that Crites *is* Jonson, or that the boundless eulogies he receives mark merely the depth of his own potations at the Fountain of Self-Love. A strenuous, combative upholder of Jonson's ideas could not but resemble Jonson; Crites is such an upholder, but he is also, like the other Court characters, a type of flawless excellence.

Mercury is describing, as he says, a creature 'more than man', and not our emphatically human Ben, when he draws his figure of Crites: 'A creature of a most perfect and diuine temper. One, in whom the humours and elements are peaceably met, without emulation of precedencie; . . . neyther too phantastikely melancholy, too slowly phlegmaticke, too lightly sanguine, or too rashly cholericke, but in all, so composde & order'd, as it is cleare, *Nature* went about some ful worke, she did more then make a man, when she made him.'[1] If the inner mind of Jonson, his intellectual ascendancy, ever finds full utterance, it is in some of these Critean invectives against the debasement which leaves the 'best and vnderstanding part' of man, the 'crowne and strength of all his faculties', to

> Floate like a dead drown'd bodie, on the streame
> Of vulgar humour, mixt with commonst dregs.[2]

Jonson often provokes comparison with his great namesake of the eighteenth century. But his Crites and Asper compel us, as nothing else in contemporary literature does, to remember the impassioned idealism of Carlyle.

[1] Act II, scene iii.   [2] Act I, scene v.

# INTRODUCTION TO
## 'POETASTER'

# POETASTER

## I

*Poetaster* was performed, as the title-page of the Folio indicates, in 1601, and probably not more than four or five months after the production of *Cynthia's Revels*. No other play of Jonson's followed so swiftly on the heels of its predecessor, and the rapid execution points to circumstances of unusual urgency. Rumours had reached him that his enemies, stung by the unmistakable references in 'Hedon' and 'Anaides', were preparing a signal revenge; that Anaides-Dekker was to 'abuse' him and 'bring him in, in a play, with all his gallants';[1] and that the Lord Chamberlain's men, who sided with his rivals in the Stage Quarrel, had commissioned the piece for production on its boards, where it was, in fact, subsequently presented.[2] He resolved to parry this attack by a counterstroke of his own; to bring his assailants themselves into a play, and arraign them for their literary sins. In fifteen weeks, he tells us explicitly, *Poetaster* was finished.[3] These fifteen weeks must have fallen somewhat early in the year, for Histrio is made to complain that 'this winter ha's made vs all poorer, then so many staru'd snakes',[4] words which would hardly have been used later than May, and if the play had been performed later, would have been altered.

Like *Cynthia's Revels*, *Poetaster* was acted by the Children of Queen Elizabeth's Chapel. These 'little eyases' were now the fashion. It was their immense popularity in this very winter that had been the chief cause of the 'starvation' of the older players, and driven one thriving company,

---

[1] *Poet.* III. iv: cf. IV. vii, 'Come, we'll goe see how forward our iourney-man is toward the vntrussing of him.'
[2] The title-page states it to have been 'presented publikely by the Right Honorable, the Lord Chamberlaine his Seruants; and priuately, by the Children of Paules'.
[3] Envy's Prologue, 14.   [4] *Poet.* III. iv.

as we learn from *Hamlet*, to 'travel'. The performance was the most sensational incident that had yet occurred in the Stage Quarrel. Here, at any rate, 'the poet' with the 'boys' at his bidding, and the player with the playwright in his pay, 'went to cuffs in the question', and there was 'much throwing about of brains'. The town, always ready to desert the regular stage for a prize-fight or a bear-baiting, crowded round the arena and tarred on the combatants to controversy.[1] The play proved, however, to be something other than a spectacle for the onlookers. A tumult of angry cries broke out amid the excited plaudits; a host of persons who had no concern in the quarrel felt their withers wrung by the large sweep of Jonson's satiric lash; citizens of standing, professional persons, lawyers and soldiers as well as players, indignantly protested against the outrage offered to their orders and to their persons; while the two or three individuals against whom the satire was principally directed, far from being struck with shame into silence and surrender, as it appears to have been Jonson's somewhat naïve expectation that they would, flew upon their assailant with the fury of wasps and hornets, and

> like so many screaming grasse-hoppers,
> Held by the wings, fill'd euery eare with noyse.

A storm of retaliatory abuse in pamphlets and satires broke upon Jonson's head. Shakespeare himself descended into the arena in Marston's behalf, to contrive a 'purge' for the doughty purveyor of the 'pill';[2] and the other principal victim, Dekker, hastened to turn his probably still unfinished *Satiro-mastix* into a retort to the play which the rumour of it had originally provoked. Of the whole bevy of 'libels' this alone survives. Even before it appeared, however, Jonson, whose vehement temper rarely permitted him to maintain the attitude of disdainful silence which he recog-

---

[1] *Ham.* II. ii. 350. There is little doubt that Rosencrantz's report has in view the performances of *Poetaster* and *Satiro-mastix*, in which the whole quarrel culminated.
[2] Kemp in *Return from Parnassus*, II.

nized as the most dignified course, had once more intervened, brandishing an olive-branch only less formidable than his weapon. The 'Apologetical Dialogue' was indeed, as he confesses in the preface to the Folio text of it, 'only once spoken vpon the stage'; a summary prohibition intervening to prevent a further application of Jonson's irritant balsam. He protests that *Poetaster* was the most harmless piece in the world,—

     I never writ that peece
 More innocent, or empty of offence.

The satire on lawyers was copied from Ovid, a lawyer himself; the abuse of a skeldering captain cast no stigma upon true soldiers; as for the players, only a few were pointed at, and these were men who had for three years been assailing him on every stage, while he had still neglected their attacks. It had been the uniform practice of his satire, he claims, to 'spare the persons, and to speake the vices'. Such professions, however, availed little to conciliate when the author, a few lines before, had flung the most unmistakable personal charges at his enemies, declaring roundly that

    in all their heat of taxing others,
 Not one of them, but liues himselfe (if knowne)
 *Improbior satyram scribente cinædo.*

However we may discount these professions of innocence, the 'Apologetical Dialogue' throws an important light upon the aims of *Poetaster*.

 He was himself, he tells us, weary of the barren conflict. He resented the obstinacy of these champions of Ignorance, who, instead of submitting to the correction of his critical lash, retaliated, on every stage, with the acrimony of their 'petulant styles'. Argument against such opponents was useless and out of place; but it might be possible to work upon their literary self-respect, to wring the otherwise impenetrable stuff of their literary conscience by holding up the image of another great historical conflict between the giants and the pigmies of literature, in which the pigmies had acted with the same shameless irreverence and the giants with the same calm but inflexible justice. He

> therefore chose AVGVSTVS CAESARS times,
> When wit, and artes were at their height in *Rome*,
> To shew that VIRGIL, HORACE, and the rest
> Of those great master-spirits did not want
> Detractors, then, or practisers against them.

There was some *naïveté* in the device, but Jonson was not the man to shrink from an effective design because it involved a comparison of himself with Horace. He had already, in *Cynthia's Revels*, conferred upon his representative and spokesman, Crites, a position of authority and prestige at Court to which his own, even in the palmiest days of the Court masque, was to make but a faint approach. To present himself in the person of Horace at the Court of Augustus was merely to substitute a real and historical for an imaginary personation. It called into play a new and fruitful source of interest, but also involved additional hazards; and in Jonson's hands the new hazard and the new interest were about equally matched.

II

No other dramatist was so well qualified as Jonson to call up before the eyes of Elizabethan London the brilliant society of Augustan Rome in its habit as it lived. The *Satires* and *Epistles* of Horace and Ovid's *Art of Love* would by themselves furnish forth a whole comedy of Humours. And the situation of Horace lent itself in some respects not ill to the satirist's special purpose. The Horace of the first book of the *Satires*, in particular, who was then about the same age as Jonson at the date of *Poetaster*, had suffered something from the persecutions, the importunities, or the defamations of various persons of the literary and artistic world, who are for the most part visible to us only in the somewhat cruel light in which they appeared to him.

Such were 'cimex' Pantilius;[1] the fashionable singer Hermogenes Tigellius,[2] and his companion Fannius Quadratus; the scurrilous backbiter 'Demetrius';[3] and the blear-eyed pedant Crispinus,[4] with his floods of moral talk. Of the really distinguished poets among his contemporaries, then or later, only Propertius and Ovid are plausibly suspected of having regarded him with ill will.[5] But for all this animosity Horace had more than adequate compensation in the admiration and friendship of the intellectual and political leaders of Roman society. So long as Plotius and Varius, Valgius and Fuscus, Pollio and Messala, Maecenas and Vergil, and Octavius himself approved or endured his lays, he could afford to ignore the cavils of the rest.

To this aspect of Horace's situation, the position of Jonson in 1601 presented but an imperfect parallel. He had not as yet, in any strict sense, either an Augustus, or a Maecenas, or a Vergil. It was only in the next reign that his fond vision of himself, in *Cynthia's Revels*, as the trusted ally and executant of his sovereign was at length in some remote degree fulfilled. With a few noble houses, of literary traditions,—with a Lady Rutland or a Lady Bedford—he probably already had some acquaintance, as well as among the young lawyers of the Inns of Court, many of them old 'Westminsters' like himself. And Tucca's taunt, in the *Satiro-mastix*,[6] that 'Horace did not skrue and wriggle himselfe into great Mens famyliarity, (impudentlie), as thou doost', may be taken to show that he had already enough incipient 'familiarity' with great men to excite the envy of less successful playwrights. But none of these relations brought him as yet into any kind of touch with the social

---
[1] Horace, *Sat.* i. 10. 78.
[2] Ibid. 80; also 2. 1–4; 3. 1–18, 129; 4. 72.
[3] Ibid. 10. 79, 90.
[4] Ibid. 1. 120; 3. 139; 4. 13–6; ii. 7. 45.
[5] Propertius is held to be the poet whose vanity is criticized in *Epist.* ii. 2. 87. Ovid omits Horace pointedly from the list of seductive poets (*Ars Amat.* iii. 329 f.) which includes Propertius, Tibullus, Gallus, Vergil, and himself.
[6] Act v, scene ii (ed. 1602, sig. L 4).

and political centre of affairs. And as little as he had a Maecenas had he a Vergil. Shakespeare, who to our eyes seems to fill so naturally the corresponding niche, was during these early months of 1601 peculiarly ill qualified to justify the parallel; the sovereign, since the Essex catastrophe, regarded him with coldness, and 'Horace' had just been the victim of his 'purge'. Shakespeare's Company had, moreover, as Jonson knew, arranged with Dekker for the very play[1] which *Poetaster* was written to forestall, and which was, the same autumn, actually performed on their boards.

Among other poets, he was probably already intimate with Chapman and with Donne. Chapman, though nearly twenty years his senior, had only recently won high repute, chiefly by his version of the first seven books of the *Iliad* and his continuation of Marlowe's noble fragmentary paraphrase of the *Hero and Leander*. Donne had perhaps already thrown off the greater part of his verse, and Jonson may already have regarded him as 'the first poet in the world in some things', who nevertheless 'deserved hanging' for his bad verse. But none of his verse was published till several years later, and Donne was still obscure.

### III

It was thus only in the number and bitterness of his literary assailants that Jonson's situation bore any striking resemblance to that of Horace at the time of his early satires. Of a close parallel there could be no question, as no one knew better than he. For Jonson's larger design, however, of presenting the master-minds of Rome at the height of their renown, yet still subject to the detraction and calumnies of ignorance, exact parallelism was in no way necessary. Enough that in Elizabethan London, unrecognized by the Queen, unprotected by her counsellors of state, one master spirit was fighting single-handed the

---

[1] This is a fair conclusion from the words of Histrio, *Poet.* III. iv.

battle of poetry against assailants who wielded more formidable arms, and had a more considerable public behind them, than any of the Augustan detractors of Horace. Jonson was drawn to his Augustan theme by several distinct kinds of attraction. To the incensed antagonist of Marston and Dekker it supplied the materials for a mordant satirical comparison, humiliating to his assailants, glorious to himself. To the doughty but forlorn champion of poetry at large against ignorance, it offered the reassuring spectacle of a company of illustrious spirits, bound together by lofty friendship and admiration, and devoid of envy, triumphing over the malignity to which they were exposed. And to the humanist, who was soon to body forth a piece of Roman History with unexampled erudition on the English stage, the Augustan world and its illustrious poets had an independent fascination. Each of the three points of view prompted a particular choice and handling of the classical material. For the first it sufficed to find Roman analogues to himself and his assailants; the second demanded a call upon the ideal figures of Roman poetry; the third invited a comprehensive picture of Roman society at large. All these interests and motives were vital for Jonson, and the unusual speed with which he here worked has permitted them all to assert themselves, with little consistency or control, in the shaping of the play. And in addition Jonson has used once more certain stock situations and characters of his social satire, which had, so far as we can see, no personal, poetic, or historic relevance at all, but simply made for comic vivacity. *Poetaster* is by no means Jonson's worst comedy, for the swiftness of the execution has tempered the over-elaboration which plays such havoc with *Every Man out of his Humour* and *Cynthia's Revels*; but it is surely the least well made.

As a piece of satirical invective, *Poetaster* centres in the little group of rival dramatists who plot and persecute, or suffer and revenge, under the transparent masks of Crispinus, Demetrius, and Horace.

Jonson's 'Horace' is a tempting butt of ridicule. In spite of rather numerous and extensive Horatian trappings [1] he is not very perceptibly like Horace; and he is also less like Jonson than the Asper and Crites through whom he had spoken his mind in the earlier plays. It would seem that Jonson, in seeking to temper his own naturally 'sharp and thorny-toothed' satire to the measure of Horatian urbanity, succeeded only in blunting its point without polishing its surface. The Jonsonian Horace is neither right Elizabethan nor true Roman. He wields no 'whip of steel', and refrains with a good-natured reluctance, foreign to this Boanerges of the stage, from taking full advantage of his enemies' fatuity (V. iii); but his courtesy is negative and colourless, and lacks the well-bred ease and mellow charm of Augustan gentility. His nervous embarrassment in the company of the bore is similarly out of keeping with Jonson's peremptory methods (III. i). The author of *Satiro-mastix* rallied Jonson on the folly of presenting 'a goodly Corpulent Gentleman', like Horace, in the person of a 'leane hollow-cheekt Scrag' like himself.[2] Jonson's 'mountain-belly' clearly belonged to a later time; but the stage Horace is called, and was doubtless represented as, corpulent ('my little fat Horace', IV. vii). It was less easy for a still struggling playwright, who had perhaps starved as often as he had feasted, to simulate the choice yet temperate Epicureanism of the Roman poet. On the other hand Jonson's vindication, through the lips of his Horace, of the clear judgement of poor men rings truer and strikes deeper than the Roman Horace's comfortable praise of temperance:

> As if the filth of pouertie sunke as deepe
> Into a knowing spirit, as the bane
> Of riches doth, into an ignorant soule.
>                                       (V. i. 81–3.)

---

[1] See especially III. i–iv, Horace and the bore in the Sacred Way, from *Sat.* ix; III. v, Horace and Trebatius, from *Sat.* ii. 1.
[2] *Satiro-mastix*, V. ii (ed. 1602, sig. L 4, verso).

Crispinus and Demetrius, Horace's principal enemies and victims, undoubtedly stand for Marston and Dekker, who had already been obliquely glanced at in the Hedon and Anaides of the previous play. Dekker in *Satiromastix* rather naïvely taunts Jonson with attacking fellow-poets, instead of, like the real Horace, the enemies of poetry. 'Horace lou'd Poets well, and gave Coxcombes to none but fooles.'[1] This was not quite exact, for the 'fools' who received Horace's 'coxcombs' included at least one nominal 'poet',—the very Crispinus whom Jonson singled out to personate Marston.[2] Demetrius appears to have been a teacher of rhetoric in girls' schools.[3] But 'poets' or not, their poetry was no part of Horace's charge against them; he did not 'tear them for their bad verses' or even exactly for their insensibility to his own good ones, but for their envious abuse of his character. The Elizabethan Stage Quarrel, on the other hand, was by no means confined to personal animosities. Even now, when he is trying to forestall a violent personal attack, Jonson does battle as much for the honour of poetry and the discomfiture of bad poets as in vindication of his own character. He ridicules the hackneyed ghost and revenge business of *The Spanish Tragedy*, to which, a few months later, he was himself to supply (in any case to be paid for supplying) 'additions', though hardly those famous ones which Lamb called 'the very salt of the old play'. Crispinus is brought forward as a most resolute and prolific versifier, in the very kinds that Jonson himself pursued; Demetrius as a 'dresser of plaies about the towne'. 'I write iust in thy veine, I', says Crispinus to Horace on the Sacred Way, 'I am for your *odes*, or your *sermons* . . .; we are a prettie *stoick* too.' Each has his special vice: Crispinus is attacked for his 'frothy' and 'strenuous' vocabulary and clotted style; Demetrius for his loose and slipshod doggerel. The

---

[1] *Satiro-mastix*, v. ii (ed. 1602, sig. L 4).
[2] 'Crispinus . . . poeta fuit qui sectam stoicam versibus scripsit' (Scholiast to Horace, *Sat.* i. 1. 120).
[3] Ibid. 10. 91.

scene (v. iii) in which the issue of their two brains is publicly produced for judgement before the tribunal of Augustus and Virgil has been compared with the great trial scene of the *Frogs*. The resemblance is only superficial. Aeschylus and Euripides are opponents in a great civil cause; they stand for two generations, and the issue is between two ideals: Crispinus and Dekker are merely a pair of criminals brought to the same bar for different offences, equally heinous, against the common literary standards of the time. It is true that both have affinities with older fashions of Elizabethan writing, just as Horace's Demetrius can declaim nothing later than Calvus and Catullus (*Sat.* i. 10. 17). But they stand for no literary principle or principles, however humble; and, with all their marked differences of manner, there is no hint of rivalry between them. Jonson himself indeed shows a certain, well controlled but unmistakable, preference for Marston (Crispinus). His tone towards him, though rough, is not altogether unkind. He rallies his well-born assailant on his pride of birth ('wee are a gentleman besides'), but he was not indifferent to the tacit claim of fellowship which that involved with himself. And, apart from this, Marston's abstruseness and violence were less uncongenial to him than Dekker's diffuse facility; they appealed to his intellectual athleticism, to his scorn for popularity: while in Dekker, who lacked the classical training common to his comrade and to his foe, Jonson saw a type of the blatant 'ignorance', against which he waged eternal and merciless war. Once more, as in *Cynthia's Revels*, Demetrius's inability to read Latin is made game of:

I know the authors from whence he ha's stole,
And could trace him too, but that I vnderstand 'hem
not full and whole.   (v. iii.)

One regrets that the man who so loftily repelled the stigma of poverty in his own case should have condescended to make capital of the poverty of his enemies;—to rally Marston on his fretted satin sleeve and Dekker on his decayed doublet. Judged, however, as a fencing stroke, the taunt was effective enough. A more dignified antagonist might have disdained it; Dekker's loud complaints in *Satiro-mastix*[1] show that it went home. Almost everything, then, in the two characters is taken directly from Marston and Dekker.

If 'Crispinus' and 'Demetrius' have at least some plausible affinities with their Horatian counterparts, Pantilius Tucca owes to his namesake at most the unsavoury epithet ('cimex') which he so vigorously translates into speech and action. Dekker's testimony makes it probable that he too derives much of his rich individual colour from a contemporary model, one Captain Hannam; a person of whom all we know is that he must have been sufficiently like Captain Tucca to make Dekker's plagiarism plausible.[2] Dekker's own version of Tucca in the *Satiro-mastix* must be a monstrous caricature of the 'honest captain': the exasperated Demetrius saw in this genial ruffian merely a piece of human artillery capable of discharging filth and obloquy with unprecedented velocity for any required length of time. Whatever Jonson's relations with Hannam may have been, he has not thus crushed the humanity out of his representative. The Tucca of *Poetaster* is a genuine comic figure,—the best and liveliest character in the play,— with the burly, insolent good nature of Sir Toby, and the thin spirit, behind his bravado, of Bobadill. He compliments with curses, and fondles and caresses in terms of the stews; 'by thy leave, my neat scoundrel', 'cry thee mercy, my good scroyle', 'I'll know the poor egregious nitty rascal', 'tis a good vermin they say';—and contrives to maintain an insecure footing in a society not too favourable to decayed and beggarly men of war by a like blending of

---

[1] I. ii (ed. 1602, sig. D).
[2] 'I wonder what language *Tucca* would haue spoke, it honest Capten *Hannam* had bin borne without a tongue?' (*Satiro-mastix*, To the World). Small (*Stage Quarrel*, p. 26) quotes from Guilpin's *Skialetheia*, 1598, a sarcastic description of a 'Captain Tucca', from which Jonson may have taken the name.

wheedling and truculence until he finds his proper conclusion in Augustus's double-faced mask of Janus.

Jonson is fond of making his disreputable old soldiers allies of the underlings of literature. Master Matthew was the associate of Bobadill; and Tucca blusteringly patronizes those gentlemanly scoundrels, the actors. He goes about attended by two of the Boys who at this time were drawing off the audiences of the great companies,—a little, docile, furtively sarcastic 'Parnassus' who takes his orders,—and incidentally exhibits his taste in drama by reciting specimens of the high-sounding Cambyses-vein that he affects, from the universally ridiculed *Spanish Tragedy*. Tucca was thus the very man to give his blustering patronage to the poetasters in their dramatic assault upon the poet. 'He pens high, loftie, in a new stalking straine; bigger then halfe the rimers i' the towne, againe', says Tucca approvingly of Crispinus (III. iv); implicitly consigning the work of the ambitious Marston to a common limbo with Kyd's notorious masterpiece. Histrio, an actor of the company which has commissioned the play against Horace, is, compared with Tucca, a lifeless figure; but his character and activities, so far as they go, are frankly Elizabethan; even his company and the theatre it plays in are hinted at[1] in a way doubtless clear to the audience but ambiguous to us. Like 'Horace's' enemies in general and like 'Horace' himself, he is impecunious; only, while poverty cannot touch the knowing spirit of Horace, it directly stimulates the struggling players to their 'abuse' of him on the stage; for the profits are likely to be great, and the times are hard. 'O, it will get vs a huge deale of money (Captaine), and wee have need on't; for this winter ha's made vs all poorer,

---

[1] He is said to *have fortune on his side* (III. iv); in other words, to have the support of the Fortune playhouse. As he is represented as having Demetrius-Dekker to write against Horace, it is probable that he is meant to stand for some member of the Chamberlain's Company, or for the Company collectively. That he is not Henslowe, as asserted by Symonds, and by one of the present editors in the *Dictionary of National Biography* (art. Jonson), may be taken as fairly clear.

then so many staru'd snakes: No bodie comes at us' (III. iv). Several other actors are glanced at whom we cannot identify; the only one who is at all distinct is Aesop, the 'politician'[1] of the company, and 'an honest sycophant-like slaue' (according to Tucca) to boot. He exhibits a second character, and probably the first also, in his insinuation to Lupus that the 'embleme' made by Horace 'for Maecenas' is in reality a treasonable 'libell in picture' on Caesar (V. iii).[2]

## IV

Jonson's aim in these characters is of course unmistakable; he was concerned simply to represent the chief persons of the Quarrel in a transparent and telling 'Augustan' disguise. But the intention of *Poetaster*, as described by himself in the lines already quoted, was larger and loftier than this, and demanded a different executive procedure. To show that the 'master-spirits' of 'Augustus Caesar's times' had detractors too required him to give an at least broadly recognizable picture of these master-spirits and detractors themselves, considered as historic figures, not merely as satiric symbols. Jonson was too angry to do full justice to this larger scheme, but it is never lost sight of. Both persons, circumstances, and details are introduced, which serve to make the historic picture plausible, and for which we must not postulate, though we need not exclude,

---

[1] 'Politician' was a cant-term in theatrical parlance, apparently indicating an actor who carried on transactions on behalf of the company with outside persons or authorities. See the Commentary on III. iv.

[2] This incident, the making of an 'emblem' for a noble patron, is purely Jacobean. It has been recently discovered that Shakespeare made emblems for the Duke of Rutland. This makes it highly probable that for some Maecenas Jonson too made the 'imprese' which his enemies so grotesquely misinterpret. That it was a recognized part of the poet's function to provide these devices with their distichs, may be assumed from our play (IV. iii):

*Chloe.* MERCURY? that's a *Poet*? is't?
*Gallus.* No, ladie; but somewhat inclining that way: hee is a *Herald* at *armes.*

a satiric meaning. Thus, if Horace serves both for satire and for history, Vergil and Maecenas, Propertius and Ovid, Tibullus and Sallust, were bound to be included in any credible picture of the Augustan master-spirits, and need have no other purpose. Jonson had, in fact, embarked, under his polemic animus, on a scheme which appealed to deeper and greater things in him than his personal controversy. The scholar had received his mandate from the satirist; but he was too independent and too keen to pause just when the satirist ceased to need him. Even the directly satirical figures are enriched with touches, like the 'stoicism' of Crispinus ('we are a prettie *stoick* too', III. i), not apparently relevant to the satire. One at least of Horace's detractors, Hermogenes, seems to owe his status in the play to the inalienable place which he occupies in our conception of the Roman Horace's entourage. ''Tis the failing of all singers,—and 'twas his,—never to be brought to sing, when they are bidden; and when they are not bidden, never to leave off.'[1] Such a hint was a direct provocation to the comic dramatist, and Jonson turned it to account humorously enough in the supper-party scene, with the 'cannot sing', 'will not sing', of Hermogenes, and then when the 'banquet' is announced, his 'Why 'tis but a short aire, 'twill be done presently, pray' stay; strike musique' (II. ii).[2]

Among the 'master-spirits' who surround Horace, Virgil[3] and Ovid are treated with peculiar and unmistakable care. They were indeed, for Jonson's time, which, like Horace himself, had not yet learned to appreciate the genius of

---

[1] *Sat.* i. 3. 1-3, of the Sardinian Tigellius Hermogenes, a distinct person from the singer of the same name, Horace's acquaintance and butt (ibid. 129, &c.), but legitimately identified with him by Jonson for the purpose of the play.

[2] Mr. Fleay's identification of Hermogenes with S. Daniel has been sufficiently refuted by Small (*Stage Quarrel*, p. 192).

[3] Where Vergil is spoken of as a person in Jonson's play, it seems right to use Jonson's spelling of the name; but not where he is spoken of as an historical character. In what follows the distinction is observed as far as possible; but consistency is not easy.

Propertius, by far the most considerable of the remaining Augustan poets. Both play roles that are in keeping with their literary renown but not very obviously related to the business of the drama itself. Both, as presented by Jonson, stand outside the impressive picture of great men subject to the envy and abuse of the base and mean, by which Jonson thought to silence his own detractors. For Ovid's tragic fate is a punishment inflicted by the greatest of the great himself; and as for Virgil, the action of the play is held suspended on the verge of the crisis, that he and we may listen, not to detractions from Momus and Zoilus, but to a series of lofty eulogies from his most illustrious fellow poets. The story of the historical Ovid illustrated the ordinary hard fate of poetry in an unsympathetic world, that of Vergil its rarer achievement of supreme recognition and authority; but neither episode bore closely upon the situation which *Poetaster* was designed to illuminate. It is easy nevertheless to understand the special attraction which may have operated in each case. Ovid's early history, in the first place, as told by himself in a famous passage (*Tristia*, IV. 10), was piquantly like Jonson's own. A dozen years before, he too had fought, probably in still more vigorous vernacular, the eternal battle of the young man bent on literature with the father bent on business. He had imitated the situation already in his first great comedy. Young Ovid's praise of poetry as

Thou spirit of *artes*,
The soule of science, and the queene of soules,

like young Lorenzo's (in the quarto text of *Every Man in his Humour*), comes unmistakably from Jonson's heart. And he has uttered few things more pregnant and more profound. But the autobiographical suggestion soon disappears. The tragic passion of the historical Ovid for the Princess Julia,[1] culminating in the catastrophe which closed his

---

[1] Jonson, in accordance with the views then generally held, makes Julia the daughter of Augustus. When Ovid was banished, in A.D. 8,

career, was a theme full of romantic opportunities, which Jonson, of all the greater Elizabethans, was the least fitted to turn to account. The design of the play no doubt precluded any adequate treatment. Where Horace was the central figure, and the glorification of the Horatian spirit in letters, original and derived, the essential theme, Ovid and his romantic story could only be an episode. A poet of another temper, a Drayton or a Daniel, planning the play, might have chosen Ovid instead of Horace to personate himself and made the romance of Delia or Idea, under the guise of Julia, the central topic. Jonson himself, had he been writing in the days of 'Celia' or 'Charis', or had he now been fighting the battle of romantic poetry, might perhaps have done the same. But he was fighting the battle of satire, and 'Celia' and 'Charis' were at most a dream. Ovid's story comes in only as accessory, as part of the Roman scenery. Unfortunately, it so far surpasses in dramatic potentiality all the events in which more important persons are engaged, that it seems to demand a more important function; a demand which, more unfortunately still, Jonson's handling, at once elaborate and ineffective, appears at once to concede and to frustrate.[1] Of the love lyric he was a master; but love in blank verse dialogue was not within his scope, and the heavy apologues exchanged by Julia and the banished Ovid invite a comparison doubly disastrous with the parting scene of Romeo and Juliet, imagined some half-dozen years before by the poet who 'wanted art'. For Jonson's art is here as inferior to Shakespeare's as his poetry. The romance of Romeo and Juliet is dissonant enough with the quarrel of the Houses, upon which background of dissension it is imposed; but the dissonance is significant and fateful, it

---

she had been in exile for nine years. Modern critics connect Ovid's banishment with the no less profligate younger Julia, who was banished a few months later than he.

[1] Swinburne justly remarked on the gross technical flaw which makes Ovid at the outset the 'apparent hero' (*Study of Ben Jonson*, p. 25).

has a tragic and a poetic value. Whereas Jonson's Ovid-romance, uninteresting and even grotesque in itself, is felt as a mere disturbing incongruity.

The sudden and unforeseen apparition of Virgil, in the fifth act, introduces another scene, no less episodic than the opening colloquy of the elder and the younger Ovid, but more problematic and arresting, and far more nobly wrought. Not much, it is true, can be said for, or need be said about, the specimen of an English *Aeneid* which Jonson, with his resolute confidence in his powers as a translator, makes Virgil recite to an applauding court. It is certainly not better than the elegy (borrowed, with a few new touches, from Marlowe) which young Ovid is made to recite to himself. Something of Vergilian grace and charm may be admitted in the poet's courtly speeches to Caesar; but, as usual, Jonson's most felicitous rendering of character is given in description, not in dialogue. For the critical eulogies which precede his entrance Jonson had no such direct authority as he had for the reading of the *Aeneid* before Augustus, but they are in keeping with what we know of the boundless admiration in which Vergil was held at the height of his career by the literary world of Rome; and of the insight and subtlety of the literary criticism conveyed, there can be but one opinion. This episode has no parallel in the Humour plays: Asper comes to flagellate, not to praise; Crites, admitted for his merits, like Horace, to the charmed inner circle of the Court, has no rival there, far less a superior, least of all a superior to whom he pays noble and unstinted homage. It does not directly further the purpose of the play, for Virgil is not represented as the mark of any special obloquy; and Horace, who is, receives no such signal and spontaneous chorus of praise. We regard it as simply a personal application of that passionate ardour for poetry, which glowed and thrilled under the hard and fretted surface of Jonson's satire from the first. Old Justice Clement's merry outburst might well be taken as the motto of *Poetaster*:

> There goes more to the making of a good *Poet*, then a Sheriffe, M*r*. KITELY. You looke vpon me! though, I liue i' the citie here, amongst you, I will doe more reuerence, to (a good poet), when I meet him, then I will to the Major, out of his yeere. But, these paper-pedlers! these ink-dablers! They cannot expect reprehension, or reproch. They haue it with the fact.

The extraordinary emphasis given to this praise of Virgil has, nevertheless, naturally encouraged the disposition to discover a modern face under the classic mask. To which of his contemporaries in poetry would Jonson in 1601 have done homage in such terms? The field of choice is in any case extremely limited. The older critics, from Gifford to Symonds, decided that 'Virgil' was Shakespeare; the more recent, like Mr. Fleay and one of the present editors in the Mermaid edition, have identified him with Chapman, or, like Small, rejected identification altogether.[1] The case for Shakespeare, which to the modern reader is apt to seem as irresistible as it is alluring, owes its plausibility to a naïve assumption that Shakespeare looked, to fellow-playwrights in 1601, as he looks to posterity after three centuries. In the first place, Shakespeare's work was, in 1601, yet but half finished; and by far the greater part of what has given him his supreme place in literature and made his thoughts the current intellectual coinage of the civilized world, had still to be produced. The noble and splendid verses of Tibullus seem, but for a phrase in the second line, to utter once for all what almost every one who has since written about Shakespeare has in some form repeated:

> That, which he hath writ,
> Is with such iudgement, labour'd, and distill'd
> Through all the needful vses of our liues,
> That could a man remember but his lines,

---

[1] The Shakespeare hypothesis, however, still finds authoritative support. At a performance of *Poetaster* in London, on April 26, 1916, Mr. William Poel dressed 'Virgil' as Shakespeare; 'the Stratford bust walked in alive', reports an onlooker, 'among the courtiers of Augustus'.

> He should not touch at any serious point,
> But he might breathe his spirit out of him.

Of a Shakespeare who had still to write all the tragedies except *Romeo and Juliet,* the Roman plays, and the later and graver comedies, who had been for not more than five or six years writing in the unmistakably Shakespearian way at all, this was not a natural assertion. It is less important that in another trait—the critical judgement and laborious art—Jonson's 'Virgil' is sharply marked off from his 'Shakespeare', the Shakespeare of his private memoranda and intimate talk. For this is a public declaration, and in the equally public memorial lines he expressly asserted the claims of Shakespeare's 'art'. Yet there is a wide interval between that passing and subordinate reference and the reiterated emphasis laid upon these qualities here. Gallus and Horace concur with Tibullus in celebrating 'Virgil' for precisely that severe critical scrutiny and self-control which Jonson in the *Discoveries* so bluntly desiderated in Shakespeare. Far from giving the full rein to an unruly wit, and dashing off a thousand lines which he ought to have 'blotted', Virgil is
> most seuere
> In fashion, and collection of himself,

his writing is 'labour'd' with extreme 'iudgement', and his ear is 'so chaste and tender'
> In suffering any syllable to passe,
> That, he thinkes, may become the honour'd name
> Of issue to his so examin'd selfe;
> That all the lasting fruits of his full merit,
> In his own *poemes,* he doth still distaste.

To all this must be added the certainty that, as already stated, Jonson was in the summer of 1601 at issue with Shakespeare's Company, and on no friendly terms with Shakespeare himself.

The case of Chapman is rather more plausible. As a poet he had held, since the publication of the first instalment of his *Iliad* and the *Hero and Leander* in 1598, a distinguished place. Meres in that year counted him among the poets who had 'mightily enriched and gorgeously invested the English tongue in rare ornaments and resplendent abiliments'; as well as among the dramatists most excellent for tragedy and for comedy. In 1600 some eighty extracts from his poems in *England's Parnassus* testified to pretty general and somewhat indiscriminate admiration. In 1601 he contributed, with Shakespeare, Jonson, and Marston, to Chester's *Love's Martyr*. That Jonson was already an intimate friend is to be presumed, though the evidence of their friendship begins only two years later with his lines on *Sejanus*. The case for the identification of Chapman with Virgil rests mainly upon this friendship. His relative standing among his contemporaries was not seriously comparable with that of Vergil in the Roman world, and the details of Virgil's literary 'character' apply to him as imperfectly as to Shakespeare. He might indeed claim to be, like Vergil, a fastidious artist, who subjected every syllable he wrote to the judgement of his chaste and tender ear. But his notion of artistic perfection was very far from that which Jonson attributed to his Virgil. Virgil is the 'rectified spirit', whose speech, winnowed and purified from the mists and confusion which darken the language of common men, yet touching common life at all points, becomes at once for all the world a standard and an instrument. Chapman, too, recognized that 'absolute poems' ought to be 'clear'; but only to those select readers who had secured a 'passport' to Parnassus and graduated in 'the divine discipline of poetry'. 'The profane multitude I hate, and only consecrate my strange poems to those searching spirits whom learning hath made noble.'[1] And he put on his title-page a motto from Persius: '*Quis leget haec?*' '*Nemo hercule, nemo; Vel duo vel nemo.*' Even the praise of Virgil's 'learning' in Horace's second speech does not apply very strictly to Chapman. Learned he was of course, but it required more

[1] Preface to Ovid's *Banquet of Sense* (1595).

than a friend's eye (and Jonson was a critic before he was a friend) to acquit his abstruse writing of all savour of 'the school-like gloss', and discover in it the very essence and spirit of all the arts, divested of all their curious and pedantic terminology. If we suppose that Jonson might refer to the translation of the *Iliad*, eight books of which had appeared in 1598, we are met by two facts. Firstly, we know that he thought slightly of 'the translations of Homer and Virgil in long Alexandrines', as 'but prose'.[1] The reference must be mainly to Chapman's version, the only one then in vogue, though the criticism is much better deserved by the first English translation of Homer, Arthur Hall's *Ten bookes of Homers Iliades*, 1581, which Jonson doubtless knew. Chapman's lines, like Hall's, were yet 'longer' than alexandrines, and Jonson probably liked them even less. Further, Chapman had, in the ardour of his Homeric enthusiasm, made himself the champion of his poet against all rivals, in particular against the most formidable of them, Vergil. In his Epistle dedicatory to *Achilles' Shield*, 1598, he contrasts them, as so many later critics have done, from the purely Homeric standpoint, inevitably so unjust to the Roman poet: 'The majesty he enthrones, and the spirit he infuseth into the scope of his work, so far outshining Virgil, that his skirmishings are but scramblings of boys to Homer's; the silken body of Virgil's muse curiously dressed in gilt and embroidered silver but Homer's in plain, massy and unvalued gold.' It was solely in order to give a crushing proof of Vergil's inferiority that he issued his rendering of this famous episode from the eighteenth book of the *Iliad*.[2]

We are thrown back then on the view that Jonson's

---

[1] *Convers.*, iii. 33, 34.
[2] It is not irrelevant to recall Dryden's scornful disparagement of Chapman beside Jonson, in the Epistle dedicatory to *The Spanish Friar*, though Dryden is referring to Chapman's plays, not to his translation. Like the modern poet Strada, he says, who used every year to burn a Statius to the manes of Virgil, he has 'indignation enough to burn a *d'Ambois* annually, to the memory of Jonson'.

Virgil is simply Vergil; that, like Gallus, Tibullus, and probably Ovid, he supports and gives verisimilitude to the partly symbolic Horace, Crispinus, and Demetrius, but is not a symbol himself. Gifford, the first critic who proposed any other interpretation of the eulogies, allowed that the first two, those of Horace and Gallus, are, as a character of Vergil, 'at once discriminative and just'. But he took exception to the speech of Tibullus and to the second speech of Horace: 'Jonson could not think that Virgil was the poet of common life, as Tibullus affirms, or, as Horace [says], that he was unostentatious of literature, and averse from *echoing* the terms of others.' Neither point is quite accurately made. Tibullus's description, taken as it must be with those that precede, does not point to some genial realist, some comprehensive transcriber of men and manners, like Scott or even Shakespeare, but to a consummate artist in speech who was at the same time a brooding thinker, a profound 'critic of life', and, shy recluse as he might seem to be, yet so penetrated with the traditions and the ideals of his people, that his delicate phrases, purified of whatever was merely casual and ephemeral in vernacular usage, touched life only the more intimately because they touched it less obviously than any transcript. From a very early time the felicitous aptness of the historical Vergil's speech, its wealth of unsuspected relevance, its mysterious depth and pregnancy, the large humanity even of its 'lonely words', were implicitly recognized by the custom of resorting to his volume for guidance at every 'serious' point. The practice of Sortes Virgilianae was current in England until long after Jonson's time,[1] and it is quite likely that he had it directly in mind. But the custom was only one illustration of this quality in Vergil. 'No poet', says F. W. Myers,[2] almost echoing Jonson's words, but hardly thinking of them, 'has lain so close to so many hearts; no words so often as

---

[1] Thus Charles I and Falkland consulted the Virgilian oracle in the Bodleian, turning up *Aen.* iv. 615.
[2] *Classical Essays*, p. 117.

his have sprung to men's lips in moments of excitement and self-revelation.'

The second speech of Horace surely applies better to the Vergil of history than either to Shakespeare or to Chapman, as they appeared to Jonson in 1601. To Caesar's question about Virgil's learning Horace replies by distinguishing the vital and significant learning of his friend from the parrot-like iteration of scholiasts and the verbose technical jargon of pedantic theorists. He did not discourse in abstract terms of the objects and methods of the several arts, but his writing was penetrated through and through with the keenest perception of their values and the subtlest mastery of their 'effects'. And just because the inert matter of pedantry and formalism was so purged away, this poetry is, in Jonson's too robust but not inaccurate expression, 'ramm'd with life',—the best security for the literary immortality which awaited it.

## V

The extraordinary interest and poetic nobility of these eulogies has won a degree of favour for this scene to which it is, dramatically, by no means entitled. On the whole Jonson must be said to have failed once more in the attempt, so curiously fascinating to him, to find a dramatic form in which satirical exposure of bad poets and the exaltation of poetry could equally find place. In his first comedy his better judgement exorcized the lyric oration of Lorenzo, the finest he ever wrote. The set speeches of Virgil's Roman colleagues, prompted by no occasion and furthering no issue, have less dramatic justification than the 'defence' which breaks from Lorenzo on the provocation of his father's taunts. In respect of dramatic technique, the *Poetaster* marks no advance whatever on its predecessors. The plot is little more than a hurried amalgam of more or less effective motives; and its 'technique', if the term can be applied, is a loose mixture of different technical methods, for the most part already employed in one or another of the previous comedies. In general scheme it stands nearest to *Cynthia's Revels*; taking over from it the Court scenery, the conspiracy of the base against the noble, the alliance of poet and prince. But the execution, thanks to the stress of the emergency under which he wrote, has recovered much of the freshness, and the character-drawing some of the checkered light and shade, of the first Humour comedy. The persons, however variously equipped with Elizabethan or Roman traits, are human beings, not personifications; and the cleavage between the friends and foes of wisdom and virtue and Jonson is by no means rigorously carried out. Jonson's invention continually recurs to the fatuities of vanity, of social pretension, of doting credulity; all his persons incline at times to the Humour type. Some of them he found already Humorists *in posse*, and he had merely to emphasize and iterate the absurd trait he found. Thus Horace's Tigellius, already noticed, was a direct provocation to the creator of Master Matthew and Master Stephen. Sometimes he rearranged his classical material for the sake of such traits. Thus Crispinus has the sins of the bore in the Sacred Way laid to his account in addition to those of his prototype; Ovid and his comrades, whose burlesque 'banquet of the gods' is cut short by the indignant entrance of Augustus, have to suffer for an escapade which history reports of Augustus himself.[1] Shakespeare could with impunity make the three masters of the world join hands in a swaggering reel. These extravagances of the lesser poets are rendered in the thin artificial vein of the 'sports' of *Cynthia's Revels* (IV. iii). And whenever Jonson enlarges on or embroiders his classical or topical material, reminiscences of the Humour plays or of the Revels take shape under his pen.

Albius and Chloe have their names, and Albius the hint of his disposition, from Horace;[2] but they prove to be one

[1] Suetonius, *Aug.* 70. The detailed conduct of the scene is modelled, as Whalley pointed out, upon the council of the gods in the first book of the *Iliad*.
[2] 'Stupet Albius aere' (*Sat.* i. 4. 28).

more variation on the theme of the meek husband and well-born ambitious wife, already effectively exploited in Deliro and Fallace and the citizen-pair of *Cynthia's Revels*. Crispinus, when he flirts with Chloe, is similarly an echo of Fastidius Brisk. Tucca, as already stated, has his origin in Horace's Pantilius, and his cue in the epithet 'cimex' with which Horace couples his name; but his particular generic character in that order of vermin is derived from the class of bragging and cowardly old soldiers, the kindred of Bobadill and Shift. Ovid's narrative of his early resistance to his father's choice of a profession, in the name of poetry, while substantially, of course, derived from his Latin namesake, is filled in, as we have seen, with reminiscences of the similar struggles of Edward Kno'well, and doubtless of Jonson himself. In many of these characters the drawing, far from flagging where it follows an old pattern, seems actually to gather vivacity from the figures it retraces. Chloe is better than Fallace, and Tucca than Shift. And the contrast is glaring indeed between Jonson stumbling laboriously after the light-footed master of the *Art of Love* through the alien fields of romance, and the same dramatist merely equipping with the name and circumstances of Ovid the situation, familiar to his art and probably to his experience, of the self-willed son and the self-confident poet.

The technique of the Humour plays prevails still more decisively in the crucial moments of the action, though here too, characteristically, it has to suffer intrusions of quite alien matter. Neither his classical sources nor his contemporary experience provided Jonson with a becoming denouement for his main plot; the Roman Crispinus and Demetrius had suffered no recorded castigation beyond that which has preserved their names in the amber of Horace's satire, and their modern counterparts were still rampant and breathing vengeance upon the modern Horace. But with the pugnacious and censorious Humour-poet, to exhibit men being buffeted out of their Humours by grimly or grotesquely appropriate cures was as ingrained an instinct as the exhibition of the Humours themselves. The primitive but rudely effective catastrophes which had temporarily suppressed the imaginary vagaries of the Stephens and Matthews, the Buffones and the Brisks, are invoked for the benefit of one or the other of the poetasters' quasi-classical attendant crew, and applied as a sort of prophylactic to the effigies of the unpleasantly actual poetasters themselves. The Janus-faced Tucca receives his 'case of vizards'; the credulous Lupus his pair of 'larger ears'; the slanderous Demetrius his penal 'coat and cap'; above all, Crispinus, the virtuoso of a 'frothy' and 'strenuous' rhetoric, has to submit to be relieved by the salutary but drastic pill. The Humour comedy had tended in Jonson's hands to these symbolic retributions; they belong neither to Elizabethan London nor to Augustan Rome, but to the tribunal at which Jonson-Minos presided within his own breast. On the other hand, the 'politician' player Aesop undergoes the unimpeachably classical punishment of castigation by the lictors; and the Nemesis of Ovid and Julia has no proper place in comedy at all, unless the unwitting grotesquerie of their love-making suffice to merit one.

Yet in spite of the strong retributive animus which impelled him, Jonson succeeds, on the whole, in maintaining the spirit and temper of comedy. He was helped by his sense of his own immense superiority in power. Caliban and his crew attacking the cell of Prospero encountered a more Olympian scorn, but hardly a more assured self-confidence. And Jonson, if he had little of Prospero's magnanimity, had the ambition and the instinct of a great artist, who meant to chastise even his bitterest enemies 'comically' in a 'comical satire'. 'Some salt it had ', he wrote afterwards of his play,[1] ' but neyther tooth, nor gall '; and the plea was just. Horace himself looks on at the machinations of his enemies with ironical amusement; and their arraignment, with all its air of judicial solemnity, has an undertone of dry fun, fit prelude to the uproarious Lucianic comedy of the Pill.[2] The terrors of

[1] 'Apologetical Dialogue', 63.  [2] From Lucian's *Lexiphanes*.

the law, whatever these were, are effectively dissolved by this abrupt transformation of the plaintiff into a physician, whose malice towards the chief offender is to dose him with pills, and his vengeance on him to prescribe a wholesome diet. Even Demetrius, whom Jonson clearly regarded with very genuine scorn, has his 'juster doom' of the branded brow mitigated at the intercession of Horace.

For the rest, Jonson's custom of inlaying whole fragments of alien matter, very imperfectly assimilated, in the substance of his own work, here as elsewhere seriously damaged his play. To represent the most fastidious and refined of Roman poets, one of whom has just uttered words as noble and as just as were ever imagined of the poetry of the other, vindicating their common art by this drastic horseplay, was not a happy notion; and it involved a sudden and disturbing change of key from actuality to symbol. There was a rigidity in Jonson's mind which impeded the perfect mastery and harmonious fusion of its complex elements and vast resources; so that things came from him in masses, with abrupt discords at the points of junction, and a strange variegation of tones. *Poetaster* is assuredly no masterpiece; but its hurried and disorderly composition exhibits in picturesque exuberance the elementary forces, the primitive tones of the Jonsonian temperament: the vehement self-will, the ardour for antiquity, the pride of the scholar and the artist, the scorn for all other forms of pride, the grim jocosity, the burly wit, the Attic horseplay, the erudite buffoonery. And it contains one of his best scenes of high comedy, one of his strongest characters, and some of his finest critical poetry.

PRINTED IN
GREAT BRITAIN
AT THE
UNIVERSITY PRESS
OXFORD
BY
CHARLES BATEY
PRINTER
TO THE
UNIVERSITY